Mom. I love pray for God protect you. Miss prosper you and provide for you.

THE INVISIBLE FATHER

Approaches to the Mystery of the Divinity

Louis Bouyer

TRANSLATED BY
Hugh Gilbert, OSB

God bless keep and watch over you all. Miss Me/

T&T CLARK
EDINBURGH

Copyright © 1999 by St. Bede's Publications
Published in the United States of America by
St. Bede's Publications
271 North Main Street
Petersham, MA 01366

This edition published under licence from St. Bede's by
T&T Clark Ltd
59 George Street
Edinburgh EH2 2LQ
Scotland

Imprimatur: E. Berrar,v.é.
Paris, 18 December 1975

The *Imprimatur* is an official declaration that a book or pamphlet is free
of doctrinal and moral error. No implication is contained therein that
those granting the *Imprimatur* agree with the content, opinions or
statements expressed.

Cover photo by Harold M. Lambert

First published 1999

ISBN 0 567 08666 6

British Library Cataloguing-in-Publication Data
A catalogue record for this book is available from the British Library

PRINTED AND BOUND IN THE UNITED STATES OF AMERICA

Contents

Part One

From Natural Religion to
Religious Philosophy

I

Ritual, Myth and Divinity

Abstract reasons for believing in God have never been the source of any man's faith. That source is invariably a religious society, be it that of a man's birth or of his own free and purposeful choice. It is from there that he receives the idea of God or, more correctly, that first instinctive belief in some god which only gradually attains an appropriate conceptual maturity. But this does not mean, as we shall see, that a man's belief is simply passively imbibed from outside. His adherence to the *Gemeinschaft*, to his natural community, is something spontaneous; the place where life was given him is the place where he will keep and cultivate it. With no less spontaneity he will accept that society's form of religion or, if need be, another's, and it is there he will develop that religious life to which the simple fact of being a living person predisposes him. At the root of all this lies what is perhaps man's profoundest instinct. But this too is not to say that religion, with its various tenets, is not a social phenomenon. Arguably it is the most social thing in human life and therefore something that could never be simply lived en masse, so to speak, but only chorally, to the beat of a single heart.

Religious societies, of course, are both synchronically and diachronically diversified. But their differences or divergences can only be fruitfully studied after grasping the processes or, better, the structure underlying every actual religion. Our first chapters will begin with this. Being anxious to avoid the common recurrent temptation of constructing systematic theological theories and of then projecting what are only subsequent elaborations back upon the reality of religion, we will adopt instead the phenomenological approach and consider that reality's life and essence as it actually is.[1]

On such a view, religion again and again stands out as that which confers meaning on human existence. Mircea Eliade in particular has expressed this and expressed it very well.[2] The obvious implication is that religious experience is not something on the periphery of life but rather life experienced as being in complete and conscious harmony with

---

[1]See Etienne Gilson's comments on this point in *Le Philosophe et la Théologie*, Paris, 1962.

[2]Mircea Eliade, *The Quest*, Chicago, 1969. The whole first chapter is to be linked with his earlier *Traité d'Histoire des Religions*, Paris, 1949, pp. 392ff. (Eng. trans. *Patterns in Comparative Religion*, New York, 1958, pp. 388ff.)

the total reality of which it must be part and, by the same token, har-monized with itself as well. We seem, after all, only to emerge from chaos by being born to relapse into it by virtue of being alive, and per-haps the happiest formulation of what religion is is to say that it delivers us from this and allows us to organize our existence in a truly satisfying way. It is because of this, as Eliade again has said, that every religion emerges as aboriginally and—*pace* the impressions of the over-civilized—indissolubly bound to what we know as being, meaning and truth.

The error to avoid and yet the one to which theologians, by virtue of their discipline, are most liable, is to take all this in a too narrowly intel-lectualist sense. Religion does not first provide us with a clear, distinct concept of the world and ourselves which, once we have simply applied it, makes us religious and, in consequence, successful persons. Religion indeed will produce such ideas and produce them in abundance. But the truth is that they are much more the fruit of religion than its root, though this again is not to say that religion can bypass these ideas or that they are not more or less latent from the very beginning. We simply want to stress that religion is a crucial thing, the most crucial thing in man's life. *Ab initio*, of course, this involves an element or aspect we can call intellec-tual and reflective. But to suppose that this element comes first or, worse, exists in isolation from the start, or worse still, is the cause of all else, would be an idealist error of the most pernicious kind possible. There is no religion without its beliefs, certainly, but no belief has ever engen-dered a religion unless it be one manifestly artificial and, so to speak, still-born. On the contrary every living religion carries its beliefs within its womb, bringing them forth when appropriate, though even then only with labor and very disparate degrees of success.

Religion is part of the life of man. It is a life, a certain kind of life. Better, it is human life lived fully, lived at what we might call its maxi-mum or rather optimum level. It is human life brought consciously into harmony, and harmonizing in consequence the individual and society and even human society and the cosmos as a whole. To close one's eyes to this is to miss the primary datum of the religious phenomenon and to condemn oneself to total incomprehension.

Hence religion, even if always implying thought (the thought behind every thought we ever have) is first and foremost not an idea but an activity. Nor is it one activity among others, but the one that assures the others of coherence and value; the activity, therefore which, however costly it may be, gives man the profoundest satisfaction. It is indeed the only activity in and by which a man can know his life "has meaning," and that this meaning goes beyond anything he could imagine or conceive, having a richness transcending every concept and every dream, even the wildest.

At this point, Rudolf Otto's insight into the sacred fits in. It is the nature or, rather, the most salient characteristic of the sacred to be the "wholly other," as he says: a mystery filling us with fear, even extreme terror, the *mysterium tremendum* but equally and even more so the *mysterium fascinans* which, the moment we encounter it, even the moment before we encounter it, reveals itself in our own spontaneous, unarguable certainty that here we are facing something not simply attractive and desirable but something which satisfies as nothing else can every human desire for better things.[3]

Mircea Eliade's view is apparently more mundane but in reality the same. The religious factor, by virtue of unveiling the unity of the whole universe to us, gives our lives their unity, a unity, though, that is no more inherent to the universe or to any element of it than it is to ourselves, since it is found only in that mysterious Other who, though other, is closer to each and every thing, each and every being, than they can possibly be to themselves.

Ritual

There is one primordial activity in which religion assumes not simply a specific form but its very existence, and that is the activity we call ritual.[4]

Moderns are almost congenitally incapable of conceiving ritual as anything but artificial, essentially peripheral to life, "formalized" they deprecatingly say, as if hieratic and fossilized were synonymous. This is to confound ritual with what ritual may become in a degenerate religion or, frankly, with how it may appear to someone whose religious sense is as good as dead. Ritual in reality is a super-natural action, not in the sense of not being natural or being less natural than other actions, but in the sense that it is more intensely and absolutely natural than any other. What exactly is ritual? It is, we might say, nothing else than natural activity retaining possession of all its primitive capacities.

We have of course learned to be wary of the ambiguity in the term "primitive." Modern humanity has, on the whole, adopted not just a historical but an evolutionary view of itself, but one may reasonably doubt whether this amounts to anything more than what Kant would have called an "*a priori* form of our sensibility" without even the com-

---

[3]Rudolf Otto, *The Idea of the Holy*, Oxford Univ. Press, 1923, 2nd ed., 1950.
[4]Gerard van der Leeuw, *Religion in Essence and Manifestation*, London, 1938, pp. 339ff.

pensation, in this case, of there being a "transcendental aesthetic" await-
ing discovery at the root of human consciousness. We are dealing in fact
with a product of definite date and a particular mentality, a mentality so
contingent upon the recent history of our civilization that it would be
extremely naive to presume upon its perdurance. We must recognize, as
do most contemporary historians, that history alone can never vouchsafe
"the meaning of history." And in any case, even if it could, the available
section of human history is so minute by comparison with the whole that
no amount of legitimate hypothesis can enable us to infer the real nature
of the primitive state.

So, if we retain the word "primitive," as we can, it must be in
a phenomenological rather than a historical sense. In which case the
primitive would be what supports any superstructure; even if not strictly
causing everything else, at least enables it to have a form and gives it
whatever intelligibility it may have. Ritual action, therefore, would be
action which has retained or even regained its capacity for embodying
the rich exuberance of lived and, still more, living meaning. We cannot
insist too much that, for those involved, this meaning would not be
the product of any *a priori*, clearly articulated vision of things but rather
the source of a continuous stream of concepts, none of them equal to
expressing its inherent richness.[5]

So, while sacred action definitely remains apart from other actions,
even from those most akin to it, it is not apart from the whole and, as
long as its religion is a living one, will not be felt as something that tends
by nature to dissolve into unreality but, on the contrary, as the most real
thing there is. One might call it super-real.

But to remain on the level of generalizations will be to remain without
understanding. These things can only be grasped intuitively, and this
means beginning with a concrete example.

Sacrifice and Divinity

Sacrifice can be considered the paradigm rite and therefore we must
at least say something about it, though without attempting a complete or
even summary analysis of it here.[6]

---

[5]Mircea Eliade, *The Quest*, pp. 23ff.

[6]R. K. Yerkes, *Le Sacrifice dans les Religions grecque et romaine et dans le judaïsme primitif*,
Paris, 1955, studies these religions in their relations to others, previous to or contemporary
with them, and has the great virtue of furnishing us with an abundance of facts without
forcing them into the mold of any *a priori* theory. See also G. van der Leeuw, *op. cit.*, pp.
341ff.

Theories and explanations of sacrifice abound. This was true even in the various "pagan" antiquities, and Christian theology itself has known no less profusion and rather more confusion, despite or because of its attempts to produce systems that obey the strict laws of logic. But if sacrifice be taken in its actual reality, if none of its many facets be excluded for the sake of some *a priori* definition, it will be seen as something considerably simpler than the theorists would have us believe and also, if we remember the vistas it can throw open to unsophisticated religious man, as something far too wide for the strait-jackets of system and definition.

Our first remark must be that, etymologically and especially semantically, the word sacrifice, the Latin *sacrificium*, having passed from a religious though non-theological usage to one that either is or is about to become highly conceptualized, has thereby been progressively and tellingly diminished and distorted. In modern parlance we talk of "making a sacrifice" when, for the sake of the divinity, we deprive ourselves of something belonging to us. Such a phrase is typically tautological and the whole idea a grievously impoverished one, an inheritance from medieval and baroque theories of sacrifice. The original meaning of sacrifice is incomparably broader. One clear-sighted analyst in particular, though lacking the courage to exploit his discovery, showed that the prime aspect of sacrifice is not destruction or mortification but rather the wholly positive act of self-oblation. Only at this point do we regain contact with *sacrificium* and *sacrum facere*, at least in its meaning of "to render sacred," "to consecrate."

Yet it seems to be the case that the original meaning is simpler still and decidedly more positive, i.e., "to make the sacred," meaning not the artificial production of something sacred nor the rendering sacred of what was not but the making of that which in itself and of itself is sacred.

This is the primitive in the sense we gave it above; the primitive form, phenomenologically, of what Husserl would understand by the essence. To suppose, as is generally done, that the notion of consecration involves a forcible introduction of the sacred by man into a world or part of it from which it is absent would be to see implied in it an idea in fact late, secondary and evidencing either decadence or a misreading of what the sacred is. When a man has a real, living apprehension of the sacred, he knows it is something totally unartificial. It cannot be fabricated. It is, we repeat, the aboriginal act, the essential act. "To make the sacred," then, means not to confer sacrality on what is without it but rather to recognize it or, at the worst, recover it if lost to sight from where it has always been as *the* reality, the very reality one is "making" and the basis of any reality worthy of the name.

Considered materially, a sacrifice is nothing but a meal. It is of course a distinctly sacred meal but this in no way means that it is not truly or fully a meal. Indeed the precise opposite is the case. It is a meal that has retained or rediscovered everything a meal can and should be and really is, if still genuine and inviolate, with its integrity unimpaired. It is a meal at which man's life is consciously recharged by the life of the cosmos; a meal at which the individual, the society in which he shares the meal and even the totality of things into which this society is reintegrated by the act of eating, all reassimilate this life; a life apprehended each time as something in and beyond each and every one of us, its source somewhere above and beyond everything in the world while it gives the world all the value it has.

By the same token and moving to a less profound, more intellectualized level, it is the exchanging of the gift that provokes realization of how "other," how "sacred," how "divine" life is—our life, the life of all men and every being. This gift is at once received and shared. It is received only in surrender, in that dispossession of what one has, even of what one is, which effects entry into a circle of life whose circumference is wider than the existence of individual and society and wider even than the cosmos itself.

Underlying such an eating, we find those pregnant ideas of communion and love that will prove so susceptible to subsequent elaboration. Such love is in one sense a desire for self-enrichment, but this very aim and its enactment make of it a desire for self-enlargement, for growth and escape from one's own limits. This ultimately means giving, self-giving, even though such is possible only within, so to speak, the original gift of life. And it is precisely this gift that the meal provides, a gift requiring our consent and that consent being impossible apart from participation.

One could continue developing these ideas almost indefinitely and, what is remarkable, do so without any explicit formulation of the idea of a god distinct from the sacrifice. On the other hand, though, once such an idea of God has erupted, it will be seen to be the dominant of the whole experience of sacrifice and primitive meal. Even if not at first adequately conceived, even if never attaining the heights of an all-embracing theory, it will, once out, immediately mobilize all those infinite implications we could only suggest above.

It is by thinking along such lines that sense can be made of a paradox which has much struck the moderns. In the oldest extant religious texts, for example in the earliest of the Vedas, sacrifice is central. But there was at that state no explicit mention of any god and, when the god Agni did feature, it is by no means clear whether he was the one to whom sacrifice is offered or its real offerer or simply the sacrifice itself.[7]

It would be to swing from one error to the other to claim that we can at this point touch the very origin of the idea of God. This tends to be the view of historians of religion in opposition to the phenomenologists. But the fact is that there is no such thing as the origin of the idea of God if by such one means a human construct made from conceptual analyses and mere deductive reconstruction of the real. God, in his transcendent unity, is present behind the most primitive experience, that is, as we have said, the experience of life in the world so far as the world is grasped from the start, however confusedly, as not mere chaos but an organic unity. It is that which gives meaning to man's life in the universe or to the life of the universe as it contains man, supporting rather than overwhelming him. Man in consequence could not enjoy consciousness without being immediately impressed by what we can at least call some kind of idea of God which, however inadequate, will inevitably provoke an incessant, inexhaustible succession of images and concepts. We can state now what we will attempt to justify later, namely that these images and concepts nourish the life of this idea in us in proportion as they develop, while suffocating or disfiguring it so far as they tend to be absorbed into or identified with it.

Every species of prophecy will raise its voice against the idolatry of identifying an image with God or of proposing concepts that claim to encapsulate his essence.

But at this stage of our inquiry we must first try to trace concretely how the idea of God emerged from ritual. This means studying the origin and especially the structure of what is called "myth."

From Ritual to Myth

"It is with fear and trembling that a historian of religion approaches the problem of myth." So, once more, speaks Mircea Eliade.[8] Facile popularizations, which have been outdated in any case by genuine scientific research into religion, have had the effect of giving the modern

---

[7]See the summary given by H. de Glasenapp, *La philosophie indienne*, (French trans., Paris, 1951), pp. 34ff. His theory, however, that it was the idea of sacrifice that absorbed the gods is not supported by the texts which witness to the opposite process: distinct gods emerge in the wake of reflection upon the ritual. Cf. the two hymns to Agni translated by L. Renou in his excellent *Anthologie Sanscrite*, Paris, 1947, pp. 13ff. For the present state of research see Jean Varenne, *La Religion védique*, in l'*Histoire des Religions de la Pléiade*, vol. 1, Paris, 1970, pp. 578ff, and particularly pp. 602ff and 610ff.

[8]Mircea Eliade, *The Quest*, p. 72. See the whole chapter.

western public a singularly distorted view of myth, and to try to undo it is a labor of Sisyphus. It was Jaspers who observed that Bultmann's attempt to demythologize Christianity is not just nullified but radically vitiated by the fact of being based upon this vulgarized idea, obsolete as it is and long ago demolished by the progress of research. Nothing is more indicative, in this regard, than the inextricable entanglement of Bultmann and his disciples in their confusion of myth and mythology.

One false persuasion that had a particularly unfortunate effect on the first phases of the modern study of myth was that Greek mythology, as represented by the *Iliad* and *Odyssey* (not to mention Ovid or Virgil), was typical of the mythical or rather mythopoetic mentality. But such a mythology, which was in any case in a manifest process of development from work to work and author to author, was a mythology not of living myths but moribund ones, myths in fact already dead and sometimes not simply dead but fully decomposed. In the face of such myths or myths in such condition it is hardly surprising that ancient Greek thought had already identified myth with fable, that is, with unreality, be it acknowledged or not. What we call classical culture inherited this misconception as something axiomatic and the popular culture of the modern world remains its victim.

One can then understand how, given such a premise, Max Müller, towards the middle of the nineteenth century, held that all myths could be explained as simple illusions of language. Man had literalized metaphors drawn from his own activity to describe cosmic phenomena. Thus, for example, to speak of the sun "going down" or "rising" was to make a magnified human being of it. The gods, therefore, would be nothing but reified images: verbal humanization imposed on the universe with the hammer-blows of misplaced personification.[9]

Behind such views lay an *a priori* vision of religion which found its definitive as well as final expression in the great French sociologist, Lévy-Bruhl's works on what he himself called "the primitive mentality," characterized by him as pre-logical.[10] This last term was expressive. Religious science, still in its own infancy, generally held that religion itself corresponded to the infancy stage of the human mind, prior to its awakening to logic and thus, at least potentially, to science. In no time, however, the researches of professional anthropologists had given the lie to this very scientific illusion. There was, for example, a study by Gerard van der Leeuw on Polynesian methods of boat-building. This indicated that the mythical mentality, which may be called meta-logical, was cer-

---

[9]Max Müller, *Lectures on the Science of Language*, 2nd ed., Oxford, 1864.
[10]See Mircea Eliade, *The Quest*, p.16 for a complete bibliography.

tainly not pre-logical. Purportedly simple minds had mastered techniques presupposing both long experience of navigation and a remarkably perceptive rational reflection upon it. The products of their skills, as a matter of fact, are on a level with those of the most advanced contemporary hydro-dynamics.[11] Lévy-Bruhl, man of great integrity that he was, had the merit of admitting his mistake in his later years and, at the time of his death, was preparing to revise his theory in the way indicated.

But at the present stage even the characterization of the primitive mythical mentality as meta-logical would seem too cautious, and a hangover from those discarded ideas of science, and of physics in particular, as a photographic copy of reality in opposition to the symbolic outlook of poetry and religion. Whitehead, one of the most eminent modern thinkers and certainly the one who had reflected most upon science itself, demonstrated, in his capital study of symbolism, that scientific knowledge is no less symbolic than religious knowledge.[12] What makes the difference is the specific orientation of scientific symbols: to the use of the universe rather than to its interpretation—though both kinds of symbol are equally humanist.

The French Structuralists have gone still further and so linked up by another route with the analyses of Collingwood,[13] the historian and philosopher of the sciences. In their view, the scientific outlook did not succeed the mythical vision of the universe, still less emancipate itself from it, but developed at its very heart (albeit almost immediately inclined to forget the fact) and remains so dependent upon it that, if the mythical vision flags, the scientific one will probably be unable to survive for long.[14]

In fact, at the turn of the century, the Scottish folklorist Andrew Lang had upheld the thesis that myth, far from being pre-logical, stood rather for a first exercise of logic: the original anticipation of the scientific explanation of the world and the first quest for the cause of phenomena.[15]

But even this view was to be corrected and apparently refuted by a crucial study of A. M. Hocart which appeared in *The Labyrinth*, a collection of essays on the problems of comparative religion, edited by

---

[11]G. van der Leeuw, "La Structure de la Mentalité primitive," in *Revue d'histoire et de philosophie religieuses*, Strasbourg, 1928, pp. 1ff. See also Maurice Leenhardt's study, *Do Kamo*, Paris, 1947, esp. pp. 220ff.

[12]Alfred North Whitehead, *Symbolism, Its Meaning and Effect*, New York, 1927.

[13]R. G. Collingwood, *The Idea of Nature*, Oxford, 1945.

[14]See the assessment of M. Foucault, *Les Mots et les Choses*, Paris, 1966. Cf. Claude Lévi-Strauss, *Anthropologie structurale*, Paris, 1958, pp. 248ff.

[15]Andrew Lang, *Myth, Ritual and Religion*, London, 1899.

S. Hooke between the World Wars, and which proved to be a decisive turning-point in the history of such researches.[16]

What Hocart established was that myth is not essentially something prescientific, cosmological or aetiological in the etymological sense of seeking causes, but rather liturgical; not simply religious, but ritual. It is not a first, more or less jejune, attempt to explain the world but a poetic explanation or, better, expression of ritual. Myths, of course, sooner or later inevitably become detached from lived religion. But once that has happened, they cease to be living. They are true to themselves only at the place of their birth, at the heart of the ritual from which they have sprung.

After World War II, E. O. James,[17] without subtracting from Hocart's conclusions, was able to show that there was less of a contradiction with Lang than might appear. Every myth very definitely includes from the start an element one can call aetiological and, more emphatically still, one that is cosmogonic. And the reason for this is simply that ritual is not one human activity among others but that in and by which man consciously coincides, so to speak, with what one can call the universe's lines of force and aligns his own life on the axle of the life of the cosmos. Whence derives the impossibility of transposing ritual into myth without at the same time lighting up, along with the human enigma, the mystery of things.

If myth therefore depends upon ritual and was subsequent to it, can one trace the mode of its emergence? Myth, it seems, provided a first instance of what we customarily name humanism; it was, that means, an initial attempt to understand reality in human terms. This attempt represented the origins of man's self-awareness. He discovered himself rather as did Narcissus, in the mirror of the real.

The matter, indeed, is more complex than it appears and one cannot, it seems, explain the origin of myth without introducing a problem which, more than any other, has divided modern specialists in religious science: that of the relations between religion and magic. And this problem in turn cannot be raised without summoning up another, that of the relations between magic and technology.

Religion, Magic and Technology

Sir James Frazer was, if not the first, at least one of the earliest and most influential anthropologists to propose that the original or earliest

---

[16]A. M. Hocart, "The Life-Giving Myth," pp. 261ff. in *The Labyrinth*, Oxford, 1935.
[17]E. O. James, *Myth and Religion in the Ancient Near East*, London, 1958.

stage of religion consisted in magic.[18] The objection to this thesis, as was quickly pointed out, lay in the massive and ubiquitous fact of conflict between religion and magic. This in turn was attemptedly explained away on the grounds that the conflict was between new forms of religion and the archaic one of magic. The Middle Ages were given as an example. So was the later phenomenon of witchcraft which, according to Margaret Murray, was nothing other than ancient paganism surviving or reviving in a Christian environment.[19]

But even in those instances that seem to justify such a standpoint, magic always had a maleficent character, and this not just because it was in opposition to the prevailing religion but because it was itself a degenerate form of religion. Invariably the degeneracy consisted precisely in man's attempt, by using magic, to take possession of divine powers, to constrain whatever gods he can and use them for his own ends, setting himself up as a god opposed to God.

Any practice manifesting a belief in the irrational represents magic. It is an infrarational irrationality, while that of religion is supra-rational, supposing as it does man's radical dependence on powers superior to him. The irrationality of magic, by contrast, always supposes that man can reduce what is mightier than he to servitude and gain control of it by his own powers of manipulation.

It appears to be the case that magic came to birth when man attained the awareness of being the operative agent of ritual At that moment, in accordance with that dialectic of nascent human freedom so well-known to every educator, he was irresistibly tempted to affirm himself by going into opposition: affirming himself against the gods by turning the sacred to his own profit, convinced of his power to exploit it at will. *Eritis sicut dei.*

Magic, therefore, was caught in an inherent contradiction. It constantly presupposed that in ritual man encounters powers surpassing himself. But so far as he was the executive of the rite, so long as he knew the gestures to make and the words to say, he appeared to be their master. Given this, myth, whether it be aware of this or not (and certainly the awareness is more instinctive than reflective), must be seen as the exact opposite of magic. It did indeed form part of the same process of humanizing reality or, to be still more precise, was rooted in the fact that ritual, although a divine and sacred action, was nonetheless performed by man, was therefore a human action and, in a sense, the most human

---

[18]James G. Frazer, *The Golden Bough*, 2nd ed., London, 1902.
[19]Margaret Murray, *The God of the Witches*, London, no date.

there is. But, though conscious of this, myth reaffirmed that only the god is the ritual's ultimate author, originator and celebrant.

This affirmation of the ultimate reality hidden within ritual can at this stage only be made by reference to an activity which was human in its mode but had the invisible God as its more than human agent. Here we find the first utterance of an idea, already contained embryonically in the fact that ritual is a human action coincident with the divine, namely that man is not merely a microcosm but is an image of the divine. Nor did this make it unlawful for him to represent God to himself by projecting upon him an enlarged self-image.

Such a way of understanding the origin of myth seems to accord both with the dialectical process of human knowledge and with the religious evidence where its development most admits of observation. It means that myth should be seen as a spontaneous reaffirmation of the religious import of ritual, made at the very moment when man entered onto the stage of his own awareness, tending to occupy it to the exclusion of all else. Myth therefore effectively re-established the dominance of the divine over reality. It re-introduced the divine under the very same human form which man, having discovered it in himself, was tending to impose on everything.

This in its turn of course entailed the further risk of idolatry: the confusion of the human image and the divine reality.

In this perspective, there is no objection to agreeing with Freud and admitting the original conjunction not so much of religion as of science, at least technological science, and magic.[20] Both aimed to establish man's self-interested mastery over physical reality. Both replaced the divine plan with a humanist one.

The only difference was that, being a more realistic and better-informed species of magic, technology was more likely to succeed. Even so, highly critical modern historians of, for example, non-scientific, magical medicine, tell us that its success-rate is scarcely any lower than that of scientific medicine and that it even works cures beyond the latter's powers of explanation or emulation.[21]

The Co-Evolution of Ritual and Myth

Whatever the validity of this last point, it is a fact that myth, having sprung from ritual under the conditions we have attempted to define,

---

[20]*Civilisation and Its Discontents*, Eng. trans., London, 1930.

[21]See Henri F. Ellenberger's studies on this subject in the *Encyclopédie médicale*, and in his book *A la découverte de l'Inconscient*, Villeurbanne, 1974, pp. 25ff.

then reacted back upon it. The ensuing process was a complex one. It demands at least a brief outline. What emerges is that, subsequent to its projection at the level of imagination, the idea of God was conceptualized. This meant that, having overcome the temptation to magic while replacing it with one to idolatry, myth had to be rationalized if it was to defeat this new enemy. This, though, in turn could only be done at the peril of having the divine evaporate into pure abstraction.

In order to substantiate our assertions and witness the above process in act, we may now appropriately refer to a particular case that will enable us to follow the vicissitudes of myth and ritual. The mysteries of Eleusis were a central component in the development of hellenic culture and it is of them we wish to speak. No other cult had such a formative influence upon the mystery religions that were so prominent a feature of the last phase of ancient pre-Christian religious development. But, beyond this, it gives us an essential key to the understanding of the whole humanist inheritance received from Greece.[22]

We have spoken at length elsewhere of this and hope to be able to return to it one day in more depth. For the present we will simply note certain of the more essential and significant data of the case.

However short we are on information about the ritual content of the Eleusinian mysteries, there are certain details that cannot be contested. They evidence its complexity. More important, they show how in the course of a gradual development this content evolved eventually beyond the mysteries themselves and became quite separate.

There appear to have been at least three distinct levels to the mysteries of the "good goddesses." The most ancient corresponded to something that remained right through as the culminating point of the mystery's celebration: "the blade of corn harvested in silence." As we will see later, a study of the different and successive cultural spheres attests that this silent rite, representing that most ancient of human activities, the harvest, was at the root of the whole mystery. It was wholly in character that the rite should have been entirely silent and that a conservative reverence for beginnings should have preserved this. Here we have proof, if proof were needed, of the propriety and primacy of ritual, not only over myth, but over every verbal expression. Religion is action before it is speech. The action, which has become banal to us, was in fact sacred from the very beginning and, most of all, sacred at its

---

[22]The latest study on the Eleusinian mysteries is that of George E. Mylonas, *Eleusis and the Eleusinian Mysteries*, Princeton University Press, 1961. This book has transformed our knowledge of the issue thanks to its being based on a detailed archeological examination of the site.

beginning: in this sense that at that point there came awareness of encountering the sovereign power who held the universe in his hands— he who would later be described as Zeus or God, that is, the heaven who rules over the earth and all that happens there.

A second element of the ritual was hierogamy, the sexual union of hierophant and his mate, accomplished presumably in the *megaron*, the subterranean grotto splicing the hill of Eleusis. This belonged to a different sphere of culture: that of the first farming civilizations. It was always connected with seed-time and supposed the conviction of a harmony between man's fecundity and the earth's, a harmony agriculture exploited in order to dominate. The cult of Demeter corresponded to this ritual. She was reckoned as someone divine, but maternal rather than paternal, part and parcel in some way of the earth from which we were drawn and which is the where and whence of our lives, and therefore not a person who came down upon us from above either in grace or judgment.

Here indeed religion risked becoming magic. Once agriculture had assured a relatively regular provision of his needs, man would all too easily imagine that the autonomous deployment of his own sexuality gave him power to unleash the cosmic energies within and around him.

But it was at this same point that myth arose, with the precise effect of compensating for this tendency. One of its characteristics was that the "great gods" had little or no part to play. Zeus was a remote spectator, who would only intervene at the crucial moment. Demeter herself was nothing but compassion, or divinized intercession. The principal role belonged to her daughter, who was almost entirely human: Kore-Persephone who was inextricably polarized between resistance and surrender to Hades, the subterranean world and its powers. While gathering flowers in the valley, she was ravished and dragged off to hell. Her distraught mother went in search of her while pleading tearfully before the supreme god. Thus was Kore guaranteed a periodic return to the earth's surface, and the earth, therefore, its rhythm of sowing and harvest.

Such, as myth proclaimed it, was the meaning of the dangerously humanizing ritual of hierogamy. It was not therefore simply a sexual union conceived as a magic means of dominating nature. It manifested rather the beneficence and fecundity of a strictly divine action (not merely sacred) performed for man's good. Far from compelling the powers above to serve human ends, the hierophant and his mate simply represented them. Strictly speaking, they manifested the sovereign kindness of the sacred towards those who showed it honor.

All this eventually reacted back upon the ritual itself, with the simple procession preceding the hierogamy and the wordless exhibition of the harvested ear being transformed into a dramatic rendering of the myth: of Kore's rape, the mother's journey through the tenebrous underworld and the culminating glory of the girl's return to the light, just as the harvest sprang from the earth where the grain had been hidden.

With this we have reached the last stage in the co-development of myth and ritual, each acting and reacting upon the other. We have also reached the first of developments that were to go beyond the specific sphere of ritual mystery, though they were never to emancipate themselves completely from it.

The myth, which was proclaimed by the Ceryx and ritually re-enacted by the initiates in a dramatized procession, was to be the source both of epic and of tragic drama. The latter was to apply the ritual's mythical meaning to the whole of human existence and thereby made its eventual laicization possible. Last of all were to come the philosophical explanations, with their wholesale rationalization of myth and their consequent tendency to dissolve it altogether.

Thus even though the thoughtful, if no one else, would still have been able to catch something of the mystery, the original rite, additions and all, had inevitably fallen victim to a desacralization. It had become a simple agricultural technique. It had become, in other words, an increasingly profane action meaning, as always, profaned, consciously or otherwise, by the ethos of humanism.

This is, of course, a highly schematic presentation. All too little evidence has come down to us and the mysteries of Eleusis remain, in many particulars, undivulged.[23] But it is legitimate to think that what has survived has done so precisely because it is so salient. Our interpretation may indeed be in large measure conjectural, but it can claim to be based upon the best established reading of the course of cultural evolution and its repercussions on the forms of religion. And, as long as one remembers the undeniable indeterminateness of so many of the phenomena under discussion, the schematic approach has the merit of underlining certain constant factors. Precise chronology is not of the first relevance. Most unlikely anticipations and no less improbable survivals mark the religious sphere perhaps more than any other. We prefer to focus upon the inner dialectic of religion and especially of religious awareness, of which the Eleusinian mysteries provide a particularly representative instance, and one that has had an immense influence upon the whole religious history of the West.

---

[23]All the available texts can be found in N. Turchi's invaluable *Fontes historiae mysteriorum aevi hellenistici*, Rome, 1930, pp. 43ff.

The first and immediate impression of the divine was of its benevolent sovereignty, of which the provision of man's primal needs was the basic and abiding sign. But as man's consciousness developed alongside his activity, the divine immanence within which we move and have our being came increasingly to the fore. This in turn entailed the temptation to magic, to securing control of divine energies for our own exclusive benefit: to humanize the divine, in other words, a process to which myth was a kind of spontaneously secreted antidote. On the very basis of the divine image which man had recognized in himself, myth reaffirmed with the utmost explicitness the divine content of the ritual in which man's life, and man's specifically, proved itself feasible in a world that was simultaneously close and remote. But in doing this, myth humanized the gods and so exchanged the peril of idolatry for that of magic.

Epic and tragic poetry only survived the temptation by gradually shifting their ground off the incomprehensible omnipotence of the gods and onto the promethean ambitions and emancipations of their heroes, while philosophy dissolved the idols but re-formed the divine into an elegantly shaped system of abstractions, and rational science, implicit within such philosophy, hastened the passage from magic to technology. All this amounted to a first secularization, a process that seems ineluctably part of what we call civilization.

The Ambiguities in Myth

What precisely was it in myth that unleashed such at least apparently fatal consequences? Why did it only fecundate culture in dissociation from it? For this was to be the burden, as we shall see, of prophecy in its various kinds. Fear of a catastrophe caused by man's very mastery of his destiny and of the universe's periodically engulfs the human race. Prophetism, as we call it, and especially biblical prophetism would withstand this. It would do more than urge a return to myth and, sometimes, beyond myth to a life purportedly pre-rational and instinctive. Neither would it follow the direction of the first philosophies in dissolving myth. Rather it rectified it and rectified it definitively, first in Judaism and then in Christianity, by exploding its structure and composing a quite new one, open rather than closed. All the enduring elements of mythic symbolism would indeed be found again, but with their significance changed forever by their new and unexpected configuration. For, as we shall see, a new content had entered ritual.[24]

---

[24]Our first treatment of this was *Le Rite et l'Homme*, Paris, 1962, esp. pp. 171ff.

What happened was the replacement of the earlier sacred history, which had been a reiteration at the human level of the seemingly unalterable circles of cosmic life by a history as much human as divine but divine in a forgotten or unsuspected sense: a history marked by the *ephapax*, by the "once for all," by a decisive and therefore definitive intervention. We will not at this stage trace this process of substitution in detail. What we want to emphasize here are the redoubtable ambiguities that myth contains. That we can perceive these so clearly we owe simply and solely to the prophetic word, that word which came to us at the furthest point of our accelerating "alienation." Yet, for those who had eyes to see, those ambiguities were already there, visible along the whole range of the myths we know.

Before this revelation, man's situation in the face of cosmic and divine reality may be compared to that of a diver raising his eyes skyward from beneath the mass of water pressing upon and overpowering him. Just as the diver would be unable to distinguish between what was happening in the air and what in the water, so, in every myth, the processes of creation and of the fall of the world were mingled with one another. Thus all hope of salvation was inevitably confused with the expectation of some kind of de-creation, any distinct existence being reabsorbed into the indistinctness of a higher and anterior existence.

What is more, the divine was not distinguished from the cosmic and divine life was equated with cosmogenesis. Hence the actual, fallen world became identified with multiplicity, understood as polytheism. Creation in other words, was the fall of God and his dispersion among the things beneath him. Salvation, therefore, would mean the reconstitution of him in his original, transcendent unity and unicity.

Hence every myth was cosmogonic while tending, for as long as fall and creation were confounded, to make theogony of cosmogony.[25] On such a view, cosmogenesis was the fall and fracturing of God in alien matter. Whence a salvation more God's than man's or the world's and which consisted in God refinding his original integrity by abolishing the world.

We will expand this critique when we come to study the Judeo-Christian revelation. But we have said enough for the present to point out the paradox of myth, how it bears within it the future of all human civilizations, indeed, but also the seed of its own demise and, at least potentially, of that of those same civilizations the very moment they believe themselves free of the gods.

---

[25]E. O. James, *Cosmogony and Creation*, Leiden, 1969.

The study, to be undertaken in the next chapters, of the most recent conclusions of modern psychology, sociology and cosmology will be seen to confirm, in fact, by its own ambivalence that of myth—whence all these sciences have sprung and against which they have all turned. But it will also evidence how myth is not merely inevitable but perennial; because of this, such studies have become for us moderns all but indispensable preliminaries to rediscovering the critique and remodeling of myth found in what we call the Word of God. The rational analysis and critique of myth form, indeed, the immediate antecedent to this Word, doing so not abstractly but in their precise location at the point of common crisis whither all civilization tends when man grows in knowledge of himself, his race and the universe.

But before embarking on this, it is worth underlining how inane and impossible a venture is any "demythization." Myth will certainly never satisfy man but, far from being merely a preliminary phase in his intellectual development or cultural maturation, it is the one and abiding foundation-stone upon which every culture must be constructed. Man cannot dispense himself from it. The structuralists of our own time, more than anticipated in fact by several of their predecessors, have provided proof of this. Whenever the human intelligence tends towards the destroying of myth it may not be imperiling its own development, even in opposition to myth, but in no way whatever can it survive without the primordial intuition contained in myth, which is not something "primitive" but essential to the very being of man. This intuition myth may express well or badly but no other form of expression is available. When man thinks he can bypass myth and dispense with it, he is deluded. The idea is impracticable and, what is worse, quite meaningless. One can no more bypass myth than be free of one's shadow, unless it be at the price of obliterating the light. But in such a case man would have not only evaded myth; he would have forsaken existence itself.[26]

---

[26]Mircea Eliade, *The Quest*, pp. 68ff. and his discussions of the matter mentioned in note 9.

II

Myth and Depth Psychology

It is no easy task to predict all the profoundly human repercussions which the present renewal of the science of religions is capable of promoting in our culture, especially as a result of its rediscovery of the meaning and value of myth. It is itself a palpable demonstration of what makes for the drama of humanism, how man simply destroys himself whenever he seeks to free and fulfill himself by loosening his bonds with God and turning away from him, whereas he can only make sense of himself, within the meaning of all else, in God, the only being who is true with that divine truth which is the supreme truth—truth itself. Myth itself had already formulated this idea, the root of which lies in the simple contrast between sacred, ritual activity and activity that is profane or, more accurately, profaned.

If religious phenomenology and the comparative history of religions are capable of regenerating a truly religious humanism, the human sciences in their turn offer no less promise, confirming and complementing, in their own invaluable ways, this same process. This is particularly true of psychology, and preeminently of those new forms called, in Germany, depth psychology or, in the Anglo-Saxon world, dynamic psychology. Sigmund Freud was the great pioneer in this, although he had precursors and more than precursors, in fact, who are worth returning to, as is happening, for instance with Paul Janet.[1]

Freud and the Discovery of the Unconscious

The personal and public fate of Freud and his work is typical of that of so many moderns in being profoundly ambivalent. In France, for example, the scientific establishment, no less than the theological one, was intent on ignoring him for as long as conceivably possible. In neither case did one have to be a prophet to predict what would follow. The

---

[1]The entire history and interpretation of the various schools of dynamic psychology have recently been recast by Henri F. Ellenberger in the work referred to in note 21 of the preceding chapter. It is a monument of phenomenal erudition and penetrating assessments, underpinned by a wide culture and long psychiatric practice.

resistance had not been rational. The dikes cracked, then, almost in a single go, collapsed and total immersion ensued. Given this background of contempt and, even more, of unbelievable ignorance, it is pathetic to see philosophers and theologians eager to outdo each other in suddenly canonizing as "science's" last and definitive word every utterance of a master who, but yesterday, was unknown and held in opprobrium. Worse still, they often merely parrot the simplifications of dubious disciples and rush into amateur psychoanalysis of anything from St. Paul to the problem of knowledge.

In fact, Freud's work, like that of his heirs and rivals, is a curious mixture. It is difficult to disentangle what is genuinely scientific from an ideology that is, in some respects, pure fantasy and, in others, infantile. It is more difficult still to isolate those elements of truth, impatient of the framework of modern science, as it is at present understood, but which would require integration once that was needed and inevitable refashioning of our knowledge and its categories has been achieved. Freud's personality remains one of the most enigmatic of modern times: man of learning, prophet, sometimes, even often a genius and yet, under the revolutionary appearances, tacitly but tenaciously conservative; discovering complexes, yet himself mysteriously complex; open-minded, curious about everything, happy to go outside his own sphere with a serendipity there, as within it, more pregnant with possibilities than he often realized, yet capable of venting outrageous lies with positively pontifical assurance or of sticking obstinately to mere whims without sense or substance.

Ellenberger adds another pertinent observation.[2] Psychology had been supposed to consist in schools of thought, each seeking the fullness of truth with the help of the others, whereas Freud has the questionable distinction of having brought back the sect, in the sense that the ancient philosophies were sects: meaning, first, common loyalty to a master for whom one has the attitude, less of a pupil for his teacher, however brilliant, than of a disciple for his guru, and, furthermore, a morose, mistrustful orthodoxy, forever refining the only supposedly true interpretations of the master's *dicta* and viciously badgering anything and anyone straying in the slightest from the party line.

But the litany of droll misunderstandings of which Freud has been and remains the occasion is not exhausted. There is Anna de Noailles hastening to thank him for the sexual liberation so many owed him, only to hear, with a comic horror, that he himself had never dreamed of betraying his wife! Freud is certainly responsible, albeit against his will,

---

[2] *Op. cit.*, pp. 345ff.

for modern consumer society floundering and drowning in a flood of filth, with its eroticism degenerated into a scatological hysteria. Without intending it, the man who discovered the sado-anal stage as the first bog where man's progressing awareness risks submerging him threw us all back into it.

Freud's own equivocations and, curiously, not so much his audacities as everything dated and old-fashioned about him were no mean cause (not simply the occasion) of these bizarre deviations. But it need hardly be said that his real merit, his unquestionable stature, lies elsewhere. It is he who has let us rediscover, or discover, the mysterious depths of the human soul: the drama inseparable from it, its astounding complexity and its still more astounding unity.

He himself drew, or believed himself to have drawn, from his own discoveries a reductionist interpretation of religion. What this meant, though, only appeared after his death when the explosive, which was its main ingredient, went off. Destructive it undeniably was, but only by virtue of the scientist confusions it included and of which his own discoveries had, in any case, sounded the death knell. Freud regarded himself in all sincerity as a strict materialist, faithful to nineteenth-century scientific orthodoxy. Yet one may credit Soviet psychologists with the greater perception. They have banned his theories and his psychoanalysis for bringing back soul and spirit, in a way they would almost qualify as diabolical, where they were to be least expected.

The unconscious was Freud's first discovery.[3] He was led to see, almost to touch, a fact totally ignored by Cartesianism and which even the penetrating analyses of Leibniz had not restored to modern thought: namely that the soul's dimensions exceed those of explicit consciousness. And this is not just a simple matter as was once thought, and by Freud himself for a while, of a somewhat tenebrous margin to the conscious mind. We are not merely faced with a subconscious but with an unconscious, a wholly unlit sphere of the psyche which is of no less influence, in its way, than its enlightened complement. It even seems to possess so redoubtable an autonomy that we begin to wonder how far the unconscious dominates our consciousness, rather than vice versa.

It must be said, though, that Freud for his part had not the slightest intention of reneging on the supremacy of the conscious mind. This whole technique had as its aim (and one must never forget that psychoanalysis is meant to be an instrument of healing and not pure scientific

---

[3]It is clearly expressed in his *Traumdeutung*, Leipzig and Vienna, 1900. (Eng. trans. in vols. 4 and 5 of *The Standard Edition of the Complete Psychological Works of Sigmund Freud*, London, 1953.)

knowledge) to reabsorb the unconscious into the conscious and thereby restore it to the latter. For to Freud, in opposition to Jung's much bolder and even extravagant view, the unconscious only held things it had taken from the conscious, this conscious being only too ready to consign them.

Thus repressed material formed the whole content of the Freudian unconscious. It was peopled, that meant, by things the unconscious could not and particularly did not dare embrace and which it had frantically pushed out of sight, in the forlorn hope of being rid of them for good.

But all this, interesting as it is, assumed its precise importance only when linked to what was Freud's truly key discovery that enabled him to put forward on a basis of definite facts, ideas which though relatively speaking, new, were hardly revolutionary, and that, above all, it allowed him to provide an unanticipated explanation and a practical cure for neuroses, things until then not just beyond treatment but beyond comprehension.

We refer, of course, to complexes: repressed memories agglutinating, organizing and eventually crystallizing themselves in the psychic under-ground. This, in the strict sense, is the revelation we owe to Freud,[4] a revelation of how factors apparently expelled from our conscious exis-tence and of which we thought ourselves permanently relieved continue to live, and to live not just a latent, passive life but an active and disturb-ingly creative one. By this means he was enabled to explain how the conscious mind could be paralyzed, inhibited or become positively deranged. What our conscious personality had thought to have ejected or suppressed was in fact still developing, not so much outside the person-ality but at a hidden level of it, unvisited as a rule by the conscious mind. In return, this wild, parasitical undergrowth would be sucking the con-scious life of its vitality, imposing on it its diminishing autonomy. A time would come when the consequences of this proliferation in the sub-soil would be such that, without exactly coming out into the open, the pres-sure they were applying would break and scatter the harmony that seemed to be in possession. It is as if, at the expense of that personality we consider truly and uniquely ours because it is the only one on the surface, one or more anti-personalities had formed themselves in its shadow. Not satisfied with silently milking its vigor, these underground forces one day erupt within it and, being stronger, literally tear it to shreds yet without having vouchsafed their own identity.

Psychoanalysis, the therapy Freud proposed, consisted in returning to the past, to that unobliterated, still subsisting past, which, by the ironical

---

[4]On this and what follows, see especially Ellenberger *op. cit.*, pp. 414ff.

means of apparent disappearance, in reality persisted in attenuating the conscious mind's dominion. Thus, by a patient process of anamnesis, the elements hidden from the conscious and causing unconscious complexes, would be brought back to the conscious level. Provided that the conscious gave them space, reintegrating the *Das* in the ego, this anamnesis would dethrone the now acknowledged complexes and restore health, that is, its own supremacy to the conscious. This would require the conscious, cost what it may, to appropriate what it had earlier wished to deny or disown, thereby investing itself with a merely specious and in fact unattainable autonomy, threatening ruin to that which was rightfully its own.

All this shows how strongly regressive Freud's psychological perspective was, and therefore his therapy. He bade the ego descend into its own hell, that is, return to its past in the sense of bringing it back to life in order to repossess it.

Before proceeding, it is worth stressing the general consequences of this. If there is one fantasy absorbing us moderns, it is that of pure futurity. We would fain believe that the future, an untrammeled, creative future, is everything, and in order to enter upon it we are prepared cheerfully to sacrifice our entire past.

But the first lesson Freud can give us is that such a sacrifice cannot be made. Any attempt only bestows a devouring, draconian freedom, progressively inhibiting our whole present until finally it does away with all chance of a real future. A past that is forgotten or suppressed is a past that imprisons us instead of leaving us free to use it as we wish. Worse still, the unstable freedom such suppression confers has the paradoxical effect of turning our present and our future into seasons of meaningless enslavement.

Only a full integration of our past allows us to master and surpass it. Whenever pride or cowardice (the two in fact go together) forbid this, we block ourselves, we condemn ourselves to a progressive deterioration, which only accelerates with the passing of time. Humility and courage are needed to take us back to the point of blockage, to remove it and make possible a gradual reconstruction of our existence and a renewal of our personality.

The Oedipus Complex and Sexuality

Freud maintains, in this connection, that no period has such importance or such abiding effects as early childhood. It is then that the first level of complexes is formed, and so long as they are not resolved, they vitiate our entire psychological development. As the years pass this encystation merely hardens.

To mention the complex that particularly characterizes life's first stage is to touch the heart of the common idea of "Freudianism," and what is perhaps its most inspired element is also its most ambiguous. We are referring, of course, to the Oedipus complex and, with it, to libido, something given such unique status by Freud and, frankly, a most elusive meaning. Freud's dilemma is at this point painfully evident, his total, unshakable and yet unquestionably tormented adherence to materialism on the one hand and, on the other, an insight which, had he yielded to its inherent logic, would have compelled him to break with his preconceptions.

The Oedipus complex, as its name indicates, consists of a hidden desire to murder one's father, held to be a rival, combined with an emotional and sensual fixation with one's mother. This represents the first expression of the erotic impulse, libido as Freud called it, and this libido, according to him, forms the primal and in fact only tendency behind all human life. Life's development is but the expansion of this tendency and the various incarnations it adopts so as to weave the fabric of our psychological life. All our other tendencies or, more correctly, since there are no others, what appear to us as such, are only different versions of what Freud called sublimation, which applies to our every aesthetic, moral and religious instinct as well as to the plain and simple urge to know.[5]

Freud himself anticipated objections by distinguishing the sexual from the genital in the narrow sense, and refused to reduce the former to the latter, although it remains—more or less immediately, more or less covertly—inseparable from it.

But this was no real answer. If the realities under review are not of themselves necessarily linked with the genital function, in the way that sexuality properly so-called of course is, in this case what Freud termed the sexual would embrace and confound a host of realities better named vital and which, granted that the genuinely sexual forms a primary, or even the primary, instance of them, cannot be reduced to it. Thus to label this disparate collection as sexual is gratuitous. It lacks justification; it lacks meaning. Or, taking the opposing possibility, if these activities *are* intrinsically related to genital activity, then the extension of the term sexual would be justified. But Freud himself never seriously attempted to prove this connection. The conclusion must be, therefore, that there is no good reason for enlarging the term sexual to the extent of applying it to

---

[5]Ellenberger, *op. cit.*, pp. 424ff.

every human tendency or activity. This becomes more evident still in the equivocal use which Freud and especially his disciples made of the term sublimation. Did they mean that activity inspired by such sublimation was only a camouflage for sexuality? This of course undoubtedly happens. There have been, for instance, pseudo-mystics, deluding others and deluding themselves, who disguised feelings that were purely physical in the distinctly sexual sense under a religiously-colored emotionalism and language. But the fact that this can occur and even occurs often does not establish that all religious experiences have this character. And in fact no other proof has yet been produced or even seriously proffered.

If, on the other hand, a genuine transition from one kind of life activity to another by sublimation be possible, in the sense that physical and moral energies which, in a given individual, had begun by being channeled into sexual activity could then be turned to a quite other mode of activity, then sublimation merely stated the truism that our life is one and that it is that one life which must be occupied with one thing or another. But in that case it was quite wrong to reduce religious activity or any other to sexual or, again, to any other activity.[6]

This is a matter of common sense observation, verified by therapeutic practice whenever it is not vitiated *a priori* by the impositions of conventional jargon, and it led Jung, previously Freud's closest collaborator, to break with him and to talk of the "metamorphoses of libido," with this last word losing any specially sexual connotation.

From Freud to Jung by Way of Adler

Adler, before Jung, had already fully established from his own therapeutic practice that it was in many cases nothing but pure dogmatism to invoke the Oedipus complex. Experience revealed that a complex of a quite different kind, which he called the inferiority complex, and which had nothing specifically sexual to it, was capable of playing an equally decisive part in neuroses, as was proved by the fact that the neurosis was cured once the complex had been resolved. Jung, for his part, progressed towards a vision of things that tended to balance in importance, aggressive instincts with the erotic, the former being the basis of the inferiority complex and the latter fundamental to the Oedipus complex. At the same time he made both relative by describing the problem behind every psychological crisis as one of "individuation," understanding by that the process of the gradual inner formation of our autonomous being. As a

---

[6]On all this it is still worth reading Roland Dalbiez, *La Méthode Psychonalytique et la doctrine freudienne*, vol. 2: *Discussion*, Paris, 1949, esp. pp. 258ff.

result, he placed the center of gravity beyond, at once, our tendencies to opposition and to union.[7]

As Jung himself observed,[8] such a point of view was indicative of the three psychological systems: Freud's concentrated on the consequences of early childhood, Adler's on the adolescent crisis, and his own on the mid-life crisis which surfaces inexplicably after first sexual and then parental problems seem resolved.

The finest historian and analyst of these systems, Henri Ellenberger, is undoubtedly justified in stressing, with a touch of irony, that the differences among Freud, Jung and Adler corresponded both to their different types of client and to their individual histories. Freud, for long, practiced almost exclusively among the bourgeois Viennese, people enjoying a comfortable, unexacting life where the sole occupation, the sole value, lay in sentimental love-making. His patients in fact had generally been pampered as children, but having discovered all the prejudices of the preceding generation they were easily led to think of themselves as having been unbearably oppressed.

Adler's work was with the working-class juvenile delinquents who were too young to be so absorbed by love affairs and had, in their own environment, quite other fish to fry. Even less was their problem that of the oppressive father. Rather, they lacked any experience of a real father and it was this that caused their adolescence to be encumbered by an instinctive conflict with society as a whole.

To Jung's patients, eminent bourgeois and liberal Protestants, both love affairs and teenage delinquency must have seemed of little moment, in fact mere nothings. Rather it was being alone with oneself, the inevitable consequence of such a Protestant upbringing, that threatened them with the unbearable.

Furthermore it seems certain that in each case the therapist himself, albeit involuntarily, albeit quite unconsciously, infused into his patients, who belonged socially and psychologically to his own world, the characteristic features of his personal problem.

Freud, as is now known, was the son of a mother who adored her eldest boy and of a parvenu father who was compelled to make an impression upon the environment into which he was intruded by the social climbing, which peaked with his marriage. Hence Freud projected his own complex upon patients who cannot all have suffered the same, but who could easily recognize themselves in it and adapt to it. They were, after all, more or less spoilt children, sons of parvenu fathers, with

---

[7]On Adler, see Ellenberger, *op. cit.*, pp. 469ff.

[8]On Jung, see Ellenberger, *op. cit.*, pp. 539ff.

a common taste for "amusing themselves" in the very, though not of course exclusively, Viennese sense of the term.

Adler came of a humble family and undoubtedly had a social handicap to overcome so that, while his biography has none of the tragedy or waste of those of the trouble-makers with whom he concerned himself, it certainly fitted him to understand them. And in return it became easier to assimilate their own criminal unadaptedness to a simple but not irremediable under-achieving such as his own.

In the case of Jung and his patients, the mutual preadaptation was closer still. Like him, certainly, the majority of his clients were afflicted by the false angelism of excessive refinement, that of the famous patrician culture of Basle, while at the same time they suffered from the vertigo of a freedom proclaimed as absolute yet emptied of occupation.

All this assuredly contains a great deal of truth and should keep us from any excessive passion for system-making while bringing home to us both the incredible variety of the human psyche and its almost equally amazing plasticity.

The True Meaning of Sexuality

The fact remains, however, that although Jung was among the first to have the distinction of detecting and denouncing Freud's confusion, like many others he failed in his reaction to recognize that Freud's intuition, however misdefined and under-developed it may have been, was perhaps Freud's greatest achievement. What Freud saw was that the sexual instinct is not simply one among the instincts of the human soul. It is absolutely central and similar in this respect to the religious instinct such as contemporary religious science is coming to locate and define. The question now is, how can both be central, even at different levels, and how should their relationship one to another be interpreted?

Freud, it seems, was torn all his life between the desire to reduce the religious instinct to the sexual and an ineradicable doubt as to the real possibility of doing so. The extremely contorted fashion in which he made the attempt in *Totem and Taboo*[9] and as late as *The Future of an Illusion*[10] is very revealing. Religion, he proposed, was an offspring of early man's archaic way of surmounting the Oedipus complex. In a society still dominated by sexual promiscuity, the strongest male would have suppressed every possible rival until his sons, in dread of their lives,

---

[9]The first German edition appeared in 1913 (Eng. trans., *op. cit.*, vol. 13, London, 1955).

[10]Appeared in 1927. (Eng. trans., *op. cit.*, vol. 21, London, 1961.) See Ellenberger, *op. cit.*, pp. 445ff.

came to do away with him. Thereupon full of remorse, they would have consecrated their murder by a cannibalistic meal designed to revive within them the life of their immolated father. Hence both totemism and sacrifice would have emerged together.

This reconstruction was, of course, a mere conjuring trick and no anthropologist could take it seriously. Primitive promiscuity never existed while it is notorious that sacrifice always antedated totemism, often being found without the latter ever appearing. Thus, when in *Moses and Monotheism*[11] Freud went on to explain the genesis of monotheism, the result was predictable: a second-rate novel bearing no relation whatever to historical reality.

The very fact that Freud felt bound to make such detours and never roundly asserted, despite pressure from his disciples, that religion was nothing but a pure and simple projection of unsatisfied sexuality indicated the great uncertainty that always plagued him on this point and, more generally, on the precise meaning of sublimation. This came to light unexpectedly in Zilboorg's revelations on Freud's childhood,[12] which explained the blend of attraction and fear that religion held for him ever after. We see him at once unable to break the chains of his native Judaism yet furiously intent on regarding it as definitely defunct—the mirror or explanation of the persisting insecurity caused by so recent a social liberation. We can register, too, the simultaneous nostalgia and repulsion that Catholic ritual aroused in him ever since an elderly housemaid had introduced him to it as a child.

This attitude, hardened to the point of insoluble self-contradiction, came out in his correspondence and dealings with Pastor Pfister.[13] Their exchange was cordial, mutually respectful, increasingly frank, but it is quaint to see both protagonists always softly circling the question of religion without ever openly tackling it. In Pfister's case, no doubt, we have the tact of the experienced ecclesiastic, anxious to avoid even a hint of proselytism—though one suspects there was more to it. With Freud, however, his habitual politeness is certainly not the real explanation; rather, it was his censored awareness of an inner contradiction between his intention, fixed yet unsure of itself, of holding to materialism and his plan of offering to humankind what may well be called an equivalent to redemption.

---

[11]First appeared in articles in the review *Imago* in 1937-38. (Eng. trans., *op. cit.*)

[12]Part of O. Zilboorg's recollections of Freud appeared in *Etudes carmélitaines*, 1947. Cf. his *Sigmund Freud, His Exploration of the Mind of Man*, New York, 1951.

[13]Eng. trans. *Psychoanalysis and Faith: The Letters of Sigmund Freud and Oskar Pfister*, New York, 1963.

There is only one possible escape from this dilemma and it surely consists in conceiving the libido, as Freud never could, neither as "sexual" in his own confused sense nor merely as capable, following Jung, of assuming a sexual form as one among others. At the root of man's whole psychic life lies what, prior to any analysis, we can simply call a desire for the Other, union with whom is a requisite of self-fulfillment. Since man is inseparably body and soul, his pursuit of the physical realization of this union is a pursuit of something more than the merely genital, more than the merely sensual, even on the level of a purely human encounter. It is indeed a most crass misunderstanding of Freudianism to use it in justification of a superficial eroticism where the pursuit of pleasure is detached from all other finalities. The true meaning of Freud's discovery lies completely the other way. There is no sexuality that is merely genital nor, *a fortiori*, merely sensual. It is always something that involves man's whole life and personality.

Yet, for both individual and couple, any mutual relationship is but the principal expression of something far wider. Man's pursuit, man's desire for the other (an ambiguous desire, as much about getting as giving) reveals him as structurally related, in his entirety, to the cosmos. However widely one understands sexuality, such a relationship far exceeds it, but it is in sexuality that it achieves symbolic expression and its primary realization. And this in turn brings to light the transcendental relationship of the cosmos itself to the supreme mystery that lies beyond it, outside man's grasp unless it should yield itself to him, and with man always and everywhere dependent upon it.

Thus there is a fundamental likeness, first, between sexuality and man's whole relationship with the cosmos, while this in its turn reflects invertedly the relationship of the cosmos, ourselves included, with God. In other words, man bears the image of the masculine before the universe, applying his mind to it but needing its material for his mind to fructify while, conversely, God plays a transcendent, masculine role in relation to the whole cosmic reality and particularly to man.

In such conditions we can see how privileged and irreplaceable an image of the relationship of creator to creature is provided for myth by what is human and, more specifically, by human sexuality. One must even say that, however analogical its application necessarily remains, this image does involve a very real participation in the model it reflects, or better, refracts. Yet it is the very reality of this connection which forbids any reduction, while any attempt to turn a legitimate induction into a simple deduction would be to open the way to idolatrous distortions.

Taking a still broader and more profound view, it is at this point not simply the meaning that the sexual relationship can have in myth that may claim to be justified, but also that of either side of the parental relationship, paternal or maternal, as of the horizontal relationship of fraternity. And here too one may foresee that, if the parental relationship, in its transcendental sense, precedes the sexual or, preferably, spousal relationship and yet in another immanent sense, follows it, then a cleavage is possible through which what we call original sin may find its way. This would be the situation of man when he wishes to be a husband without being a son and yet being unable to kill an unassailable father, only becomes a father himself by begetting children for death.

This is merely a preliminary notice of what we intend to develop later, but it is worth bringing out an intuition of Freud's that came to him late in life, was wholly unexpected and yet is in remarkable concord with our own thesis. It was so unexpected indeed that it threw even his closest disciples into confusion. He affirmed that the sexual instinct seems to be doubled by a shadow of its own projecting. He called it the death instinct.

Eros and Thanatos

The term itself—death instinct—has been rightly criticized for skating over the essential dissimilarity of the libido and the fascination for death.[14] Instead of an instinct, it would be better to talk of a presentiment of, a fascination for, death which the sexual instinct, including all that surrounds it as much as what it itself incorporates, reacts against in the most fundamental fashion while apparently at the same time embracing it to its own destruction. Here, even more than hitherto, we rejoin myth —every myth where death is seen not simply as the inverse of birth but inextricably caught up—and Oedipus is the classic example—with the development of Eros.[15]

Freud's intuitions often lacked direction. They were badly expressed. They tried to rationalize everything and are, to that extent, unsatisfactory. But provided their superficial logic be superseded, they serve to confirm, by means of the most recent psychological experience, the abiding meaningfulness, value and relevance of myth.

---

[14]This is the great surprise of *Jensists des Lustprinzips*, Vienna, 1920. (Eng. trans. *Beyond the Pleasure Principle*, in *op. cit.*, vol. 18, London, 1955.) See Ellenberger, *op. cit.*, pp. 434ff.

[15]Despite its being somewhat superficial, it is worth mentioning E. Gargam's thesis, *L'Amour et la Mort*, Paris, 1959.

Jung and the Collective Unconscious

Jung stumbled about with Freud in the same twilit labyrinth until, by giving his master the slip, he lost hold of the thread of Ariadne which the latter had clung to. On the other hand, he must be tributed with a far greater appreciation of the size and complexity of this labyrinth, even though he too was to lose his way, as Freud had done, and finally sit himself down, complacently, in total confusion.[16]

Jung's merit consisted above all, not so much in desexualizing the unconscious, where there was as much loss as gain, as in his frank acknowledgment of its super-individual character. Freud himself had certainly anticipated this. His maladroit attempts at religious phenomenology drew what validity they have from their recognition of what we may call the collective dimension attaching to the Oedipus complex and everything connected with it. Yet Freud never really moved beyond his vision of the unconscious as nothing more than the repository of material suppressed by the conscious. Jung had no hesitation in saying and showing that the unconscious contains material of which the individual's consciousness can never, at any stage however early, have been the source, and which must be regarded in consequence as lying outside that person's history and even their existence.

Jung claimed that what he called the collective nature of the unconscious was attested, above all, by material emerging through recollection or simply in dreams which could not possibly have sprung from the history of that person's conscious mind and which showed a remarkable structural similarity with the great religious myths. The name he used for this was archetypes.[17]

The engaging description he gives of them, though, leaves one with the uncomfortable impression of clinical observations having been somewhat contaminated by a jumble of information drawn from the comparative history of religion. This information, even before being harnessed to the material in question, had undoubtedly been subjected to a good deal of imaginative refashioning and then, seeming to have been empirically verified, provoked the imagination of Jung, and even more of his enthusiastic but uncritical disciples, to the wildest excesses. The works of Jolan Jacobi, for example, give the impression that this part at least of the Jungian corpus is nothing but a self-generating gnosis about

---

[16]Ellenberger, *op. cit.*, pp. 539ff. Ellenberger knew Jung personally.
[17]See in particular the last part of *L'Homme à la Découverte de son Ame*, French trans., Geneva, 1994, pp. 215ff. (Eng. trans.: *Modern Man in Search of a Soul*, New York, 1933.)

as substantial as cotton candy. *Symbols of Transformation*[18] was already moving in this direction and to read *Memories, Dreams and Reflections*[19] is to have one's fears confirmed.

But it would be unjust and erroneous to retain this aspect only of Jung's view of the unconscious and his archetypes, along with his own penchant for erratic and elaborate systematizing. Undoubtedly his imagination would, at the least opportunity, take over from his scientific knowledge, and its very exuberance could not hide its platitudes. Nevertheless he succeeded in detecting the amazing structural continuity there is between the waking and sleeping dreams of civilized man and the myths of primitive man. Does this mean we have a racial memory, retaining the history prior to our personal histories? Or is it that the human soul has a congenital structure, representative, in its turn, of the appearance in the psychic world of the structure of the universe itself? We cannot possibly go into these questions here, except to say that the two propositions are not mutually exclusive.

Jung's undeniable contribution, after his opening, rather jejune affirmation of the impossibility of reducing religion or culture in general to mere sexuality, was to reveal the continuance of the mythical world in the unconscious of civilized peoples. This may well imply that we are bound not only to our collective, human past, but to the very texture of the cosmos, attached to it in every fiber of our sensitive, vital, instinctive and even chemical being. It will only be possible for us to interpret this discovery once we have examined recent sociological research and gone on to chart the course of the cosmological question.

Another and by no means negligible achievement of Jung's was, not indeed to replace the regressive perspective by the prospective, but to give a clear primacy to the latter. He did this far more overtly than had Freud, even though the latter, without stating it or even being aware of it, had begun to move in that direction. If the conscious mind was to attain integral well-being in the present, it was neither possible nor desirable merely to recall the past but necessary for that past to be integrated into a prevision of the future. Thereby Jung gave us back a truly dynamic view of the psyche within the universe, while at the same time he extended Freud's vision, not just by avoiding his narrow view of sexuality but by looking to the future as well as to the past.

---

[18]*Wandlungen und Symbole der Libido*, published in articles in 1911 and in one volume the following year. (Eng. trans., *op. cit.*, vol. 5, *Symbols of Transformation*, 2nd ed., 1967.)

[19]*Erinnerungen, Traüme und Gedanken*, Zurich, 1962. (Eng. trans. *Memories, Dreams, Reflections*, New York, 1963.)

These achievements, however, should not hide from us the fact that, despite appearances of greater breadth and profundity, Jung was no less subject to the reductionist temptation than Freud. Mircea Eliade's judgment on this point formulated in *Myths, Dreams and Mysteries*[20] is undoubtedly to be endorsed, however much its severity might have surprised some. Like Freud, Jung could not resist the temptation common to the medical profession of explaining the healthy in terms of the sick. But we mean more than that. He failed to appreciate the necessary distinction between the archetypes as simple psychic data and the essential mark of the hierophanies, as Eliade himself calls them, which are at the root of myth, namely that of revealing a reality that transcends the psyche, unconscious as much as conscious. So it was that while Jung seemed to open up immense horizons for the human mind, he was in fact subject to a latent solipsism, all the more exclusive, paradoxically, for ego. Jung simply bypassed the fundamental, inveterate objectivity of the unconscious and the conscious. He took the subjectivity of our representations for granted, forgetting of what late development such subjectivity is and how, even then, any of its deliverances only retain their meaning because they imply an objective value to our thought. Myth's prime achievement is not that of reflecting any unalterable structure of the psyche or, derivatively, of the universe. It is that of proclaiming, incessantly and insistently, from the very moment of its birth, that the human spirit can never be closed upon itself, but only exists and only experiences itself in reference to something beyond itself.

Certain of Jung's declarations towards the end of his life seem to betray an awareness of the problem, and one may believe that, well before then, as his bizarre but enthralling memoirs reveal, he had regained or simply preserved, beneath his scientism, a genuinely religious sense of the world and human existence. But one cannot avoid the thought that his religion, real though it may have been, never rose above a lasting fascination for a kind of gnosis, that is, a religion in which religious reality is admittedly acknowledged to be the *Grund* of our existence, even its *Urgrund*, but never as truly transcendent, as an *Ungrund*.

We shall presently show that precisely such an acknowledgment underlies the poorest myth, even if the more refined sometimes apprehend it less than fully. Freud and Jung were men of bold vision, but ultimately the first was adrift and the second confused. Adler, on the other hand, arrived at a religious and Christian conversion through

---

[20]Mircea Eliade, *Mythes, Rêves et Mystères*, Paris, 1957, pp. 48ff. (Eng. trans. *Myths, Dreams and Mysteries*, Magnolia, MA: 1992.)

practicing an individual psychology that was speculatively modest but wholly honest in practice, and it is he, one may think, who in the end grasped most fully the final implication not only of the human psyche's reinsertion into the cosmic whole but, simply, of the created personality and the universe in which it features.

III

Myth, Sociology and Cosmology

Just as the psychological discoveries of modern times exceed those of the three masters and three schools we have just treated, so modern psychology's contribution to our understanding of the religious phenomenon and its central importance to the phenomenon of man as such cannot be restricted to the admittedly fundamental aspects just examined. There is, for example, the light that Szondi's analysis has shed upon that supremely religious problem of inherited conditioning and individual freedom. No less worthy of mention in this context is the psychological cosmology of Minkovski. This has plainly shown that we cannot live in the world without representing it to ourselves and that this representation is less a projection of our personality upon our experience of the cosmos than the discovery of that personality in the presentiment we have of a super- or rather ultra-personality standing behind the whole universe.

The very existence of such material would lead us to expect that the religious understanding of reality, registered in myth, is as much corroborated by cosmology or sociology as by psychology. Yet a superficial study of the results of modern scientific sociology and cosmology is all too likely to give the impression that they have done nothing but expose the mythical, religious view of reality as an old-fashioned illusion. Closer analysis, however, proves that this is in no way the case. The modern sociologies or cosmologies intent upon reducing the religious phenomenon, or claiming to have done so, when put under the microscope betray the inevitability of religion, if only because of the self-contradiction and self-frustration to which their pseudo-reductionism reduces them.

Myth and Society

This was particularly evident in the fruitless attempt of the French school of sociology to treat religion as a mere social phenomenon. What emerged in fact with startling clarity and in complete contradiction to the intentions of the authors was that religion is not a mere side-show to society's early development, but that without religion there is no society, society itself being only one of religion's most indicative products.

In this context, the studies of Lévy-Bruhl[1] and Durkheim[2] yielded two major insights, badly elaborated and unsatisfactorily expressed but nonetheless distinctly worth retaining. The most important was perhaps the one that at first sight seemed most extravagant. This was the idea propounded by Lévy-Bruhl in order to justify Durkheim's theory of social constraint being the origin of moral conscience, and at the same time to give as much of a rational basis as possible to the totemistic conception of both society and religion. According to Lévy-Bruhl, individual consciousness is not inherent to human nature. It appeared relatively late, long after its ancestor, collective consciousness. It emerged only gradually, along with the first rational analysis, of what he called "collective representations." In this view, moral consciousness would be the survival of this original consciousness, which is something greater than the individual's consciousness and the latter's interior root.

By the same score, we have an explanation for religion. It originated in the collective "I," so much vaster than the individual who for long lived in utter dependence upon it.[3]

There is a real kinship here with Jung's collective unconscious, with the individual consciousness gradually emerging out of it, without ever achieving that total emancipation which would be equivalent to suicide.

Again, it is not uninteresting to connect such speculations of sociologists and psychologists with the musings of a mind whose philosophical claims are usually unjustified but who now and then lets fly an intriguing intuition. We refer to Maurice Maeterlinck and the sketch of technical man's future with which he concludes La Vie des Termites. According to this, the immersion of individual consciousness in the collective will occur, not at the beginning, but at the turn of the human spirit's evolution. This will be the inevitable result of increasing specialization and of the ever stricter co-ordination of human effort in a scientifically organized society. Such a view is not that remote from the excogitations of Teilhard on the Omega point, towards which converge all the apparently individual lines of the human phylum. The only difference is that such a

---

[1]Lucien Lévy-Bruhl, La Mentalité primitive, Paris, 1922. Cf. also what he had already written in 1910 in Les Fonctions dans les Sociétés inférieures. His development can be traced in L'Ame primitive, 1927; Le Surnaturel et la Nature dans la Mentalité primitive, 1931; and La Mythologie primitive, 1935.

[2]Emile Durkheim, Les Formes élémentaires de la Vie religieuse, Paris, 5th ed., 1968. The most remarkable treatment of the problem of religion and society is undoubtedly to be found in Joachim Wach's Sociology of Religion, Chicago, 1944, and in his posthumous The Comparative Study of Religion, New York, 1958.

[3]Lévy-Bruhl, La Mentalité primitive, esp. pp. 49ff., 295, 310, 403ff.

prediction appears wholly sinister to Maeterlinck, while Teilhard seems delighted.

Lévy-Bruhl, of course intended to be rigorously scientific and would not be flattered by our comparisons with these rather fuliginous theories. (Maeterlinck and Teilhard would of course claim the same, but in their cases and without analyzing their respective equipment as men of science, amateur or specialist, it is more obvious that they deceived themselves as to the true nature of their ideas.) If our comparisons prove anything it is especially that which Arthur Koestler stressed so emphatically: that in every inspired man of science there is, behind the most strictly rational exterior, a background which one may call mystical or illuminist and without which it would not seem possible for science to progress.[4] Further, there is no doubt that to introduce, at the end of an attempt to provide a rationalized explanation of the religious phenomenon while by-passing God, such a notion as that of the collective consciousness is not progress but a regression to primitive views under their most chimerical aspects.

But any attempt at a phenomenological analysis of the concept proposed by Lévy-Bruhl must be preceded by an examination of the earlier proposals of Durkheim which were what moved Lévy-Bruhl to his rather disconcerting conjectures.

The author of *Formes Elémentaires de la Vie Religieuse* is remembered as the father of totemism;[5] not for discovering the anthropological phenomenon of the totem, but for having aimed to explain the whole genesis of the religious idea by means of the totem. A totem, we recall, is, among certain Native North American tribes such as the Iroquois and the Algonquins, a mythical tribal ancestor represented by a sort of heraldic symbol on which he is generally assimilated to a fabulous animal, akin to those that occupy the life of hunters. Since not dissimilar phenomena appear elsewhere, in particular among the Australians, it was thought to admit of generalization.

If there ever were anthropologists who thought that religion could be explained by totemism, there are certainly none today. The phenomenon, in the first place, is emphatically not universal, and, secondly, even where it exists it belongs to a secondary stage of human evolution, following and not preceding the more primitive manifestations of religion such as sacrifice.

Yet Durkheim's researches have not lost their interest. He succeeded in showing effectively, on the basis of the totemistic cult, how that col-

---

[4]Arthur Koestler, *The Sleepwalkers.*
[5]See especially his Chapter IV, pp. 123ff.

lective spirit which every genuinely organic society requires for its birth and survival, supposes that all the members of that society refer themselves to an enigmatic being, finding themselves in him even though he be "other," as much in relation to all as to each.

The totem is only one mythical form among others of this reference. What gives it value is the way it signals the conjunction, so clearly seen by Otto, of remoteness and sympathy, something so characteristic of the sacred in all its forms. On this point Durkheim undoubtedly saw straight, but what he saw was not the totemistic and so, social origin of religion, but the religious origin of society whether that be expressed in a totem or quite otherwise.

We can perhaps best elucidate the implications of Durkheim's insight by recalling the enlightening distinction we owe to Tönnies, between natural societies of the *Gemeinschaft* or community type, and artificial societies, simple associations of the *Gesellschaft* type.[6] The mark of the first and the source of their specific character is that they are founded upon the conviction common to all of a general and individual relationship to a mythical "father," in whom everyone can recognize himself, though without any confusion between one another or with him, because it is no less essential for this father to be wholly distinct as it is for him to be unbelievably close. Whereas a *Gesellschaft* is a society of which men are consciously the exclusive authors, every *Gemeinschaft* is essentially religious.

But the religiousness characterizing such societies is certainly marked by that ambiguity inherent to every myth and which we have already mentioned. Hence there is a semblance if not of identity at least of indistinction between the community and its totem, sufficient to explain though not ultimately to justify Durkheim's conclusion that the totem is only the group's collective soul. It does indeed seem, in many respects, to have played such a role. But to conclude that that exhausted the meaning of the totem for primitive man (it was of course *a* meaning) is for the civilized man of learning at once to project his own naiveté upon him and to credit him with a radical rationalizing that is quite alien to him. But from another, equally essential and far more penetrating perspective, the totem was and remained "wholly other." Were this not so it would have no more sacrality for him than it does for the professor who attributes his own style of reasoning to primitive man.

Once this has been said, we can talk purposefully about Lévy-Bruhl's still undifferentiated collective and primitive consciousness, Jung's collective unconscious and the groping, sometimes floundering speculations

[6]*Gemeinschaft und Gesellschaft* was published in 1887.

of Maeterlinck and of Teilhard de Chardin, not to mention the late Renan and Loisy.

The first remark must be that the very idea of a collective consciousness is profoundly unsatisfactory. This applies whether we talk, as with Lévy-Bruhl, of a consciousness anterior to individual consciousness and from which this latter only gradually distinguishes itself or, as with Maeterlinck or Teilhard, of a final, complete consciousness into which all individual consciousnesses would be called to immerse themselves. Both Teilhard when he speaks of atoms of consciousness which must successively cohere at different levels of complexification and Lévy-Bruhl when he pictures a global primitive consciousness called to shatter into atomized consciousnesses, forget that every consciousness requires a unity which is not accidental but constitutive. In this sense, one can no more speak of adding consciousnesses than of dividing them. Consciousness is nothing if not a unity. To suppose that this unity can be added to others to produce a greater unity or, with equal ease, be smashed into fragmentary unities is to betray crass incomprehension of the subject under discussion and ultimately to vent nothing but hot air.

But it still remains to tackle the problems which the unhappy notion of a collective consciousness sought to illumine.

It is not enough to say with Jung that all our individual consciousnesses emerge from a collective unconscious and are still swimming in its waters even when it has been forgotten. The social phenomenon—as embodied in primitive societies or rather in societies that are true and not simply artificial conglomerations with strictly limited goals and responsibilities—certainly supposes a great deal more than this.

In the first place, it is incontestably the case that in such a society, the society is more and other than the simple sum of its component individuals. In his *Psychologie des Foules*,[7] Gustave Le Bon justly remarked that the collective soul of a society, however one understands that term, can certainly manifest a quasi-personality alien to those of its members and, in some cases, even among the most civilized, not merely alien but terrifyingly barbarian. We will shortly return to this point, but such a lowering emphasizes the fact that this collective soul is not equivalent to the individuals of a society and not even to their sum (if the notion of sum has any real meaning).

But, generally speaking, the society we are envisaging is not the crowd. The crowd represents a regression of society, a neurotic contraction. True society, albeit unsatisfactory, "fallen" as Christians would say, assumes towards the individuals who comprise it, so long as it is not

---

[7]Gustave Le Bon, *La Psychologie des Foules*, Paris, 1895.

definitively corrupted, a character best described as maternal. We mean by this that the individual, the individual consciousness, draws from his society both his existence and his growth. Society gives him the material means of subsistence but, more than that, by its history, its traditions, its culture, it continues to nourish the growth of his intelligence, his heart, and all one may call his soul. He cannot become himself except by a process of assimilation, of recapitulation, consciously making his own the whole human development lived by the society of which he is a member. In this sense it is as true psychologically as it may be biologically that each individual's ontogenesis reproduces the phylogenesis: the most personal development resumes that of the race.

But it is equally true that all this only provides the living humus for the development of unrealized possibilities within each individual, within his own particular consciousness. These all proceed, undoubtedly, from the virtualities concealed in the collective soul. But they are revealed only in each individual consciousness and always in a mode unique to each. They spring up afresh each time from some unsearchable depth. However rooted each individual consciousness may be in the becoming of the collectivity, and in a sense, the more rooted it is, it is always a new, unpredictable and even to some extent unprecedented revelation of the genius of humanity.

Szondi's analysis of fate may be mentioned as a confirmation of this. His analysis is singularly precise.[8] Struck by the importance of hereditary factors in every neurosis and psychosis, Szondi began his study of individual psychological development from a trenchantly determinist perspective. But seeing the created possibilities evidenced by the conscious minds repossessing and dominating every hereditary factor, even the most negative, Szondi became convinced of freedom's reality. This was no abstract freedom, but concrete freedom experiencing itself as a capacity for drawing unforeseen achievements out of the conscious assumption of hereditary predestiny.

An awareness of this other aspect to the relationship of individual and society shows that any recognition of the maternal character of natural society—in which and of which one is born—implies recognition of a mysterious paternity to which no actual society, nor even the whole of humanity, can set limits. And by the same token, one sees both the ambiguity inherent in the totem as in all mythical data, and the illuminative value of Bergson's fertile distinction between closed and open societies.

---

[8] Leopold Szondi, *Schicksalsanalyse*, Basle, 1944.

It is not too much to say that no society will continue to live and generate persons except in the measure that it remains open, without qualification, to the infinite. But at the same time every society seems to be branded by a fatal tendency to close in upon itself. It is then that it becomes a crowd in Le Bon's sense, and manifests a quasi-personality more perverse than every possible or actual perversion of its members, as if a demonic incubus were applied to it. In truth, the society only progresses, is only truly spiritually fertile, according to the measure of its conscious dependence upon and permanent, living openness to the mystery of the divine Other, in whom the unlimited, the infinite is positively revealed. Only there does it become possible to link together all the members of the society alive or dead, without crushing some against the others or mashing them altogether into an impersonal mess of putty. Rather, it would nourish each one at his most intimate level in a common devotion and a common service to a human society which is not indeed ideal, but renders progressively possible a humanity neither uprooted nor arrested, nor falling back on and beneath itself, but a humanity in flower, tending to what transcends it.

In this sense, the experience of a society, assuming it remains fecund, is the experience neither of some unthinkable collective personality anterior to individual persons nor of some even less conceivable future personality where all individuality would be abolished. Rather, it is of developing towards a fullness where all people obscurely feel that they will only meet together not in mutual confusion but full-grown, united because recognizing themselves as children not only of a terrestrial mother, but of a heavenly father.

This being so, religious experience is very far from being only an elementary form of social experience. Rather, social experience envelops the elementary forms of religious experience. This is still so, and the drama of closed societies, our societies, lies, in spite of the best that is in them, in their continual peril of being suffocated in this original enveloping placenta. Hence idolatry. Hence, more specifically, idolatry in its tribal form, the first perversion of any religion and, without any doubt, a perversion that should be dubbed demonic. The heavenly father is caricatured into a Saturn devouring his sons, and the mother-society the first victim of the tyranny, becomes an evil stepmother.

If this analysis is true, it shows that there is no such thing as a collective consciousness, but that actual, always individual consciousness is rooted, throughout the whole biological and psychological history of natural society, in a mysterious interior, simultaneously disclosing the beyond towards which it must never cease to tend if it is not to degenerate or to pervert itself. Hence it is that society (and therefore, certainly, consciousness as it emerges from the collective unconscious) is *at the source* of religion.

That does not mean that it is its source but rather that religion itself is a source from which human existence, both individual and collective, proceeds just as it is also the goal which draws it, so long as it does not turn fatally in upon itself.

So we come back, at the level of collective life, not only to this first, indissoluble datum which is religion as the unifying factor of experience, at once transcendent and immanent, and transcendent at the very heart of its immanence, but also to this second datum, its shadow, which is the blind and ungovernable tendency to reduce religion to the sacred which expresses it, to confuse the Wholly Other with the known good, only too well-known, of our finitude erected into an absolute. Hence, among other things, the ambiguity of the totem, a super-human god and a sub-human animal, a permanent attestation of the divine otherness within the instinctive confusion of that Other with ourselves, never achieving anything except our reduction to a sub-human level.

But to appreciate this fully, we must look at it in its historical embodiment at the heart of social experience. This embodiment is two-fold, in feast and language, a duality echoing that of ritual and myth.

The Religious Meaning of the Feast

What Andrew Greeley has called "pop-sociology" has, these last few years, put the notion of the feast to grotesque uses, while a cheap theology has made such capital out of it that it has become difficult to introduce the idea without promoting derision. These *deliramenta*, though, have only served to veil, while affirming it, the vital importance of the feast. That the subject can be so easily trivialized is due to the degradation of the feast in our modern societies and is an index of their own decadence. In most of our languages, the feast is synonymous with the vulgarest kind of *dolce vita* or simply designates a break in serious life, marked by amusements as insignificant as they are inoffensive.

But in societies where religious influence is still deep and of real quality, to feast has a quite different meaning.[9] It corresponds exactly to what has come to be known as returning to the sources. Essentially cultic, it is religious celebration in its fullness and, on the same count, the occa-

---

[9]See especially G. van der Leeuw's, *Religion in Essence and Manifestation*, pp. 388ff. and Mircea Eliade, *Myths, Dreams and Mysteries*, pp. 27ff. and above all his *The Myth of the Eternal Return*, pp. 83ff.

sion when a society rediscovers the directly religious character of its origin and essence.

It may be said that a feast offers all the members of a society a golden opportunity to become collectively aware of this, since it is an epiphany of its religious soul. Hence it is that a feast is synonymous with joy. But the joy it renews is not any joy. It is the joy of regained fullness. A true feast is a discovery of real life at its source, irrigating anew the whole of existence. A feast that is an interruption of life is no true feast.

It is essential to a feast that it be a commemoration, a recalling of the memories that created the community. But it is not restricted to commemorating them. It re-actualizes them. They are summoned, all of them, to live again. Tradition, which guarantees the continuity of every society, thereby revives, re-lives because present. Culture ceases to be a heap of relics and becomes or re-becomes a living experience.

At a feast, a society reassembles and rediscovers itself in its entirety. The dead are no longer dead. They mix with the living, but not as mysterious fearsome ghosts. It would be truer to say that they return to life with and in the living. These feel themselves enriched with all the experience and vitality of their fathers, restored to its first freshness while paradoxically immortalizing the fruit of earthly experience. In this community, which is more than its members, all become aware of a common fraternal soul, for they all rediscover, beyond the line of generations, a common dependence upon a supernatural fatherhood, the creative energies of which remain as fresh as they were in the beginning.

At the same time, it seems, this warm, human motherhood that has brought them into the world, and this whole world itself, regains its significance. Ceasing to be hostile or alien, it becomes a friend to them. They feel at home. Every element of it contributes to their welfare, the welfare of their human and more than human community.

All this is expressed, inevitably, in a particularly solemn celebration of the sacrificial banquet. But every simple communal meal of the feast-day shares that sacrality and is soaked in the incomparable joy proper to the feast. In English the word *feast* does still evoke a meal, a sacrificial banquet.

The same applies to all the highly diversified cultural forms celebration assumes. At heart they are profoundly one, and show how all folk-lore is the product of ritual. The frontier between the two is practically erased. This does not mean that the feast becomes something artificial and secondhand. Rather, it spreads its own vivacity and éclat around itself. Lyrical and dramatic poetry, music, dancing come together or rather have a common origin in the feast. They radiate from that primal fire. It is in the feast that this beauty rises, the most mysterious product of human art because it both registers the perfect humanization of reality and yet it is what reveals truth to man and gives him his first real sight of the world.

Once one has grasped something of this, one sees how pathetic and contemptible are the contemporary attempts to have a feast by putting a carnival-mask on top of an ideological conference or a political demonstration. An artificial feast can only ever give a miserable ersatz of the sacred. To be able to keep a feast again presupposes a rediscovery of the sacred at the place where it is, a reacceptance of it as it really is, namely as that supernatural which is the most natural thing, in the true sense of the word, that there is: the sur-real real, the source-reality.

Yet a feast, a true feast is not without ominous and maleficent features. The least thing can turn its joy into frenzy, the recovery of vitality into debauchery, enthusiasm into violence.

It is not simply that when life has gone stale, flat and over-organized, it must be smashed to bits so that true life can course through it again. More than this, there is to actual human life something troubled and ambiguous, something voracious and destructive. There is a sort of wild enjoyment which is the very opposite of creative fecundity and yet is its shadow, haunting us ineluctably. Hence it is that a feast is always menaced by the possibility of orgy, and orgies do not regenerate life. They weaken, muddy, and damage it. Euripides' *Bacchae* embody better than any analysis the uncertainty that besets a profoundly religious man when reflecting, and not in spite of it, upon a feast. There is far more involved than the distinction between the Apollonian aspect of order and clarity and the Dionysian of intoxicated exultation. In giving this explanation, even if it is not utterly valueless, Nietzsche gave himself away as an exegete trafficking in palliative interpretations. It is far more a matter of that fatal vertigo which Freud rightly saw lying at the heart of the urge for life...on the natural level, there is no reconciliation possible. We would waste time looking for it. The contradiction can only be resolved in another way, from outside.

A feast, however, is by its nature an exceptional event, usually recurring annually, and giving a society a chance to renew its youth by contact with its sacred beginnings. But there is also something that serves as a permanent affirmation of these beginnings, something part and parcel of daily social life: language.

The Sacredness of Language

Every religious tradition represents language as a gift of the gods that makes society possible and continues to hold it together like a divine thread. Conversely, Genesis sees in the fragmentation of speech into mutually incomprehensible languages a curse from heaven upon a persistently sinful society. Closer to our own times, the Traditionalist school of the nineteenth century multiplied aberrant speculations on language's supernatural origin, but failed to decode the mystery. Contemporary linguistic research has itself been scarcely more cogent. It has failed as well. It is only a little less unconvincing and has served merely to emphasize the mystery.[10] Every language is a paradox to its users. Without it, our consciousness seems to be unable to come to life. It is now a known fact that children who have not acquired a language at the proper time cannot make the loss good later and are permanently intellectually paralyzed as a result. Yet, language is for each person the vehicle for expressing his or her own uniqueness. I am not thinking here simply of the creations of poetic genius. I am thinking of how in ordinary life it is by means of language that each person voices his or her own personality, his or her new and inalienable uniqueness. Our first conclusion, then, is that language, being both the fruit of the efforts of all the individuals of a society and yet, prior to that, the very principle of their formation, is as it were the expression of a society's collective or, rather, maternal soul. This itself makes for a considerable mystery. But then there is the inexhaustible and unpredictable possibilities that any language is constantly realizing, not only in works testifying to an emerging new idiom, but in plain, ordinary daily use. And this surely attests to the presence at society's heart of a continual creativity that it would be misguided to restrict merely to its origins.

What modern linguistic research has more specifically revealed is that language exists in society as a live structure, stable and yet infinitely adaptable, both transcendent as regards a society and yet immanent to its whole existence.[11] This is what renders all authoritarian attempts at blocking or regimenting a language impotent. It was Ferdinand Brunot who first stressed this. Many have followed in his wake. But there is more to his observation than his own glib populism made him capable of seeing. Language has a life of its own. It is, undeniably, subject to a society's ups and downs. It can also, though, stand up against it, sometimes in a way quite contrary to its members' desires and particularly to the

---

[10]There is an excellent introduction to these researches in the volume of the *Encyclopédie Bordas* on *Les Sciences humaines*. On the creative power inherent in every language, cf. Noam Chomsky, *Language and the Mind*, in *Columbia University Forum*, Spring 1908, pp. 5ff.

[11]Cf. J. Vendryes, *Le Langage*, Paris, 1921, pp. 274ff., and E. Benveniste, *Problèmes de linguistique générale*, Paris, 1966, pp. 49ff. See also E. Gilson, *Linguistique et Philosophie*, Paris, 1969, esp. pp. 104ff.

desires of its more intellectual members. It is precisely the great masters of language who know this. The most successful and original use of language is often the one least in harmony with conscious art. Sometimes it is even quite indifferent to it, and an author's "inspiration" often means that language is speaking in spite of the speaker.

All this of course does not admit of easy ordering and definition. But to have let us divine the structures of our unconscious repeated in those structures of our language which take shape with such mysterious spontaneity represents a real advance on the part of contemporary linguistics. And these structures of our unconscious are in turn rooted in our physiology, itself the epiphany of the innate physical structure of the universe which remains without a voice until it finds it in the common speech of human minds.[12]

This corresponds exactly with Eliade's definition of religion as a vision of the unifying form of the universe, grasped when reality's lines of force break surface in a hierophany. This explains why there is no more constant factor throughout social life than the religious substructure underlying the use of language. It is not merely some mysterious tribal spirit who speaks in what we think of as merely our own words. It is, to use the image from Genesis, the spirit of God who breathes into our nostrils every time we vent a thought in speech. The expressing of it is as much for each and for all as for ourselves. It is a means for together taking possession of this world of ours which, for all that, always exceeds our grasp.

Exploring the Cosmos and Discovering God

By speaking in such a way of the feast, and especially of language, we have already passed from sociology to cosmology. Here again, perhaps more forcibly than before, it is the most modern scientific research that has given evidence of how natural and innate to all reality religious experience is. Once again it has done this in spite of itself. It has been done by the very efforts of those scientists, caught in the adolescent phase of scientific development, who aimed at by-passing the idea of God. And so it is that the most resolutely materialistic developments of physical science are the very ones which at the present time have brought us back to religion with an almost disconcerting explicitness.

Collingwood, in particular, pointed this out. An examining of the effata of those thinkers who wished, in the name of nineteenth-century science, to exclude the idea of God and replace it by a strict materialism

---

[12]Cf. Claude Lévi-Strauss, *Anthropologie structurale*, p. 258.

revealed that they surreptitiously transferred to matter, or to what they called matter, the traditional attributes of divinity. This goes both for the exponents of mechanistic materialism, like Haeckel and for the creators of dialectical materialism, beginning with Engels. A self-originating vitality, prevision, omnipotent will, even unlimited fecundity and generosity: all these things which embody so much of what man has been able to imagine of God were not got rid of but attributed henceforth to matter. Both schools of thought did this, and so doing failed to see that such a conception of matter is, point by point, plainly opposite to what matter had hitherto been understood to be.[13]

Two options then present themselves. Either, without any justification and in a strictly contradictory fashion, divinity is attributed to matter. Or, without explicit affirmation of the fact, matter is dubbed the face or veil of divinity. This, of course, is playing with words and entails a return to the most banal kind of theism.

The same goes for the "philosophes" of the eighteenth century, such as Holbach or Helvetius. It goes, of course, for every materialist there has ever been, except when they engage in the vain attempt to suppress the most human part of human experience. Lucretius is the classic instance of the paradox. He prefaced the most furious diatribe against every god there was with the invocation: *Aeneadum genetrix, hominum divumque voluptas, Alma Venus...*and the whole poem is nothing but a glorification of cosmic life carving out its road and overwhelming every obstacle.

This would be enough to show that it may be easy enough to sheer one's vocabulary of a word like God but impossible, either before or after to avoid the reality it denotes.

But a still more interesting observation is this: the modern systems which one thinks of as dispensing, in their explaining the universe, with all recourse to what Laplace called "the hypothesis of God," all presuppose the very hypothesis they intend to exclude. The men who made the systems, of course, *did* forget the foundation they were building on. The sadness is that this foundation was nonetheless there and gave intelligibility to all they did. By neglecting this and all the more by contesting it, they drained their systems of explanatory power and turned them, quite literally, into nonsense.

Take the vision of a universe ruled by mechanical laws, the post-Newtonian universe. It was no mere coincidence that this vision was conceived by a mind, Newton's, which pictured God as a mechanic and his creative work as the assembling of a machine. The whole subsequent

---

[13]R. G. Collingwood, *The Idea of Nature*, Oxford, 1960, p. 104.

intellectual reconstruction depended for its validity, willy-nilly, on whatever objective truth this fundamental conception possessed. Forget it, exclude it and the whole construction becomes a castle in the air. From that moment, its consistency has vanished, its meaning gone. It may still render some services. It can be of great practical utility in accounting for a considerable quantity of experimental relationships. But as an explanation its value has entirely ceased. It literally has nothing more to say.

The same can be said of Darwin's scheme of evolutionist explanation. Recent science has of course been based upon it. It presupposes a projection onto the screen of the whole universe of the image of nineteenth-century man organizing himself for a victorious and very Victorian existence in a liberal economy where only the fittest survive. The whole transformist vision of the world, in the Darwinian or neo-Darwinian version of natural selection, depends upon the implicit validity of extending such a human model to the whole cosmos. If one protests that this is pure fantasy and that nature contains no such anthropomorphic divinity to direct it, the explanation, once again, falls flat. It becomes no more than a factitious support to what is a literally meaningless system for tabulating a considerable number of factual data. More than this it cannot do. If behind nature there is no God in the image of that kind of man of which Darwin was so perfect a representative, if reality need not be conformed to the image of Darwin, then Darwinism with all its consequences becomes simply a handy means, to one particular kind of mind, of imposing a satisfying order on a multiplicity of facts. It tells us nothing of the actual fabric of reality. It explains nothing.

From this angle, then, the apparent ease and success with which materialism, be it mechanistic or dialectic, has by-passed God in order to consider and explain everything, are quite illusory. They only hold as long as one looks at one side of the picture. But if one wants to account for the way in which such organizing of reality satisfies the human mind, one must turn the picture over. There one cannot but discover that God, fashioned in man's image and thought to have been excluded. In fact, he had only been excluded from the field of vision because man had put himself in his place. But if he does not exist, the perspective man had thought to locate turns into a mirage. It only has validity, it only exists, in relation to him.

Indeed, the most recent developments of physics have made illusion impossible. It is no longer possible not to question the point of view one adopts to look out upon things. It is always a divine point of view presupposing God's existence and at least some resemblance between himself and man. It is in the phenomena themselves that atheistic materialism has been exposed as unfeasible and absurd. First came relativity physics, then quantum physics, and each subsequent development has merely added a nail to the coffin.

The conclusions of the new physics in fact allow of only two interpretations, though one of them is not an interpretation but a capitulation which if accepted would involve science in total agnosticism.

One can follow the Copenhagen school and restrict science to the proposing of models or constructs committing the mind to combine in a satisfying way a mathematized collection of factual relationships, but without conceding any objective value or any correspondence to reality to these models or constructs.[14] This of course is to strip science (*scientia*) of its cognitive character. Or rather, it is to equate the knowledge it gives, outside a mass of unexplained and inexplicable, experimental data, with what Kant would have called the *a priori* forms of our sensibility but which in fact turn out to be nothing but the gratuitous projection of our imagination, bound to a given epoch and passing with it.

The unanswerable objection to this kind of attitude was commonsensically expressed by Einstein. Science, human science, may be always beginning, always needing not merely perfecting but revising. Yet it works. It must therefore correspond to something in reality.

But what can this "something" be? Our images of matter seem to have lost their objectivity for good and all, whether they be of elementary bodies envisaged as small elastic, indestructible balls, or of waves pulsing through some medium or other, or of fields of force ceaselessly intersecting and modifying one another. Scientific truth is therefore left with no other objectivity but that of being, however imperfectly, a coinciding of our thought with a transcendent thought. In other words, matter itself or what we call matter becomes, in the last analysis and in the judgment of science itself, a basic language by which absolute mind expresses itself to our minds and which at the same time permits them to hold converse in a common universe.[15]

Thus modern physical science, however materialistic it may have intended and still intends to be, appears, the more it advances, to have no choice except between a pure nescience which is its own denial and

---

[14]It is striking to witness the growing power of these ideas among those American scientific circles that reject the neo-theism of what they call "the Princeton gnosis" (recently studied in Raymond Ruyer's *La Gnose de Princeton*, Paris, 1975).

[15]See the very thought-provoking essays of Ian T. Ramsey's *Religion and Science; Conflict and Synthesis*, London, 1964. One of the most original pieces of philosophizing by a contemporary physicist is that outlined by Olivier Costa de Beauregard in his *Le Second Principe de la Science du Temps*, Paris, 1964.

the acknowledgment of Thought thinking itself. In other words, logical thought must either, at the end of the day, destroy itself or return to its origin. That origin was myth.

IV

From Myth to Rational Theology:
The Cosmological Proofs of God's Existence

The last two chapters have shown how deeply rooted myth is by way of ritual experience, in our experience of ourselves, of our societies and of the world in which we and they live out our lives. Modern science and scientists may use their science to justify their unbelief. But their psychology, and even their sociology and cosmology, have given them the lie and revealed that all man's living and thinking depends upon religious presuppositions. They have turned their backs upon these presuppositions only to find them staring them in the face.

Not that we simply find God in ourselves or society or the cosmos. Rather, ritual experience, of which myth is the expression, functions as the starting-point for all the simultaneous exploration and exploitation of ourselves, society and the universe in which human life consists once it has emerged from animality and as long as it does not give in to self-despair. This corroborates the Structuralists' contention that the "death of God" was not, as Feuerbach thought, the liberation of man but the signal for his demise. God, though, does not die. If the man who proclaims the death of God were to analyze himself adequately, he would see not only that his very denial attests God's existence but that even at the very moment he is contorting himself in negation he is ineradicably professing his faith.

Myth however, every myth, like the experience from which it springs, is nonetheless afflicted by insoluble contradictions. Man cannot affirm life without death affirming itself. He realizes he is a creature and confuses this with being fallen. The gods he worships are fallen gods. The salvations they proffer lead to annihilation.

Hence myth had to be criticized. Precisely its positive insights made this inevitable. Merely negative criticism could never satisfy mankind and, as we have said, can only ever have one effect. Trying to suppress the problem of religion only serves to set it in greater relief. The witness to the divine running through all experience only sounds out louder for being attemptedly muted. Rationalist criticism may think to disavow the truth undoubtedly present in myth, however ambiguously; but such an intention betrays its blindness. In the process of executing it, it will have undermined the foundation of its own rationality and when the process is complete it will be confronted, unless it yields to the abyss where it had thought to banish myth, with the very God myth proclaims.

Mythos and Logos

We can see all this verified in the Platonic dialectic of *mythos* and *logos*.[1] Plato held that resolute criticism of traditional myth was essential for the progress of the rational *logos*. It is fascinating to see how completely he changed the Greek idea of God. Father A. J. Festugière has recently shown how convinced Greek tragedy was, all the way from Aeschylus through Sophocles to Euripides, of the mythical belief in the gods' jealousy of men. Aeschylus' answer was resignation; Sophocles' disdain; Euripides' hopeless rebellion. Plato set himself to show that divinity was necessarily *aphthonous*, without envy. Divinity is Good itself. And what is the Good if not diffusive of itself?[2] But he knew too well that the immortality such reasonings seemed to offer the good man amounted to no more than a possibility. To the man wanting more, he could only counsel going back to the myths, his understanding of them, of course, transformed. But is there any human mind capable of exhausting them?

It is in this interstice that we must situate what are known as the proofs of the existence of God and what might better be called efforts at rationalizing myth. They are essential for avoiding idolatry. Without them we would fatally confuse the reality of God with the images drawn from our human experience by which alone we can hope to conceive of that reality. But while the proofs dissolve the idolatry latent in every myth, they run their own risk of vaporizing into mere concepts. The only way that can be avoided is by returning to the myth which is the source of their vigor but with which they can never be wholly satisfied.

This explains an apparent paradox: that it is Muslim, Jewish and Christian theologians who borrowed their rational proofs of God's existence, based on natural data, from pagan philosophers. Yet only at the hands of these theologians of a divine Revelation did the proofs begin to assume a satisfactory shape. And it was only in the climate of Christian faith that they lost all appearance of sham. Yet, when this faith ceases to nourish itself at its own sources, the proofs, the more they are refined,

---

[1] Among the many studies on this subject, one of the most penetrating is W.K.C. Guthrie, *Orpheus and Greek Religion*, London, 1952.

[2] A.J. Festugière, *De L'Essence de la Tragédie grecque*, Paris, 1969.

show a remarkable capacity for reducing that faith to lifeless abstractions.

Lived religion, then, is the matrix of these demonstrations. Modern thinkers, in their naively rationalist way, think of them as a dialectical process geared to producing a god who was until then absent from man's thought. But the truth is simpler. They seek to express in a logical form the belief engendered, not by them but by the lived religion of those who produce them.

What makes them new and important is that, for better or worse, they inevitably reform our ideas of God. They have a cathartic effect, valuable in eliminating idolatry and, more profoundly, not in emptying out the mystery involved in every idea of God that is not unworthy of its object, but in heightening our awareness of it and disclosing its true dimensions.

Concomitantly these proofs, assuming they do not turn into mere word-games, must lead to a discovery or, more precisely, to a better articulated awareness of that analogy of being supposed by myth. But at the same time they must include a truly tragic appreciation of the mystery of evil, something which appears in myth as part and parcel of the mystery of God. We speak of a tragic appreciation, because it was that which Greek tragedy prepared for philosophical reflection. In this respect, one can assess the philosophical rationalizations of myth by the light they shed on a religious man's conception of evil.

Again, of course, there is the danger of a meretricious clarity. There is no hope of ideally solving the problem of evil. Such a solution would only be verbal. It would mean too that the philosophy of God had turned the divine into a tissue of abstractions. But when the critical purification of man's spontaneous ideas of God is really effective it makes the problem of evil more acute and at the same time it makes itself incapable of explaining it away by speculation.

The Various Forms of the Rational Argument for God

Like their progenitors ritual and myth, the proofs of God's existence have their roots in our experience of the universe, society or the individual soul. They would only be wholly adequate in fact when, like myth, they attempt to take in the salient points of this threefold unity. But it is then that the strength of rational analysis shows its weakness. In order to succeed, it must necessarily limit and distinguish its objects. Whereas myth is immediately comprehensive of the whole variety of human experience, a rational demonstration is valid only so far as its analyses are precise and its application, in consequence, exclusive. Only afterwards is synthesis possible when, for better or worse, the partial demonstrations are combined with the aim of matching the all-embracing continuity of myth. But success is always less than complete and the results invariably awkward and imperfect.

Such is the nature of rational analysis and it means that it will yield its most assured results in the field of cosmology. Of all the reality forming the subject-matter of our experience the cosmos is the only element or aspect which we can envisage, at least partially, as lying over against us. Only there, to echo Gabriel Marcel, does the logical mind feel fully at ease, facing problems in the data of which we ourselves are not enmeshed. If then our aim is to prove and so define God's existence *more geometrico*, in a fully logical fashion, we would be well advised to stay with the cosmological arguments.

Contrariwise, life in society is such a mystery that if we invoke the moral arguments, we thereby necessarily involve ourselves and so obscure the possibility of rational objectivity and logical rigor.

Even more is this the case if we embark on an analysis of the thinking mind. We are stopped dead by the inconceivable chasm between the I who observes and the Me observed. Perfect coherence with the laws of abstract reasoning can, in such circumstances, only be obtained at the cost of an illusory formalism. This is why most of the philosophies that call themselves transcendental give the impression of being conjuring tricks.

But we must hasten to balance all this with another crucial observation. It is true (at least to an extent) that cosmological speculations can easily be logically satisfying. But there is a price to pay. Their yield is poor in the extreme. The classical cosmological five ways of proving God's existence beget in the end an exceedingly impoverished idea of God. This is truest of the one that is apparently the most convincing. They only become acceptable if their god is given features properly belonging to the living God of living religion. And this imposition, of course, cannot be dialectically justified.

How, in any case, can this be achieved except by reverting to the mythical expressions which were available prior to undertaking the argument? And what becomes then of the catharsis wrought by reasoning? Naturally everything literal-minded in myth, everything incompatible in it with reasoning, will be cut out. But what about the remainder? How can it be sorted and reorganized? There is no criterion by which to do it.

This is not the case with the moral arguments. It is true that they lack the detachment and proportion of the cosmological proofs. They involve convergent probabilities rather than strict demonstrations. But they have the great merit of incorporating a considerable amount of the same actual experience as was the matrix of myth. Their ultimate idea of God, too, is far richer and while being more mythical in content they include definite criteria for interpreting and correcting myth.

Yet this kind of argument is not wholly free of the danger of anthropomorphism, not precisely that of myth but all the more perilous for being subtler. God can be reduced to a name for purely human experiences. We may take an example typical of contemporary errors. Lived Christianity teaches us that God is Love. But it seems to be the supreme temptation of personalist philosophies, on the other hand, to insinuate that love, meaning the love men experience in society, is God.

There remains, then, not any particular transcendental analysis of the human soul but an analysis that would bear upon the highest mystical experience of which the soul is capable, seeing there, actually embodied, how the ego can be invaded by another who is God. This would not of course constitute properly speaking a logical demonstration. The rules governing such would long since have been broken. Nor would it even show God to exist on the basis of him acting as the sustaining and moving power of the whole moral life. Rather it would simply attest that within the mystery of our own being there is a deeper mystery, namely, the active Presence of a self-revealing God.[3]

Then, as never before, God would perforce be acknowledged as the *Deus revelatus tamquam absconditus*, the God who is never so hidden as when he reveals himself.

The Ontological Argument

Before dealing with the cosmological attempts at putting our belief in God on a rational basis, it is necessary to say something of those more paradoxical approaches which, on various grounds, have claimed to cut all knots and show how immediately obvious God's existence is. They took their classical form, with St. Anselm and then Descartes, by their extension beyond the cosmos which is the object or our sense-experience. We can indeed explain the universe scientifically by tracing its causal lines. But we cannot go beyond analyzing that idea of perfection which is innate in all of us.

God, said Anselm, is that being than which nothing greater or better (*maior*) can be conceived. But this fullness belonging to God by definition

---

[3]It is no coincidence that Fr. J. Maréchal, who was responsible for the first example of what is known as transcendental Thomism, should also have produced some of the finest philosophical and theological analyses of mystical experience in the two volumes of his *Etudes sur la Psychologie des Mystiques*, Paris, 1924 and 1937.

necessarily includes his existence. Descartes refined the argument by replacing the *id quo non est maior* by the idea of the perfect being.[4]

The objection is obvious, as St. Thomas observed. What is proven is not that God exists but simply that our idea of him implies his existence. The actual correspondence of this idea with reality still remains to be demonstrated.

It is difficult to counter this objection. Unless our thought is to be credited with an obviously untenable realism, how can one jump without any transition from an idea, however firmly it can or may be implanted in our minds, to a conviction of existence?

Yet many excellent minds, from St. Bonaventure through Descartes to Schelling, persons one cannot accuse of lacking the critical spirit, have accepted St. Anselm's reasoning and even affirmed it to be the most satisfying that there is. With this in view, one is inclined to think that the argument holds something more and other than meets the eye. Perhaps the best indication of this is that St. Thomas, in one of his famous five ways, uses an argument which seems to be nothing but a cryptic variant of St. Anselm's. We will come to this shortly and then conclude by reconsidering the implications of the ontological argument.

The Five Ways

The traditional cosmological arguments proposed by St. Thomas after his waiving of St. Anselm's, were synthesized by him in five convergent ways which have in their turn become classical. On several occasions modern Thomists have attempted, understandably, to reduce them to one: the contingency of everything in the world requiring a necessary being without which all existence would have had to come from nothing —an unthinkable proposition because meaningless.

Etienne Gilson, on the other hand, was certainly right to maintain that St. Thomas intended a multiplicity of ways in his cosmological proof. God cannot be the necessary conclusion of merely one line of thought about the world but rather of all those by which our understanding of the latter is deepened and rationalized.[5] Hence, too, it is obvious that St.

---

[4]The Anselmian argument periodically arouses passionate interest. A masterly examination of recent work can be found in *The Openness of Being* by E. C. Mascall, London, 1971, pp. 36ff.

[5]For what follows we are considerably indebted to E. Gilson, *Le Thomisme*, in the 4th French edition, Paris, 1942, pp. 85ff., as well as to E. C. Mascall, *op. cit.*, where the chapter on the proofs for God's existence contains a sizable bibliography on recent discussion of the "five ways."

Thomas did not consider the five ways, even within their cosmological sphere, as exhaustive but simply as complementary.

The First Way: Movement or Change

The first way is the one presented in greatest detail. It came from Aristotle but after the shipwreck of his works in the early middle ages only resurfaced with Adelard of Bath. It was Albert the Great, however, who completely restored it, being indebted in this to Maimonides. This is the proof from movement. To St. Thomas himself it obviously seemed the simplest and most rigorous. Other disciples of Aristotle have felt the same. It is based on the distinction, fundamental to Aristotelian physics, between act and potency. The necessary consequence is that nothing in this world moves itself. A moving being only moves because it is in potency as regards that towards which it is moving. But nothing moves except so far as it is in act, because to move a thing is to make it pass from potency to act. But, of course, the same thing cannot be at the same time both in potency and act under the same aspect. Therefore, every-thing moving in this world is moved by something else. But an infinite regress is impossible because this would be tantamount to saying that nothing in existence is capable of provoking the general movement. Hence it is necessary to suppose a "first unmoved mover," who is God.[6]

Modern thinkers, as opposed to St. Thomas and his contemporaries, have inevitably considered this argument to be particularly inadequate. The first principle of Newtonian physics appears to nullify the argument at its root. The principle is that any body will, if free from external inter-vention, persist in the state in which it is, whether that be one of uniform movement or of immobility. But the difficulty is only apparent. The meaning that St. Thomas and Aristotle attach to the word motion is at once more general and more precise than the one it has in Newtonian physics. When they speak of motion, they mean change. Once this has been grasped, the objection becomes a confirmation.

A more interesting observation perhaps is that the contradiction ap-parently latent to the argument has in fact the immediate effect of coun-tering the fundamental objection Kant raised against every cosmological argument.

Kant contested that the logical impasse to which all rational principles lead when applied to the infinite forbids their extension beyond the cos-mos which is the object of our sense-experience. We can indeed explain

---

[6]*Summa Theologica*, Prima Pars. q. 2, art. 3.

the universe scientifically by tracing its causal lines. But we cannot go beyond this into the metaphysical sphere.

It seems to us though that this is avoided by the argument we are discussing, and avoided, paradoxically, by what might seem to be the internal contradiction of which is the victim.

Beginning from the idea that nothing moves in this world unless moved by another, it arrives at the idea of a first unmoved mover. What is this if not to admit that the laws in force within our universe cannot apply outside it? But how has this conclusion been reached? By grasping the idea that attributes autonomous activity to the sum of the objects of our sensible experience comports a necessary contradiction. It is no riposte to say that the contradiction only appears when one wishes to go beyond the limits of sense-experience. All thought locates itself in such a beyond. If it refuses to do so, it thereby refuses all distinction between truth and non-truth. For, while numerous truths obviously only apply to what is relative, the idea of truth as such being relative is a contradiction, simple non-sense. By accepting the truth of the phrase "everything is relative," one implies, consciously or otherwise, that at least that proposition is an absolute.

If this be so, the argument of the first way—and the same applies, albeit less obviously to the others—is not guilty of evading the antinomies inevitable in passing out of the bounds of the cosmos into the divine infinity. Rather, it alone makes the only possible logical deduction from them which is not destructive of all logic. This is what Anton Günther called the principle of counter-position and it applies to all reasoning which makes the transition from the world to God.

Another interesting point is that it is the principle underlying this way which has led many, mainly though not only American scientists, to reintroduce, under the compulsion of their own specialties, that "God-hypothesis" which Laplace rather prematurely thought science had rendered superfluous. If, they say, the physical world has, at least in us, produced a thought and if this thought is capable of turning back, so to speak, upon the world, then the latter itself must proceed from a transcendent thought.[7] But this of course is the kind of transcendental reflection which Kant himself much preferred to the cosmological proofs and it takes us beyond our present stage. It is worth saying though that this shows how the "proofs" hang together and cannot be limited to a single type to the exclusion of all others.

Let us turn next to the second way.

---

[7] See above, R. Ruyer, *op. cit.*

The Second Way: Efficient Causality

St. Thomas himself attributed the proof of God's existence from efficient causality to Aristotle. In fact, however, it was only in the wake of Avicenna that Alan of Lille and then Albert applied to this proof the more general Aristotelian principle that none of the four causes (material, efficient, final and formal) admit of an infinite regress.

At first sight so similar does this way seem to the first that it has sometimes been regarded merely as another form of it, for the first is nothing but its preparation. Its point of departure is the fact that no object can be its own efficient cause, that is, the source of its own existence. This requires, since an infinite regress is impossible and irrelevant, that this whole world in which nothing is self-subsistent depends upon a being who does not receive existence from any other but is the Existent in pure fullness.[8]

There is in fact a fundamental difference between the first two proofs. The first is concerned only with the source of movement or, in general, changes presented to our experience, while the second is concerned with the source of existence as such.

In his *Compendium*, St. Thomas displayed great ingenuity in deducing the principal attributes of the biblical God from the proof by movement and its simple idea of God as the first unmoved mover. But it is obvious that the second way takes us far closer to that fundamental notion of Thomistic theology which makes it so consonant with scripture, namely that of God as Pure Act or, equivalently, as the being whose essence is existence.

On the other hand, the analogical application of efficient causality to God (or of any other of the Aristotelian causes) raises a problem. In this case it seems more difficult to disarm Kant's objection. For Aristotle's efficient causality presupposed material causality, of which it itself cannot not be the cause. How then can it be attributed to God except by a transposition which would seem self-invalidating?

It is precisely here, though, that the third way comes on stage, as if to dissipate the uncertainty apparently clinging to the second.

The Third Way: Contingency and Necessity

This is the way opened by the distinction between what is only possible and what is necessary. It is owed ultimately to Avicenna, though the formulation of the *Summa Theologica* seems to come directly from

---

[8]*Summa Theologica, ibid.*

Maimonides' re-statement of the proof.[9] In parenthesis, it is ironical that this proof does not feature in the *Summa Contra Gentiles* whereas we are inclined nowadays to reckon it the surest and profoundest.

It is evident that all the beings known to us through our experience of the physical world are merely possible. All of them are capable of appearing at one moment and disappearing at another. Not one of them, therefore, has in it that which would make it exist rather than not exist, since at any moment it could equally well not exist. Hence the existence of all these things must depend upon that of a necessary being, who is God.

It has been justly remarked that the obverse of this proof is the real distinction between essence and existence in all beings except God. The whole proof depends upon whether or not this is accepted. Here especially then we see how essential to Thomist thought is the idea, obviously owed to the Bible, of the being who is the pure, absolute Existent.

The Fourth Way: The Degrees of Being

The fourth way by contrast seems to be a continual embarrassment to modern Thomists and though Gilson brilliantly showed that it impugns none of the masters' principles, this in turn imposes the acknowledgment that these principles are a good deal more complex than Neo-Thomists are in general prepared to admit. In other words, the idea of Thomism as a fully logical Aristotelianism cannot stand.

The fourth way is the proof from the ways of being. Those most disconcerted by its seeming Ontologism and definite Platonism have tried in vain to oppose the supposedly correct and watertight form it assumes in the *Summa Theologica*[10] with that of the *Summa Contra Gentiles*. The latter, they say, limits itself to affirming that there is necessarily, in one being, a maximum of relative being. Thus there is no hint of Ontologism, nothing making the pure idea the measure of the real. But if this is so, nothing has been proven, least of all the existence of so rigorously transcendent a god as is the God of St. Thomas.

Correspondingly, the sudden final recourse to efficiency in the text of the *Summa Theologica* cannot aim to complete the proof, as is maintained, by deducing an absolute maximum (the only universal cause of being) from a relative maximum. If this were so, then the fourth way would simply boil down to the second. In fact, St. Thomas' concluding reference

---

[9]*Ibid.*
[10]*Ibid.* Cf. *Contra Gentiles*, I.13.

to efficiency is not made to consummate the proofs but to draw from the latter the confirmation of the proof from efficiency.

But isn't this to relapse into the confusion with which St. Thomas reproached St. Anselm: unwarrantably attributing existence to what is true only in thought, demanding existence of the perfect absolute? No, says Gilson with considerable subtlety, because St. Thomas' reasoning evidently presupposes the participation of created things in the being of God in the sense of God being their Exemplar. Yet for St. Thomas, participation and efficiency are only two aspects of the same reality. Hence it is undoubtedly from an existent, evidenced by the senses though obviously interpreted by the intelligence, that the transition is made to the supreme Existent.

This is fine, but again there is a difficulty of directly applying to God the notion of efficient causality. Though only patent in the second, this underlies each of the various ways. Aristotle himself, as we have said, would have been the first to object that a so-called efficient cause which did not presuppose a material cause and, what is more problematic, was claimed as the cause of matter itself, would no longer be what he understood by an efficient cause. Undoubtedly, St. Thomas did achieve a synthesis between efficiency and participation. But this does not mean, at least as regards divine causality, that participation can be reduced to efficiency. Rather it seems to be complementary to the latter, so much so that without it efficiency would no longer have meaning or application in the context.

However he be interpreted, then, it seems that St. Thomas in this fourth way was far closer to St. Anselm than he perhaps intended. In any case, he was injecting a strong dose of Platonism into his Aristotelianism. The best indication of this, and Gilson himself admits it without hesitation, is that St. Thomas' source for the fourth way was less those texts of Aristotle which speak of how the level of truth in beings corresponds to the level of their being as the famous passage of the *City of God* where Augustine applauds the Platonists for recognizing that the mutable character of empirical beings leads us on to the sole being who is immutable.

The Fifth Way: Finality or the World's Order

The final way starts from finality or, to be more exact, from the order which in general holds sway in the universe.[11] St. Thomas invoked as his source a text of St. John of Damascus. But this proof of course is a presupposition of the whole sapiential literature of the Bible and has always

---

[11]*Summa Theologica, ibid.* Cf. *De Veritate*, q.5, art.1.

been a commonplace of Jewish and Christian apologetics. It is note-worthy that, in each of these cases and even in the Old Testament, the argumentation incorporated several elements of Stoic philosophy.

This proof presupposes that order cannot arise from chance. Order implies not merely being which cannot come from non-being, but thought. Leaving aside the teleological details of which popular apologetics has always been fond but to which there are no end, it is clear that this way links up with that profound induction to which modern scientists have been unavoidably led by reflection upon science.

In other words, despite using the Aristotelian framework of causality, this way too, no less than the fourth, goes well beyond Peripateticism.

It is certainly true, as Gilson pointed out, that the moment it has recourse to the axiom *de nihilo nihil fit*, this proof shows that it too is based upon sense-experience of existent things, while involving an intellectual analysis of the meaning of the sensible serving to take us beyond it. But here again, as with the fourth way, it is clear that the cosmological proofs cannot be fully developed without obliging us to leave their own terrain and move either to the level of the moral life (where we meet the Good which is, as it were, the top side of merely physical being) or to the transcendental level, the only one where the Truth of being can be justified.

If this be so, how short-sighted are those modern Thomists who would have us eliminate the moral arguments from any rational scrutiny of our belief in God. It seems, in fact, that St. Thomas preferred cosmological arguments for merely pedagogical reasons. They lend themselves more readily than any other to clear and coherent formulation if only because, in Thomas' view, our knowledge, albeit obviously rational in character, is directly ordained to the sensible. But his treatment of the arguments more than authorizes us, in fact it obliges us, to climb higher.

Then again, there is the inherent poverty of any idea of God drawn merely from the cosmological arguments unless, that is, they are in the hands of a Christian who knows, the moment he begins, that the God he is seeking is the living God of Scripture.

Gilson proved beyond doubt that it is this God who lies behind St. Thomas' understanding of Pure Act. But the point we wish to conclude with is this, that the inevitable distinction such an idea involves, in every being outside God, based on concepts taken from our own experience, is analogical. Indeed, as St. Thomas was quick to point out, it is a matter of the analogy of simple proportionality; not a direct analogy between him and us, but an analogy restricted to the level of the respective relationships between, on the one hand, God and his actions and, on the other, we and ours.[12]

Of course, there is certainly a privileged exemplarist relationship between God and man. At this point, the biblical vision of our creation to the image of God takes on its full meaning. But this meaning seems to be that man is to the image of God so far as capable, like God, of interpersonal relationships. It is true enough that, given the primary ordering of our intelligence to the sensible, such relationships, ever restricted to created things, are already full of mystery. But the moral arguments, although (or perhaps because) their application to God intensifies the mystery, are as a result incontestably superior.

---

[12]*De Veritate*, q.2 a.11; cf. *Summa Contra Gentiles*, q.1 a.3,4; cf. E. C. Mascall, *Existence and Analogy*, London, 1949, especially the synthesizing note on p. 114. Considerable importance also attaches, in our opinion, to the treatment of the matter by Cornelio Fabro, CPS, in *Participation et causalité selon S. Thomas d'Aquin*, Louvain-Paris, 1961, esp. pp. 509ff. and 634ff.

V

From Myth to Rational Theology (continued): The Moral and Existential Proofs for the Existence of God

If it was St. Thomas who gave the cosmological argument its classic form, it was of course St. Augustine who gave shape to the moral argument. One must add, though, that there are also in Augustine the seeds of other forms of the moral argument, which modern thinkers like Newman, Blondel and the Christian Existentialists have developed.

The Augustinian Argument from Happiness

The characteristically Augustinian argument is practically the leit-motif of the *Confessions*. The simplicity of its expression is somewhat deceptive. Its semantic banality and the sheer ordinariness of the experience from which it starts is liable to hide its depth and subtlety. It begins with the desire for happiness (*Beatitudo*) which is at the root of all human aspirations. Experience, however, shows that all the various objects, high or low, in which man seeks this happiness deceive him. It is not simply that some yield a false happiness, only appearing good, or that even when genuine there remains an insecurity or transience about them. Even the most satisfying forms of happiness, the purest in other words, in fact fail to sate us fully, having the contrary effect of arousing a purer and more elevated desire, so that man's quest never ends and every apparent end merely compels him further. From this, St. Augustine concludes that there must be a *Summum Bonum*, which we are made to attain and which is free of any limitation. This *Summum Bonum* is the *Summum Amabile*, God.[1]

There is an easy objection: the fact that I feel thirsty in the desert does not mean I will necessarily find the water I want. To which the no less easy answer is: is it conceivable that beings should exist capable of an uncontrollable desire for water in a world in which water did not exist?

---

[1] E. Gilson, *Introduction à l'étude de saint Augustin*, Paris, 1949.

More searchingly, many minds and often very religious ones, have been embarrassed by the Eudomianism involved in the proof. Surely it is wrong to reduce God to a simple object of desire. But against this, the *Beatitudo* of Augustine, even more than is the case with the *Summum Desiderabile* of Plato, is not just any happiness, even less just any pleasure, however refined. It represents the concrete attainment of that for which man knows he is made, that which makes sense of his existence. It involves him at his noblest and most disinterested (understanding interest in a strictly egocentric way).

This is why, as is already the case with Augustine himself, the moral argument tends to pass from being an argument from happiness into a complementary argument from duty.

Newman's Argument from Conscience

Here we turn to Newman and his remarkably forceful but simple statement of the argument. The voice of conscience, however uncertain it may be as to the specific nature of the duty required of us in a particular situation, is quite emphatic as to the duty of accomplishing the Good, whatever it may be, the moment it is recognized. Indeed, recognizing it must be our primary preoccupation. We may refuse to heed this voice of conscience but we cannot fail to hear it, and it reveals itself both as that which makes us persons and as evidence not just of the existence, but of the presence, at the heart of ourselves, closer to us than we are to ourselves, of another Person, possessed of a perfect personality of which our own, in its freedom and rationality, is but an echo.[2]

There is no weight to the objection drawn from sociological studies on social constraint, such as those of the Durkheim school. Moral obligation is, specifically, at its most precise and imperious when affirming itself against every constraint, even the subtlest. Bergson's analyses of open, as against closed, consciousness shatter the objection.

Father J. H. Walgrave was perfectly right in stressing the absurdity of those so-called Thomists who rejected this form of argument for being contaminated with Plato's idealism. In fact, the strongest support available to this argument could be taken from St. Thomas' wonderful analyses, in the *Summa* and *De Veritate*, of the divine law and synderesis. Synderesis is that superior form of practical reason by which human freedom realizes that it can only positively fulfill itself by adhering to the

---

[2]J. H. Newman, *An Essay in Aid of a Grammar of Assent*, London, 1870, pp. 101ff. The best commentaries are those of M. Nédoncelle, *La Philosophie Réligieuse de Newman*, Strasbourg, 1946, pp. 91ff. and J. H. Walgrave, *Newman The Theologian*, New York, 1960, pp. 203ff.

divine freedom which is itself one, not with some or other necessity, but with absolute reason, namely the divine Wisdom that imposes an order on all created beings which is at once identical with their true good and the means by which they glorify the Supreme Good.

Kant's View of Duty and Virtue

We have already said that these two principal forms of the moral argument can be harmonized at different levels. The simplest way of doing this is that chosen by Kant in his *Critique of Practical Reason*. He presents eternal life as the reconciliation of duty and virtue, their final identification, and God as the one in and through whom the two are joined.[3] It is this conception that gives such stature to Kant's philosophy and explains its lasting power over some of the finest minds and noblest spirits among us. It would therefore be wrong to dismiss it as a simple *deus ex machina* summoned up to avoid the fearful difficulties raised by, on the one hand, the radical anti-eudomianism of the categorical imperative and by, on the other, wholesale autonomy of consciousness. Whatever one may think of these two points, and we are not discussing them here, there is no doubt that Kant saw clearly how every antinomy of moral conscience can only be resolved in God, in the relationship between his freedom and ours.

God and the Meaning of Human Life. Blondel's *Action*

But the moral argument, fully deployed, calls for a far broader synthesis than Kant's. It should enable us to connect the meaning of human life with the meaning of reality as a whole. Man's most authentic experiences become meaningful through the relationship with God brought about by moral action, and above all by prayer which draws more consequences from conscience than mere morality ever can and while supporting moral action surrounds and surpasses it. Among authentic experiences, first place must go to those inter-personal experiences involved in friendship and the highest forms of love. These both reflect and prepare for that knowledge of God which is so much more than mere knowledge. At this point, in fact, we are so far along the path of rationalizing the highest human experience that we can already see that this human experience is called beyond itself to a superhuman experience.

---

[3]See René Le Senne's analyses in his *Traité de Morale générale*, Paris, 1949, pp. 232ff. and also pp. 343ff. and pp. 450ff.

Here we can turn to the best thinking of Maurice Blondel[4] and of the Christian Existentialists, from Kierkegaard to Gabriel Marcel. One may also maintain that those Existentialists who halt on the brink of theism, such as Jaspers and Heidegger, and even those who deny theism, like Sartre, in fact corroborate their analyses.

Hitherto, for clarity's sake, we have distinguished the cosmological and moral approaches to God. This may have given the impression that intelligence and free will are two not only distinct but unconnected faculties, the first applying itself, as objectively as possible, to the primary sense-presented objects of our intra-mundane experience, the second entrusted with the similarly intra-mundane task of constructing (or destroying) our personal life through what we do and in particular through what we do in relation to other persons. In truth, of course, this is a merely abstract view without correspondence to reality. This is the basic contention of Blondel's *L'Action*. In fact, it is a view that tends to denaturalize reality. As Blondel said, it is our intelligence which is free and the vision it attains of the whole of reality in its ultimate unity necessarily depends upon the use intelligence makes of its freedom. Hence it is that a gap always yawns between what Blondel called our will willing (*la volonté voulante*), namely its deepest motivating aspiration and our will willed (*la volonté voulue*) embracing our actual achievements and also our intentions at their most ambitious.

One could say in fact that the drama of our will lies in its encountering determinism at almost every step, within us as much as outside us. We are compelled to avow that ours is a liberty which can only realize itself by acknowledging the determinations imposed upon it, accepting them, yet always going beyond. But how can it "go beyond" except by recognizing that it is itself placed in existence by a higher wholly undetermined freedom, and that it cannot fulfill itself except by adhering to this freedom, not just by an act of the intelligence but by an intellectual act posited in harmony with the self-giving will and meaningful by means of that coincidence?

Such, according to Blondel, is the "great option" (*grande option*) to which a close analysis of our action in the world, inseparable from total commitment to that action, must lead us. It is by accepting this option that one comes to an acknowledgment of God which is also an acceptance of the supernatural.

Blondel has not always been fully understood on this point. He did not mean that metaphysical analysis of human actions as such leads of

---

[4]Henri Bouillard, *Blondel et le christianisme*, Paris, 1961. See too the excellent introductions by Alexander Dru and Illtyd Trethowan in their *Maurice Blondel*, London, 1964.

itself to acceptance of the Christian supernatural, of the revelation of Bible and Gospels, with all its ethical consequences. This would be a complete misunderstanding. The acceptance of the supernatural, as Blondel conceived it from the earliest edition of *L'Action*, does not mean that. It means the precise opposite. It means a readiness for encountering God, not as an abstraction nor even as a living idea, but as a reality: the supreme and supremely personal reality, encounter with whom necessarily involves consent to all that this Reality may disclose of itself and its will for us. And such a disclosure cannot be made, cannot even more be communicated, except on God's initiative.

Thus, not indeed by a proof but by a way that Blondel was not wrong in calling "scientific," i.e., experimental and rational, we arrive at the life of the living God.

Thus, too, Blondel echoes—by an anticipated echo as has been well said—the positive conclusions of the existentialist explorations and analyses of man's situation in the world.

Existentialist Approaches to the Reality of God

Blondel's approach vindicated the importance of history, especially in its relationship to the discovery of God and its rational justification. Kierkegaard had already emphasized this. But Blondel saw and said better than Kierkegaard that while this is certainly a matter of individual personal history, it cannot be abstracted from the history of the whole race.

But the history must be real. It is fatuous for the dice to be loaded beforehand towards a junction of our own persons and God's in some nameless, wholly abstract idea, like telescoping the tubes of an opera-glass into one another and reducing the scene to darkness. This is the besetting sin of Hegelianism and its offshoots, and it is against this that Kierkegaard and his followers have continually protested. If history be where man meets God, the history must comprise creative events, which are obliged to be meaningful but with a meaning so much their own that it cannot, even a posteriori, be abstracted from the history.

Hence such analyses of relevant human behavior as Gabriel Marcel's of fidelity[5] or Jaspers' of what he has called the "encompassing" factors of every experience[6] can be at this point color in the outline of Blondel's *Action* with a rich variety of actual human experiences.

---

[5]See especially his *Creative Fidelity*, New York, 1964.
[6]Xavier Tilliette, *Karl Jaspers*, Paris, 1960, pp. 170ff.

From the Problem of God to the Problem of Evil

But at this same moment when the free mind, by recognizing the drama as well as the dynamism of its freedom, begins to unfold the meaning of the word God, other highly disconcerting discoveries ensue. If they are honest and clear-sighted, the very analyses that disclose, in a sense, the hidden presence of God behind human life in the world, must also expose this presence's necessary shadow: the correlative presence of evil in the same world, the fatal absence of God. This is something so grafted into the human condition that it leads us either to push God back into an inexpressible and unthinkable transcendence or to reject him as pure nonsense. Heidegger's thought is perhaps best understood as typifying the first reaction, whereas the second defines the meaning a Christian will see in Sartre's specifically atheistic analyses.

We may pause here for the sake of a first provisional conclusion, worth stating if only to debunk the facile optimism to which we might be led by exclusive consideration of the cosmological ways of rationalizing the idea of God.

These ways reveal God as the unique fullness of being: the moral proofs show him as the source of all good as well as all being. The inevitable corollary of this is that evil cannot be a quality of being. But then it is all too easy to say, as has been said again and again since Proclus, that being is nothing but non-being, a statement meaning either nothing or that evil is nothing.

The truth, however, is—and any existential analysis brings this to light—that evil is a flaw in being, a lack of being *precisely where being was legitimately expected*. Hence the insubstantiality of evil, its ultimate unreality or rather its plain counter-reality, even if possible in a world sprung wholly, matter and all, from the pure Existent, does not in any sense justify the presence in a world created by him of the actual evils we observe.

Further, the higher one's idea of God, the more problematic becomes the presence of evils in our world and not just problematic but insolubly so, at least by speculation. Hence this problem cries out for some fuller revelation of creation's history, it being but one sign of how dramatic this history is. And if there is a solution it can only be in a salvifically eschatological denouement, bringing this history to its fulfillment in a way commensurate with that creative plan, once revealed, which has permitted the evil.

St. Thomas said all this, and said it very well, in his *De Malo*. This, however, has not prevented those disciples of his who understood his philosophy better that he did from confining the problem of evil to mere philosophy, and so making it susceptible of a purely conceptual solution, without the need for any recourse to history. But, as practically any analysis of human experience would suffice to show, these solutions are fraudulent pseudo-solutions, their inevitable exposure ensuring the dishonorable ruin of the factitious theories and the idiocy involved in them.

The Moral Argument, The Cosmological Argument and Aesthetic Experience

A second, still more surprising conclusion may be provisionally drawn from what we have so far seen of philosophy's reconstruction of the God-idea. It is called for by the unavoidable urgency of the problem of evil, or better mystery, for into that mystery the problem is absorbed and, at the same time, out of that mystery comes, ever clearer, not indeed God himself, but that reflection of his presence which our rationality is capable of detecting and delimiting within the field of our experience of human life in the world. The conclusion is this: just as the rationalizing of our idea of God based upon the cosmos requires completing by reflection based upon and sustained by moral experience, so both of these must be fulfilled or simply continued along the lines which only aesthetic experience seems capable of opening to the thinking mind.

We are well aware, once again, how unexpected and even discouraging at such a point this observation may seem. But did not Kierkegaard locate aesthetic experience midway between the pure objectivity of an exclusively rational approach (the very purity of which is suspicious) and the moral approach? And does not this make him a final echo of a tradition going back at least as far as St. Augustine? What, then, do we mean by "aesthetic"?

The Beautiful is not simply the pleasant. Even less, with all due respect for the author of *Art et Scolastique*, is it simply that which pleases the senses. There is a truth in the Platonic myth which makes of our sense of beauty a reminiscence of that vision of the Perfect Good which the soul possessed before its present existence and which it glimpses again whenever it comes upon some vestige of that Good among those material things entombing it. This is not far from the famous exclamation of the converted Augustine: *Sero te amavi o pulchritudo tam antiqua et nova!* "Late have I loved thee, oh Beauty so ancient and so new!"[7]

The most striking characteristic of the Beautiful is that it extends to inanimate as well as animate things, to bodies as well as to souls, and thereby seems to harmonize the physical and moral worlds, making them concertedly suggest, not just the vaster world of which they are but

---

[7]See the whole beginning of the *Confessions*.

the outer fringe, but a Presence. An ambivalent Presence, like the scent from an emptied vase, a Presence mixed with absence, or rather the nostalgia for a Presence now gone, but of which some trace yet remains, perceptible at certain times, in certain circumstances.

This is no merely passive perception. On the contrary it incites us to seek, to go in quest of a paradise lost and yet, in a sense, surviving behind all the rank cancerous growth of an archaic world, seemingly perfected only in its corruption and degeneration. Certainly, aesthetic experience, in this about-turn that it implies, the regression to which it seems to summon, can constitute a serious temptation for the created mind: that of retracing its steps and, having failed to find the paradise, of using art to make an artificial ersatz of it. Then, all it does is assemble from without according to the whims of sense or imagination the *membra disjecta* of this paradise. This is not merely a sense-temptation. It is embodied also in the dream of rational reconstructions that dispense with redemption, and even in that supreme and saddest fantasy of generous human love which is nothing but a subtly collectivized egoism.

But this temptation can be mastered. Art does not have to save the failing beauty of the world by adroit cosmetics that only congeal what they mean to bring out. It need not yield to the meretricious magic of conjuring up paradise lost by dreams and counterfeits. Its vocation is to puncture boldly the opacity of the present world. Even at the risk of losing itself in the night, of being stripped of all spuriousness, even losing its present counterfeit self, true art pierces its way, as if with a prophetic instinct and free of all falsehood, before the forgotten Presence. That at least is what true great art and inspired poetry attempt and suggest. They are far removed from the ineffectual or mystagogic nostalgia of a purely ornamental art or of poetry that is only a game, a diversion in Pascal's sense. Hence it is that the beauty they recall, the Presence they evoke, is no mere reminiscence, forcing us back beyond our existence, but a beauty transfiguring the ugliness in power and a presence abolishing absence but only gained when that absence has been experienced to the bitter end.

In our own time, it seems that it is Heidegger who has had a quite exceptional grasp of this. He has expressed it in perhaps the most revealing of his writings: the essay inspired by Hölderlin and his supremely tragic yet victoriously serene poetry and destiny. One might somewhat naughtily, though not unfairly, say that these stunning pages tell us more about Heidegger than about Hölderlin. More than that, they reveal how a modern man, overwhelmed by the fall of so many idols and especially of those most pernicious idols put in place of the true God by his unfaithful or incapable servants, can yet have a presentiment of that God in the lightning-flash of beauty at once consuming and consummating a poetry and poetic journey which truly touched on prophecy. Here indeed we find verification for Henri Bremond's own presentiment of the definite kinship between poetry and mysticism, even though it is found on a level quite different from that on which that aesthete, in the bad sense of the word, ordinarily moved. He too, though—and who does not?—had his moments of vision.

VI

From Myth to Rational Theology (continued):
The Transcendental Proofs or
Traces of God's Existence

One might ask to what extent experiences such as Hölderlin's may be rationalized and provide us, if not with demonstrations nor exactly a "monstration," at least with evidence, presentable in ordinary language and thought, of that God who is neither a mere concept nor even a living idea but a presence and the presence of a Person par excellence. The answer would require a philosophy of the creative or rather re-creative imagination, a philosophy such as Coleridge dreamt of and sometimes outlined but which no one yet has really undertaken to produce.

In its absence, we propose to conclude our study of the rational arguments for God's existence by a brief examination of those approaches usually known as transcendental. They aim specifically, by returning to the very springs of our knowledge, not in the cosmos or in human society but in ourselves, to regain contact with God—that God apparently absent from a world and mankind immersed in evil, that God whom beauty allows us momentarily to touch but only as hidden behind our past, whom all successful poetry stimulates us to pursue as the only possible goal of our life, the only end to that quest precipitating us into the world.

One can truthfully say that all transcendental philosophy aims to return to and enter into the living spring of knowledge within us and thereby, in a wholly rational fashion, to attain to that beyond, outside ourselves and the world which is, in the Platonic myth of reminiscence, the origin of all thought and even all being. Kant's undying greatness lies in his simply having conceived such an ambition.

But one must add that this journey of Kant's, so far as concerns what he called the pure reason, proved impossible or at least fruitless. Our subjectivity proved to be a prison. There being no door out, it was futile to look for a key. As regards what he called the practical reason however, the results were less disheartening. By the practical reason Kant meant reason acting as a guide, not to our knowledge of the world such as it might be in itself, but to our knowledge of what we should do with our existence.

This practical reason, certainly, as little allows us to come face to face with God as does the pure reason. But it postulates him behind, so to speak, the categorical imperative and, at the same time, as the source, in another existence, of the final reconciliation of virtue and goodness.

Yet, this division and opposition between pure and practical reason has for long appeared as an unacceptable defect in Kantianism. For knowledge to capitulate in the face of a phenomenon apparently unrelated to the noumenon it nevertheless attests has always seemed particularly unacceptable to minds formed to philosophy by the Greek tradition and by what one may call the classical tradition of Christian thought, its heir. Yet some of this tradition's more alerted exponents have not thought it possible simply to brush aside as *magni passus extra viam* everything that has been thought since Descartes. In particular, they have deemed it impossible to persuade the moderns that the criticism of all actual and possible metaphysics inaugurated by Hume and endorsed by Kant in the name of scientific reason should simply be reversed by an unmitigated return to the objectivism of all pre-Cartesian and especially pre-Nominalist philosophies.

Among those so minded was a Thomist—at least it must be admitted that he *meant* to be a Thomist—who was more intelligently informed as to medieval thought than even Suarez, in his day, was able to be. He did not hesitate to rethink the philosophy of St. Thomas, or at least what usually passes for such, in transcendental terms. The result was that God was once more rationally posited, not in the inevitable obscurity of the practical reason, but in the clear daylight of the pure reason, at the luminous source of its own luminosity.

This bold thinker was Father Joseph Maréchal, S.J.

Father Maréchal's Endeavor

The thought of Father Maréchal was for a long time more esteemed than followed, even in his own Society. But more recently a whole series of thinkers, all of them in their different ways remarkable, have applied themselves to exploiting and developing it, while reshaping it in a variety of forms.[1] Whether or not they are to be considered successful, they cannot be bypassed. In order to understand them, we must begin by tracing as precisely as possible what it was their master intended to do.

---

[1] Here again we are greatly indebted to the critical analyses of E. C. Mascall, *The Openness of Being*, pp. 59ff.

This is relatively easy. But we have also to trace how he did it, which is rather more problematical and one reason at least why the various efforts of his most outstanding pupils are often not in harmony with each other.

One can easily be discouraged by the sheer mass of material produced by this school. Even to draw up an inventory is daunting. And as a commentator, who has done his best to facilitate access to one of the best of these thinkers, once ingenuously remarked, they need to be expanded rather than summarized if they are to be understood. Eric Mascall has rightly observed that, given their aim, such prolixity is inevitable. Attempting a critical analysis of our knowing, down to its very source, before deciding whether one can make use of it or not, is like trying to sail without a wind. After a great deal of tacking, it will still be unclear whether or not one has got anywhere.

Hence, however cavalier it may seem to give them only these few pages, it is probably true that a great deal more would only add very little.

Father Maréchal's whole endeavor, by way of critical analysis of knowledge, was to establish that absolute being was not just the regulative principle of our knowledge (which indeed it is) but a ˙constitutive principle. Given this, he thought, it could be seen that our noetic activity has the structure that it has precisely because polarized by this absolute, necessarily positing and apprehending it in every act of knowing, even if not explicitly or consciously. Hence, while taking up Kant's critique, he brought into it St. Thomas' dynamic interpretation of knowledge, in which the knowing subject is not merely passive but active, tending to become the object, if not entitatively at least intentionally. Doing this allowed Maréchal and his heirs to go on calling themselves Thomists— that is, of course, transcendental Thomists—despite sarcastic remarks from the Thomists of the old school.

His enterprise had a lengthy preparation in the first four volumes of *Le Point de départ de la métaphysique*,[2] which abound with observations and analyses of the greatest interest. It came to its climax in the fifth volume which, by way of contrast, is outstanding for that kind of ingenuity in which Suarez excelled but which is more suggestive of patchwork than a philosopher's synthesis.

Something of this impression, one suspects, is shared by Maréchal's contemporary successors. Each of them, in fact, has restarted his work on a different tack and got involved in similarly tortuous circumnavigations.

---

[2] The first of the five volumes appeared in 1937.

Emerich Coreth

This is certainly the case as regards Fr. Emerich Coreth,[3] who has kept the closest to Maréchal. His sphere has been the exercise of the judgment, leaving aside what constitutes its content so as to delimit the conditions of its possibility. He submits every act of judgment which would contradict its latent metaphysical presupposition to a succession of *reductiones ad absurdum*. In other words, he maintains that one can only bypass Kant and resurface in metaphysics by being more transcendental than was Kant himself: beginning from the concrete activity of the questioning mind and showing that such questioning presupposes, as given, the realm of being. Following from this, each particular being returns as the material object of our intelligence, with being as such its formal object. The tables are turned by this dialectic, and the cosmological approach to God characteristic of Thomism ends up justified by the transcendental critique itself.

Karl Rahner

Fr. Karl Rahner, however, is not interested in such a return to cosmology, nor in the accompanying rediscovery of objectivity. Influenced by Heidegger, he is fully convinced that the only philosophical attitude appropriate to the modern mind is necessarily *existential* as well as *existentiell*, that is, not just originating in the subject but aimed at deepening his subjectivity.

He too has made copious use of the Thomistic analyses of the act of knowing but, in order to purify them of their inherent objectivism, he so constantly transposes them that *Geist im Welt*[4] reads like a perpetual allegorization. His goal, it is true, remains that of having being itself emerge on the horizon (Coreth is fond of the same image) of the intellect's vision, but he has no intention of changing this non-thematic knowledge, as he calls it, into something explicit by bringing it back to objectivity. Rather, he wants to evoke the necessary, hidden presence of an absolute, transcendent subject at the root, so to speak, of that automatically knowing subject that we ourselves are.

Rahner tries to reach this point not, like Coreth, by analyzing the judgment but by using, in his own fashion, the Thomist analysis of the

---

[3] Emerich Coreth, *Metaphysik. Eine Methodisch—Systematische Grundlegung*, Innsbruck-Vienna-Munich, 1961. See also Bernard Lonergan's discussion of this work in the volume of essays, *Collection*, edited by F. E. Crowe, New York, 1967, pp. 202ff.

[4] *Geist im Welt*, first published in 1939, revised in 1957. See Bert van der Heijden, *Karl Rahner. Darstellung und Kritik seiner Grundpositionen*, Einsiedeln, 1973.

conversio ad phantasma (what Kant would call the phenomenon), an action that implies, so he maintains, a *Vorgriff*, a pre-apprehension of absolute being. So we do not have some *a priori* proof of God's existence. Rather God is necessarily implied a posteriori, behind the apprehension of every real existing thing. Rahner defines this relationship to God underlying all our intellectual activity as a "supernatural existential."

One might be tempted to think that all this, instead of taking us out of our particular limited subjectivity, in fact ends up by bringing down into it the subjectivity of God and that gratuitous relationship of ours with it, which the Christian tradition has in mind when it uses in a precise sense the term supernatural. But Rahner denies the charge by recourse to the essentially, if we may say so, historical nature of man, it being wholly dependent on God's summons to him in history by his living and incarnate Word, Christ.

There is no reason to question Rahner's sincerity, but this last concession or compensation surely proves too much. Man's supernatural historicity is made so much a part of him that he is stripped of any nature of his own, even when it is conceived as being open or, simply, as openness to the supernatural. Indeed, an examination of the theological anthropology with which Rahner is increasingly replacing theology as a whole makes one suspect that his system is taking him to a goal exactly opposite the one he intended to reach, while the rather disconcerting developments he has recently made of his idea of an "anonymous Christianity" coextensive with all human history can only confirm one's suspicions. Just like Hegel, though in a different way, Rahner, instead of having historicized to the utmost his conception of humanity and of God himself, has without realizing it plunged God, Christ and the Christian supernatural into the pure subjectivity of our human nature, naturalizing all these realities by the very fact of relieving us of our own proper human nature.

Bernard Lonergan

The vast, difficult but incredibly enriching work of Bernard Lonergan is less presumptuous, more coherent and, for that reason, at the end of the day a good deal more enlightening and constructive. It also seems more genuinely Thomistic than Maréchalist, despite his method being transcendental and his debt to Maréchal, which Lonergan freely admits, being very considerable.

If it is possible to compress into one sentence Lonergan's analysis of the concept and of the judgment which unfolds in great concentric circles or rather spirals upward through the 800 pages of *Insight*, one might say that he means to show how the relative transcendence which makes for everything we know being referred, so far as knowable, to an object greater than its immediate one, is ultimately underlain by an absolute transcendence, implied by that intelligibility of the real presupposed by all knowledge.[5]

Hence it is that knowledge is essentially *insight*: a vision of the thing in itself and not merely a superficial viewing of it. Given this, all reasoning seeking to give reasons for the existence of God boils down to saying: if reality can be understood, God must exist. But reality can be understood. Therefore, God exists.

The God thus arrived at, as Lonergan stresses, is Aristotle's God, the first unmoved Mover but so far as "the Thought of thought." He is therefore, as in St. Thomas' formula, *ipsum intelligere, ipsum esse* and *summum bonum*, but with this precision, which would have so rejoiced Meister Eckhart, that in God intelligence, and not being, is the ultimate (or primary) reality.

It seems then that, unlike Rahner and even unlike Coreth who is wholly preoccupied with man as a questioner, Lonergan, while doing full justice to the latter's approach, is completely unaffected by Heidegger's existentialism in the sense that, thanks to his great common sense which never deserts him even in the subtlest flights of thought, he sees no meaning in and does not even deign to discuss the tension between the subjective and objective.

Eric Mascall and Illtyd Trethowan

The conclusions of Bernard Lonergan seem to us very akin to those of two other English-speaking philosophers and theologians, despite the diversity of their own starting-points. One of them was among the finest Anglican thinkers of our time, Eric Mascall, a loyal Thomist, however unusual such may be in his environment, and yet extremely open and perceptive. The other was a born Augustinian, but of exceptional intellectual acuity, Dom Illtyd Trethowan, a Benedictine of Downside Abbey.

They were in dialogue for over twenty years. The results can be seen in Mascall's Gifford Lectures, *The Openness of Being*, and Trethowan's two volumes on *The Absolute*. The former, having pondered over the things we have just been summarizing, concluded that every rational demonstration of God's existence supposes not any initial or immediate intui-

---

[5]*Insight, A Study of Human Understanding*, London and New York, 1957. Lonergan discusses the criticisms of him in *Collection*, pp. 152ff. His study, *Verbum, Verb and Idea in Aquinas*, University of Notre Dame Press, 1967, is also most enlightening as to the starting-points of his thought.

tion of God but what he unmusically if expressively calls a *contuition*, underlying all rational thought. On his side, Dom Illtyd Trethowan preferred to say that everything in our thinking springs from a mediate intuition of God as the unconditioned who is presupposed by every rational apprehension of our wholly conditioned experience.

It seems impossible to us either to reduce to each other two such differently conceived yet convergent expressions, or to choose between them. But, and this seems to be the view of the authors themselves, we may regard them as more complementary than contradictory.[6]

Realism and Idealism

If we can attempt any conclusions to these somewhat high-flying metaphysical exercises, even at the risk of playing the Peasant of the Danube, the first would be to agree with Gilson's own analysis of the different species of transcendental Thomism. He spoke from the point of view of an extremely clear and critical Thomism, but refused to fly so high at the risk of breaking his neck, and he was surely right to stress that philosophy took a wrong turn with the *Cogito* of Descartes and ended in an impasse with the *Critique of Pure Reason*. Any thought, the starting point of which allows the possibility of all thought being an illusion or even immures itself in such an affirmation, denies itself all right to any kind of affirmation, beginning, of course, with the one it has chosen to rest in.

Nonetheless, the modern drift towards idealism (meaning, thought itself creating what it thinks it knows) cannot be explained as a simple perversion. Or, rather, the perversion, so far as it is one, itself requires an explanation, as the Peasant of the Danube would be the first to admit.

One may reasonably regret that the finest among contemporary Thomists, including Gilson, have not seemed to realize that this idealism is latent in their master himself. One cannot but agree with the exuberant and slightly ferocious final chapter of that great book *Le Réalisme Méthodique*[7] as it ruthlessly exposes the sophistry inherent in any philosophy which claims to avoid solipsism and yet to extract the whole of reality out of its own inside. But one would have liked to hear the *altera pars* citing the universally revered Doctor in its own defense (even if it be a defense that will ultimately have to plead guilty).

---

[6] Cf. Mascall's Gifford Lectures, *The Openness of Being*, London, 1971 and the two volumes of Dom Illtyd Trethowan, *The Absolute Value*, London, 1970, and *The Absolute and the Atonement*, London, 1971, as also *Mysticism and Theology*, London, 1975.

[7] Paris, 1935. *Réalisme thomiste et Critique de la Connaissance*, Paris, 1939, should also be read.

It would be possible to plead that, according to *De Veritate*, while in us our thought is necessarily dependent upon an object existing outside and independent of itself, to which it is bound to turn and turn continuously if it wishes to exist, in God, on the contrary, it is the thought he has of beings and things that is the cause of their existence as the exemplar of their essence. We must be realists. But in God it is idealism which is true.[8]

Now, as is well known, man's primordial temptation, usually fatal since the Fall, is to forget that he is in God's image and take himself, innocently or not, for his model. The only way for him to overcome this is to go out of himself, that is, to recognize himself as essentially historical. On this point, Karl Rahner is wholly correct, though if historicity, as happens with him, goes so far as to de-essentialize man, it itself perishes. Man, in other words, in order to realize himself must turn away from himself in order to go, or at least intend to go, and encounter others and, behind and even in these others, *the* Other, who is also in a unique way like another self to ourselves, *intimior quam ego interiori meo.*

Hence our inquiry must now pass from the synchronic to the diachronic. This is a requisite of our phenomenological approach to religious activity. Or to put it simply, *pace* the erudite: since we are aiming at an integral description of man's religious activity, we must now proceed to trace its history, the profoundest aspect of the history of man.

---

[8]See *De Veritate*, q.2, a.14. (Cf. articles 2 and 8 of q.1.)

Part Two

From Natural Religion
to the Word of God

VII

From Primitive Religions
to Religious Civilizations:

Egypt, The Amerindian Religions,
China and Japan

One of the inescapable paradoxes of rational thought is that man's reason aims to be universal in its results and yet in its actual exercise is wholly individual. Its ambition is to say something effective to everyone who cares to listen, whoever he may be, yet it is only the single solitary thinker who can say his say. And this requires of him that he temporarily separate himself, spiritually as well as physically, not just from some blind mob or confused mass but even from the most living of collectivities. The rational criticism he adopts necessitates this at least provisional disjunction between himself and society, its cardinal principle being the questioning of every tradition, indeed of human tradition as a whole.

Religious Tradition, Rational Criticism and Prophecy

Religion, on the other hand, is essentially traditional and therefore social. And while, by rational thought, the thinking individual stands in opposition to the world itself, consciously and deliberately detached from it, a society in which religion is born and flourishes must necessarily and voluntarily be profoundly integrated into the physical universe. Conversely, in societies in which rational thought is paramount—society being considered as a purely human construct, severed from and opposed to the cosmos—religion declines and degenerates. This does not mean, strictly speaking, that it disappears. Rather, it bifurcates either into crass or refined forms of magic or into a State-worship in which a purportedly humanist mechanism having reabsorbed the cosmos finally assimilates man to the Moloch of the hypertrophied State. Any reactions, even the so-called atheistic ones, are only attempts at returning to a savagely naturistic religion, practically equivalent to the suicide of everything human.

Then in the midst of this process of disintegration, sometimes a part of it and sometimes partially succeeding to arrest it, the divine suddenly and irresistibly invades. This invasion does more than rejuvenate traditional religion. It transfigures it, at the cost of real death and resurrection. We call it prophetism. It occurs, it seems, in most, perhaps in all religious societies. But its only real lasting success appears to have been in the Judeo-Christian tradition. Hence only in that tradition has the critique of myth issued in something other than futile attempts at solving the insoluble problem of evil or the transmutation of the idea of God into a lifeless game of words.

It is only by an anamnesis of this whole process that the religious understanding can hope to arrive at the true goal of its age-old quest. For here again, and here especially, ontogenesis necessarily reproduces phylogenesis. Any thinker wishing to escape this necessity will end up thinking in a way contrary to life. A religious thinker, more than any, would thereby volatilize his religion or, worse still, produce an illusory substitute according to his own views of the sublime, appropriating religion to himself only by plunging both it and himself into solipsism.

Genuine religious philosophy, on the other hand, re-echoing the religious history of all mankind, is essentially a quest. It is a quest in that venturesome, most mysterious, most sacred sense of the word, as when we speak of the Quest for the Holy Grail. The tales built round this theme make a fascinating study. It is not hard to see in them how Christianity has projected itself upon a foundation of archaic stories in which the old primitive magic was striving to become mysticism. The quest of man stumbling in the dark as he seeks the sacred is taken up again and given answer by the quest of God made man for a pure heart to which he can give himself. Only the humble man, who had innocently sat in the perilous Seat can, by way of the trials to which he had unwittingly committed himself, reunite with God on the sanctifying Cross where he is hidden only to be revealed. Only he will see the Grail for one fleeting moment and yet be drawn by it, beyond the *flammantia moenia mundi*, towards that secret City where the Wisdom of God has set her table and prepared her banquet.

It is now incumbent upon our inquiry to try to follow as faithfully and intelligently as possible this human quest for God in the midst of which there suddenly appears, to use the title of Abraham Heschel's fine book, God in quest of man.[1]

We will begin with what is inappropriately called primitive religion and proceed to the three major religious civilizations in which that primitive religion came to full flower. They were civilizations enduring for thousands of years, unique in stature, apparently unchangeable through long fable-filled centuries, but in fact constantly changing and

---

[1] A. Heschel, *God in Search of Man*, New York, 1966.

constantly being deepened. It is not that they were ignorant of the developments proper to rational wisdom. But, in their case, these developments were either graven at the very heart of traditional religion or remained outside it and so, in either case, were powerless to effect a critique of the tradition.

The first seems to have died of introversion. The second was obliterated at a stroke, at the hands of what we might think a dramatic judgment of history but which is also perhaps the greatest crime on the Christian conscience. The third, in our own day, is caught between the giddy forces of self-destruction and an opportunity for renewal which some think will allow Christianity itself the chance of consecrating a general renaissance. We intend to treat respectively of ancient Egypt, of pre-Columbian America and of China, without forgetting its close and yet in some respects very distant neighbor Japan.

After that, we will enter a vast religious universe, apparently inexhaustible though it seems at present to be showing signs of fatigue. We are speaking, of course, of India—a universe within the universe—and at the same time of all those Aryan civilizations either directly dependent upon it or more distantly subjected to its influence. Unlike the aforementioned, Indian religion is one in which primitive religion has been so fully penetrated and permeated, and at the same time soaked up by critical reflection, that it is impossible to say what remains of it or to distinguish it from what has replaced it. It is also the remote source of the varied developments proper to Greece and Rome, and of the religion of the Germanic, Scandinavian and Celtic peoples.

But at the very heart of this Aryan flood, or rather deluge, it is necessary to mark out the small world of the Fertile Crescent, Mesopotamia and Syria. This world cannot be reduced to a conjectural "Semitism" in opposition to a (hardly less problematical) "Aryanism" since many of the people of the area were not Semites. But they had something which the civilizations of the first type held in contempt and restrained and which India and her disciples calmly ignored, namely an interest for the historical and an increasing appreciation of the person, things which were perhaps the happy reverse of a naively materialist attachment to the concrete.

Prophetism made a brilliant but brief breakthrough in Egypt, with the reign of Akhenaten. In pre-Columbian America, it scored at least two successes, permanently transforming the earlier religious structures. But it is hard to say how far it succeeded in impregnating them rather than just saving itself by means of them. For a while (and no more) it invaded ancient India. But in this case it was at once so radical and yet so restrained in character that one hesitates to call it prophetism. It only survived in Ceylon before taking possession of China and Japan, and in the process undergoing a highly problematical change. We refer, of course, to Buddhism.

In fact, it was only in the midst of Mesopotamian civilization, among a people, small, territorially insignificant and then dispersed, though not destroyed, that prophetism seems to have scored its one complete and lasting success—that is, in the faith of Israel, thereby preparing for the break-out and worldwide spread of the Christian faith.

Zoroaster, too, in neighboring Persia, represented a distinctive echo of prophetism. This then re-echoed itself. Islam, for its part, represents a delayed and unconsciously reactionary echo of the same phenomenon.

It is in such a framework that we must set what we call biblical revelation, both Jewish and Christian. This will enable us to see both its great humanity and its quite unique originality.

It would of course be fatuous to attempt a complete synthesis of so vast and complex a human experience. But the simple vision of Christian theism calls on us at least to sketch certain perspectives from which it is possible to look upon the great diversity of man's religious experience in the light of the Catholic faith. Conversely, if we wish for a renewed understanding of this faith, we must at least attempt to define, so far as possible, its insertion into this whole experience. If the Incarnation is a reality, if the Word of God has an abiding meaning, we are bound to seek understanding of everything wrought by that flesh of historical humanity of which the spirit has taken hold. Correspondingly, too, we are bound to sound the depths of the possibilities of expression offered to God as he searches for man in the language providentially prepared for this by general religious experience, be it elementary or highly elaborated.

So-Called Primitive Religion

Henri-Charles Puech in his introduction to *Religious History* in the *Encyclopédie de la Pléiade*[2] has shown, with great restraint and precision, how prudent should be our use, nowadays, of the expressions "primitive man" or "primitive religion." By definition, our knowledge of man's pre-

---

[2]Paris, 1970, pp. xivff. For what follows, the present state of historical studies in comparative religion can be found in Mircea Eliade, *The Quest*. See also Michel Meslin, *Pour une Science des Religions*, Paris, 1973. M. Meslin himself says that any lacunae are not the product of ignorance. One would like to know, in that case, why there is no mention of such unquestioned masters as H. Frankfort, E. O. James, Sigmund Mowinchel, G. Widengren, and others.

history is so fragmentary, so full of mystery, so patchy, that it is impossible to generalize in any authoritative way.

To have recourse to what we can know of actually existing cultures, different from our own and distinctly archaic, is one means of seeking light on our pre-history. It is not entirely fruitless. But there are two major difficulties. The first is that it is certainly false to consider these cultures as unevolved. All we can say is that they have not—as ours has. Nor need this mean that they are at an earlier stage of evolution. This would be an unprovable assumption, and in many cases can be clearly seen to be wrong.

Secondly, even if, in comparison to the few remains of the pre- or proto-historical periods, documents are not lacking, there is almost as much difficulty in understanding and interpreting them as their predecessors. This has been very well shown, on the basis of long experience and much reflection, by Michel and Francoise Panoff's book *L'ethnologue et son ombre*.[3]

This raises a question mark over any evolutionist view of religion, once it claims to be not just an *a priori* philosophy but a science worthy of the name.

The late nineteenth and early twentieth centuries saw a succession of such reductionist views of religion. One by one they foundered before the profusion and complexity of the facts. Yet the highly ambitious apologetical enterprise of Fr. Wilhelm Schmidt, who proposed a kind of regressive evolution, with "universal monotheism" as the basis of all later polytheism, can no longer hold.[4]

There was Tylor who urged that animism was the origin of religion.[5] Marrett replaced this with an impersonal *mana*.[6] Frazer, following Robertson Smith,[7] took everything back to the totem, then changed his mind.[8] Durkheim took it over, but made it a projection of social consciousness. And so on...

---

[3] Paris, 1968.

[4] On what follows, see M. Eliade, *The Quest*, pp. 37ff. and Maurice Leenhardt, *La Religion des Peuples archaïques actuels*, in *Histoire des Religions* of the Editions Quillet, vol. 1, Paris, 1948, pp. 108ff.

[5] Edward Burnett Tylor, *Primitive Culture*, London, 1871.

[6] R. R. Marrett, *Preanimistic Religion*, in *Folklore*, London, 1900, pp. 162ff.

[7] William Robertson Smith, *Lectures on the Religion of the Semites*, 1st Series. *The Fundamental Institutions*, London, 1894.

[8] His *Totem and Exogamy*, 1910, is certainly the source of Freud's *Totem and Taboo*, (see M. Eliade, *The Quest*, p. 14).

Andrew Lang,[9] always perspicacious, had shown that it was impossible to make the idea of the soul the origin of the idea of God. The idea of a universal Father-God appeared—in Australia, for example—precisely where animism was only minimally developed. Fr. Schmidt[10] made this the starting-point for his research, basing it on Groebner's confronting of ethnographical with linguistic data. He distinguished successive "cultural circles" and maintained that the earliest, that of the harvesters, gave evidence of a primitive monotheism. This lingered on, through the later stages, in the form of the "great god," who never fell entirely into oblivion, but became inactive and was thought of as distant and remote.

First, the hunters and fishermen set this figure in the shade of the divinity attributed to the putative sources of animal fertility. Their preference was for lunar and aquatic deities. Shepherding peoples, for their part, celebrated solar and heavenly gods in conjunction with their seasonal transhumances. Sedentary cultivators then introduced the earth-gods, the powers in vegetation. Finally, with technical progress came early urbanization and industrialization and thereby the passage from religion to magic.

These opinions are all based on interesting observations, interpreted however, too hastily and excessively generalized.

It is certainly true that the cult of the dead has occupied considerable space in all religions of every period. This is attested by—to give it a name—the "cult of skulls," revealed by discoveries of the earliest prehistoric remains. Nonetheless, as Lang long ago observed, death constitutes the unbreakable barrier separating souls from gods, and making it impossible to reduce the latter to the former. On the other hand, the totem while serving, as we have already said, as a focus for a variety of interesting religious phenomena, is itself a decidedly secondary phenomenon, evolutionarily, nowise universal and, further, however great its sociological significance, not in any sense capable of being reduced to a simple projection of the society choosing it for its emblem.

Again the studies of magic by Hubert and Mauss, albeit highly interesting, do not allow us to equate the religion of supposedly primitive man with magic.[11] Magic seeks to actuate supernatural forces—*mana*,

---

[9]Andrew Lang, *The Making of Religion*, London, 1898.

[10]The vast work of Wilhelm Schmidt, *Ursprung der Gottesidee*, the last volume of which appeared in 1955, shortly after the author's death, runs to over 11,000 pages. See Eliade, *The Quest*, pp. 25ff.

[11]H. Hubert and M. Mauss, *Esquisse d'une théorie générale de la Magie*, in *Année sociologique*, vol. 7, 1902-1903, pp. 1ff., and *Origine des pouvoirs magiques*, in *Mélanges d'Histoire*

orenda, etc.—but these forces are obviously more powerful than the one trying to manipulate them and are already possessed by mysterious beings from whom the magician is specifically aiming to wrest them.

What, then, of Fr. Schmidt's huge edifice? He undoubtedly descried a real correlation between the complexity of civilizations and that of their beliefs; he pointed out how the differing levels of the sacred and of our ideas of the divine follow a historical sequence, with a constant grasp of underlying unity subsisting beneath the apparent dispersion. But to elaborate from that his notion of a primitive monotheism was to impose an anachronistic intellectualism on the facts he was aligning.

Returning to Mircea Eliade's proposed definition of the religious and sacred, we could say that what Schmidt actually brought to light as something at the origin of every religion, and surviving even in its most highly developed forms, was not conscious, reflective mono-theism but the confused perception of the unity—both transcendent and immanent—of our experience. It is this essential unity to the divine, springing from the radically unifying character of our sacral experience, which, giving birth at the further stages of development to critical reflec-tion, would produce monotheism, and not vice versa.

In other words, we can once more see how the emergence of myth and of magic represent two possible options for man when he tries to take possession of his religious consciousness. In magic man performs a ritual and tends to attribute its efficacy to himself, thereby absorbing his consciousness of God into his consciousness of self.

Myth, on the other hand, though similarly humanizing, reaffirms the autonomy and transcendence of the god, who functions as a true agent in the ritual over and above the human celebrant. This though, in turn, runs the risk of humanizing the gods—something that the divine Word of Judaism and Christianity will call idolatry.

In what we call the primitive religions (or primitive religion), magic and idolatry thus represent two opposing and yet frequently superim-posed dangers. One way out is what we have described as prophetism. Apart from that there lies only the path of purely rational analysis, and the danger in this is that of volatilizing the divinity into abstractions.

Shamanism

Probably one of the most important of recent contributions to our understanding of primitive religion lies in the study of what is now

---

des Religions, Paris, 1909, pp. 131ff. On magic and religion, see the bibliography in Micrea Eliade's *Patterns in Comparative Religion*, New York, 1958, pp. 34ff.

called Shamanism. Mircea Eliade has been prominent in this.[12] It has taken over from the many studies in the last two or three generations, initiated by Frazer and especially developed by the Anglo-Saxons and Scandinavians, which were concerned with the mythical figure of the king. These served to reveal the important fact that religion, however social it may be, is always connected to certain exceptional persons. To some extent, it is true that these people can be considered as heirs of a whole collective tradition focusing on and in them, but it is no less the case that it is only in these providential men that a particular race, or the mass of men or even the whole of humanity, can see revealed the full richness of the realities they bear within themselves.

Shamans constitute one variety of those personages to be found at the heart of all the magical activities of purportedly primitive peoples. For long, it has been fashionable to equate them to our magicians and sorcerers. But the recent study of Siberian Shamans has shown that they represent a human type and a kind of activity wholly different from that of the popular sorcerer who is only, in fact, a miserable survivor of the ancient magician and his dubious practices. The original attempt to see the Shaman as a psychopath have proved fruitless. Even if it is true that he does not assume his role until after a crisis marked by undeniably pathological traits, he only becomes a Shaman when he emerges from the crisis. From that moment, he presents a personality a great deal more integrated and self-possessed than that of the ordinary people round about him, even to the extent of being able to work unquestionably authentic cures, sometimes purely psychological, sometimes even psychosomatic.

But the Shaman is more than a man uniquely endowed with supernormal powers. He is wholly at home in a world vaster than that of his congeners. He sees "spirits"; he communicates with them; he shares their radiance as well as their superhuman capacities. Because of this he is able to put his brethren in human nature in contact with superior realities. He teaches them about this higher world. He grafts their lives into that of a richer, more real sphere. Finally, it seems that he gives them in his own person, a privileged image in which the unity and unicity of the divine becomes explicit for the first time, by means of myth.

In more highly developed societies, the king (as studied by Frazer, then in greater detail by S. Hooke and his school, by the Scandinavian historians of religion and finally, more recently, by H. Frankfort and his colleagues) is obviously the successor of the shaman and his equivalents.

---

[12]Mircea Eliade, *Le Chamanisme*, Paris, 1968 (2nd ed., rev. and expanded); Eng trans. *Shamanism*, Princeton, 1970.

He is the source, at one and the same time, of the functions of the priest, the wise man, the judge, the warrior, the administrator. He is the key-stone of every traditional civilization, while his single but complex function becomes, so to speak, the axis along which myth and ritual will develop.[13]

Hence the king functions as a natural transition from archaic or primitive religions to the great and, in the strongest sense of the word, traditional religions, beginning with that of ancient Egypt.

Egyptian Religion

It was Herodotus who remarked that the Egyptians were the most religious of peoples. But he too saw the other side to this: how any examination of this all-pervading religion soon reveals the monstrous superstition in it. Egyptian civilization can only be called colossal. So long-lived was it that it could claim immortality and give apparent substance to the claim. Yet this in itself is disturbing. It never moves beyond highly primitive insights and practices, and the very frenzy with which it returned to them was a mark of death.

At first sight, religion in Egypt was ubiquitous. More than that, everything was god or liable to become such. Hence local gods proliferated. They were carefully included in the national pantheon and there confused with the leading cosmic gods and a plethora of divinized abstractions. Hence, too, the persistent appetite for representing gods in animal form which led to the divinizing of every conceivable creature, great or small.

To this was added a macabre preoccupation with death. Egyptian gods were either dead or dying. Their statues were venerated as the equivalent of mummies, while the general divinization of man (no less of the cat and the beetle) went hand in hand with an obsessional passion for mummifying as many things as possible.

After reading any simple description of gods and their worship— A. Erman's[14] for example , even if it is too glibly contemptuous, or even that of Mme. Desroches-Noblecourt[15] which is at the opposite extreme of benevolent interpretation—it is hard not to be filled with repulsion and

---

[13]Reference may be made to our earlier work, *The Eternal Son*, (Huntington, IN: Our Sunday Visitor, 1978), for a bibliography and for a comprehensive study of the mythical theme of kingship, pp. 86ff. We should also add H. Frankfort, *Kingship and the Gods*, Chicago, 1948.

[14]A. Erman, *Die Religion der Agypter*, Leipzig, 1934.

[15]In *Histoire des Religions* of the Editions Quillet, vol. 1, pp. 205ff.

fright. Egyptian religion seems to be that of crank collectors and maniac morticians.

However, any familiarity with Egyptian art and wisdom, while not getting rid of such an impression, can at least serve to correct it. Certainly, it was a strange religion. There it stood, century after century, rejecting any attempts to criticize it and withstanding any progress which might have, even only slightly, severed it from its roots. But there was a humanity underneath it all. A genuinely phenomenological approach would be capable of showing the unity and the religious, metaphysical depth of the Egyptian conception of the divine, despite external appearances. Hence, a synthesis like Philippe Derchain's[16] can give the impression of treating a completely different subject than that of the authors mentioned above.

Henry Frankfort,[17] in fact, had already powerfully intimated this by showing how Egyptian religion, for all the apparent diversity of its notions of the divine and its attachment to wholly animal representations of the gods, possessed a dynamic and ultimately unified vision of divine reality along with a marked preference for living, actual anamnesis over against abstract intellectualisms. Such a view seems to be corroborated by S. Morenz's minutely patient analyses, even if one cannot accept them in every detail.[18]

The Egyptian pantheon can be stripped of its nightmarish character if one realizes that in their thought, as in their religion, the Egyptians were almost uninterruptedly dominated by the sense of being beneficiaries of a beneficent order in which life was the victor and the forces of chaos, even if requiring repeated reconquest, were definitively vanquished from the beginning.

Egypt then was in a privileged position. It was the center of the world. Egyptians themselves were the only men worthy of the name, the word for Egyptian being the same as the word for man. And it was the discovery of Maat that made this possible. Maat was the source of all wisdom, and wisdom was the recognition and acceptance of a divine order imposed on things. This order gave men justice and happiness by way of the existence and action of the Pharaoh.

---

[16]Philippe Derchain, *La Religion égyptienne*, in the Pléiade *Histoire des Religions*, vol. 1, Paris, 1970, pp. 63ff.

[17]H. Frankfort (and others), *The Intellectual Adventure of Man*, Chicago, 1946 (reproduced in Pelican Books under the title *Before Philosophy*, 1949), the chapter on Egypt, and especially his book *Ancient Egyptian Religion*, new edition, Chicago, 1949.

[18]S. Morenz, *Ägyptische Religion*, Stuttgart, 1960.

For the Egyptians, the king was always the supreme epiphany of the divine.

Maat, however, was never the object of any definite teaching. She emerged gradually out of traditional experience, an experience which grew richer with time while never relinquishing anything of its past. The understanding of this past experience was progressively clarified, but on that very count none of it was forgotten.

In connection with this, the wise men, the "King's people," whose inspiration was personal experience but understood as cohesive with collective experience, never separated themselves from the priests nor the priests from the humblest of ordinary people. This was true even though the wise men pushed thought to its limits while the priests repeatedly refined their traditional rites and their meaning. The people left the mark of their piety in inscriptions; the priests in hymns and rituals which could be very highly wrought but were always full of traditional allusions; the wise men in their, on occasion, very free and far-ranging meditations. But for all their obvious differences of mentality and culture, continuity was never broken. Their vision was a single vision; their practice a unity. One fact in particular reveals this: leaving aside the pharaohs, and prior to the general divinization of the dead, wise men were the only individuals divinized by the priests, and popular devotion accepted this without demur. Imhotep was a favorite. He had belonged to the priestly caste but was glorified for having been an architect (he seems to have laid the plan for the Temple of Edfu in the third dynasty), a wise man and above all the founder of medicine. Another instance is Amenhotep. He was also an architect, and a confidant of Amenhotep III. But he was honored especially as the greatest master of wisdom.

However, the mention of Amenhotep leads us to another observation. Just as Imhotep was held to be the father of medicine, so he was regarded as the father of magic. Egypt's wisdom, in other words, like its priestly and its popular religion, was deeply enmeshed with magic.

At the heart of everything Egyptian was the king. It was always supremely through him that men, i.e., Egyptians, could participate in Maat. He was the epiphany of divinity, to the point of being confused with it. In consequence, he was the archetypal wise man, the archetypal priest. He had been begotten either by Ptah, the demiurge who had emerged from chaos at the very moment of drawing the universe, beginning with the gods, out of it, or by Amon, the sky, or by Ra, the sun-god who restored life each day with the light and determined its annual rhythm of rebirth.

Above all, however, as long as he lived, the king was Horus, the falcon god, and therefore the son of Osiris, the god of the fertility guaranteed by the overflowing of the Nile. When he died he became Osiris himself.

This is the clue to Egypt's thanolatry. Egyptian religion seems to end in an omnivorous mortuary. The reason was, as Morenz rightly shows, that Egypt was nothing but a long oasis fertilized by the Nile and surrounded by a barren desert which only necropolises could occupy.

This meant that Pharaoh was more than just the chief celebrant of Egyptian religion. It meant that Egypt's worship was centered on the liturgical unfolding of the king's whole existence and reached its climax in the pomp of his funeral.

Conversely, the daily liturgy before a particular statue in the temples of the multifarious great gods was essentially a court ceremonial with a heavy dose of magic (as for example in the priest's morning embrace of the statue, reckoned to revive the god). On feast days, the god emerged from his secret apartment, without leaving the ark which gave him a halo of glory. Usually Pharaoh accompanied him. The god processed while the people acclaimed him, and the king in person, or a priest as his representative, presided over the liturgical reenactment of the appropriate myth.

But, here again, the heart of this liturgy lay in the celebration of Pharaoh's death, embalmment and burial, and in the enthronement and coronation of his successor. The dead pharaoh was assimilated to Osiris, whose body had been torn to shreds by the jealous god Seth. Isis, Osiris' sister and spouse, had collected the remains and restored him to life by the magic of embalmment. It was then that Horus had been conceived. By being embalmed, the dead king had become another Osiris, while enthronement made his son Horus. The funeral barque took the immortalized body of the king to the West, towards the valley of tombs where he was to be buried. He was carried in the very same catafalque by which Osiris himself, in the wake of Ra (the sun plunging into the night), had traveled through the underworld in order to rise again victorious in the sky of a new morning.

The scope of this liturgy, with different degrees of schematization, was progressively widened as part of what has been called a democratization of ritual and belief. All the dead, however humble, came to be embalmed and simultaneously divinized in the hope of being identified with Osiris. Finally, when its very existence and religion came under threat, Egypt tried to somersault itself, by way of magic, into whole-scale survival. Every creature was mummified and divinized, beginning with those ordinary animals Egyptians had long acknowledged as manifesting mysteriously the life they experienced in themselves.

Behind this passionate conservatism and the obsessive desire to score a magical victory over death lay the very opposite of a static view of things. It cannot be emphasized too much how convinced Egypt was of the world's origin in chaos and its tendency to revert to it. Its whole worship was an immense attempt at exorcising, in the name of every conceivable god, the serpent Apophys, representing chaos and threatening to reabsorb everything into it. Yet, even in the midst of the benevolent deities, evil and death constantly reappeared, personified by the enemy, Seth, the jealous one. They threaten us from without, but also from within. Hence the judgment of the gods was always being invoked. Hence too everyone was subject to it. The magical interpretation of the funeral rites, the ritual counsels of the books of the dead accompanying the dead to their tombs, had the purpose of overcoming the terrible fear of this judgment. But the wisdom writings, echoed both by the most highly refined of the priestly hymns and by the plainest of popular inscriptions, subordinated these rituals, without in any way rejecting their effectiveness, to a practical implementation of wisdom. This was the only sure way to righteousness. One of the very ancient wisdom men, Ptah hotep, despite his stress on the laborious learning needed for wisdom, never forgot that it can be found, pure and living, on the lips of the simplest, and not only in sophisticated traditional writings. A solemn confirmation of this conviction is preserved in *The Story of the Eloquent Peasant*, in which the peasant's violent protests win the unhesitating approval of the monarch.

This insoluble ambiguity was embodied in Thot, the god of the divine word and the corresponding wisdom vouchsafed to men. He gave simultaneous expression to the order governing the universe despite the everpresent imminence of chaos, and to the derisory nature of man's hope of ever laying hold on it, his abiding incapacity to master it. The destiny to which man was subject was itself subject to a god in whom justice was paramount, but the evil negating this justice was apparently incapable of ever being overcome. Egypt regarded itself as a kind of miraculous interlude, miraculously held in being by a word both magical and divine.

H. Junker maintained that the apparently insuppressible polytheism of Egypt had been preceded by monotheism, and that this monotheism was never effectively revoked.[19] Behind Atum, the demiurge of Heliopolis, and Ptah, that of Memphis, behind Horus also stood the faint outline

---

[19]H. Junker, *Die Gotterlehre von Memphis*, pp. 25ff. and 76ff., cf. his *Christus und die Religionen der Erde*, vol. 2, 1951, pp. 570ff.

of the sky-god Ur. What is certain is that the priests, both at Heliopolis and Hermopolis (the sanctuary of Thot) and then at Memphis, strove to organize and unify the world of the gods, without however abolishing every distinction between them, either in triads or enneads. The ennead of Heliopolis was so successful that it gave its name to any group of ten or more gods.

Parallel to this, the priests also rehearsed and refined the distinction between the statue or, more often, the image it clothed, and the *ba* by which the god revealed himself. Finally and most importantly, the wisdom men always spoke of God as if he was unique. They seem to have done this without any awareness of opposing the deepest level of priestly or popular piety, nor did anyone ever take offense.

The Religion of the Amarna Age

Only during the eighteenth dynasty (1562-1309 BC), however, did monotheism emerge in a fully self-aware and coherent form. The way had been prepared by Amenhotep II and Amenhotep III. With Amenhotep IV it became a doctrine, preached with passion and yet sincerity. It was explicitly opposed to every kind of polytheism, seeking to eradicate it once and for all. This was the extraordinary interlude known as the Amarna Age.

Its precise significance is still under analysis and discussion. Undoubtedly political reasons, both inside Egypt and outside, favored and prepared for Akhenaton's ephemeral reform, just as they brought it to a sudden and unhappy end. Amenhotep II had earlier been concerned to reduce the power of the Theban clergy of Amon, built as it was upon a gigantic economic substructure of "sacred" goods. He was the first to set up Aton, the solar disc, as an opposition—a synthesis in which Atem, the supreme God, manifested according to the priests of Heliopolis in the sun Ra, would absorb Thebes' heavenly demiurge. Tuthmosis III, his successor, was able, thanks to the support of the Heliopolitan priests, to diminish the political power of the prophet, i.e., high priest, of Amon, while at the same time favoring the worship of the solar disc. Amenhotep III brought this policy to its conclusion: the Theban priesthood became politically impotent and Aton's sanctuaries multiplied. At the same time, all these rulers seem to have done their best to rally their newly-conquered Syrian subjects to a worship which was now regarded as no less universally applicable than pharaonic sovereignty.

Amenhotep IV, however, went much further. He changed his name to Akenaton, the servant of Aton. He declared himself the high priest of the sun's disk. He organized a new system of worship, stripped of all images, and built a new temple and a new city, El Amarna, for the purpose. The new religion was proposed as the only unadulterated worship of the one and only God, the creator of everything, invisible in himself but made manifest in the sky in the burning disc of the sun and on earth in Pharaoh his son. He had excised from inscriptions the names (*nets*) of any god other than Ra, even Amon, while discharging and expelling his priests and even, it seems, setting fire to the new sanctuary at Karnak, only finished at the beginning of his reign.

Akhenaton's personal religion which he hoped to have Egypt and perhaps the whole world adopt, was expressed in his own great hymn to the sun.[20] One of the most magnificent cosmic psalms of the Hebrew Bible (Ps. 104) echoed this hymn centuries later.

His reign drew to its end amid defeat at the hands of the Syrians. After his death everything he had labored for collapsed almost at once.

Undoubtedly Akhenaton and his work have been the victims of a rather naive romanticism, attributing a greater purity to his words and deeds than perhaps they merit. Nor has the fidelity shown him, even after his death by his wife, Queen Nefertiti, been uninfluential in this respect. For the first time, the frescoes of El Amarna show us a graceful female silhouette alongside the august image of the king, and in their train a host of little princesses striking their sistra while mother and father practice what has been called the offering of the divine names.

Yet when all is said and done, Amenhotep IV cannot be explained merely politically. What E. Drioton has well described as "his decisiveness and its negative capacity for opposing every belief refusing submission to his synthesis" indicated how inspired, how much a man of conviction Amenhotep IV was.

Amenhotep had tried to trample the traditional spirit of Egypt underfoot and inevitably it took its revenge. Under his successor and erstwhile collaborator there began a restoration of the proscribed forms of worship, starting with that of Amon. The process triumphed under his grandson, the feeble Tutankh-Aton, who willingly or not was renamed Tutankh-Amon. Yet the very fact that the priests of Thebes then thought it necessary to produce a "trinity," in which Amon in his turn strove to incorporate Ra and Ptah, was a sign that the reformer's radicalism, though condemned as heretical, answered to a certain instinct in the Egyptian soul, an instinct no longer admitting suppression.

Amenhotep IV, however, remained a solitary figure, and Egypt's traditional religion lasted into the time of the Ptolemies. They them-

---

[20]For an English translation see D. Winton Thomas, *Documents from Old Testament Times*, London, 1958, pp. 145ff.

selves, not without some measure of success, tried to extend it beyond Egypt in a hellenized and factitious form, in the mystery of Serapis and Isis.

But once Egypt lost an indigenous monarchy, its religion drained of life. Christianity, and then Islam, replaced it with ease.

This, though, does not mean that nothing has remained of Egypt's religious legacy. The *Hermetic Books*, it must be said, do not contain much that is specifically Egyptian. This may be less true of the sections treating of magic, but it certainly holds for the philosophico-religious treatises, which have nothing Egyptian about them apart from a superficial local color. Their intellectualized mysticism is simply a blend of Stoicism and Judaism, the former already tainted with Middle Platonism and the latter highly hellenized. Egypt's spiritual heritage, however, does exist. It must, though, be looked for elsewhere.

Survivals or Preparations

Certainly this spiritual inheritance was taken up without difficulty by the Bible. This is true of the riches of rationalized experience in the wisdom writings with their remarkable progressive concentration on the problem of innocent suffering. It is true, more particularly, for the concept of Wisdom itself, which the inspired word was to rejuvenate and to develop in unpredicted ways.

Morenz, however, for all his critical caution and keen perception of the irreducible originality of things, sought to claim more. He saw in the pharaonic function and, more generally, in the theology behind the worship of statues, an Egyptian preparation for the Christian theology of the Incarnation, and in the various triads of the priests the same for the Christian Trinity.

Before assessing such suggestions usefully, the differences need to be underlined. These are so considerable as to prevent any facile transference of Christian formulas onto ideas or realities whose resemblance to those of Christianity is merely superficial. Thus, it is essential to what we call the Incarnation to have in mind a unique historical individual, who in person is none other than the second Person of the eternal Trinity. On the other hand, it is equally essential to the concept of the Trinity that, rather than reflecting various cosmic phenomena, it express the wholly transcendent inner life of the Godhead. It is not just any triad, but the mutual interrelation of three subjects of whom one is the source of the other two.

But, as regards the special presence of God in the pharaoh or statues, this admitted of extension to any number of individuals, successively or simultaneously. Then again, the more Egyptian thought dwelt on the king's divinity, the more explicitly it affirmed the subsistence, within the union, of his limited, even imperfect human personality.

As for the various triads (also the enneads and other more complex groupings), they consisted of either distinct local divinities or different cosmic powers. Only occasionally within a particular triad can we see a sketch or some distant equivalent of the Christian processions, usually in the form of two gods emanating from another. But even when, as was by no means always the case, symbolism cleansed these relational images of their materiality, they remained images purely of the relationships between various aspects of cosmic life.

What the Bible did accept, however, applying it to God and to the Messiah, was Egypt's mythical view of the king, a view more fully developed in Egypt than anywhere else. But the application involved a radical transformation. Thus, on the one hand, we have the case of the closest link between a mythical figure and the major themes of the inspired word. On the other, as we shall shortly see, we have the most striking example of the total reworking such ideas could undergo.

It can also be conceded that Egypt, with an unrelenting vigor unmatched by any of Israel's other neighbors, highlighted the twofold problem of the relationship between cosmic and divine life, and, within the latter, between its contrasting unity and multiplicity. This was a real contribution. But if Judeo-Christian monotheism was to emerge, with its resultant vision of God as Creator and Savior, the Egyptians had to be rejected, even more forcibly than they had been by Akhenaton.

The thing closest in Egypt to the forms of expression common in what we call the "Revelation" of the two Testaments was the Egyptian understanding of the divine word. But, as has often been observed, this word never precisely involved a revelation of God himself. The Egyptian gods did not reveal themselves, not even Maat who transposed into the world the transcendent order those gods represented. They merely appeared either in the more salient beings or phenomena here below, or in the thought and experience of those who, by the help of the gods, had achieved spiritual union with the world's order.

From the point of view of Hebrew and Christian sages, the Egyptians had certainly made great progress in exploring the order imposed by divine Wisdom on the course of life. Their greatest achievement undoubtedly lay in the courageous clarity with which they raised the problem of evil and innocent suffering. But the mystery by which the Wisdom of God transcends all merely worldly wisdom remained inaccessible to them. They were never to know how what was, to their wisdom, a problem, had been resolved by a revelation of sheer grace. Under

Akhenaton, there had been a fleeting flash of light; it was never completely forgotten, but neither was it ever acknowledged.[21]

Amerindian Religions: Mexico

There are many apparent similarities between the religion of Egypt and those of pre-Columbian America,[22] i.e., first the Toltec and then the Aztec in Mexico, the Mayan to the south of central America and that of the Incas between the Andes and the Pacific. There were the same astonishing feats of architecture, performed according to magical numerical laws and involving skills we find it hard to reconstruct. There was the same juxtaposition of undeveloped primitiveness—witness the animal gods—and the greatest refinement in art and sometimes in speculative thought. In both cases, the worship of sun and stars predominated, bound up, especially in Peru, with a cult of the dead involving mummification. In Peru again, more than elsewhere, royalty appeared to occupy the center of the cosmos and of cosmic life, making the king, the Inca, not just the supreme pontiff but the Sun-god manifested on earth.

But there is one signal difference between these civilizations and that of Egypt. The latter's unity was age-old and lived on in isolation for centuries. That of the former coalesced out of a host of peoples, fragmented culturally and linguistically throughout a history marked by violent confrontations.

Two revolutionary reforms were particularly notable and, as in Egypt, they were brought about by royalty. That in Central America ended in failure, even if less of a failure than it seemed at first sight, whereas that in the Andes was relatively successful.

It is usual to distinguish three major eras in the development of the civilizations of Mexico and Central America. After the pre-classical period (at its apogee between 1000 and 500 BC) came the civilization of Zacatenco, surviving in some graceful figurines, probably deities of fertility and life after death, then that of Ticoman, in which the god of fire featured (who would survive to be familiar to the Aztecs as "the old

---

[21]One curious characteristic of Egyptian religion is its tendency to see a twofold aspect to all reality. Many rituals had to be performed twice. This might, though, like the double crown of the pharaohs, be no more than a hang-over from the separation of Upper and Lower Egypt. For a brief account of recent developments in the study of Egyptian religion, see the final chapter of C. J. Bleeker's contribution to the collective volume edited by him and G. Widengren, vol. 1, *Religions of the Past*, Leyden, 1969.

[22]In this section, we are particularly indebted to W. Krickeberg *et al*, *Pre-Columbian American Religions*, Eng. trans., London, 1968, and the works of Jacques Soustelle, summarized by him in his contribution to the Quillet *Histoire des Religions*.

god"). This period culminated in La Venta. The earth pyramids belonged to an earlier age, but now had enormous heads added to them, in which the human face can be seen gradually developing out of the mask of the jaguar—for long the preferred image of God for all these peoples. Stone, originally basalt, began to be used for these buildings and jade objects for worship. Both of these would be inherited by Mayas and Aztecs.

The two great pyramids of Teotihuacan, in the Mexico valley, bring us to what is called the classical period. From now on the plumed serpent, the Aztec Quetzalcoatl, held sway. But at this stage he was a rain god, bestowing food in the present and life hereafter, a life placed by the cultivators of that appallingly dry region in a paradise of exuberant vegetation.

After the transition period of Monte Alban (below the Oaxaca valley) and El Tajin, where the remaining traditions of La Venta, plus others apparently coming from the southeastern Mayan cities, blended with those of Teotihuacan, we come to the historical era.

It began with the Toltecs, the people of Tula or Tolan, in the state of Hidalgo, fifty miles north of the site of Mexico. It was from them that the even more warlike Aztecs received their particular style of human sacrifice, i.e., excision of the heart, the practice of flaying alive, and the magician god, Tetzcatlipoca, the warrior of the north, who was identified with the Great Bear (and hence was one-legged) but always represented by the jaguar. The Aztecs referred to themselves as the Mexica, after their tribal god, Mexitli, identified with the sun and usually known as Huitzilopochtli. They only arrived in the valley of Mexico at the end of the twelfth century. There, a hundred years later, they built their capital Tenochtitlan. They owed Quetzalcoatl, the feathered serpent god, however, and their priestly calendar, to the Mixtecs of Puebla, a people who did not belong, as the Aztecs and Toltecs did, to the Nahuatl linguistic group. Quetzalcoatl was identified with the wind god of the Huaxtecs, a Mayan people who harked back to El Tajin.

The Aztecs have often been compared to the Romans. Like them, they were adept at conquest and organization while borrowing most of the elements of their culture from those they conquered. At the summit of their pantheon they always retained an ancient great god, Tonacalicultli, "Master of our flesh," the "only true god" (Nelli Teotl), whom they described as omnipresent, incomprehensible, both father and mother "by whom we live." They honored him with fervent prayers but, at the time of the conquest and presumably well before, with no other kind of cult.

Their own tribal god, Huitzilopochtli, a solar divinity who was represented by the eagle (still Mexico's emblem) was for them essentially the Master of war. The sun's rays were his mark, and to him was transferred the sacrifice of human hearts, inherited from the blood-filled worship of the Toltecs.

They also took over the Toltecs' own tribal god, Tetzcatlipoca, the astral magician who saw everything, even at night, in the obsidian mirror with which he was identified. Their cult of the plumed serpent Quetzalcoatl was again derived from another people, in this case the Mixtecs. The Aztec priesthood bore his name, their rites following a mysterious calendar of 260 days, the *tonalmatl*, also taken from the Mixtecs.

In the Aztec view, Nelli Teotl, the "true god," created everything, availing himself of this incongruous couple as intermediaries. Tetzcatlipoca, however, overcame Quetzalcoatl by magic (the latter now being regarded, as we have said, as the god of wind and sky, and founder of the sacred rites and of art and civilization in general). Pursued by his rival, he deliberately destroyed himself above the Gulf of Mexico and his heart became the planet Venus. It was a particularly inauspicious moment when Venus came into conjunction with the sun.

The exiled god, however, was expected to return on a date prescribed in the priestly calendar: in the year 1 Acatl. He would then regain his power. Cortez disembarked at that very moment and owed his astonishingly easy conquest to the coincidence.

This myth, one would feel, is the outward expression of the conflict that the Aztecs must have sensed between the different components of their syncretist pantheon. But only when we proceed to the Mayans will the puzzle become clear.

A further mark of Aztec religious complexity lies in their three calendars. That of 260 days, inherited from the Mixtecs, provided chronology for all the ritual they had taken from them along with Quetzalcoatl. But they also used a solar calendar, apparently personal to themselves and, most remarkable of all, a calendar of 584 days, corresponding to the revolution of Venus. This is reckoned to have some connection with the myth of Quetzalcoatl.

They also believed in four earlier ages of the world, each of which had been brought to an end by a disaster. The present fifth age had been preceded by a flood, which features throughout Amerindian myths, and the world was due to come to an end in a general conflagration. A final point to note is that, for them, the four cardinal points each corresponded to an elemental god, a series of years and a color: the north to red, the east to yellow, the south to white and the west to blue.

The Mayas

The Mayas came from the south and, except for the stray shoot of the Huaxtecs who remained relatively stable, evolved on their own. They too had a pre-classical period of civilization during which they developed certain architectural and sculptural elements inherited from La Venta in their own distinctive, baroque-like style. This can be seen at Uaxactun, where the first Mayan writing, dating from 328 AD has been discovered. Only later, however, between 692 and 810, did their sculpture reach its golden age, despite never moving beyond bas-relief—unlike that of the Toltecs, Aztecs and even La Venta. This golden age may be seen embodied in the figures at Yaxchilan, representing Itzamma, the heavenly god (with "the Roman nose" as the archaeologists call it), or Chac, the "long-nosed" god of rain.

In the ninth century, however, for some unknown reason (perhaps because of virgin forest intruding after a climatic change), the Mayas forsook their former towns and high civilization, though not their religion, and moved from the equatorial plains to the more mountainous region north of Yucatan. Their short-lived, authoritarian and centralized empire, based on Mayapan, fell in the fifteenth century. Thereupon decline set in. Some elements of their earliest beliefs and rites have survived in Guatemala for centuries. (A parallel case was the survival of the ancient Nahuatl religion among undeveloped peoples such as the Nicaraos; this was still in existence at the Spanish Conquest.)

The Mayas had the same ritual 260-day calendar as the Aztecs, calling it *tzolkin*. They also went in for similar speculations about the cardinal points, except that, for them, the south was black and the west white. But the chief parallel lay in their belief in a supreme god, whom they too called the "one true god," Hunah Ku in their language. However, since they always remained an agricultural people, they gave greater attention to the rain-god Chac (also known to the Aztecs, as Tlaloc) and to the maize-god, Yam Kaak (Xipe to the Aztecs). The "crosses" which so intrigued the Spanish when they met them in such places as the famous sanctuary of Palenque were connected with the last god. But they were nothing more than the representation of a cosmic tree.

Their own sun-god Kin (eventually to be fused with Itzamma, the god of heaven) was certainly connected with war, like Huitzilopochtli among the Aztecs. But the connection was not identification. In general, for the Mayas, each sacralized natural power had either a benevolent or malevolent aspect.

But most remarkable of all, perhaps, has been the discovery of the genuine historical basis underlying the Aztec myth of the struggle between Quetzalcoatl and Tetzcatlipoca.

From the History of Ce Acatl to the Myth of Quetzalcoatl

The buildings of Chichen Itza, in the heart of Mayan territory, are so outstanding in both style and splendor that only events of epic proportions can adequately explain them. They were the fruit, in fact, of an upheaval in Toltec history. The date is in the last years of the first millennium AD, and the crisis unexpectedly culminated at Yucatan, only a little while after the Mayans had emigrated there.[23]

It seems that Ce Acatl, fifth of the ten Toltec kings, sought to introduce a profound religious and cultural reform among his people. It would have outdone even that of Akhenaton in Egypt. Presumably the first to do so (setting a precedent followed by Toltec and, later, Aztec priests), he assumed the sacred name of Quetzalcoatl, regarded as the heavenly messenger, and then tried to suppress all the blood-sacrifices at Tula and restore, or initiate, the one worship of Nelli Teotl, the "only true god," father and mother of all beings. At the same time, he proposed a wholesale cultural transformation, affecting art as well as thought, and drawing inspiration from the renewed worship. The astonishing originality of the art of Chichen Itza became the monument to this.

The supporters of Tetzcatlipoca, the god of magic, chased Ce Acatl from his throne and country. Accompanied by a notable group of his own faithful, he set out for Yucatan. There his remarkable genius was to provide a lasting witness to itself in the holy city of Chichen Itza: an amazing synthesis of Toltec art and such Mayan techniques as the use of the arch. It was completed only after his death, however, and bears marks of his disciples having quickly resumed the crueler practices of their religion, apparently provoked to this by a revolt of the Mayas against their initially peaceable invaders.

But, under the Mayan name of Kukulcan, a literal translation of Quetzalcoatl, Ce Acatl, with the Morning Star as his chosen emblem, lived on among the Mayas as the prophet of their "only true god," Hunah Ku.

The Aztecs, on their part, identified him with the Plumed Serpent, his supernatural alter ego. In a richly significant way they also associated him with the various rites of purification, common to most Amerindian peoples: ablutions, confessions, penitential practices, sexual abstinence before the major cultic events and so on. It was Ce Acatl who had

---

[23]On this reconstruction of events, see Krickeberg, *op. cit*, pp. 48ff.

stressed the importance of such rites and seen the deeper meaning in them.

Peru and Inca Religion

Inca religion was far closer to the dreams of Ce Acatl than to the old Central American religions and their less developed South American equivalents. From the time of the Inca Hatua Tupac, c.1347 AD, it was dominated by the vision of a pre-Inca creator god, called Huiracocha on the plateau and Pachamac on the coast, where he gave his name to the city in which he was worshipped. To him was attributed the flood, which the Incas, too, believed had put an end to the period of human history preceding our own.

However, the Inca, along with the sun to which he claimed to be related, remained the principal manifestation of the creator god, and worship was essentially solar and astral. In the Coricancha, the great temple at Cuzco, stood gold and silver images of Inti, the sun, and Quinta, the moon. Mummies of emperors surrounded the former, those of their wives the latter, around an altar where Orion and the Pleiades were represented.

The Incas all but completely dispensed with human sacrifices. Instead they sacrificed llamas, made libations of maize-beer and held solemn lustrations followed by a ritual banquet at which everyone, even strangers and mummified ancestors, was invited to share a cake of maize kneaded with the blood of the sacrificed llama.

The way in which this Inca civilization, in particular, was wiped out and its last representatives massacred by the bestial cupidity of supposedly Christian conquerors has remained a sort of original stain on South American Catholicism. It was obviously no coincidence that decadence almost immediately ensued upon so shallow an implantation.

Further, the savage suppressions of these Amerindian civilizations, with the destruction of so many documents that might have lessened our ignorance, have served to add a pathetic postscript to the mystery surrounding them.

Even among the Incas, with whom ritual and myth gained, or regained, a striking simplicity and purity, we see a process similar to that so marked in Egyptian religion. In both cases, a highly developed civilization emerged without ever outgrowing what we regard as the primitive mentality. Also striking is the oscillation between the two extremes of Mexico and its sanguinary rites on the one hand, and Cuzco and its apparently pure and brotherly religion on the other; between the complete dualism of the one, most manifest among the Mayas, and the

monism of the other which aspired towards a demiurgic kind of monotheism. The most moving general characteristic, however, is the one that
reached its climax with the reform of Ce Acatl: the sense of culpability
and of man's duty to overcome it within himself, even more than death,
so as to rejoin the gods. Then, too, there was the supreme god, man's
friend and the author of civilization as well as creation, who in the end
was to triumph over the demonic spells temporarily cast on man and
exiling him, as it were, from his true home.

On the other hand, the blood rites, especially among the Aztecs, stand
in brutal contrast with the nobility of their art and, despite its military
ambitions, with the ultimate broadmindedness of their political outlook.
However, we should not forget that the Aztecs were always ready either
to risk death in war or to offer themselves spontaneously for their horrible sacrifices, and that this was expressly done with the idea of
restoring to the gods the life they had given. The notion of thereby
preventing the putative exhaustion of the gods bordered, of course, on
the magical. Nonetheless, all this was not without its grandeur. And the
hecatombs of Toltecs and Aztecs surely seem trifling when set against
those of the last two centuries of our post-Christian and supposedly
enlightened world, the repeated holocausts perpetrated in the name of
nationalism or liberty or the class struggle, all of them unavowed
religions.[24]

The Religions of China

Whereas source-material for the pre-Columbian American religions is
scarce, for those of China it is abundant.[25] One aspect of Chinese religion
was for long predominant, and it is the one which makes by far the most
stunning parallel with ancient Egyptian religion, namely the cosmic,
almost divine function allotted the sovereign, along with the place given
to the dead. In China, too, a civilization, though even more refined,

---

[24]Though obviously out-dated in many respects, Prescott's two classics, *The Conquest of Mexico* and *The Conquest of Peru* are still worth reading for their astonishingly evocative re-creation of these ancient civilizations and their religion.

[25]We have made particular use of Marcel Granet, *La Civilisation Chinoise*, Paris, 1919 and *La Pensée Chinoise*, 1934 (both re-edited in 1968) and of Max Kaltenmark, *La Chine antique*, and *Le Taoïsme religieux*, of the Pléiade *Histoire des Religions*, vol. 1, pp. 927ff. and 1216ff.; Paul Demiéville, *Le Bouddhisme chinois, ibid.*, pp. 1249ff., and also H. Steininger's contribution on China's religions in vol. 2 of the *Historia Religionum* (ed. Bleeker and Widengren): *Religions of the Present*, Leyden, 1971. But our greatest debt was to our late and esteemed confrere, Fr. Vincent Ou, whose own father was the last minister of the ancient Chinese rites.

developed for thousands of years without ever overstepping the primitive framework of religious thought. Only Buddhism could do something like shake the foundations and, even then, in highly paradoxical fashion, the repository of the most archaic kind of Chinese thought (what we call Taoism) practically took Buddhism over, with the Taoists, in their humorous Chinese way, driving the Buddhists to fury by changing Buddha into an ingenious disguise assumed by Lao-Tse to bring Tao to the barbarians of the West.

Perhaps the most thrilling thing, however, about the three Chinese religions is that they are still alive now. It may even be that we stand unawares on the eve of a new victory for their assimilative power, this time over Marxist Communism (which seems incapable of developing in the West). Christians in the know as regards the Far East think that such a victory could prelude a wholly new beginning for the Christian mission and, above all, provide twentieth-century Christianity, which so often seems moribund, with an unexpected instrument for the vigorous re-expression of its eternal truths.

But can one in fact speak of three Chinese religions? It is true they have often been locked in bitter combat, but it may be truer to see these as three never completely separated and ultimately inseparable aspects of a common religious outlook. And it has been well said that Chinese religion is often indiscernible to the foreigner precisely because it is indistinguishably enmeshed with the Chinese sense of what life is about.

The first foundation and continuing ground of Chinese religion lies in Taoism or, to be more precise, in that sense of the dynamic unity in nature and the universe as a whole which Tao articulates, calling it the "way," with everything unceasingly springing from and returning to this unity. Tao is capable of degenerating into popular or, equally, sophisticated superstition, into a vitalist species of magic, or of rising to the heights of mysticism. It is not easy to say whether this mysticism can be called genuinely pantheist or not rather, in Krause's term, panentheist. Confucianism humanized Tao to the point of apparently secularizing it completely. Chinese Buddhism, on the other hand, purified it, one could say, almost to the vanishing point. But neither of these two rivals has ever freed itself from Tao. However much they might have transfigured China's original "way," that way remains. It continues to impose its logic of universal participation, so baffling to the Western mind.

In Confucianism, as much as in ancient Taoism, the Emperor, the Son of Heaven, was the center of everything. He was *the* manifestation on Chinese soil (and no other deserved the name) of the divine goodness and harmony. But in Buddhism (of which it could be said more truly than of any of our own forms of wisdom that its center was everywhere and its circumference nowhere) the Buddha, once sinicized, became in turn a heavenly Emperor, an Emperor of jade, with the Emperor on earth as his most zealous devotee, intent only on his being his perfect reflection.

This did not mean that at the primitive stage the Emperor was conceived of as an autocrat. Man was the microcosm whose endeavor was to align and identify himself with the cosmos. And so in Tao it was notdoing, which best defined the highest activity of man and *a fortiori* of that most highly-placed of men, the Emperor. His duty was simply to be what he should be, to live in perfect accord with the immanent law of Tao, so that, placed at the very heart of the reverberations of cosmic harmony, he could mediate that harmony to the human, i.e., Chinese world.

We find here as in Egypt, though the two cases are not identical, a law governing everything and therefore meant to govern everything human, and which was essentially twofold. It both alternated and harmonized: *yang* and *yin*, male and female, light and dark, hot and cold, living and dead, with life's very heart-beat expressed in the unending rhythm and everything incessantly proceeding from and incessantly returning to a center and a heart.

How, then, formulate Confucius' endeavor? Did he strive to make the cosmos human by absorbing it into that ideal society to which Chinese society was intended to conform? Or did he rather seek to bring his dreamed-of Chinese humanity into accord with a perfect cosmos, forever renewing itself, harmonious in all its parts and never waning into decadence? But such a question is probably meaningless. Either or both are no less true. The essence in any case lies in the adjustment of human relationships to the profoundest postulates of nature and specifically of human nature. Such an adjustment had to be precise and spontaneous, even though the spontaneity be a supremely studied one. It was to be achieved by a constant watch on linguistic usage and by a meticulous (as opposed to scrupulous) ritual observance, which would have the effect of steeping these relationships—of parents and children, of brothers, friends, masters and subjects—in a tonality whose accord with the cosmic register was the guarantee of its truth.

Forget the profound inspiration of all this and it would have every appearance of formalism gone berserk and artificiality at its ultimate. This indeed was what happened in neo-confucian scholasticism. Man, stripped of personality and stripped of nature, was trapped like a fly in amber in the frozen embrace of a factitious universe produced by victoriously pedantic sophisticates.

Then the Taoist reaction set in. This was not popular Taoism, which sought to guarantee facile well-being through the use of undemanding logic. Nor was it that refined Taoism which by conserving breath, blood and sperm, blocking those body-orifices (which folk medicine was wisely anxious to keep open) aimed at physical immortality by preventing out-flow of the life-force, mummifying that force in imperial cinnabar even at the cost of poisoning the body. The reaction, rather, was that of Taoist mysticism, whose intent was quite other, namely to give man back to himself by giving him back to mother nature, withdrawing him from the too self-conscious, self-reflective, over-deliberate and positively narcis-sistic humanism of decadent Confucianism, so that he could find his life, quite literally, by losing it.[26]

The identity of contraries here reaches a high point that makes for nonsense at the conceptual level but which is perfectly reasonable, if not rational, at the level of practical common sense: the most widespread thing in the world and possessed, if not by *homo sapiens* in general, at least by that very special *homo sapiens*, the Chinaman, whose humanity, nothing if not realist, could be claimed to represent the finest instance there is of humor.[27]

The Chinaman, overcome, having drunk the intoxicating intellectual rigor of hyper-cerebral Confucianism to its dregs, always bounced back to this Taoist naturalism with an ease quite inexplicable to us. And Bud-dhism, or rather the unique Chinese conception of it, grafted itself on to this, and by replacing the naturalist, cosmic character inseparable from Tao with its own ultra-cosmic or even non-cosmic outlook, formed its exact counterpart, its twin, or better, its mirror-image. But in the Chinese perspective that very fact would constitute the supreme glorification of Tao, for where the opposition of Yang and Yin was at its most stubborn and irreconcilable, there precisely contraries would be definitively re-solved and transcendence rediscovered at the very heart of immanence.

Consideration of one of those exquisite Sung landscapes would be enough to quell any doubts on this score.[28] We do not even see, at first, the diminutive man who is there unassumingly in a hidden corner. Yet, just as his personality which, far from having disappeared in the Tao, had discovered in it refuge and salvation; so the abyss of unknowing into which he had willingly become absorbed now restored him and the whole of the cosmos that had vanished together with him, to a state free of all contradictions, so that, once again, everything became eternal, unalterable harmony.

---

[26]Jean Grenier, *L'Esprit du Tao*, Paris, 1957.

[27]Liou Kia Hway, *L'Esprit synthétique de la Chine*, Paris, 1961.

[28]See on this point (although devoted to a neo-confucianist) the wonderful work of Nicole Vandier-Nicolas, *Art et Sagesse en Chine*, Paris, 1963.

What is the meaning of all this for us? He must, in spite of every best effort, realize that we shall always border on utter misunderstanding, while the Chinese wise man—kind Lao-Tse, fatherly Confucius, or commiserating Buddha—looks at us from the corner of his eye with varying but unmistakable irony—whatever his particular style at the moment. At any rate, if we interpret as sheer nothingness this supreme subterfuge of Chinese Buddhism, through which Chinese religiosity seems to have finally delighted in dodging every one of its own traps, we have obviously understood simply nothing of China, from beginning to end, especially its tremendous and serene love of life.

But, we might ask, where exactly is God to be found in this (or these) religion(s)? Once again, God is just everywhere—though nowhere tangibly.

Yet, note carefully, if we fall back with delight on universal love, caring little for all hierarchy, for all law (including the august Tao), for that Me-ti wherein we delight to recognize ourselves, to find our "Christian charity" as we have diluted it into a universal, do-good-ism, then let us beware, for the charitable Chinese themselves will be the very first to point out to us how mistaken we are. To take a typical Chinese anarchist for one of our Western saints would be pitiably to misrepresent the sublime devil-may-care attitude of which the Chinese soul is capable, as though it were another form of our clammy, lachrymose humanism, which could not possibly be more alien to its instinctive, invariable sense of decorum.

Japan

Japanese Shintoism, despite evincing a different temperament, is another specimen of the same persistent primitiveness, proving more resistant to any evolution even than Egypt, if that were possible, while at the same time assenting to every kind of external transformation.

Everything was sacred or liable, in some inexplicable, indefinable way, to become a revelation of the *Kami*. What were the *Kami*? Demons, or gods? Or anonymous magical powers? None of these questions are to the point. They made the sacred present. At first sight, there seems to have been no limit to their multiplication. Yet, the sacred they represented was always one and the same, while always eluding any kind of circumscription.[29]

---

[29]Hartmut O. Rotermund, *Les Croyances du Japon antique*, in the Pléiade *Histoire des Religions*, vol. 1, pp. 968ff.

What was peculiar to the Japanese was their brand of instinctive, spontaneous loyalty, binding worshipper to worshipped by a romantic bond. On the emotional level (though less so intellectually), the relationship was intensely personal. The only comparison would be with vassal and suzerain. We see it in the relationship of a samurai to the mikado (and every Japanese was a potential samurai), or of the mikado to the Japanese imperial mother and, finally, to the sun-goddess, Amaterasu (another paradox for us).

China and Japan, against a background of constant familiarity, have often been in opposition, and nothing reveals this so eloquently as the paternalism of the Chinese Heaven, absorbing everything in its super-cosmic masculinity, set against the fundamental and never-abandoned materialism of the Japanese. Yet the sun, which the latter took for their mother, has everywhere else been the cosmic emblem of fatherhood.

VIII

The Ganges to the Tiber:

From Indian Religion and Religious Philosophy to Greece and Rome

It is tempting for a naive Westerner to think of the religions of India and China as nothing more than related variations of a common "oriental" spirit. After all, did not Buddhism, which came to birth in India and then all but disappeared from there, go on without a break to China and Japan while, if not conquering, at least coloring everything it met? This may or may not be so. But, in any case, to associate China and India is a fallacy. There are, perhaps, no two intellectual worlds further removed from one another.

"Chinese" can be a synonym for foreign and strange, and first appearances can certainly be bewildering, but the great paradox is that the European mind, formed on a Christianity which has either subsumed or been subsumed by Greco-Latin humanism, can find itself at ease in Chinese thought with amazing rapidity. By way of contrast, the slightest acquaintance with the Indian or Hindu world suffices to expose the fundamental misconception underlying the immense nineteenth-century Western effort to translate and interpret Indian thought in terms of its own idealist categories (which run counter, of course, to man's innate realism). Nor does the fact that certain modern Indians have taken to expressing themselves in this kind of language suffice to change the failure into a success. Nineteenth-century knowledge made it look as if India had been perfectly understood; the twentieth century has seen the illusion collapse.

One could sum it up roughly by saying that Chinese and Western man (unless the latter has been unduly sophisticated) have a common passion for the concrete. In China, as nowhere else, *homo sapiens* has remained *homo faber*—to his fingertips, or even his nailtips! On the other hand, to categorize Indian thought as idealist is a pathetic simplification. It would be better to speak of a dream within a dream, an indefinite series of gear-changes or a game of mirrors with reflection after reflection. Our most finely honed categories are left stranded or quietly over-

ruled, with the apparently most pellucid of our oppositions being immediately outmaneuvered with an unchecked and protean dexterity.

One factor, however, common to Indian and Western thought alike is
a relationship with religion, both having usually unfolded in conscious
tension with a living religion. But, whereas in the West thought reaches
the point, at least temporarily, of volatilizing religion in order to replace
it, in India thought pervades and absorbs religion to such as extent that it
becomes impossible to tell which is which. Thought replaces religion but
by so deft an imitation that one fails to see that religion has not just been
refined but emptied.

The result of or, rather, reaction to this is sheer paradox. Here was
religion worm-eaten by religious philosophy. Buddhism came to its
rescue—but only by affecting complete atheism!

Subtlety or refinement are words that come to mind in characterizing
Hinduism and its philosophical development. Man's spiritual history
holds no greater example of such highly-wrought elaboration. It reaches
the ultimate in verbal and intellectual virtuosity. But, for all its astonishing success, there is a price to pay. Distinctions follow distinctions. They
multiply to such an extent that there is a danger of falling into plain
confusion of mind. Nor is the danger fictitious. If everything possible
is said on every possible subject, this very totality will inevitably end,
at least sometimes, looking embarrassingly like nothing and leave one
wondering whether one is at the high point of refinement or in a welter
of balderdash.

Hence, we find in Hinduism (especially, though not only, in the
export brand, symbolized by Katmandu) a bewildering juxtaposition of
the most high-flying ecstasies or "enstasies" and the coarsest, shallowest
kind of charlatanism, and, at the theoretical level, the sublimest thoughts
alongside a muddy-mindedness as inappropriate as flatulence. In such
circumstances, one can be forgiven for feeling lost. On the one hand is
the genius of Sankara, on the other the paranoia of Annie Besant; the
holiness of Aurobindo, and the dissolute duplicity of his partisans.

More simply, this luxuriant world of overcharged intellectuality and
oppressive spirituality sometimes creates the inevitable and not always
unjustified suspicion of being made of marshmallow or of chewing-gum
masticated for thousands of years. Similarly, it is often hard to dis-
criminate between grandiose temples and papier-mâché pagodas, and
yet, once again, given such uncertainty, one is led to understand and
appreciate the splendid simplicity with which Sakya Muni could brush
all such things aside as trifling—though he too was exposed to the
danger of being sucked back into the world of dream or nightmare by his
own disciples.

The fact, however, remains that this same India undoubtedly lies at the root or basis of everything developed by the West. This is true of thought and of religion, even of that religion which we, Jews or Christians, regard as revealed. So it is India we must begin with or return to if we want to understand ourselves and, so far as is possible, our faith.

From Mohenjo-Daro to the Vedas and Upanishads

Indeed, our own beginnings were Indian. The great European Indianists of the nineteenth century, from the Schlegel brothers onwards, were quite right about this. Their mistake was to consider the Vedas as man's first bible (they are not even India's first) and to imagine that all later Hinduism sprang from there. Our own century's archaeological discoveries at Mohenjo-Daro[1] have shown the Vedas to be a secondary, non-autochthonous stratum in Indian religion.[2] They were the properly Aryan contribution, and the earlier culture underwent, rather than accepted them. Correspondingly, it now seems quite clear that even present-day Indian religion proceeds from the primitive origins unveiled at Mohenjo-Daro, while the Upanishads,[3] which glossed the Vedas in a particularly trenchant way, provided the justification for returning to these origins at the same time as making possible radical transformations of the material they explained in their own distinctive way.

This means that the original basis of Indian religion, in direct opposition to the heavenly or solar religions we have seen so far, was the oldest known example of those fundamentally matriarchal earth religions in which the object of adoration was the life of the cosmos with its alternation and intersecting of fertility and death. The horrible, devouring, blood-stained mother, Kali, was the post-Vedic "translation" of this. But she was only a survival of the mother-goddess, rediscovered at Mohenjo-Daro, and who was at the center of all earth-worship. Siva, whose dancing represents the perpetual play and loving combat of life and death, began by being nothing more than her consort, along the lines of Tammuz, Adonis or Attis.

---

[1] Marshall, *Mohenjo-Daro and the Indus Civilisation*, London, 1931. Cf. in *Historia Religionum*, vol. 2, the beginning of R. N. Dandekar's chapter on Hinduism.

[2] Jean Varenne, *La Religion Vedique*, pp. 578ff., in the Pléiade *Histoire des Religions*, vol. 1.

[3] The Belles Lettres editions have made available excellent French translations of several Upanishads. On Hinduism in general, a good introduction, along with Dandekar's study cited above, will be found in Anne-Marie Esnoul's highly condensed summary, *L'Hindouisme* in the Pléiade *Histoire des Religions*, vol. 1, pp. 995ff. (For English translations, see S. Radhakrishnan, ed. and tr., *The Principal Upanishads*, New York, 1953.)

On to this, the Aryan invaders tacked their rigid arrangement of sacrifices and their worship of Agni, the sacrificial fire, later identified with the breath of life, both cosmic and super-cosmic, namely Brahma.

Here then was a highly-organized system of worship which contrived to ritualize the whole of man's life and the whole of the universe's. The Upanishads claimed to do no more than add a few glosses. In fact, though, they took the first and decisive step towards the kind of religiousness characteristic of the Hindus. This flourishes freely on the fringes of ritual. It respects ritual. It even justifies it by way of symbolic explanations. But it goes far beyond it. It even goes so far beyond it as to get beyond any kind of god, the Vedas themselves not having always clearly distinguished particular rites from the gods at their heart.

Here lie the roots of that extraordinary, calmly self-contradictory profusion of the most varied interpretations and contrasting devotions which gradually came to make up the warp and woof of Hinduism. It is not even enough to say that every conceivable position is represented. There is the worship of a one and only god who is all-loving benevolence for his faithful, and apparently transcendent and personal. The classic expression of this is found in the Bhagavad Gita. At the other extreme is the practical and theoretical atheism of the Sankhaya Upanishads. In between fall all the various cosmic and acosmic forms of worshiping the Self, the "breath." This can, if one likes, be identified with what Tillich called the "ground" of the human soul. It is the reality of everything or the opposite, the reality contrary to everything's unreality.

On the one hand, we have a wide and ever-widening range of interpretations, tolerating one another without the slightest embarrassment, and at the same time a chameleon-like capacity enabling any one such interpretation to give way to any other and even to change itself at will into any one of them, going through the most disconcerting metamorphoses in the process. In the face of this kaleidoscopic variety, the dedicated labors on the part of Western intellectuals to translate and pigeon-hole it all seem rather pathetic, even ridiculous.

We may take a typical example: *maya*, the relentless variability of things, the constant plasticity of the world of sense or of matter. It is generally translated as illusion. But is it an illusion created by the weakness of the individual mind or, rather, a mirage recreated over and over again by *prakriti*, herself a derivative divinity or perhaps an anti-divinity? Or is it God's dream, or is it, whether it be a dream or not, a reality of some kind, even though wholly relative; having objectivity in us as well as in God? And if so, is it perhaps an eternal counterpart, the outside as it were, of *purusha*, the living flame of mind? A Hindu, even though personally inclining to one or other of these views, will also probably think that they each, separately or together, have their own value and should not be rejected.

India's ethics, also, have risen and fallen as profusely and fluidly as her metaphysics. Curiously, there was complete agreement about respecting the Vedic ritual prohibitions affecting castes. Sacred cows were venerated, etc. But, beyond that, one could indulge in the most orgiastic kinds of worship or the strictest asceticism and even see the latter as the meaning of the former. Or again, one might be in the most indigent condition possible or, alternatively, comfortably devoted to pursuing the goods of this world while practicing detachment, in word and thought, of the most idealistic kind. And Hinduism proved fully capable of accepting all this, rationalizing and harmonizing it; making light of it and getting bogged down in it and then again and again going effortlessly beyond it, like a swimmer bobbing up from the bottom after being pushed under.

So, on the one hand, one is tempted to regard Hinduism as the most inorganic form imaginable of religious thought and practice and, on the other, forced to evoke consummate examples of amazingly organized speculation. Yet in the latter, it must be said, so fine is the thread of deductions that, no matter where the argument began from, any conclusion escapes the naked eye.

However, there is one thing which acts as the framework or structure of Hinduism. It is not speculation, even though Indian speculation goes far beyond the wildest projects of our scholastics. It is something practical. It is not the official rites, pursuing their perpetual round in the shaded temples and never more than a back-drop for lived, especially fervently lived religion. It is, as Mircea Eliade has rightly insisted, the practice of yoga.

Yoga

But what is yoga?[4] Undoubtedly, an ancient ritual engrafted with a very strict yet markedly flexible method of meditation in which form seems to be more important than content. This meditation extends into a kind of gymnastics, penetrating to the meeting-place of mind and body. All this generates and is fed by a mass of speculation, a world within the multiform world of Hinduism, its best microcosm, even though there is hardly anything in the almost horizonless Indian world untouched by the ramifications of yoga.

---

[4]Mircea Eliade, *Techniques du Yoga*, Paris, 1948, and especially *Yoga: Immortality and Freedom*, 2nd ed., Princeton, NJ, 1969.

What is the aim of yoga? In theory, it will culminate in *samadhi*, marvelous tokens of a total mastery of reality which appear miraculous to the uninitiated and win veneration for the yogi. The latter, however, if faithful to what is reckoned the most orthodox doctrine, will disclaim this and pass on to a wholly interior experience, proper to him alone.

But then, what is this experience? Is it ecstasy or enstasy? Is it the discovery of true reality, or of the divine beyond it, or of a blissful indistinctness in which such distinctions are absorbed and abolished? All these explorations can be and have been maintained. There are many others and anyone is free to add some new ones.

But you can also quietly turn your back on yoga and hope for everything from *bhakti*, a divine grace owing nothing to your merits and practices. Or again, you can practice yoga systematically while only trusting in *bhakti*. Nothing need prevent your gaining it.[5]

Then, what about this *bhakti*? Will it be Vishnu who gives it? But who is Vishnu? Is he anything more than the name or outward form of a personal though hidden god, or of the self, or of anything else? There are no answers to these questions—or every and all possible answers.

Then again yoga can ally itself with Tantrism, i.e., an interpretation and especially a praxis that are definitely magical. We, of course, would be tempted to say that this was to be expected. Yet, at the same time, yoga can maintain its independence. It can even be in opposition to Tantrism, while Tantrism itself is, at its most quintessential, curiously liable to link up with *bhakti* at its most refined.[6]

All this marks something of the impression Hinduism tends to make on us Westerners. Perhaps the passion with which we try to extract its one or many secrets is the very reason it always seems to be receding into an increasingly incomprehensible inaccessibility?[7]

---

[5]The *Bhagavad Gita* is the classic text on *bhakti*, trans. with commentary by R. C. Zaehner, Oxford, 1969.

[6]On Tantrism, see Eliade, *Yoga*, pp. 200ff. Cf. H. von Glasenapp, *Buddhistische mysterien*, Stuttgart, 1940.

[7]Louis Renou's *Anthologie sanscrite*, Paris, 1947, gives a good idea of Hinduism's unbelievable variety, even in its classical period. His *L'Hindouisme*, Geneva, 1951, gives one of the latest and best general accounts of the subject. (It was summarized in advance in a short book with the same title in the "Que sais-je?" series, Paris, 1947.) H. von Glasenapp's *Die Philosophie der Inder* (Stuttgart, 1949) is an excellent introduction to Indian philosophy. Its only weakness is that it makes things a little too clear!

Buddhism

After that, it is tempting to regard the original form of Buddhism, that of Sakyamuni,[8] as a reaction akin to our own. It seems like a cry of "Stop!" uttered sweetly but strongly and definitively before the riotous exuberance of Hinduism. But once again, we are back on the merry-go-round. Two diametrically opposed historical interpretations may be found not only among the best Western Indianologists but also among the finest Hindu experts on Hinduism, and Buddhist scholars. One school sees Buddhism as a particularly successful distillation of Hinduism's hidden essence and, as a result, as was the case with Ananda Coomaraswany and his disciples, claimed to be reabsorbing Buddhism for the good of Hinduism.

Others, however, have continued to regard Buddhism as a total negative of actual Hinduism, even more radical in its rejection if that were possible than Jainism,[9] its close relative.

What makes it even harder to decide between these two conflicting views of Buddhist origins is that Buddhism itself, as it developed, rapidly reproduced characteristics remarkably similar to those of the highly developed Hinduism from which it had originally broken away. This was especially, though not exclusively, the case with *mahayana* Buddhism, that of the "Great Vehicle" and the more popular form, in contrast to *hinayana* Buddhism, that of the "Small Vehicle." The tendencies of the latter appear as the more authentic, or at least more primitive. Then, beyond *mahayana* itself, once transported to Japan, stands Amidism, which in many respects seems very close to the Indian *bhakti* and even seems to surpass it in a way we would be tempted to consider Christian.[10]

Certainly, however, Buddhism always expressed itself and acted within the intellectual and spiritual framework of Hinduism. It used it to formulate its message, doing so with a perfect ease verging on polite indifference. Certainly, too, the message was one of liberation—the liberation which all the mystics, so to call them, and wise men of India had been seeking.

But it is not enough to say that this liberation was conceived of in Indian terms. It was a total liberation, freeing from the framework as well as from anything else. The Upanishads had discreetly disentangled

---

[8]On Indian Buddhism, see André Bareau's competent introduction in vol. 1 of the Pléiade *Histoire des Religions*, pp. 1146ff. One should also see at least H. von Glasenapp, *Brahma und Buddha*, Berlin, 1926.

[9]On Jainism, see Colette Caillat, in the Pléiade *Histoire des Religions*, vol. 1, pp. 1472ff.

[10]Henri de Lubac, *Amidisme et Christianisme*, Paris, 1954.

themselves from Vedic ritualism, nonetheless leaving it carefully undisturbed. Buddhism freed itself not just from all Indian ritual, belief and speculation but even from its yoga, its *bhakti* and, *a fortiori*, its Tantrism.

This, however, did not prevent Buddhists, outside as well as inside India, from reintroducing into Buddhism rituals, beliefs, speculations, an equivalent to yoga in Zen and many other sects, to *bhakti* in Amidism and to the ultimate in Tantrism in Tibetan Buddhism. Yet one need only read the memoirs of the fourteenth Dalai Lama to recognize the distinctively Buddhist savor persisting despite the reintroduction of all this lumber. Buddhist spirituality remains able to use, play with or do away with any or all of these props. This is a measure of the deep freedom it aspires to, a freedom we see attained not only by great religious personalities but also by the simple faithful.

As everyone knows, Buddhism aims at *nirvana*. Is nirvana, though, something positive or negative? That is a question which can be discussed interminably. What is certain, however, is that it lies beyond not just definition, but any experience capable of being described or expressed or even intimated.

Hinduism hesitates before or flirts with every possible interpretation of the precise relation between self at its most intimately experienced and the final object of religious experience. It seems to want to hold onto everything capable of being said or thought, however contradictory, and proceeds to do this with an ingenuity of imagination, a philosophical fecundity and a hyper-intellectual subtlety which we find positively overwhelming. Buddha brushed all that aside like a fly, the self included. What he said, it must be stressed, was not that none of this had reality or was unrelated to reality, but that none of it must be an object of our definitive interest.

What then was Buddha after? What was he hoping for? He simply knew that liberation from absolutely everything must precede any encounter. But who or what was to be encountered? He did not know and was patently too honest to palm people off with any substitute. He simply fell silent.

Even the endearing Ananda, devoured even more than we are by a craze for questioning, could not penetrate this silence. However, before he entered it, Buddha did make some very simple but pointed remarks. They stand in complete contrast to anything Hinduism could have said or inspired. They are humble, precise and yet remarkably open and have the effect of a cold shower after so much clammy, tropical fug.

First came a morality, wholly negative in expression like our Decalogue but of a crystalline purity: no murder, no theft, no adultery or fornication of any kiud, no lying. Then, an ascesis, balanced but tending markedly to simplicity, restraining every unbridled desire and pacifying all the way from the most carnal areas to the center of the soul, while never proposing to suppress or destroy anything of either soul or body.

Then came the paradoxical affirmation that the soul is no more real than the body, even though what the soul does in the body loads it with a *karma*, a weight from the past burdening the future, only to be lightened or cast off by total present detachment.

Then again, in equally paradoxical contrast with this ascesis of indifference, came what might be called a mysticism of pity and universal compassion. It is after all this that *nirvana* is found—the unimaginable, the unthinkable.

These precepts, and even more the underlying world-view, can seem negative. Yet this is not how man, and specifically religious man, appears to Buddhism. A remarkable proof of this is in the Buddhist reaction to Rudolf Otto and his attempted description of the object of religion as the "Wholly Other," supremely terrible in his total otherness and yet more fascinating than anything else. Westerners were baffled; the Indians only vaguely interested, but the Buddhists of China and Japan were conquered at a blow and have not stopped saying that no one, not even among themselves, had so happily expressed the object of their search.

In view of all this, it is extremely tempting to agree with Soloviev. For him, Buddha was no atheist. His rejection of every satisfactory form of religion was made in silent expectation and with a real presentiment of the one true God who would one day speak and make himself known as transcending every thought about him that might rise in the heart of man.

Be that as it may, the Buddhist *nirvana* was not ultimate extinction, the disappearance of being into pure non-being. The ironical sign of this was that everything Buddha had calmly thrown out of the window would be carefully gathered up and reintroduced by those apparently unfaithful disciples who attached themselves desperately to his person, experience and doctrine.

One may legitimately think, in particular, that the Chinese of the Sung period assessed Buddhism rightly as completely transcendental, the very leaven they had lacked, capable of lightening the pastry of their immanentist Taosim and of conferring a "heavenliness" on the very source of their otherwise so earthly Confucian humanism. Nor, it seems, were the Japanese mistaken when they thought to find in Buddhism the elusive object of their civilization's quest, an object for supra-cosmic devotion and loyalty, lying within and yet at the same time going beyond their extremely "primitive" religious spirit.

Greek and Roman Religion

In the far West, however, the religious complexity of India was to find another kind of resolution. In Buddhism, it had transcended itself; in the West, it bifurcated into the religions of Greece and Rome. It is droll to see the Alexandrine culture of hellenistic Rome doing its best to identify them, when in fact they represented a reduction of the Indian compound into its two major antagonistic compounds (though both would tend to simplify themselves to the extent of becoming unrecognizable).

It seems that with the Greeks,[11] the heavenly and solar deities, the Olympians, triumphed over the old maternal residue of chthonic, lunar, aquatic and finally subterranean gods—though these preserved enough strength for later revivals. With the Romans, on the other hand, until they discovered Greece for themselves, it was definitely the gods of mother-earth who were in the ascendant. At the most, there were a few consorts of a rather specious masculinity, aggressively virile but infertile, like Mars. They have visibly receded to the status of "powers" which, like the Japanese *kami*, could be differentiated *ad nauseam* without ever becoming persons.

These two opposite evolutions both let the other marginalized divine world continue to subsist, despite withdrawing attention from it. And there remained (as in India), both in Greece and more cautiously in Rome, a besetting nostalgia for God, the "Wholly Other," beyond all cosmic gods terrestrial or heavenly. However, it triumphed later. Nor did it arise as a search for wisdom within lived religion (even if progressively tending to estrange itself from it). Rather, it came as an unexpected explosion of wisdom, and a wisdom which almost from the very start inclined to establish itself outside official religion and even any definite form of religion, sometimes indeed opposing it.

This trajectory, at bottom, was not so different from that of the Indian soul from orthodox Hinduism to Buddhism. But it differs from it as the discoveries of a somnambulist differ from those of someone wide awake, even if the latter, in its hyper-lucidity, ends by wondering whether all life is not perhaps a dream. This, no doubt, rather than any unlikely direct influence, is what can make Plotinus sometimes look so like Buddha. For in him, like Hinduism in Buddhism, Greco-Latin humanism was to reach a climactic conclusion that seemed like a self-contradiction.

---

[11]Martin P. Nilsson, *Greek Piety*, New York, 1969 (original Swedish: *Grekisk Religiositet*), and his other volume, *Greek Popular Religion*, New York, 1947. See also Jane Harrison, *Prolegomena to the Study of Greek Religion*, New York, 1955, and L. R. Dodds, *The Greeks and the Irrational*, Boston, 1951.

The Greek Gods

If we want to grasp something of what Greek and Latin religion was actually like, we must begin by recognizing the misleading character of what we call "mythology." This mythology was nothing but a highly artificial literary transcription. Nor, in particular, must we be fooled by the forced identification of Greek and Latin gods, practiced by hellenized Latin literature, and which even threatened the Greek gods with the imposition of Latin names.

The Greek gods were mainly local, although they had ceased to be tribal gods and had become identified with the natural forces representing their particular hierophany. Zeus, being the god of Olympus, was necessarily a sky god, just as Apollo, or Delos, was identified with the rising sun. At Delphi, however, he was to be above all a purifying, expiating god, having supplanted Python, the serpent, a god of the earth, later regarded as a god of the underworld. In like manner, Pallas-Athena, on the Acropolis, took over from Erectheus. This represented sovereign reason, the source of city and civilization, taking over from primitive instinct which was increasingly viewed as sub-human. Aphrodite of Cyprus, a water-goddess of fertility, became mother of Eros and so of all life, disputing this title, however, with the fierce Artemis, from Ida, a goddess of woods and moon. Artemis was a huntress and, in consequence, thoroughly rustic, intolerant of any of the yokes of civilization and of marriage especially.

Nietzsche, albeit slightly over-organizing the evidence, was not completely wrong in dubbing the Bacchic cult of the Thracian Dionysus a reaction against intellectualism. The old pantheon was being progressively rationalized, humanized in rather a glib way, and seemed to be on the brink of evaporation into insubstantial symbols. In such circumstances any over-refined civilization, conscious of its inanition, will proceed to swing back to the forces of instinct—this, in turn, as in Euripides' *Bacchae*, always disappearing into animal orgiastics.

Another more discreet but undoubtedly deeper reaction occurred in the very midst of the "Greek miracle," a miracle of luminous rationality if ever there was one. This was the return of the most religiously-minded to the Eleusinian mysteries. Plato and Aeschylus are instances. The Olympian gods of sun and daylight suffered a real defeat at the hands of the resurgent ancient divinities of nourishing mother-earth. Nor were these latter travestied, as they might have been, by being changed into the powers of the underworld, of death and darkness. Rather, they re-emerged as the gods of life after death, life eternal.

Still, it cannot be denied that, in Greece, these gods, at least as regards the intellectuals, very soon ceased to be anything more than suggestive poetic images. They became enveloped, gradually, by a world of religious thought more religious than official religion and in which any serious, personal religion progressively tended to take refuge.

We must not be taken in, again, by the brilliance of Greek literature. The ordinary people, in Greece as elsewhere, would certainly have remained faithful to the old gods and never have had much truck with the reductionist symbolism of the intellectuals. As for the imaginative literary treatment of the gods, this no doubt amused the populace, but one cannot but notice how conscious the tragedians in particular were of the need to keep their imagination and especially their critical spirit on a very tight rein. Had they not, the people would have taken scandal and they themselves been ostracized.

The Gods of Rome

Roman religion was undoubtedly quite different,[12] *pace* Cicero. Cicero, after all, only spoke for a tiny elite which was much more Greek or, rather, hellenistic in outlook than Roman. The gods of Rome did not blossom out and defoliate into semi-poetical allegories. They seem to have had a contrary tendency to restrict themselves to their traditional functions, and give the no doubt unjustifiable impression of being nothing but simple abstractions. In fact, these numerous powers, permeating everything and everywhere, were most like the Japanese *kami*, seeds of sacrality scattered on every object and action. Man was never alone nor his own master in any activity, however down-to-earth. It was from this that sprang that *gravitas*, which so marked the ancient Roman character.

Certainly, such a mentality had its ambivalence, like any primitive mentality. It is hard for us not to be continually and often justifiably suspecting it of magic pure and simple. Nonetheless, it was characteristic of the ancient Roman mind that the more "advanced" Romans regarded it as a matter of *superstitio*, that is, in their terms, an exaggeration of piety.

It would no doubt be misguided to regard Virgil's *Aeneid* as a straightforward specimen of the old Roman religion. But it did represent an effort by the most hellenized Romans, anxious to retain their ancient *religio*, to have it survive or revive at the heart of their "Greek" humanism. Such an anxiety would in fact, have been unknown to the Greeks.

---

[12]Jean Bayet, *Histoire Politique et psychologique de la Religion romaine*, Paris, 1957, and Raymond Bloch, *La Religion romaine*, in the Pléiade *Histoire des Religions*, vol. 1, pp. 874ff.

The most Roman, and primitive, trait in such an outlook was a respect for ritual. This far outran any respect for the gods, who probably appeared as inadequate to them as they do to us. The Roman respect for ritual outlived the Roman gods (or at least their outline before it had been fixed), and it outlived them because it pre-existed them.

Dumézil seems to have established beyond all doubt that the form taken by the Roman gods and their no less unbelievably persistent relationships with ritual and myth were simply survivals from the ancient mythical-ritual deposit of Vedic India. In fact, the connections with ritual were always closer than those with myth, Rome always being poor in myth, when not borrowing from Greece. The gods remained embedded in societal structures long after losing any capacity to inspire coherent thinking and long after having faded from the Roman consciousness.[13]

The Scandinavians, Germans and Celts

Beyond the two major resting-places of the Indo-European religious tradition, in Greece and Rome, lay its outposts among the Germans, Scandinavians and Celts. The religions of these peoples, despite or because of their remarkable proliferation of myths, remained mobile and indeterminate.[14] This explains Christianity's relatively easy conquest, in contrast to the four centuries or more of resistance which it met from the Greco-Roman synthesis.

Germanic religion can be seen as having developed the mythology of the Indo-European heritage along the line of the irreducible freedom present in the life of man and in the life of the gods, with comradeship and pugnacity going hand in hand.

The Scandinavians, with their romantic epic, the Edda, and reaching the furthest limits of the habitable world, reinterpreted all this material in the light of their own migratory instinct, making life an exodus to the heroic existence of Valhalla and deliberately ignoring death and any earthly limitation.

The Celts give the impression of having gone beyond even this and reached the point of living a waking dream, a magical existence in a supernatural world, where tangible talismen evoke the presence of the beyond. The ordinary world was no more than a frail outer crust or, rather, an enchanted sea, with fairy vessels bearing men away to the aurora borealis of the Happy Isles.

---

[13]See above all, G. Dumézil, *Mitra Varuna*, and the two volumes of *Mythe et Epopée*, Paris, 1971.

[14]See the good summaries by Frans Vyncke, Jan de Vries and François Le Roux in vol. 1 of the Pléiade *Histoire des Religions*.

Recapitulation

It seems possible, at this point, to draw some conclusions, at least provisionally, from the data of this and the preceding chapters.

Three kinds of evolution have so far come to light. They all start from a ritual basis common to all mankind and from an analogous mythological basis.

The great religious civilizations of Egypt, pre-Columbian America, China and Japan have every appearance of immutability. However, it would be wrong to maintain that the human mind in such instances refused to grow and develop. The opposite seems to have been true. In Egypt and China, at least, there was a more rapid development than anywhere else. It scarcely drew breath at any time until the final disintegration, and this latter seems to have resulted from exterior disruption rather than interior decadence, even though the decadence cannot be denied. Previously, however, periods of equally disturbing decay had been surmounted by a return to the sources and had never led to final collapse precisely because no destructive element came from without.

The truth is that in these traditions the sense of the fundamentally religious character of civilization went uncontested with the result that, as the human intelligence progressively rationalized experience, it did so, even when critical, within religion and hence in support of it.

The religious world of India seems, at first sight, to have been very much the same. But, be it due to the complexity—the initial Indo-Aryan duality—of Indian religion or to a different cast of mind, any wisdom, even while remaining within religion, seems not to have nourished that religion so much as undermined it from the inside. The result was that religion was either absorbed into speculation or into a technique which, though still deserving the name of spiritual, in fact shifted the object of religion to a place of peripheral unimportance and gave its full attention to subjective experience.

In Greece and Rome, we can witness inverse factors ultimately concurring in a different type of development. The Greek soul itself, perhaps, was weak on religiosity. Certainly its religion was. It was a hang-over from an ancient heritage, a heritage that changes of habitat or lifestyle had rendered an enigma to the very people retaining it. It was this that seems to have driven the Greeks to develop their wisdom not solely outside their religion but in opposition to it, so much so that it was to wisdom they turned in search of authentic religion. Greek "theology"—that produced by Greek religion—is devoid of interest. Of itself, it degenerated into "mythology." Only philosophy attempted to furnish the Greeks with a credible theology. Nor was the attempt, for all its ambiguity, without a certain success. It was to be found along one of that philosophy's possible lines of development: in Platonism, then in Stoicism and, in its definitive form, in that Neo-platonism which might be better called a Neo-stoicism.

With the Romans, a contrary tendency arrived at similar results. Their instinct was to hang on to their ancestral religion at any price, despite the almost total lack of intelligibility it eventually had for them. The reason for this, undoubtedly, was that the Romans had the most lively ethical sense of any of the peoples of antiquity, and practically no aesthetic sense, the Greeks of course being the complete opposite.

Yielding to hellenization at the very moment when the old Greek religion finally perished and Greek philosophy was soaring to new religious heights, Rome borrowed this philosophical religiousness, used it to reinforce her moralism while giving to it in return that seriousness and tension characteristic of late Stoicism and not to be found anywhere else, even in the "beautiful risk" of original Platonism, which after all was conscious of probably being no more than "a dream with which to enchant oneself."

Throughout the world, religion has assumed multifarious forms and followed the developments of very different civilizations. Yet, for all that, there is a striking homogeneity to the structures of man's worship, to the hierophanies accompanying or arousing it, and even a close relationship between the myths which emerge from it.

Everywhere we can see the same centrality accorded to sacrifice, that sacred meal for which gods sat down with men, acting as their hosts and their guests, becoming their food, their life and also the destination of their offerings, themselves being, in the last resort, that offering itself, and so giving human existence its ultimate meaning, even if by way of death.

Everywhere lustrations served to prepare or re-adapt man for the sacrifice, functioning as active symbols of a rebirth from and through death. Everywhere, too, anointings or even brandings of the living flesh, sealing an irreversible dedication to God, served to consecrate man for the sacrifice and mark him as his servant, adopted one and minister.

Everywhere the hierophanies followed a similar pattern. In heaven reigned the "great gods," always kings in name if not in fact. They were gladly acknowledged, by the Amerindians for example, to be "both father and mother" of everything existing. More widely still, they were regarded as the source of all that is, or even as its one true reality, however the mysterious process governing the relationship of man and the cosmos with them be envisaged. Then, at the other pole, were the dark and redoubtable powers lurking in the bowels of the earth, holding life and death in their hands.

At its surface, however, the earth was regarded as the mother of life, thanks to the life-giving waters shed on it by heaven. These waters in turn were subjected to the phases of the moon, the moon itself being the supreme source of reflected brightness.

The sun, on the other hand, was expected to provide the initial incitement and the periodical regeneration of life. It was the chief and even the only theophany of paternal divinity. Our own conscious mind was the daughter of its rays, and the earth's annual rhythm of decline and rebirth was the rhythm of the sun's own spring and fall.

Myth, for all its variations, always began from the same ritual patterns and made the same connections between the various hierophanies, which manifested the sacred. There was the archetypal story of the god who came down to a mysterious anti-world and created it as if by his own dismemberment There was also the struggle of the divine element to overcome chaos and draw out of it, anew each year, a fresh if ephemeral world. Or, contrariwise, the divine united with this same chaos, now seen not as an enemy to extirpate but as a potential mother to fecundate in view of a new birth, short-lived though that union might be.

Everywhere, again, was to be found one who, in his sacred *persona* as the prime agent of the liturgy, re-established or maintained the permanent actuality, here and now, of what myth proclaimed, namely that a divine activity incessantly subtends, inspires and restores all human and cosmic life. This was true even where the "lay" state was first outlined, as in Athens and Rome. We can see it in Pharaoh, in the death of Osiris, in the consecration of Horus. We can see it in the Inca, who was always the same whoever was actually bearing his name at a given moment; in Quetzalcoatl, who periodically sacrificed himself so as to be reborn in another person and regenerate his empire; in the Son of heaven who entered alone each year into the heavenly Temple of the forbidden City to re-engage the finishing year; in the Mikado who, faithfully punctual to the same fatidic date for two thousand years, came to meet his ancestral goddess, Atemeratsu, at Ise; or, failing these, at least in some Archon king or *Rex sacrificulus*.

Anticipation

However, what we have called prophetism was no less ubiquitous. It sprang up from the heart of those liturgies which were so impressive in the deep way they persisted unchanged beneath their varied mythical drapery—itself thematically unvarying. Prophetism was a protest, and that protest was ubiquitous.

Prophetism denounced the temptation proper to magic, that of getting possession of the gods by ritual. It denounced the temptation of idolatry to fashion the divine in the image of the all-too-human which necessarily represented it. It denounced the confusion of the gods with the world and of cosmo-genesis with an unacceptable theogony and, at the same time, the short-sighted identification of salvation with the death by which it was sought, and of the divine love with a devouring fire.

The prophet was often a king-priest, like Akhenaten, Ce Acatl or the reforming Inca, and in more than one case, he was a priest who sacrificed himself. Ce Acatl-Quetzalcoatl was one instance. But he could also be, like Buddha, a lay lord, or like Socrates, a *uomo qualunque*.

The precise stimulus of the protest varied but, with greater or lesser clarity, it always represented a clean sweep of the whole field of religion and, therefore, of the religious life of man.

In the case of Akhenaten, it was a particular hierophany—the sun's disk, rising on the horizon and then making its way to a zenith of universal domination—which provoked the affirmation of monotheism and, beyond that, of the exclusive and absolute sovereignty of God, coupled with his gracious, unwearying, inexhaustible benevolence.

It was the same with the Incas.

With Ce Acatl, it was a case of the breath of heaven, bringing everything into existence from on high, blowing away every other image of rival divinized reality, scattering at a blow all the magic and murder of ritual and politics, and reinstating life in the light of the Morning-Star.

In Buddha's case, the protest was more radical still. Every image and every concept of the divine, every means of approaching it, was not just called into question but blithely ignored. In order to go and meet the invisible, ineffable, inconceivable Wholly Other, there had to be a total stripping of every object, every thought and, above all, of our own self. Yet we are to go in peace and in an exultation prepared and evidenced by universal compassion, that compassion which seems to foreshadow some indescribably radiant Face shining out of the depths of a luminous darkness.

Buddha's protest was so discreet and humble that it seemed scarcely possible that Socrates' could be even more so.[15] Yet it was also more decisive in what it affirmed. He methodically disproved, dismissed and went beyond our every idea of the Good, and offered nothing by way of a substitute. Xenophanes had already completely rejected every idol and

---

[15]See Festugière's *Socrate*, Paris, 1934.

Socrates tacitly followed him, being a-theist himself, therefore, as regarded any defined deity, but unhesitatingly identifying the only being worthy to be called God with the indefinable and inconceivable idea of the Good.

All these prophets were like men who have seen lightning flash in the night. Their retina retains an ineffaceable impression of a day-lit world and even if, for those around them, there was as yet no sign of the dawn, it was somehow no longer possible to remain immersed in the dark. The vision peculiar to the prophet only repercussed in a confused, dream-like way on others, yet it was enough, or should have been, to leave everyone with a presentiment that what had been hitherto taken for real was perhaps no more than a nightmare and that morning would efface it.

Yet it seems to be only in Israel that a prophetic vision was able, little by little, to spread and develop, passing from one seer to the next, and, what is more, to take possession of the collective consciousness of an entire human community becoming, as we shall see in Christianity, not so much the vision of a community set apart as the matrix of one destined to embrace the whole world.

IX

From the Gods of Canaan
to the Israel of God

It became fashionable in Germany after the First World War and then more widely after the Second to contrast the "Semitic mentality," which was identified with the message specific to the Bible, and the "Greek mentality," thought to represent a merely human wisdom. This was an unexpected side-effect of the triumph of Barthian dialectic. It was James Barr[1] who, more tellingly than anyone else, denounced this strange kind of theological racism. It confused the wholly gratuitous discovery of the transcendent self-revealing God with a particular cast of mind attributed to one group of peoples and denied to others—those, particularly, whom the West had long regarded as the avant-garde of humanity.

The first point to be made is that the characteristics of the so-called "Semitic mentality" were in fact common to a variety of peoples not all of whom were Semites: those peoples who had fought and mingled with each other and successively supplanted one another in that part of the Near East commonly called "the Fertile Crescent." Then one should also point out that these characteristics may be found in civilizations and especially in religions which were very different: those of the Far East and, despite what is said, those of Greece and Rome, even if the Semites and their closest neighbors did add some remarkable emphases of their own. These, however, were perhaps not so exclusive as some would have us believe.

But what must be emphasized above all is that, if there was a "biblical mentality" capable of definition and if it belonged to this Semitic background, as it undoubtedly did, it nevertheless quite as much reversed the ambient values as privileged them. And in any case, when the latter process was in evidence, it involved so much of a reworking of the characteristics thus employed that they finished by appearing quite as new as they would have been had they been reversed.

---

[1]James Barr, *The Semantics of Biblical Language*, Oxford, 1961.

History and Person

It is generally admitted that the East (i.e., the Far East, which is then blithely limited to India and to a very simplified India at that) is the world of the intemporal or eternal. On the other hand, the Greek world is considered as the home of Socratic individualism and hence of the emergence of rational consciousness from a universe polymorphous to the point of formlessness. Midway between the two lies the so-called Semitic world, better simply called the world of the Fertile Crescent, and it would be there, according to this view, that there first appeared a genuinely historical consciousness. By this is meant a consciousness possessed by the idea of a "becoming," not only of the individual but of the race and even of the whole human species. In such a world, humanity does not so much detach itself from an anonymous universe as associate it with the processes of its own formation, making it reflect the human form, impressing this gradually-emerging form upon a mass that up till then had remained undefined or with its final possibilities no more than dimly intimated.

All this, of course, is something of a simplification, although not completely arbitrary. "History," we are told, "begins at Sumer." The truth is that Sumer,[2] so far as we know anything about it, seems to have emerged around a typical personality: Goudea, whose image and tomb have been discovered and from whom something has come down to us of the action by which he set his mark upon the city, pushing his way in among the gods he venerated, not as their equal but as their accepted companion.

To be more precise still, it seems to have been the case as early as Sumer that the king had ceased to be a god made visible, like the Egyptian Pharaoh, or to be the heir or temporary representative of an apparently eternal and therefore divine kingship. The same was true a little later at Nineveh or Babylon, or again in Canaan or among the descendants of Ugarit, the biblical Tyrians and Philistines. The king was now one adopted by the gods or by the god who, at least for the moment, retained a superiority over the king. In other words, the king was a self-made man. He had turned circumstances to his own advantage, dubbing them providential with a blend of piety and cunning. The Mesopotamian king, it seems, was a clan-chief accepted or raised by his peers to a position of pre-eminence, usually in critical circumstances. The success he

---

[2] Andre Parrot, *Sumer*, Paris, 1962.

had gained amid them guaranteed him a more or less permanent position as an acknowledged and unrivaled "servant of the god."[3]

Hence, a quite distinct type of kingship emerged. A history became essential to a king, and a particular city, constituted around the king, became an obligatory effect of the history. It was not necessary that the king be the sole actor in the drama, but he did have to be the chief protagonist.

The climatic conditions peculiar to Mesopotamia, and very different from those of Egypt, should be closely connected with this new kind of kingdom and kingship. The Nile would flood and fertilize regularly and predictably and so enable social life to be generally organized on a secure agrarian basis. By contrast, the floods of the Euphrates and Tigris were unpredictable and could be catastrophic. Individual initiative was called for. The organization of society required much greater inventiveness and the economy was necessarily regularized either by war, the earlier method, or, later, by trade.

These conditions were reflected in religion. At the very least, they guaranteed a reinterpretation and rearrangement of the ancestral myths. The god protecting the victorious or prosperous king, the "Lord of the Covenant," himself took on the characteristics of a divine hero. He imposed order on chaos. He might even be so high-handed or be so discreetly assisted from the highest quarters as to lay hold of and make off with the tablets ascribed with the destinies of men.

Marduk, the great Babylonian god (himself very much a self-made man!), was a prime example of this. He was the lover of the heavenly goddess, Ishtar, and therefore continually supplied with clandestine information as to the secrets of the higher powers; and it was he who stripped primitive chaos of its power in the person of Thiamat, the universal, anonymous mother who was also the jealous dragon always threatening to reabsorb what she had given birth to.

The Baalim of Babylon and Its Environs

A close study of the mythical material of the Mesopotamian religions, however, can leave the impression that it contains nothing essentially original.[4] It seems to do no more than furnish another instance of what

---

[3] See the bibliographical note on mythical kingship given above, p. 93, as well as E. O. James, *The Ancient Gods*, London, 1960, the whole fourth chapter, and also Sigmund Mowinckel, *He That Cometh*, Oxford, 1956, especially pp. 21ff.

[4] See the respective studies of Raymond Jestin and Jean Nougayrol on Sumer and Babylon in vol. 1 of the Pléiade *Histoire des Religions*, pp. 154ff.

we have already seen in India, at Mohenjo-Daro, and elsewhere, namely a mother goddess or, rather, a universal matrix, gifted with an inexhaustible yet thoroughly ambiguous fecundity. Ambiguous, because however much the mother may have renewed or kept in being the many forms of life, she nonetheless continued to devour them by death. The male god, to begin with, was nothing but a faceless consort, standing at her side. Every so often he would be immolated or even emasculated, as in the cases of Tammuz, Attis or Adonis. A life-giving act of copulation would involve his periodic annihilation, an annihilation demanded by and contributing to the unceasing renewal of living things.

Nevertheless, a new emphasis does appear in the religious world of the Fertile Crescent. Marduk is its most striking example, though by no means its only one. The male god rose in status. He ceased to be a nonentity, condemned to perish at the dreaded moment of his short-lived annual marital triumph. He became a continual conqueror in a continual conflict. The moment of danger was his moment of triumph and he emerged, radiant, as the lord and master of the equivocal powers of night, that night he made fertile, even if at the price of his own blood.

The specialist historians of Near Eastern mythology have given us descriptions or explanations of the above kind, but it is often difficult to make clear distinctions between what was already latent or already present in the ancient Mesopotamian, Ugaritic and Canaanite religions, and the biblical echoes which we are liable to project back upon the earlier data.

The Bible, of course, right from its beginning to its culmination in the Gospel, expressed itself in the set of symbols already used and even already recycled by the surrounding religions. But, at the same time, there is no doubt that it recast them. In fact, it operated a complete metamorphosis. We are so accustomed to this that it is hard for us not to retroject the final biblical form on to what were possible preparations or, at most, first, rough drafts of it. We forget that these images were in fact, as the Hebrew prophets themselves averred, deformations or inversions.

An over-analytic comparison between these myths and their biblical equivalents is misleading. It inevitably leads to an automatic transposition of biblical patterns upon material which, certainly, they took over (but they alone) and imposed upon in such a way that it would be impossible for us to discover them outside the Bible had the latter not conditioned us to see them. It is instructive, from this point of view, to compare the respective work of Gressmann and Gunkel on the sources of

Genesis.[5] The minute but myopic analysis of the former gives the impression that there was nothing in the biblical accounts of the creation, fall and flood that was not already present in Babylonian myths. To travel the same path with Gunkel, on the other hand, is to realize that there is nothing in these myths which has not been turned inside out, transposed and thoroughly transformed by a flood of new light and a change of perspective.

The Kingship of the Biblical God

As Mowinckel has emphasized with particular effect, the best way to measure the extent of this metamorphosis is to consider an undoubtedly central notion, or, rather, reality, namely kingship. In Egypt, as we saw, the king, Pharaoh, was the visible god. In the Fertile Crescent, the king was no longer god but he was all but raised to the status of divinity, in the sense that he was the uniquely privileged intermediary used by God to communicate with men and, as a result, his committed representative towards them. In biblical Israel, all this was turned around. The human king was not so much the representative of God in the eyes of men as the representative of Israel in the eyes of God.[6]

Henceforth, far from the king being god or his necessary intermediary, God alone was, properly speaking, the acknowledged King of Israel, and not of Israel only but of the whole universe in its invisible as much its visible elements. The affirming of his dominion did not depend on anyone. On the contrary, all men, whatever their rank, and kings no less than the rest of mankind, were nothing without him.

Again, it must be stressed that this was not the produce of speculation, which would have been unheard of even at that time. Rather, it was the result of an incomparable experience. That experience was Israel's history. It was no ordinary history, but one into which Israel saw itself being pulled or projected in spite of itself. It was a history interpreted to Israel, or rather served willingly or otherwise (and prior to their own awareness of so doing), not by one or other isolated prophet but by an astonishing succession of prophetic personalities. Even they, however, were eclipsed by the vastness of the revelation which encompassed and surpassed them. The deeds of Goudea, Sargon or Hammurabi appear in their true and ultimately derisory proportions when set beside this historical revelation, and this revelation, this history it was which brought

---

[5] Cf. H. Gressmann's *Mose und seine Zeit*, 1914, and H. Gunkel's *Schöpfung und Chaos*, 1910.

[6] Mowinckel, *op. cit.*, pp. 21ff.

the seers of Israel to a fundamental reversal of perspective and to a wholly unexpected re-ordering of levels which had hitherto been chaotically confused.

In the first place, God—the God who had revealed himself to Israel by revealing himself in the history into which he had thrown his people— was more than the master of this one people. He was more than a Marduk who could be called a king of Babylon by virtue of his self-manifestation in succeeding kings. He was the master *of all peoples* and, further still, the Lord "*of heaven and of earth*," in other words, of the whole universe. Hence he could upturn everything in order to bring a people that was all but obliterated and all too conscious of their own insignificance to a destiny which wrenched them out of themselves, confused them, terrified them quite as much as it exalted them and plucked them away from the freshly-founded cities of the earth where they had hoped to settle, only to lead them through a literal and metaphorical desert to an unknown destination.

Here we touch upon the paradox inherent in biblical revelation. The God who revealed his kingship to Israel did not do so by making of Israel one more kingdom among others of the same kind. Rather, he plucked Israel out of all such kingdoms and made it an everlasting wanderer, a living sign of a kingship of which it could already be said that it was "not of this world."

It was the kingship, in fact, of a God who was not only a "god of heaven," as all the leading gods claimed to be, but "*the* God of heaven," the only one there was; and this, not in the dangerous sense of a distant, dormant god, but as "the God of heaven *and of earth*," that is, present and active everywhere, wholly and immediately.

But it was also the kingship of the hidden God, because of one who could not be confused with any of this world's powers; the God hidden from men's eyes by their own rebellion and ensuing disobedience; the God, in consequence, who could only retrieve his creatures by detaching them from every kind of installment in this world; the God of perpetual exodus.

The discovery of God, involving as it did such an uprooting, was in one sense progressive. Israel was necessarily compelled to reject repeatedly and deny herself any settling down, any stagnation. Yet the discovery was also sudden, unprepared and unpreparable. It was a discovery in one sense given all at once and from the very beginning. God was there when it was never even suspected, and when he so willed the realization would be complete and abrupt. We can think of Jacob at Bethel exclaiming: "How awesome is this place! This is none other than the house of God, and this is the gate of heaven; *and I did not know it!*"[7]

The Progress of Biblical Revelation

This is what invalidates, as more and more exegetes are realizing, all those attempted "evolutionist" reconstructions of the idea of the biblical God, in which nineteenth-century exegesis was so immured. There was supposed to have been a "progressive" transition from a simple, naive henotheism to systematic monotheism, from a tribal god to the God of the universe and, most impossibly of all, from the quasi-tangible gods of vegetation to an invisible creator of everything existent.

It is certainly true that, for Israel, God was originally distinguished from other gods by virtue of being the only God Israel recognized, or, rather, by virtue of Israel being recognized by him, that is chosen and set apart to be his witness. To this extent, therefore, God did not instantly emerge as the term of a process of reasoning exclusive of all other gods. But it would be no less true to say that Israel never denied existence to the "other gods." Even when the later prophets, like Second Isaiah, call them "false gods" or "nothingness," this did not mean they had no existence. Rather, it meant that they were as nothing before the only God. He was the living, life-giving God and Israel, by an extraordinary, incomprehensible vocation, belonged to him far more than he to it. This belonging was by way of the covenant, a setting-apart, and Israel had not bargained her way into it. God had brought her into covenant with himself; how or why, Israel did not know except that it was in spite of herself. Obviously great lengths of time would be needed to draw out all the possible implications of such a situation, such an unimaginable experience—supposing that they ever could be. But, from the very beginning, there must have been a real if inchoate grasp of the uniqueness of this God. The destiny he had given her was itself unique and Israel took shape—a new, unheard of shape—within that unique destiny.

Israel realized this decisively at the time of the Exodus from Egypt under Moses. But it was not an illusion to project this back to the first beginnings, the summons of Abraham, the first "father of the people," in the call: "Go from your country and your kindred and your father's home...and I will make of you a great nation,"[8] even though it was certainly only much later, during the great common trial of the Babylonian exile, that the implications of the mosaic Exodus became completely

---

[7] Genesis 28:16-17.
[8] Genesis 12:1-2.

clear. And it was this which henceforth would make the content of the liturgy, above all of the Pasch which, from being a seasonal feast, became the "Memorial" of the saving event.

The God Without Images and Man in His Image

This throws light on the problem posed by Mowinckel: "When exactly did Israel's worship become free of images?"[9] The most recent research and especially archaeological discoveries in the field of Judaism during the early years of Christianity show that the answer is even more problematic than Mowinckel thought. Moses himself, in fact, was not able to eradicate all representations from Israel's worship, such as the enigmatic Nehushtan, the bronze serpent, who was not finally removed from the sanctuary of Judah until the time of Hezekiah.[10] Similarly, the "calves" of Samaria remained at Bethel, despite prophetic invectives, until it was destroyed. Most tellingly of all, it was only as a result of the anti-Christian reaction that all representations of the Godhead, even the most oblique, were banished from the synagogues.[11] Yet the Torah itself implicitly seemed to allow such images, in the three men or angels, Abraham's three mysterious guests,[12] which passed into the Church as a prophetic image of the Trinity revealed in the Incarnation and communicating itself through the Eucharist. And again, the most spiritual prophets, such as Isaiah and, even later, Ezekiel, saw the invisible present in the Holy of Holies, in the latter's embarrassed expression "in the likeness of a man."[13] And this, even though he was radiant with consuming fire; even though the inaccessible light in which he dwelt could only blind men's eyes; even though he could not be seen without dying!

The transcendence of the biblical God in no way impugned the proposition that man had been made "in his image and likeness," even though that did not justify making an image of God.[14] God's transcendence, in other words, did not mean he could not be "seen," but that the sight of him was like the sight of lightning, just as the difference between his life and ours was not that he was less alive than us or was an exile, so to speak, in the chilly abstraction of an intelligible world. So overwhelm-

---

[9] An article which appeared in 1934 in the Strasbourg *Revue d'Histoire et de philosophie religieuse.*

[10] 2 Kings 18:4.

[11] E. L. Sukenik, *Ancient Synagogues in Palestine and Greece*, London, 1934, pp. 61ff.

[12] Genesis 18.

[13] Cf. Isaiah 6 and Ezekiel 1.

[14] Genesis 1:26. Cf. by way of contrast Judges 13:22.

ing, in fact, was his life that just to touch the hem of it would mean the loss of our own. God remained quite as incomprehensible to the highest heavenly powers, the Seraphim, as to us. It was not strictly speaking that he could not be seen. Rather, he could not be looked at, though this did not prevent him being light itself nor his light our medium of vision, just as he is the living one who gives life, because with him is the source of life.

The Shekinah

Hooke has justifiably brought out, even if it sounds paradoxical, that if there was one mythical theme apparently exclusive to Israel at the very moment she was making havoc with myth, it was that subject of so much Rabbinic speculation and unsuccessful rationalization, namely the Shekinah.[15] The word designated that presence under the tent of the nomads, both revealed and veiled in the bright cloud, journeying through all the accounts of the Exodus and giving justification to the worship first in the tabernacle and then in the Temple of Solomon.

It signified that "the God whom neither the heavens nor the heaven of heavens can contain" appeared at the same time as the one who came close to his own "as no other God has come close to his people." He went so far as to pitch his tent in their midst. But then again, there could be no possibility of enclosing him, of having him at their disposal, even less at their mercy, in any "sanctuary made by men's hands." The Shekinah, which came down of its own free will upon the mobile tent "of meeting," as it did upon Sinai, was always capable of withdrawing unexpectedly, while leading further into the desert those who wished to remain faithful to it. Yet, after having seemed to refuse David, it deigned to rest for some time in the stone Temple consecrated to it by Solomon and which became, as it were, the cornerstone of the holy city where God dwelt with his own to make them his people and, no less, to be himself their God. But their infidelity, prior to their own exile and the destruction by their enemies of the sanctuary they themselves had already profaned by idolatry and injustice, provoked the Shekinah into spontaneous exile, as described by Ezekiel. Yet, as he said, it still remained, invisible but closer than ever, with the faithful exiles, in the very land of their exile.

---

[15]S. H. Hooke, *Middle Eastern Mythology*, Baltimore, 1963, pp. 145ff. See *The Eternal Son*, Huntington, IN, 1978, pp. 54ff.

The Merkabah

This was why, in Jewish apocalyptic and beginning with Ezekiel's visions, there was joined to this theme of the Shekinah, of the "dwelling" of God with his chosen ones, that of the Merkabah.[16] This was the chariot of fire, in which, seated upon the Cherubim and Ophanim and transcending all human attempts to confine him to a particular place, God could take up his faithful from the earth, drawing them, like Elijah, in a wake of flame above the *flammantia moenia mundi*.

Only the paradoxical myth, in fact, of the Shekinah of the God of heaven coming down and making himself the companion in exile of his chosen ones, and of the Merkabah, the sight of which would ravish them out of the world and of themselves, could translate, however feebly, that profoundly mysterious identity of the God who only revealed himself to Israel, yet revealed himself as supremely hidden: *Deus revelatus tamquam absconditus*.

It is only in this way that one can understand, without making havoc of the evidence, the strict connection established by the book of Exodus and the double appearance to Moses, at the burning bush and on Sinai,[17] between the revelation of the divine Name and that of the Torah which gave their identity to the holy people.

God had revealed himself, then, in the history of his own people. Not that his revelation evolved, which would have been merely to prolong the old mythical theogonies. Rather, the Exodus experience, an experience which was continually being renewed and deepened, was the experience of having been seized by the "Living One who gives life," but a life which, for every kind of earthly life, meant death to oneself.

In order for them to perceive something of this, the people to whom God spoke and communicated himself needed to undergo many experiences or, better perhaps, one long, complex experience. But this did not mean a progressive accumulation of complementary ideas about God, juxtaposed one upon another, such as a wholly static view of revelation and, ironically, of its "development" might lead one to believe. And it would be an equal, if not a greater misconception, to think in terms of a more or less Hegelian evolutionism, involving a passage from thesis through antithesis to an ultimate synthesis: a sequence of denials progressively correcting views of diminishing naiveté. Rather it was a matter

---

[16]*La Bible et L'Evangile*, new edition, Paris, 1953, pp. 154ff. (Eng. trans. *The Meaning of Sacred Scripture*, Notre Dame, IN, 1958, pp. 153ff.). Cf. G. Sholem, *Major Trends in Jewish Mysticism*, New York, 1946, pp. 40ff.

[17]Cf. Exodus 3 and 19.

of growing intimacy, of a discovery always renewing itself in the measure that it deepened itself. And the discovery was of Someone whose wholly unique identity had made its mark at the very first encounter; Someone whose identity would never finish unfolding all its implications or, rather, unveiling all its mystery, but only by leading us ever deeper into itself.

Part Three

The Revelation of the Father

X

From the Old Testament to the New

In one sense, it could be said that there was an abrupt and total change in the knowledge of God from the Old Testament to the New, as there had been from the myths to the Word of the Bible. However, just as it required a certain length of time and a whole mental evolution for the implications of the Gospel to be defined and formulated, so it did also, though even more so, for the Word of God to man, in the Old Testament, to acquire the full force and distinctness of which it was capable, even though this progress only unfolded what had been there already and had been there manifestly since the revelation to Moses and, it is not too much to say, even since Abraham.

The original Word had, so to speak, blown its way out of myth while using and re-arranging all its means of expression, and it was the progressive penetration into, the unfolding of, that Word which, in turn, not merely prepared but also presaged, summoned and even, in a certain sense, provoked and delivered that Word of God which we regard as definitive, the Word said in Jesus Christ, God made man.

The Freedom and Holiness of God

There is, to begin with, in the biblical Word, God's Word on God, something which harmonizes with and confirms, but also completely surpasses the purest and most austere elements in Buddha's protest. The Shekinah was enveloped with a dazzling glory and, for that very reason, could only be described as a cloud, later rightly to be called "the cloud of unknowing." It was said that God "manifested" himself on the covering of the ark, or that he "appeared," carried by the Merkabah of the Ophanim, those "wheels" "full of eyes round about." The ark was his throne, but the throne was empty. He who rode on the Merkabah did so, it was said, "as on the wings of the wind,"[1] meaning that his presence or, rather, in the significant usage of the mosaic Torah, his "passage"[2] could not be laid hold of. We cannot take possession of him just because he unexpectedly presents himself to us. Rather, it is he who snatches us

---

[1] Ps. 18:11.

[2] Ex. 33:19 (see the parallels and the note in the Jerusalem Bible).

away from the world and ourselves to take us on our unending "exodus."

One can put this another way by saying, as the Bible itself does, that God is at once omnipresent and omnipotent. But these expressions have a certain aura of the static about them, of an immobility and completeness which is the exact reverse of everything the Bible meant to say. The biblical representations of the bright cloud and of the chariot of fire, seen only in the flash of its passing, are of course uncouth images, but they are far more effective than any concept in evoking the reality involved: that unexpected initiative of God's, always surprising and surpassing us, and that agility of which we can only think ourselves the master at the very moment we realize that it has completely escaped us.

The Greek Fathers, especially the Cappadocians, gave expression to the same idea when, faithful to the terminology of Scripture, they spoke of never being able to "see" God except "from behind," when he has already passed in front of us. The moment we recognize he was there, he has gone.

Etienne Gilson has made us realize that this, too, was what St. Thomas meant when he interpreted the ambiguous declaration from the burning bush: "I am Who am" or "I am who I am," not as a definition of a divine essence which would thus be subject to conceptualization, but as an identifying of this incomprehensible essence with pure existence—admitting of recognition as it springs forth ever new and always inexhaustible.

But at the same time the God who spoke to Israel (and who refashioned the one he spoke to in his self-communication) took over or, rather, went beyond, from the very beginning, what we have called the Socratic protest. In other words, he identified himself with the ethical demands of rigorous justice: a justice going far beyond the *cuique suum* but always including it and demanding it absolutely. Amos and Isaiah said this with incomparable force, but they said it in agreement with all the prophets and were only confirming a demand certainly formulated long before them in the mosaic Decalogue.[3]

But, as Hosea seems to have been the first to highlight (though he again was not inventing), this justice was to be referred back, lifted up, to a Goodness which was not only "free of envy," as the best theology of the Greek philosophers was able to say, but merciful and compassionate. This was the *hesed* of the Bible, implying an affectionate loyalty suffused by pity, but going beyond both to what was already an intense, burning

---

[3] *La Bible et l'Evangile*, pp. 57ff. (Eng. trans. *The Meaning of Sacred Scripture*, pp. 52ff.).

love. And this did not mean that the demands of justice were to be waived, but rather that they had a fresh and unrestricted dimension.

Nonetheless, the justice and mercy of the God of the Bible, albeit not in conflict, were at least inevitably in a certain tension. But Hosea had already made it clear that only God's mercy could accomplish his justice. Only pardon, in fact, which was not just a forgetting but a succoring and restoration, could draw purity out of the impure, not only restoring the prostitute, by the unique power of love, to refound virginity, but raising her to the undreamed-of status of a fruitful spouse. The pity of Buddhism was, as it were, expanded into a communicated grace which was more than simple indifference to merit. It was *gratia gratum faciens*. It even created a merit open to, or rather, which it opened to, the unmeritable.

To recognize this freedom and liberality of the biblical God is to understand that he was not simply a Creator, but created creatures in his own image, endowed with a freedom reflecting his own.

God's holiness, then, his utter separation from every conceivable being, had been what manifested his transcendence, and this holiness itself had ultimately been shown to mean justice, a justice of which our attempted emulation was nothing more than a shadow. Justice, in turn, had disclosed itself as identical with unparalleled love, a love of which creation yielded a preliminary glimpse. But the full meaning of this creative love was only to be found in the adoption offered to the creature, and the depths to this adoption only fully revealed when those who had rejected it were to be given pardon.

The Free Creation of Free Creatures

Inevitably the revelation of God as Creator made use of the different images available from human activity: the potter shaping the clay, the heavenly hero dominating chaos and, lastly, the wise king making all things concur to his own ends. But, unless one realizes that the creative act lies beyond all these comparisons, even while using them, one will have missed the point of the Bible's teaching, a teaching which, yet again was present from the beginning. There was no pre-existing matter for the divine potter to work on. There was no real chaos antecedent to the order which was the fruit simply of his will. There was not even any literal foreknowledge of pre-destining on his part: God is no more before or after time than subject to it. Rather, he traverses it. He surrounds it, he sustains and contains it, without in any sense being contained and measured by it, rather like the prenatal water which does not merely carry the fish but engenders it or the air which gives life to the bird it supports.

At this point, of course, every image fails and we have to take recourse in the paradox of creation *ex nihilo*, with the *ex* being canceled out by the sheer negativeness of the "nothing." There remained, nonetheless, a radical difference between Creator and creature while, paradoxically, so freely did God create that the freedom he made proved to be freedom with respect to himself, even in opposition to himself.

From this came another paradox. On the one hand, the whole universe, or each of its parts, and in its cosmic entirety, could be called good, obviously with a limited goodness but still substantially and integrally good because it all proceeded from God. On the other hand, the only evil came from the creature, although, being made in the image of God, the creature was never truer to itself than when it freely conformed to its model, returning love for love: a love which was all gratitude in return for a love that was wholly free, the love of the bride for her Bridegroom.

This view of God as Creator was exclusively biblical. And one must go further than this. Even if this view was only made completely explicit, and even then always in imagery, in a few pages of Scripture, such as the first chapters of Genesis, it was always latent or, often more than latent, necessarily presupposed on every page.[4] If this were not so, how could they all constitute such a pressing, even passionate exhortation from "God in search of man," to use the profound title of Abraham Heschel's magnificent book? The whole Bible presumes to be free, and God's freedom to be the source of our own, even to the extent that we can only measure the meaning of God's by taking full cognizance of our own.

At this point, we might well feel that we had gone as far as any revelation on God and ourselves was capable of taking us. Strange to say, there was another people, very close to Israel, for whom what we have been outlining was, precisely, the last word of revelation. It was a people whose destiny often intersected Israel's and who, without doubt, occasioned or, more than that, positively induced the reception of some of the latest and highest revelations of the Bible. We refer, of course, to the people of Persia and the revelation of their prophet Zoroaster.

---

[4]Ludwig Koehler, *Old Testament Theology*, London, 1957, pp. 61ff. Cf. Edmond Jacob, *Theologie de l'Ancien Testament*, Neuchâtel-Paris, 1955, pp. 110ff. (Eng. trans. *Theology of the Old Testament*, London, 1958, pp. 136ff.).

Zoroastran Prophecy and Biblical Prophecy

Zoroaster, or rather Zarathustra,[5] was undoubtedly the greatest prophet outside the Bible. But is prophet the right word? To begin with, his actual teaching, such as it has been rediscovered by modern criticism, must not be confused with the various over-simplifying dualisms which have claimed his patronage. Manicheism was the prime example, with its eternal and irreconcilable opposition between two irreducible and equally immortal beings: one of good and light and spirit, the other of evil and darkness and matter. Zarathustra's dualism, however, was voluntarist and like that of the Bible was centered on the creation of free wills. The biblical teaching itself, of course, has not always been spared a parallel confusion with metaphysical dualism, thanks either to the exegesis of misguided disciples or to the imposition of interpretations wholly foreign to its native spirit. But for Zarathustra, as for his close neighbors in time and place, the Hebrew prophets, there could not be any evil that was not a bad employment of created freedom—a freedom which was owed entirely to the only creator in whom all was light and goodness.

However, unlike the biblical prophets, Zarathustra seems not to have gone beyond that point—which has also been a recurrent temptation for Judaism and Christianity. He had no view of the possibility of salvation in the Christian sense of the term. Or, which was the same thing, this possibility was restricted to the last judgment: to the separation which God would accomplish on that day in his great power and wisdom. Then the faithful, holy wills would be freed forever from the oppression of perverted wills and these latter, definitively separated from the former, would be left to their own destruction, to the abyss of darkness to which they would be condemned.

In the interval of the present world, however, the prophetic voice summoned them to repentance and conversion. Zoroaster, just like the biblical prophets, exhorted them to enter the arena courageously and to fight, not just with the external enemies, but with the worst of all our enemies, the one we find inside ourselves. But, contrary to the teaching of the greatest biblical prophets or at least of those who bring us to the threshold of the New Testament, the only way the divine judge could show himself as a savior was, once again, by his judgment, which the prophet called us to forestall by our penance. The Saoshyant, who was

---

[5]R. C. Zaehner, *Concordant Discord*, Oxford, 1970, pp. 25ff. See also the chapter he dedicated to him in *At Sundry Times*, as well as Jacques Duchesne-Guillemin, *L'Iran Antique et Zoroastre*, in the Pléiade *Histoire des Religions*, vol. 1, pp. 625ff., and, above all, G. Widengren, *Die Religionen Irans*, Stuttgart, 1965, pp. 94ff.

the universal restorer, could only accomplish his mission by fearlessly executing the just decrees of God, decrees which were incorruptible and inescapable.

The God of the Bible, on the other hand, utterly demanding though he was, went contrary to this kind of severity. He consecrated pity, Buddhist compassion, but here again he went further. It was true that he did what Amida had done. He took upon himself the full weight of the wretchedness the sinner had brought upon himself, even the ignorance, in the sense of present non-possession, of the true good lost by sin. But, further still, he lay hold, at its very roots, of man's sin and disobedience, so as to free him not just from the bitter fruits of sin but from sin itself. And, ultimately, he was even to take upon himself sin itself in order to free the sinner from it.[6]

In other words, the God of the Bible, having made what would have seemed to have been the ultimate in revelation by creating our freedom, went beyond even this by disclosing himself to us as the savior of this same freedom: lovingly identifying his own holy freedom with our sinful freedom and, to do this, bringing his divinity into union with the whole reality of our humanity, even in its fallen state. Here, truly, is something simply overwhelming. All man's imagining, all his thought is left gasping.

This, of course, would only be formally expressed when it came to be realized in the New Testament. But one can say that the whole Old Testament moved in that direction, that it came very close to it when God supported Job against his pious friends and that it all but touched it in the Songs of the humbled Servant in Second Isaiah.

It was clear from the very beginning that the Old Testament was more than a call to conversion. It was a promise of grace, and the grace promised was not simply any grace, any redemption, any deliverance from one or other secondary aspect of our present captivity. The grace was, above all, the grace of deliverance from ourselves. It was deliverance from the very captivity we had chosen for ourselves by our disobedience.

More importantly still, it was equally clear from the very beginning that God was only going to lead us back to himself by becoming our companion along the roads of life. What needed to be healed was our own free will, that free will which came from God, was in the image of his and itself had wounded itself. Hence any deliverance from outside, falling upon it, as it were, from on high, would only confound the evil,

---

[6]Cf. 2 Cor. 5:21, which is the climax to the whole prophetic orientation, most saliently represented in the Old Testament by Isaiah 53.

would only obliterate our freedom instead of restoring it by returning it to its author.

Hence the descent of God from heaven to earth. Hence that presence among us, increasingly tending to become a presence in us. Hence the progressive inclination towards the most extraordinary identification possible, that of a holy God with the lot, condition and very reality of sinful man.

This identification was adumbrated in the mysterious proximity and incomprehensible solidarity of the Shekinah with the wandering people. First, it led and delivered this people from Egypt, through the desert, to the promised land; then into a further exile, to a foreign land and the Babylonian captivity, into the apparent failure of the most precious promises, which failure would prove to be the unexpected, unbelievable way to a realization which would go far beyond the wildest hopes.

In the Suffering Servant, we see one with whom God, who sent him, identified himself as he never had with any of his principal "servants," be they kings or prophets. We see one, the injustice of whose condemnation will wipe out the unrighteousness of the chosen people and even that of the distant nations ignorant of God. But all this was only a final consequence of and an unbreakable seal attached to God's original, overwhelming commitment to sinful man.

This was something much more than some anonymous general immanence of the transcendent God diffused throughout creation. It was a fully actualized, active, compassionate, redemptive, salvific presence at the very heart of what we call sacred history. This history was a history of redemption, deliverance, salvation, not just for the righteous confirmed in their righteousness but for sinners reconciled and freed from their sin. But it would become such only because God, the holy one, would deliberately immerse himself, so to speak, in the history of sin itself.

One thinks of the astonishing prophetic action of Hosea.[7] This was more than a parable of divine activity; it was a revelation of God's very physiognomy: that love driving God to wed a whore, with the intention—surely sheer madness!—of restoring her to virginity and of making that virginity a well-spring of motherhood. If all this has a meaning, it can only be that final meaning given by God himself, beyond the Old Testament, to the word he applied to himself, the word Savior, *Goel*, Redeemer. Ezekiel's prophecy has the same significance.[8] If anything, it was even more emphatic than Hosea's. God adopted an aborted, dena-

---

[7] Hosea 1 and 2.
[8] Ezekiel 16.

tured child, whose birth had been deliberately turned into a disgrace. He covered her with his own glory, washed her in the living waters flowing from his own heart and destined her to share his own throne—all this being simply the other side of that love which made God the invisible companion of man's exile and the guest of his fallenness.

From the Gods of Myth to the God Who Speaks

The Bible did not hesitate to take up all the themes of myth: the struggle between confronting powers, their nuptial reconciliation which was a union of earth and heaven and, thereby, the re-birth found in death to self. These were all so many spontaneous expressions which religious humanity had given to its rites of purification or communion, its lustrations and banquets, and which reappeared in the liturgy of the tabernacle and Temple. But the religion of Israel, as interpreted by the teaching of the prophets or, rather, the Word of the Bible, decisively and definitively dissipated the three confusions we had discerned in the corpus of myth. These were the confusions of the god and his existence with the world and its genesis; of cosmogenesis and the fall, which thus became the fall of divinity itself into the cosmic order; and, lastly, of salvation with a symmetrical separation or, what amounted to the same thing, a reunification of the divine, which had to annul creation in order to undo the fall.

Henceforth, neither God nor his life would ever be confused again with the world and its existence. Conversely, the distinct existence of this world's beings was clearly distinguished from evil and it was no longer possible for such distinct existence to be regarded as culpable condescension on the part of divinity towards an inferior and ultimately negative reality. Rather, such existence, as much in the lowest, most material beings or in the highest and most spiritual, was nothing but a pure outpouring of the divine goodness and power. Neither was the fall some kind of external corruption of what was superior thanks to its collusion with what was inferior, of spirit with matter. Rather, it was an act of the highest thing in creation, created spirit, attempting to push itself forward to the uncreated level.

Consequently, salvation would no longer be a case of the divine disentangling itself from what was not itself and would always remain alien to itself. Rather, it would be revealed as the supreme condescension on the part of the holy God, raised infinitely above all his creatures: God lowering himself to the level of his humblest creatures and even sharing the degradation to which their fall had reduced them. And then, in return, this unequaled love, this compassionate condescendence would raise them up to himself—not in the way that they had presumptuously imagined, but in an infinitely better way, making them sharers in God's love to the unheard of, unimaginable point of sharing in the love with which their creator had loved them.

All this, of course, throws unexpected light on our own existence and destiny. But, above all, it represents the ultimate in the revelation concerning God himself. The New Testament, of course, and more so in this case than in those already mentioned, would extend the Old Testament beyond itself, even though obeying its deepest logic. Yet there is no doubt that the Word of the latter holds preparations and even presentiments of the New, even of what would become the doctrine of the Trinity.

Naturally, we could not have seen these preliminary traces, we could not have detached them and elicited all their consequences had not the New Testament been given us. But this does not mean that the Old Testament did not actually contain them, and it means positively that one cannot study the teaching of God without taking the greatest account of its ultimate basis in that same Old Testament.

The Grace and Fatherhood of God

If one follows the development of the idea of divine grace, one is soon given a kind of pre-perception of what the Gospel will know as the fatherhood of God. This was present from the start. What could have been more gratuitous and gracious than the call of Abraham, the revelation to Moses at Horeb, the covenant of Sinai? Time will merely bring out that this grace, this *hesed*, is love in the strongest sense of the term: love of the most ardent kind, but also of the most pure and most generous. Nor is this love some accidental, non-essential attribute of God. It envelops the whole revelation. It envelops the fullest gift of self that can be made, God himself being revealed as wholly present in the giving.

This amounts to saying that if the grace shown to us necessarily appeared in total contrast with our created and, *a fortiori*, sinful nature, it appeared, at the same moment, as the clearest expression of the divine nature. The final word—St. John's "God is love"—was only the climax to a line of teaching going back to Hosea and Ezekiel.

Hence God's fatherhood was already manifest in the Old Testament. A superficial assessment might only be willing to concede it about as much meaning and importance as we concede to the fatherhood generally attributed to the heavenly gods such as Zeus or Jupiter. They, of course, were fathers not in the affective sense of an ever-intimate begetter but as objects of the prostrate veneration due to the power on which one wholly depends. But what of the Babylonian and Canaanite gods? They were surely regarded as fathers by the sovereigns of these peoples. The sovereign was an adopted son, adopted by the covenant God extended to the king as his representative, his *locum tenens*.

Certainly, it was with this implication of adoptive sonship and always in close connection with the covenant, that Israel called God its Father, just as God called Israel his son: "Out of Egypt, I called my son (Israel)" and: "For thou art our Father, though Abraham does not know us."[9] Yet what we said previously about the Israelite king should be recalled. By virtue of the covenant, he became not so much the representative of God with respect to his people, as the latter's representative before God. The same would be true of the ideal, future King, the "Messiah." Even more surprisingly, it would even apply to the heavenly "Son of man" of Daniel and other apocalypses. Their privileged proximity to God was never anything but the consequence of representing the people before him—but a people to whom God had drawn close in an utterly unique way.

This adoption, then, which directly concerned the people and not the king, meant far more for that people than did the adoption of the Mesopotamian and Canaanite kings, without however falling back into something like pharaonic idolatry. For the adoption of grace given Israel was something more than a legal fiction. It led to the "children" being really assimilated to their Father. When, in the Sermon on the Mount, Jesus translated the leitmotif of Leviticus: "Be holy as I am holy" into "Be perfect as your heavenly Father is perfect,"[10] there lay behind him a long, unrelenting preparation running through the whole old covenant.

The perfection, here, was that of *agape*, the divine love, that is, *hesed* in its integrity, bearing fruit in the communication of God's heart to those whom he had adopted.

It was this which had been embodied, concretely, in the development of the prophetic "knowledge of God." As St. Paul was to say, it was a matter of knowing God as one had been known,[11] known by a knowledge which was an exclusive, not just a preferential, choice. "You only have I known of all the families of the earth," God had said to Israel by the mouth of Amos.[12] From this there would flow demands which Israel alone would be able to satisfy. But they were only the other side of that reciprocal knowledge which, on the part of the one adopted, had to take

---

[9] Hos. 11:1 and Is. 63:16.

[10] Cf. Matt. 5:48 and Lev. 19:2, 21, etc.

[11] 1 Cor. 13:12. Cf. the book of Dom Jacques Dupont, *Gnosis, la connaissance religieuse dans les épîtres de saint Paul*, Louvain-Paris, 1944.

[12] Amos 3:2.

the form, as Isaiah especially taught, of the "obedience of faith." Yet this obedience was the complete opposite of servile obedience. It was a distinctly filial obedience, because an obedience of conformation. It was a matter of reflecting the holiness proper to God by practicing the justice he demanded as he revealed it in his own person. But if this was to be a reality, union was necessary—the union of God with ourselves. God bent over us; he concerned himself with us. Our lot became his; his being joined to ours. He was the husband, we his spouse. And in return, the spouse became capable of surrendering herself entirely to her husband, giving a perfect love in response to the incomparable love shown by God himself.[13]

It is a remarkable paradox that the Bible which, in its intransigent monotheism and emphasis upon the divine transcendence, had banished the imagery of sexual relationship from the divine nature itself, took it up again to apply it to the ultimate relationship between the creator and his creature.

The Fatherhood of God and the
Bridal Vocation of the Creature: The Spirit

Here, yet again, the revelation of what God had made of us, done and become for us, involved or rather unveiled a manifestation of his own divine physiognomy. But there is clearly a tension between the fundamental revelation of God as Father and this, so to speak, final revelation of God as Bridegroom. How could one and the same God simultaneously appear to us in both relations, and in such a way that these relations, far from contradicting one another, far from one designation reducing the other to a vague metaphor, in fact confirm and confer substance upon one another?

This first tension then provokes a second. In the perspective of the covenant, the biblical God appeared not just as above us, in some sense, as Father or facing us as the Bridegroom coming to meet his bride, but as present in the bride herself, present as the Spirit inspiring her own response of love.

It is true that in the Old Testament the gift of the Spirit first appeared as something out of the ordinary.[14] It was, above all, the gift of the

---

[13]See the texts of Hosea and Ezekiel quoted above.

[14]There is an excellent summary of all the Old Testament texts in the introduction of H. B. Swete's *The Holy Spirit in the New Testament*, Grand Rapids, MI, 1964. Despite letting an *a priori* system dominate his explanations, Daniel Lys's *Ruach, le Souffle dans l'Ancien Testament*, Paris, 1962, is nonetheless the only work which studies all the texts.

prophets, making them bearers of the Word which was God's and not their own. But others beside them—the kings, in the first place (even as early as Saul[15]), and all those who like them had been chosen for a work towards the people and its vocation, from military leaders[16] to the craftsmen of the tabernacle[17]—were regarded as having equally been gifted with the Spirit of the Lord. This was tantamount to saying that God became, as it were, an extra soul within them, enabling them to accomplish a task beyond their powers and revealing himself, even at this stage as, in Augustine's phrase, *intimior interiori meo*, "closer to myself than I am."

What comparisons are there for such a relation? Language all but fails. Motherhood would be an attractive approximation. There is the same interiority, the same lived intimacy. But here, it was a case of the dependent being discovering in himself the vibrant presence of the one on whom he was wholly dependent. Nor could it be regarded as a first even merely preparatory phase of a distinct existence but of an undreamed of perfection and consummation of the latter.

A prophecy of Joel,[18] known for its impact at Qumran[19] and on other groups full of similarly apocalyptic expectations, specified the spread of this "inspiration" to every individual member of God's people as the prime object of eschatological hope. And this surely provided the principle, as it were, capable of bringing about the new and eternal covenant of which Jeremiah[20] and Ezekiel[21] had spoken: inscribing God's law on the tablets of our heart, replacing the stony heart of the old Adamic humanity with a heart of flesh, a heart beating with the very breath of God's life.

Here yet again, we see that what God did and willed for Israel was, as it were, a translation and attestation of what he was in himself.

The Trinity Foreshadowed

The Fathers, then, were not deceived when they discerned a preliminary revelation of the Trinity in the Old Testament. As is well

---

[15] 1 Sam. 10:10.

[16] Judg. 15:14.

[17] Ex. 35:31.

[18] Joel 3.

[19] See the whole of col. III of the *Rule of the Community*, (Eng. trans. G. Vermes, *The Dead Sea Scrolls in English*, Pelican books, 1962, pp. 74-76).

[20] Jeremiah 31.

[21] Ezekiel 34–37.

known, this was how they interpreted the plurals used by the Bible to speak of God: in the first place, the term Elohim and the "we" that served to express God's deliberation after the transgression of Adam and Eve and again before the destruction of the Tower of Babel.[22] Still more justified was the interpretation given to the theme of Abraham's hospitality[23]—bequeathed to Christian iconography from that of the synagogue—where the three angels were from very early on regarded as foreshadowing the Trinity: "*tres vidit, unum adoravit*," Philo himself having already identified them with God and his two chief Powers.[24] We can note too how such imagery automatically evoked the connection between the Eucharist and the revelation of the Trinity: the life into which God has taken us is the very life most personal to himself.

Word and Wisdom: The Son and His Bride

Continuing our investigation of this idea of introduction into the divine life, though now from a different point of view, we must also mention a particular duality or bi-polarity manifest throughout the whole Old Testament. This takes us into the innermost recesses of God. We refer to the very ancient distinction between God considered in himself and his Angel in whom and by whom his presence and activity are realized among us. It is the distinction, already mentioned, between his inaccessible presence "in heaven" and his presence with us, involved in all the weal and woe of Israel's history. It is the paradox of the Shekinah, the earthly presence of the heavenly God in a glorious cloud, a presence which was not content with simply resting on the mountain or the tabernacle but which had already introduced into itself such leaders of the people as Moses and others. Nowhere, though, was this duality more clearly expressed than in the ideas of Word and Wisdom.

We have already shown at length, elsewhere, how, in Israel, the Word of God came out, as it were, from the heart of myth, but reshaped it entirely in the process with unprecedented explosiveness. The consequent new picture of reality could not, in turn, take shape without the Word performing yet another complete and drastic overhaul, this time of human Wisdom.[25] Wisdom, itself, had tended in a variety of ways to prolong or deepen the myth from which it had sprung, sometimes even supplanting it but without ever being able to emancipate itself from it or

---

[22]Gen. 3:22ff. and 11:7.

[23]Genesis 18.

[24]Philo, *De Abrahamo*, 22, 113 and 24, 119-122.

[25]See *The Eternal Son*, chapters 2 and 3.

even replace it. But what the Wisdom of the Near East had certainly done was achieve a concrete, historical vision of the world, especially of the human world, particularly in its encounter with the problem of evil and innocent suffering, and it was this of which the Word of God laid hold in order to bring to perfection. But here again, Wisdom had to die, and to die more completely even than myth.

Wisdom was in origin a rational reflection upon experience. It was triggered by myth but aimed at a humanizing of the whole reality in which man is immersed. But, once touched by biblical inspiration, Wisdom became the design of God himself for man and all creation. It became, above all, the mystery of God's sovereign, loving plan by which he would ransom, free and reconcile with himself the perverted wills of men.

God inhabiting light inaccessible, and the cloud of glory enveloping the Shekinah and resting on us, were not two things. Nor were the Lord and the Angel of the Lord who was sent to us. Even less can the Wisdom of God be separated from the Word. One might even ask whether they can be adequately distinguished at all, except in relation to us. The Word, though, is essentially the revelation of God himself, God intervening in our history by his action and communicating himself to us by his presence. The Word comes down directly from God, refers to him and is, as it were, a living image expressing all he bears within himself and all that makes him what he is.

Wisdom, on the other hand, consists precisely in his plan for the world, the world as seen and willed by him from all eternity: his creation destined for adoption and sustained in that perspective from the very beginning. The outpouring of grace, given in ways known only to him but with complete commitment on his part, would be simply the realization of this plan.

So it can be said that it is the sending-forth of the Word which in some sense expresses and realizes that divine sonship which we are called to put on and which is a participation by grace in God's own life. Conversely, this gift of filiation, the reception of which meant the crowning and climax of the freedom of creation, a freedom lovingly adhering to the freedom of the creator who is Love, emerges, in the Wisdom of God, as present in him from all eternity. Following such a line, the New Testament would be able to resolve the tension between the two ultimate themes of the Old: the divine sonship made available in the "recognition" of God as Father, and the marriage with the creator through which we attain to it. The revelation of the eternal Son in his incarnation would in fact bring us that adopted sonship which is a participation in that most real of all filiations in the bosom of the Father.

The Word of God would wed created Wisdom, and uncreated Wisdom would henceforth be perfectly reflected in it. It was surely significant that Philo the Jew had already named the Logos (the rendering hellenistic Jews gave to the Word of Scripture) not simply the heavenly High-priest of earthly creation but *the* Son of God.[26]

Revealed Knowledge and Natural Knowledge

What we have just been saying about Wisdom leads us, before we leave the Old Testament for the New, to ask how the Bible itself, from the Old Testament onwards, envisaged the relationship between its revelation and what may be called the natural knowledge of God.

There is a fashionable thesis today, derived from the Protestant theology of the last generation and now echoed in many Catholic manuals, that the vision of the God who reveals himself in the Bible has nothing to do with man-made demonstrations or, more generally, with anything the human mind could infer or deduce from its examination of the universe. The first chapter of the letter to the Romans contains a vigorous affirmation that the visible things of the universe are capable of allowing the pagans themselves knowledge of the invisible qualities of God, and Karl Barth had to subject this text to some desperate exegesis rather than contradict this false presupposition. It is sheer self-delusion to see on this page an imposition of Paul's Greek culture upon the Judaism of this "Hebrew, son of a Hebrew" as he called himself. Neither the rabbis of Antiquity nor those of the Middle Ages recognized any incompatibility between biblical revelation and a natural knowledge of God using rational techniques of greater or less refinement. More to the point, they always believed that this was the teaching of the Bible itself. And it is not merely the late Wisdom writings which provide an Old Testament justification for this. The denunciations of idolatry in the second half of the book of Isaiah witness to the same conviction, and so do the oldest of the Psalms. And this in turn only made explicit something involved in the whole biblical view of man in the world and underlying not only the accounts of creation but the whole of Scripture.

According to the Old Testament, man, being a spiritual creature, fell by a failure of his will, and this fall certainly darkened his understanding. However, it has remained within man's powers, according to the Bible, and therefore within his duty, to reflect upon his experience in the world and, on that basis, realize the emptiness of idols and attain at least an indistinct conception of the transcendent existence of a wholly good

---

[26]Philo, *De Agricultura*, 12, 51.

and wise creator. In fact, the biblical Word began by purifying our natural knowledge and restoring it to that integrity which it would have had but for the fall, before taking us above it.

The Word, which we may call supernatural, supposes on every page that God speaks to man in everything, and that the fundamental employment of man's reason should be the understanding of this language. It is because of this, conversely, that the heart of man, in the biblical sense, that ultimate root of his consciousness, where reason and free will are inseparable, could only become a heart of flesh and not of stone, could only become a truly human heart with the humanity God desired and had made at the beginning, when the Spirit of God in person had regenerated it.

Only in such a perspective can one understand how Wisdom, however human and natural it was in its beginnings, was first restored to health by biblical inspiration and then became, in apocalyptic literature, the point of departure for some of the most supernatural, as one may call them, revelations of the Bible. This is as much as to say that the biblical supernatural is in no way anti-natural but, if the expression be admitted, hyper-natural.

There was, however, a kind of adumbration of the opposite view in Philo's idea that biblical inspiration—the inspiration of the Spirit in its loftiest sense—must necessarily abolish the human knowledge of the one inspired.[27] This was a sign of that radical pessimism which judged everything created as either foreign or even hostile to the divine, and which was to stand fully revealed in Jewish and Christian gnosticism, having already perverted Zoroaster's solitary prophecy into the pregnosticism of Iranian dualism.

The Bible, as a whole, for all its inflexible denunciation of idolatry, stands at the opposite pole to such attitudes. It is permeated by the conviction that man was made to the image of God and that his soul had been breathed into him by the divine Spirit himself. This is why it can maintain so intrepidly the complementary truth, that God can be expressed, albeit imperfectly, by analogies drawn from human life and human nature.

It is sometimes said today, in order to justify modern secularization, that the Bible stripped the world of all the personal presences with which paganism had stocked and secularized it. Nothing is further from the truth. In the first place, the Bible in no way denied the many personal presences which paganism had believed to be behind cosmic phenom-

---

[27]Philo, *Quis rerum divinarum heres*, 53, 265. This was certainly influenced by Plato, *Timaeus*, 71c.

ena. What it did was simply to reduce them to the rank of created powers, angelic or demonic, faithful to their creator or fallen. Above all, though, the Bible led man to recognize that the whole universe was a language in which one personality, the supreme personality, God himself, was expressing himself.

Here we come to the supreme and most deliberate anthropomorphism of the whole Bible, its supreme revelation. God is not just Someone rather than something, but Personality itself. This is why the sacred writers had none of our inhibitions about describing God as one would a man. Our minds are formed to abstract. They knew that it was much more perilous to mummify God in the swathes of lifeless notions than to anthropomorphize him in a way that might seem naive. It is highly significant that Pseudo-Denys, the patristic theologian who was the most permeated by hellenistic thought, did not hesitate to say that such images, for all their infantile crudity, were by their very character in the last resort less of an obstacle to a deep intuition of God's transcendence than were the most refined concepts, which were in fact no less resistant to literal application than the anthropomorphisms.[28]

Hellenic wisdom never rose to the concept of person, and even Christian wisdom still seems to have a long way to go before it can be said to have elaborated it fully. (Our recent so-called personalist philosophies have been somewhat of a disappointment in this respect!) But formed as we are on Jewish and Christian wisdom, we all feel, however confusedly, that the person is the most real thing in reality for the very reason that God himself is the only one to whom the term can be applied in its fullness. And this, of course, is the high-point of biblical revelation.

---

[28]Pseudo-Denys, *De divinis nominibus*, chap. 5, 6-7; PG 3, col. 821ff.

XI

From the Gospel of Jesus to
the Gospel of Paul

There has been a tendency in one school of contemporary exegesis, represented most markedly by Bultmann, to deny that anything in Jesus' general teaching, and especially that on God, went beyond contemporary Judaism. The same exegetes, including those like Schoeps, for example, who are most aware of how much Paul kept of his Jewishness, attribute the decisive rupture with Judaism and its theology to the latter. He was the first, they claim, not merely to teach formally Jesus' pre-existence (something several authors of apocalyptics had already attributed to the Messiah and, *a fortiori*, to the heavenly Son of Man) but to characterize him as divine.

This view, of course, represents an exaggerated reaction against the unconscious monophysitism of so many supposedly traditional representations of Christ. Against it, in turn, we must maintain that the transition from Jewish theology to the beginnings of Christian theology was undoubtedly owed to Jesus himself. It was owed to what he expressly said, not simply to what he did; owed to every aspect of his behavior which manifested the consciousness he had of himself. One could even go further and say, as Pannenberg has so well, that even if Jesus had said nothing about himself, what he said about God as Father would be enough to bring about the mutation—even though it be best described as a "fulfillment" in the sense of the evangelist Matthew and of St. Paul.

The finest justification of all this will be found in the penetrating analyses accomplished by Jeremias.[1] He has managed to give one of the best examples of how a subject which had long been thought exhausted can be renewed by patient investigation, progressive correction and a corresponding deepening of insight.

It is of course certainly false to repeat, as so many even of the "Liberal" Christian exegetes have done since Harnack, that the doctrine

---

[1]For what follows we are particularly indebted to Joachim Jeremias, *New Testament Theology*, vol. 1: *The Proclamation of Jesus*, London, 1971, and his other volume, *Abba*, Göttingen, 1966. Cf. *The Eternal Son*, pp. 179ff.

of God's fatherhood was unknown to Judaism or that the Jews did not call God "Father" when they prayed to him. The truth is that, though such a form of speech remains rare in the Old Testament, it is to be found repeatedly in the prayers of the synagogue and certainly prior to the time of Jesus. Like all his co-religionists, he would have said again and again: "Adonai, Elohenu, *Abinu...*," i.e., "Lord, our God, *our Father...*" This invocation, strangely enough, occurs as frequently at the beginning of Jewish prayers as does the *Omnipotens aeterne Deus* of the Latin collects. Which means that these latter, despite deriving from the former, fall well short of them.

This immediate context, however, far from diminishing the originality of Jesus' teaching and his whole religious attitude, only serves to highlight it. What happened with Jesus was that the customary use of a highly significant metaphor became something much more. It became a matter of direct application. It was not just that God had first claim to the title of Father, but that fatherhood was his exclusive property. Paul said the same when he spoke of God "from whom all fatherhood, in heaven and on earth, proceeds." St. Athanasius, with rare felicity of expression, would in turn be still more precise. Men, he said, are only ever fathers accidentally, fatherhood at the most being only one aspect of their personality, while we know from the Gospel that God is Father entirely, wholly and uniquely.

This meant, on Jesus' part, what must be called an experience of his own relationship with God, an experience unknown to any other man, except in dependence upon Jesus and the faith he evokes. Had Jesus said nothing more, that alone, once the resurrection had certified the truth of his teaching, would have enabled his disciples to call him "the Son of God" in the strictest sense. Pannenberg has been aware of all this, and Fr. Jacques Guillet, in his studies on the Gospels, has brought it out with the utmost clarity.

In the synoptic Gospels, the clearest indication lies in what has been called the Johannine meteorite, found in both Matthew[2] and Luke[3]:

> No one knows the Son except the Father,
> and no one knows the Father except the Son
> and anyone to whom the Son chooses to reveal him....

Jeremias' exegesis has served to bring out the full meaning of this text and at the same time has done away with any doubts about its authenticity. At first sight, his exegesis seems to minimize. On reflection, however,

---

[2]Matt. 11:27.
[3]Luke 10:22.

it becomes clear that it reveals more than explanations which align this text too precipitately with the Johannine formulas. The text, though, does contain embryonically all later developments. Jesus, according to Jeremias, was not here intending to give us direct teaching on his own, unique relationship with God. He restricted himself to developing, by way of a parabolic explanation, all that had already been implied in what the traditional teaching had affirmed on God's fatherhood towards Israel. Its heart lay in intimacy, in the equality springing from the mutual knowledge every true son has of the Father as the Father has of him. Paul would say the same thing when qualifying our eschatological experience as a knowing of God answering to the knowledge he has always had of us. According to Jeremias, Jesus, here, had the same thing in mind. He was not speaking directly of himself, but of what we must eventually become. Yet the very fact that Jesus could suppose such a capacity and propose it to all as something to be realized meant that he himself enjoyed an absolutely unique and unprecedented experience of God. He could not have done this, could not have proposed or even, as he did, imposed upon us this new law which was his law and the fulfillment, not abolition, of the old law—the basis of the whole Sermon on the Mount—except by virtue of the innate possession of it that he himself had.

In this sense, obviously, it belongs and always has to Jesus and to him alone to be truly "Son of God," so truly, in fact, that he can communicate this "knowledge" to others. The *logion* of Matthew and Luke begins then, in what Jesus himself invited us to appropriate, what he offered to us as the miraculous possibility constitutive of his "good news," namely sonship, but it contains in germ, albeit no more than in germ, the whole Johannine theology of the "only-begotten" Son.

This *logion* shows, in a summary way, how the *evangelium Christi* of the Sermon on the Mount—the revelation of a fatherhood of God which has become so real for us that we can really become sons of God—involved an *evangelium de Christo*, which was an inevitability even if Jesus had not expressly formulated it. On the one hand, the Sermon on the Mount brought to its climax the prodigious grace known to the prophets, Israel's grace of being "holy as I am holy," substituting for it the call to be "perfect as your heavenly Father is perfect." On the other hand, it raised this idea of God's fatherhood to infinite heights by disclosing the profusion of *agape* revealed in it: a love which does not just give all there is to give, but gives to those to whom it is revealed the capacity to live, like their Lover, in similar self-giving.

Even a superficial consideration of all this shows how far removed such a teaching was from what liberal Protestant exegesis, so memorably expressed in Jülicher's book *The Parables of Jesus*,[4] claimed it to be: namely, nothing more than a paradoxical formulation of what was, at bottom, nothing but plain common sense. Harnack's version of this was to say that the Gospel's fatherhood of God was nothing but a roundabout way of proclaiming the "infinite value of the human soul." The truth is that it involved, inseparably as ever, the promise of and demand for a phenomenal transformation of human nature. The only explanation for the sovereign facility with which Jesus introduced such a declaration is that, in his case, this human nature enjoyed a relationship with God which compels us to attribute a divine personality to him. This personality was that of the Son who, in St. Paul's words, could only make us sons also "in him" by making us, as Paul again said, "one stock with him"; that is, a single living entity, ourselves grafted on to him and made co-heirs of everything belonging to the only "heir" of the Father, of everything he is and has.

This communion into which Jesus and his Gospel bring us, involved too, a complementary aspect. It involved Jesus himself in a freely assumed communion with our condition as creatures, and as fallen creatures. The full manifestation of this lay in that full Gospel embracing all that he did, embracing above all his cross and passion.

Throughout all this, Jesus appeared to be and manifested himself to us as "the Son" in that full sense in which Christians would take it. He did this, though, not in the first place through what he said of himself but through what he alone said and could say of God as "the Father." His whole existence, like all his teaching, reflected this. It translated it into experience, into a human life without precedent and, in one sense, utterly incomparable.

Even if the only historical element in the Gospel was what we have been discussing, this *evangelium Christi*, wholly concerned with the revelation of the Father, without any explicit *evangelium de Christo*, that alone would be sufficient justification of the Church's developments to the latter and of the whole Trinitarian doctrine issued from it. However, it seems that so restrictive a view is unnecessary.

The Son in Jesus' Own Teaching

There is something artificial and over-calculating in the notion that Jesus only appeared implicitly as "the Son of God," in the sense that the New Testament tradition has transmitted to us. No doubt one cannot over-emphasize the fact that his human consciousness, like any normal

---

[4]*Die Gleichnisreden Jesu*, Tubingen, 1910.

human consciousness, was not initially or chiefly self-consciousness. On the contrary, it was spontaneously objective; and the object which drew it, riveted it and absorbed it, was God—God acknowledged as Father in a way no one had ever imagined. It was this that, by antonomasia, made it the consciousness of the Son of God. And it inevitably followed that the very fact of having so much to say about this Other disinclined him from speaking to us about himself. But it would be no less unreal to conclude from this that Jesus never paused in self-reflection, never turned his mind to what made him unique among men or, if he did, never revealed what he thought.

We shall return to this in more detail when we come to Johannine theology, but the point is still worth making at this stage. Jeremias has been right to maintain that, to use his own terminology, Jesus had, beside his esoteric teaching which was addressed to any who came, another which Jeremias does not shrink from calling esoteric, reserved to his close and chosen disciples, despite their all too obvious inadequacies (even if they were excusable up to a point). If "esoteric" is hard to swallow, we can simply call this teaching an intimate one. The synoptic Gospels themselves do not dwell on this fact but this only makes their testimony to it more convincing. They give it away by various observations. It is hard to believe that this teaching, at least that part of it which was addressed to the closest associates of his work and preoccupations, never treated of the secret of the King behind the mystery of the Kingdom. His identity, in any case, hardly admitted of being separated from the latter.

At the heart of Mark's Gospel, in fact, which is so dominated by the theme of Jesus, the Son of God (Günther Dehn, for example, entitled his commentary *Der Gottessohn*), we find an extraordinary phrase that can scarcely be attributed to any later stage of the Gospel tradition but must have come from the lips of Jesus himself. We refer, of course, to the saying about the day of judgment. No one knows it except the Father, "not even the Son."[5]

It does not seem possible here to agree with those critics, Jeremias included, who have attributed this phrase to the evangelist or his source and denied it to Jesus. One need only think of the difficulties such a text would provoke in environments extremely anxious to give Jesus' unique filiation its full sense to realize that it would not have been invented or retained had it not come from Jesus himself. Conversely, this explicit acceptance by Jesus of his sonship, at the very moment when he was throwing into such clear relief the abasement, inclusive even of igno-

[5]Mark 13:32.

rance, to which his solidarity with men had led him, bears the mark of his own inimitable manner. It was, as it were, the last word in that juxtaposition, which was so familiar to Jesus and yet eschewed by every New Testament writer, of the "form of a slave" of the humbled Servant and the glorious figure of the heavenly Son of man.

So we are bound to say that Jesus' own Gospel compels us to trace back to him and even to his own words the paradox of an eternal fatherhood in God necessarily involving an equally eternal sonship on Jesus' own part. This sonship was revealed to us in the gift of it made in Jesus' own work, in the complete and mutual solidarity with us established by his own earthly existence.

So sharply did Jesus' Gospel throw into relief God's fatherhood and the historical revelation of the eternal Son, that the New Testament, from the synoptics onwards, and even the oldest Fathers (including a St. Basil as late as the fourth century!), if read superficially, have given many commentators the impression of propounding a duality rather than, or at least prior to, a trinity of persons in God.

Jesus and the Spirit

However, it is also certain that, from the preaching and ministry of Jesus, the Spirit of God—given to men and closely bound to Jesus and his work but nonetheless quite distinct from him—appears with a clarity that is not found in the Old Testament.

Once again, it is certainly the case that we lack clear pointers to what was precisely Christ's formal teaching on this subject. But we must remember how general was the current conviction—of which the documents of Qumran give such striking evidence—that the last times were to be initiated by a universal outpouring of the Spirit. When this occurred, after the resurrection, it would have been recognized as the definitive seal upon Jesus' mission. As Newman pointed out, all the New Testament authors shared the conviction that Jesus' entrance into glory, his "ascent" to the Father and the "descent" of the Spirit were two complementary aspects of a single salvific event, and were recognized as such from the very beginning.[6]

However, more can be said. It has been rightly remarked that Luke's Gospel, and also the Acts of the Apostles, contains, among its archaic elements, what has been called a Christology before the Christologies. This consisted in the simple certainty that Jesus, who was "full of the Spirit" in a way no prophet had ever been, appeared from the very

---

[6]J.H. Newman, *Lectures on Justification*, p. 218.

beginning of his ministry as the one who unleashed this effusion of the Spirit or, better, as the one from whom the Spirit was poured out. The whole of Luke's Gospel, as we have shown elsewhere, was constructed around this theme. It is no coincidence that the first biblical words Luke's Jesus reads in public in the synagogue at Nazareth, are "The Spirit of the Lord is upon me." And Jesus comments: "Today this scripture has been fulfilled in your hearing."[7]

Once again, even the critics who see nothing more in this wonderful conjunction than a deliberate construction on the part of the evangelist are nonetheless persuaded that its origins go back to an earlier stage and an already existing conviction. From the start of Jesus' actual ministry there was evidence that God's Kingdom had come. Its presence was manifested by a positive explosion of the Spirit. This alone gives meaning to the famous saying on the unpardonable sin against the Spirit when even a sin against the Son of man could be pardoned. This could only mean that in the manifestation of the Spirit lay the irrefutable testimony to Jesus.

It is remarkable that, however individual their interpretations, all the evangelists teach that Christ's baptism was an epiphany of the Spirit. It was this before being anything else: it had to be this so as to be the theophany of the Father manifested in the Son and testifying to him. It does not matter whether it involved a collective vision, or was seen only by the Baptist, or was even personal to Jesus, though he was unable to conceal it from his own disciples. All the evangelists agree in affirming that the Spirit then came down upon him, manifested itself throughout his ministry and was finally bestowed on his own in the lavish and decisive communication of Pentecost. This latter did nothing but manifest in Jesus' disciples, symmetrically as it were, at the end of Jesus' earthly career, that the new and eternal covenant, brought about by his life and death, had now been inaugurated for them as it had been for him from his baptism. This, of course, represents the climax to a long process of collective meditation. Luke did the final systematizing. But the seed of it lay in the impressions made by Jesus' earliest public appearance, impressions which all that followed only confirmed.

In Mark, as much as in Luke or Matthew, it is the Spirit who after his baptism "throws" Jesus (the verb is Mark's[8]) into the desert to confront and conquer the devil. In other words, Jesus drives out the hostile spirit by the Spirit of God present within him. His every cure and miracle, not simply his exorcisms in the strict sense, are shown as so many materiali-

---

[7]Luke 4:16ff.
[8]Mark 1:12.

zations, as it were, of this substitution of one Spirit for the other. Consonant with this is his promise of direct inspiration for those who testify for him before men. Similarly, the Letter to the Hebrews interprets his life and death as an expiatory oblation accomplished "in the Spirit,"[9] while the Fourth Gospel leads us to see in Jesus the one who makes the "gift of the Spirit"[10] to men, and this not meanly but lavishly. The authors of these formulas were, of course, the ones responsible for them, but their use presupposes a unanimous conviction on the part of the early Christian community, a conviction that Jesus' passage had been a kind of world-wide conflagration in the Spirit and the fire. In retrospect, even the Baptist seemed to have predicted this,[11] even if only in terms of the old prophetic image of judgment wrought as if by a winnower, throwing the chaff to the wind and fire.

We are less clear here as to what Jesus himself actually said on the subject than we were in connection with his own sonship. But the fundamental pattern must have been the same. Everything Jesus said and did gave birth in the primitive community after Easter to the conviction expressed by the centurion but now given its full sense: "Truly this man was Son of God!"[12] In the same way the conviction came to this community that he was the heavenly Bridegroom and that she, the Bride, the Bride called to the eschatological espousals with him, had, as St. Paul would say, not merely the future guarantee but, here and now, the actual first-fruits of that communal experience into which the Bridegroom would lead her: that of being "one single Spirit" with him, in "the Spirit of Christ," the "Spirit of God" the Spirit of holiness and sonship, the Holy Spirit.

St. Paul, the Community and Jesus

It fell, however, to St. Paul[13] to explicate and to make the first systematic organization of Jesus' renewal of the whole of Judaism's doctrine on God. St. Paul, though, was of course wholly tributary to the spontaneous conviction enjoyed by the Jerusalem community since Pentecost. And, as we shall see, Paul's refinements and systematizing were ultimately nothing other than a considered application of Jesus' own teaching, used to interpret the effect that Jesus himself had had upon his disciples.

---

[9]Heb. 9:14.

[10]Cf. John 1:16 and 33, and 3:34.

[11]Luke 3:16.

[12]Mark 15:39.

[13]For more details on Paul, *The Eternal Son*, pp. 221ff.

However, there is no paradox in maintaining that even though the Christian Trinitarian belief goes back to Jesus' deeds and even to his words, yet until St. Paul it had not yet emerged from that deepened revelation of the fatherhood of God which, in Jesus' own Gospel at the heart of so unprecedented an experience of the Spirit, constituted this new belief's point of origin.

Elsewhere, we have shown at length just what the point of departure for St. Paul's own teaching was. It was the message he had received from the primitive Church: Jesus, by his death and ensuing resurrection, had revealed himself to be the heavenly "Son of man" featured in apocalyptic writing, but manifested in fact in the suffering Servant of Second Isaiah. As a result, he could fulfill what he had promised. He could introduce us, here and now, into the definitive Kingdom of God. He could now associate us with his glory just as he had associated with the full extent of our wretchedness. He could make us "the Kingdom of the saints of the Most High."[14] Faith in him made us "sons of God," and this sonship, derivative of his, was made manifest by the Spirit he sent to us. From the Spirit true *agape* was spread into our hearts, the very love with which God had loved us from all eternity.[15]

The Pauline ordering of these themes which, we repeat, had come to him from the preaching of the early Church, was due above all to Jesus' own basic teaching. It was this teaching thrown into a new perspective by the fact of his resurrection and the diffusion in us of his Spirit. We ourselves are now sons, as the Spirit within us itself attests.[16] We are sons because, by baptism,[17] we are one with Jesus, grafted onto him, living in him, living by his dead and risen life, nourished by his body in the Eucharist and thereby made members of it.[18] All this supposes that he, prior to us and of himself, is the Son. He is the first-born in relation to all creation[19] and has now become the first-born of countless brethren[20] by virtue of being the first-born among the dead,[21] that is, the first to be raised to this new life to which we in turn have been led by the Spirit.

The same thing also found expression in a second Christology which, in St. Paul, intersected with the first. The first, reflecting Jesus' own

---

[14]Dan. 7:27.
[15]Rom. 5:5.
[16]Gal. 4:6 and Rom. 8:15.
[17]Romans 6.
[18]1 Corinthians 11 and 12.
[19]Col. 1:15.
[20]Rom. 8:29.
[21]Col. 1:18.

Gospel, showed that our sonship, something we already enjoy, was an association with his eternal sonship, testified to in us by the gifted reality of the Spirit. The second was also an explication of something already given by Jesus himself, and was again part and parcel of this experience of the Spirit, namely the teaching on the Son of man manifested in the humbled Servant. Jesus, once risen, revealed himself as a second Adam. According to the teaching of the Letter to the Romans,[22] to which that of the Letter to the Philippians would give the optimum clarity,[23] just as Adam's single act, which was an attempt in disobedience, to equal God, plunged us all into death, so Jesus' single act, in the humbled obedience of the cross, has brought all of us into a new life, none other than the life of God in us.

Hence, as the first Letter to the Corinthians was to explain,[24] Jesus should in this light be understood as the Son of man come from heaven. He has come in consequence of having risen, and the resurrection was the term of the Servant's voluntary humiliation. Henceforth, it is clear that this heavenly Man is "Spirit," the Spirit of God giving life in him to our mortal body, just as the first man had been no more than a "soul" breathed into an earthly body. Nor is he simply the second Adam. He is the ultimate Adam: "the *last* Adam," the new Man, the Man become Spirit who gathers us all to himself in a definitive way. The Letter to the Ephesians would prolong the vision, showing him reaching in all of us, called to be his members, "the fullness of mature manhood."

The Pauline Eucharists

The result of this meditation appears in what progressively emerged, from one letter to the next as the "blessing," the great eucharistic-style prayer with which all the Pauline letters open. It tended to encroach further and further until, in the Letter to the Ephesians, it absorbed the whole epistle and thus made it the definitive summary and the ultimate articulation of Pauline thought.[25]

Paul's vision was now full. It embraced Christ, his work for and in us, the whole of Christianity and hence the whole of the Bible and the whole history of salvation. It now became sheer "thanksgiving/acknowledgment" (*reconnaissance*), in the richest, warmest and most overflowing

---

[22]Rom. 5:12ff.

[23]Philippians 2. (See *The Eternal Son*, p. 231.)

[24]1 Cor. 15:24ff.

[25]Markus Barth, *Commentary on the Epistle to the Ephesians*, in the *Anchor Bible* series, 2 vols., New York, 1974.

sense, for what had received its name from God alone, received it from the Father by antonomasia, the Father from whom comes all fatherhood in heaven and on earth. For everything, by way of Christ Jesus, in and by whom "the Spirit who searches the depths of God"[26] manifests himself within us, comes to believers as being nothing other than the manifestation of this love which surpasses all knowledge and is, as it were, the last word in the "knowledge of God." It is to this "knowledge" we are all called "in Christ Jesus." It is the final fruit of that very knowledge by which God, because "the Father," has known us, that is, loved us in his "beloved" before the world was.

St. Paul, therefore, throws light both on the conviction of the Church of Pentecost and on the Gospel of Jesus. He does so by taking everything back to this unique contemplation of the Father, now our Father, in that Son of his who has become our brother. Or rather, with his work completed, Jesus now appears as the only Spouse of the whole Church,[27] which is also his body and in which he attains his own fullness as being everything in everyone. This Church lives by his Spirit, which is also the Father's Spirit and who lives in the Son and by whom the Son was raised, just as that Son himself died *for us* in order to rise, finally, *with us*, in us, so that God, the Father, might be all in all.

"God was in Christ reconciling the world with himself in his body"[28] on the cross. This formula in no way goes beyond the language of the whole primitive Church, but St. Paul knits into it Jesus' whole teaching or, conversely, throws light on this teaching by his own experience of the faith. He brings together the original trinitarian theology and the most purely Christian theology of *agape*. But, more than this, he shows once and for all, by the use he makes of it, how such a theology necessarily flows from and to a vision of God as Father, given to us by the Son's gift of the Spirit.

This means that he also shows how such a theology only makes sense in the context of the eucharist: the oblation which is our thanksgiving, our "recognition" involving our whole being,[29] made in the person of Jesus who made that being his, made to the person who remains forever the fountain-head of everything, the Father, made by the presence, in us as in Jesus, of the person in whom everything is given, even the recipient's gift of himself: the Spirit of holiness, the Spirit of the Father, the Spirit of the Son, the Holy Spirit.

---

[26] 1 Cor. 2:10.

[27] Ephesians 5. Cf. 2 Cor. 11:2.

[28] 2 Cor. 5:19. Cf. Col. 1:22 and Eph. 2:16.

[29] Rom. 12:1.

XII

The Johannine Gospel or the
Evangelium Amoris as *Evangelium de Patre*

There can be no doubt that God's revelation of himself in the New Testament reaches its high-point in the Fourth Gospel and, more generally, in what we call the Johannine writings. But to understand in what sense this is true, and is even the ultimate truth of the whole biblical Word, of Old and New Testament, we must first progressively bypass three errors. The first error is to see in John's Gospel, for all its sublimity, a Gospel which bears little relation to that proclaimed by Jesus himself, the *evangelium Christi*. The second error is to see no more in it than the finest representative of what one might call the *evangelium de Christo*, the Gospel concerning Christ himself. The third is to think that one is plumbing the depths of this *evangelium de Christo* by treating it as an *evangelium de amore*: a Gospel proclaiming love and nothing more than that.[1]

The Johannine Problem

If we want to be cautioned against brash proclamations of "definitive results" in biblical criticism, we would do well to re-read what such a learned and religious figure as Friedrich von Hügel was capable of writing without any hesitation on the Fourth Gospel, about half a century ago. It could no longer be maintained, as had been for so long, that this Gospel gave us the direct testimony of the "beloved disciple," and thus Jesus' own deepest teaching on himself in its *ipsissima verba* delivered to and retained by his closest disciple and most faithful confidant. Rather, here was a meditation—of genius, certainly—on the message, work and person of Christ, produced by an anonymous thinker. All that could be said about him was that he had certainly not belonged to the inner circle of first disciples, was not a Palestinian, not even a Jew, but undoubtedly Greek. This unknown philosopher—with the utmost audacity!—had rethought the primitive gospel in the categories of religious hellenism and thereby given the Gentiles an "eternal gospel."

---

[1]See *The Eternal Son*, pp. 262ff.

This whole self-confident reconstruction was based on a colossal mis-understanding. Its point of departure was simply the vague impression of a Platonizing atmosphere, suggested by the Gospel's radiant symbolism, and intent, so it was said, on opposing spiritual and timeless truth to historical and concrete realities. It had been decided, following the apologists of the second and third centuries, that the *logos* of John's prologue, albeit so obviously coincident with the Word of the whole Bible, beginning with the first page of Genesis, could only be the *logos* of the Stoics and Neo-platonists. Hence John, the poor little Galilean fisherman who was quite incapable of having woven such awesome speculations around his Master, was inevitably replaced by an anonymous mystic, a sort of pre-Plotinus, who, as Holzmann boldly specified, must have been converted by some late disciple of St. Paul!

It strikes us now as something of a bad joke that such fantasies should have been taken, even by authentic scholars, as the last word in irrefutable "knowledge." But what is even more incredible is how many of their successors, despite the overwhelming accumulation of countless counter-indications, still insist on salvaging some remnants from the wreck.

In the first place—and this alone should have been sufficiently decisive—there has been the progressive discovery of more and more Egyptian papyri which attest that this purportedly late Gospel, dated to the end of the second century, was in fact widely known and an object of quite special consideration at a time in which no trace has yet been discovered of the three other Gospels, i.e., from at least the first quarter of the second century.

Yet, even before these facts had become fully appreciated, the more perceptive philologists had noticed how their supposedly pure Greek author had written in a Greek more charged with semitisms than any other in the New Testament. Some, like Burney, have even thought it possible that if any Gospel were likely to have been written originally in Aramaic, it was the Fourth. Even those unconvinced by his evidence have had to acknowledge that the evangelist used Aramaic notes or at least continued to think in this language when writing in Greek.

More tellingly still, recent archaeological discoveries have established that this purported "pure philosopher" who had no interest in facts, knew the topography of Palestine better than any of the other Evangelists and had a concern with precise dates and historical context to which the latter never approached. Even Renan, who suspected something of this, admitted finding in St. John more of the concrete details which evidence an eye-witness than in any other of the four.

Finally, there have been the discoveries at Qumran. These have shown to all what the best students of first-century Judaism had never doubted, namely that the intellectual and theological context of the Fourth Gospel lies not in some more or less late Hellenism but in Palestinian Judaism. And the crowning revelation is that it seems to belong to a form of the latter which did not survive the disaster of the year 70!

Put all this together, and it becomes understandable how Markus Barth can have come to consider the Fourth Evangelist, who seems to be ignorant of his three colleagues, as the earliest rather than the latest of them. We may be unwilling to go so far, but we must realize that the only reason for assigning a relatively late date to the Gospel lies in its seeming to represent the most elaborated New Testament meditation on the primitive data. Indeed, there are certain portions where it is not clear when the evangelist passes from what he wants to present as Jesus' own words to his own commentary upon them. But even this fact has another side to it. We can go back to what we said about Saint Paul: how he comments upon the primitive Church's confession of faith precisely by reverting to Jesus' own words, even though interpreting them in the light of this confession. The same may apply, and more so, to John, whoever it may be we want to stand behind that traditional name. One might even say that he does no more than comment on Jesus by means of Jesus.

We have already seen that it is impossible to contest the authenticity of the famous *logion* of Matthew and Luke and how firmly it pitches Jesus' teaching in the supposedly Johannine key. But we can claim still more. This *logion* can assure us that both the theme which is the most apparently peculiar to John and his own particular manner of treating it go back to the historical Jesus. We refer to Jesus' sonship and his communication of it to us, both of them being presented to us as springing from the mutual knowledge of Father and Son.

Jesus, too, undoubtedly had an "esoteric" teaching, of the kind we find in John. Jeremias, once again, has shown how the synoptics evidence this, and not only in the *logion* mentioned, although it is not as a rule their intention to transmit it. The predictions of the Passion and the account of the Supper are particular areas where Jeremias has established this.

If this is right, the consequences are weighty. It means that when we follow the Johannine meditations, we are not bidding farewell to the world of biblical religion. We are not being suddenly transported into some realm of hellenistic mysticism, which has been elaborated and justified by an essentially Platonizing religious philosophy. On the contrary, we are listening to the last word in biblical revelation. We are penetrating as far as may be into the most intimate sphere of Jesus' lived experience. We are encountering the fullest possible communication of this experience, the communication made to his closest disciples. And the fact that we are assimilating it by way of the deepest meditation that any of these close companions were able to make does not, it seems, remove us in the slightest from the Master's own world of thought and expression.

In this light, the Fourth Gospel, along with the other Johannine literature, can claim again the very importance which Christian tradition has always ascribed to it: not that of a simple, albeit highly original commentary, which would have been fundamentally alien to the Christianity of Christ, but rather that of the most far-reaching introduction into the depths of that revelation of which Jesus was not simply or initially the object but the author. But in that case, we have to be especially careful not to mistake the proper object of the Johannine Gospel.

Divine Sonship and the Knowledge of God

One might think, and it has certainly been said *ad nauseam*, that the purpose of John's Gospel is summed up in what must have been its original conclusion: "these things are written that you may believe that Jesus is...the Son of God, and that believing you may have life in his name."[2] This is taken to mean that John's Gospel is wholly preoccupied with Jesus' divine sonship. Undoubtedly, the theme does occupy a quite central place, and is the object of an especial orchestration, with all the other themes of the Gospel connected to it. But if one fails to go beyond that point, one will miss the specific originality, the final, distinctive note of the Fourth Gospel. The fact that the theme of Jesus as Son of God is so central and even dominates the whole spiritual horizon is not something unique to John. It is found, deliberately and explicitly, in Mark's Gospel, the first words of which: "The beginning of the gospel of Jesus Christ, the Son of God,"[3] denote precisely, according to the most recent exegetes, that for Mark the whole basis of the gospel is contained in that reality.

It is, then, not precisely Jesus' divine sonship which constitutes the specific contribution or, even less, the ultimate object of John's Gospel, but rather, as is sufficiently clear from the concluding phrase quoted above, a certain way of understanding this sonship, which gives us "life in his name." John's message stands out for its deliberate and thorough development of what had only been implied in the saying highlighted by Matthew and Luke, on the relationship between the Son and the Father, and on the way in which we are destined to be introduced into that relationship by the Son.

---

[2]John 20:31.
[3]Mark 1:1.

It is worth noticing how, in this text of Matthew and Luke, as in the great christological texts of St. Paul, the contemplation to which we are called engenders in us a eucharistic disposition, i.e., a vision of gratitude and recognition ("reconnaissance" in the strongest sense of the word), in the wake of which we return to the Father everything come down to us from him, ourselves included. This is precisely why and how Jesus' sonship, however much his own, is also intended to become ours. Everything in this case is a matter of knowledge, but of that knowledge of God characteristic of the teaching of the Hebrew prophets. We may recall that the essential note of this knowledge is what one might call its reflectiveness. It is the reflection in us of that knowledge which God has of us and has had from all eternity, in accord with St. Paul's highly traditional formulation "that we know him as we have been known by him."

The outstanding characteristic of John's Gospel, therefore, is not simply the continual referring of us to Jesus' divine sonship, but the continual setting of that sonship in the context of this knowledge and, more specifically, of the communication which Jesus has made of it, thereby associating us with his own sonship.

On the one hand, St. John sees this divine sonship as so exclusively proper to Jesus that, as opposed to the continual usage of St. Paul, he never calls us "sons." Thus, while for St. Paul Jesus was the "First-born," for John he always remains the "Only-begotten," the "beloved" of the Father, in the sense of being his only Son.

We, on the other hand, are always designated, in the Johannine writings, as "children of God." The First Letter, however, makes it perfectly clear that this is no mere pious appellation, but a reality: we are not simply "called" children of God but "we are" such.[4] This shows that the strict reservation of divine sonship to Jesus is no diminishment of us, but has the effect of bringing home to us just how much divine reality there is in the "grace" given us in Christ.

For St. John the genuineness of Jesus' divine sonship seems to be attested by the fact of having, like the Father, both the capacity and the will to communicate fully everything belonging to him. Need we stress how close we are to the teaching of the Sermon on the Mount on *agape* as the mark of sons and of the "perfection" which is to be the sign of their sonship of the one who is the Father par excellence?

John gives us two major expositions of this theme, the first being the commentary on the parable of the shepherd and his sheep,[5] the second

---

[4]1 John 3:1.
[5]John 10.

being the Last Discourse.[6] In both of these Jesus is shown revealing and explaining the sonship in terms of knowledge. We are taken from mutual knowledge, or rather from knowledge giving birth to knowledge—so biblical—to love giving birth to love by its sheer generosity. In both these expositions, Jesus draws the parallel between the knowledge he has of the Father and the Father of him, and the knowledge his disciples are called to have of him, just as he knows them. Yet to speak of a parallel is doubly inadequate.

It is inadequate in the first place because the mutual knowledge of the Son and his disciples is nothing but an extravasation, so to speak, of the mutual knowledge of the Father and the Son. But what makes it especially inadequate is the fact that the disciples are not called just to know the Son, even with his unique knowledge of the Father, but *to know the Father* and to know him with that knowledge which is and remains the property of the Son: "And this is eternal life, that they know *thee the only true God*, and Jesus Christ whom thou hast sent."[7] In other words, the disciples' knowledge of Jesus does not in any way come between them and the Father and, in the last resort, is identical with it. "He who has seen me has seen the Father, for the Father and I are one."[8]

This knowledge, which is equivalent to divine sonship, obviously goes beyond every possible notion of knowledge. It does so in two directions. At its root is an underlying unity, a unity of life and even of being: "I and the Father are one,"[9] "that they may all be one; even as thou, Father, art in me, and I in thee...that they may be one even as we are one, I in them and thou in me, that they may become perfectly one."[10] But, because this ontological unity is a living unity, is life itself, it brings with it a unity of perfect love or rather bears its fruit precisely in this ultimate unity: "Father, I desire that they also, whom thou hast given me, may be with me where I am, to behold my glory which thou hast given me in thy love for me before the foundation of the world. ...I made known to them thy name, and I will make it known, that the love with which thou hast loved me may be in them, and I in them."[11]

We seem to be bound to say that this glory belonging to Jesus which we must contemplate, is the glory of the Son, the glory of being the Son, a glory which, paradoxically, can only be his and yet is something he

---

[6]John 13:31ff.
[7]John 17:3.
[8]John 14:9.
[9]John 10:30.
[10]John 17:21-22.
[11]John 17:24-26.

wishes to give us: "...the glory which thou hast given me I have given to them'"[12]..."glory as of the only Son from the Father."[13] And, parallel to this, surely the divine name made known to us by the Son is the name of the Father which can only be truly known when one has come to love the Father as only the Son loves him, with the very love with which the Father has loved him.[14]

On the other hand, the Son manifests the love with which the Father has loved him by the love of the shepherd for the sheep—as the parable of the shepherd and his flock had already said—a love which goes so far as to make the shepherd freely lay down his life for them.[15] Hence it is no surprise that at the Last Discourse such love is made the touchstone of true "disciples." "Love one another"..."Love *as I have loved you*"... "Greater love has no man than this, that a man lay down his life for his friends."[16]

Gospel of Love, Gospel of the Spirit, Revelation of the Father

All this amounts to saying that one has only grasped the ultimate originality of John's Gospel when one realizes how this Gospel *"de Filio Dei"* is an *"evangelium de amore"*: the Gospel of that charity, that super-natural love which God communicates to us in his own Son, his Only-one given to save the world. The First Letter sums it up by saying "God is love": *ho theos agape estin.* "Beloved, let us love one another; for love is of God, and he who loves is born of God and knows God. He who does not love does not know God; for God is love."[17]

However, it is at this point that we might perhaps be in peril of the last of the three misunderstandings we mentioned. To say that God is love, as John obviously understands it, does not in the least mean, as we automatically tend to imagine, that Love is God, *Agape* itself the God revealed in the New Testament.

There is of course absolutely no doubt that the ultimate in biblical and gospel revelation lies in this revelation of *agape*—that love which, as St. John again says, is not any love by which we can love God but that with which he has loved us[18] and does love us, the love with which he loves his creatures, loves his Son, loves them all in him and enables them all to

---

[12]John 17:22.
[13]John 1:14.
[14]John 17:26.
[15]John 10:11ff.
[16]John 13:34; cf. 15:12-13.
[17]1 John 4:7-8; cf. 4:16.
[18]1 John 4:10.

love themselves by loving this Son and thus loving him, the Father, the beginning and end of everything.

But this is entirely different from confusing God with love, even with that utterly unique love in which he manifests himself. In the last resort, the most important characteristic of this love is that it cannot be considered and, *a fortiori*, possessed in itself. It is nothing but a relation, and a relation which is meaningless and non-existent without its constitutive reference to the Father, from whom alone it can come and to whom alone it must return. This is why John's Gospel, which is the culmination, as it were, of Jesus' Gospel, should not be taken to be an *evangelium de amore*. Certainly it is an *evangelium amoris*, of that love which only love can teach, "God's love poured into our hearts through the Holy Spirit who has been given to us," as St. Paul says. But this can only mean that the Johannine Gospel is the *evangelium de Patre*, the Gospel which has everything return to the Father from whom everything has come.

Here we touch on the final aspect of this Gospel, and on the fullness of the whole Christian Gospel as such: the full revelation of the Spirit. It is not that John identifies the Spirit with love, as do the Trinitarian theologies derivative of Augustine. But the Spirit reveals himself, in John, as specifically the personal character of divine love, as bearing the stamp, completely and abidingly, of *the* personality, the only source-personality, the only absolute personality, that of the Father.

St. Paul showed us the Spirit to be the one given us by the Father to make us his sons in the Son, the one, also, whose presence in us attests to the fact that we are now sons. And it was he too who showed us the Spirit communicating to us, by his presence, that *agape*, by which the Father is father and which, in the Son, is the proof that he is "the Son of the Father": the only, the one, true Father.

In the Last Discourse, the promise of the Spirit is not just the supreme "consolation" for the Son's "exodus" to the Father from whom he had come down to us. He is the goal of this coming. With the Son, the "Comforter," the "Paraclete," who gives simultaneous evidence to the world, to ourselves and before the Father that we have become "children of God," was himself "with us." But once the Son has returned to the Father, the Spirit can at last be, and is, "within us."[19] For St. John, the diffusion of the Spirit within us does not simply follow the ascension of the risen one. It coincides with that departure *ad Patrem* implied in the resurrection itself. We can recall the words to Mary Magdalene: "Do not cling to me" or "do not hold me back, for I have not yet ascended [in other

---

[19]John 14:17.

words I must ascend] to my Father and your Father, to my God and your God."[20]

We are told that the Spirit, on the other hand, has nothing of his own. It is his mission, rather, to communicate everything belonging to the Son.[21] He will do so with such liberality that we will be able to accomplish even greater things than did the Son during his life on earth.[22] For the Spirit, just as he "proceeds from the Father"[23] alone, is the one who finally brings everything back to the Father, just as the Son only completes his own work among us by returning to the same Father. It is by means of the Spirit that the Son is able to prepare us now for his climactic return when he will set us where he has always been: not just "with the Father," however closely, but *ad Patrem*—tending wholly towards him just as he comes wholly from him.[24] And so it is the Spirit himself who cries to the Bridegroom, cries with the Bride and in the Bride: "Come, Lord Jesus! Come quickly!"[25] Why should he come? Surely to consummate his sonship, to return to us in order to lift us definitively out of this world and establish us forever in his relationship to the Father.

The Spirit, in the Fourth Gospel, is freedom itself, like the wind which blows where it wills with no one knowing where it comes from or where it is going. But this freedom, in the last analysis—whether it be the freedom found in everything proceeding from the Father or in the Father himself, whether it be the freedom found in time or in eternity—can only ever be the freedom of love, *his* love. The Spirit has to uproot us from our every attempt to settle down in ourselves. He has to tear us away from any magical or idolatrous fixation with ourselves or anyone else. Only then will we be those true worshippers in Spirit and in Truth whom the Father seeks, worshippers who will worship him as Father, in the truth recognized in his Son, by the power of that Spirit whom that same Son has given us.

Knowing the Father

For St. John, then, the mutual knowledge of which he speaks can never be isolated from its object, the Father; its environment, the Son; its moving power, the Spirit. And it is this highly existential, personal character which explains one remarkable fact. The Fourth Evangelist never

---

[20]John 20:16.
[21]John 16:13-14.
[22]John 14:12.
[23]John 15:26.
[24]Cf. John 14:2-3 and John 1:1-2.
[25]Rev. 22:17ff.

uses the noun *gnosis*, "knowledge," but only the verb *ginoskein*, "to know." This is not to be explained by fear of having his teaching misread for that of the heretical Gnostics. In the first place, it is only the moderns who have adopted the habit of giving the word *gnosis* a technical meaning, reserved to these particular heretics. All the early Christian writers saw nothing heretical in the idea of the "knowledge of God." The prophets had spoken of it, and it was used to designate the highest aspect of Christian experience. Here Irenaeus, for example, never spoke of the *gnosis* of the heretics but of their "pseudo-gnosis," and made it quite clear that the only true *gnosis* was that transmitted by the apostles to the Church.

Further, what would be better called heretical "gnosticism" only developed after the Johannine writings and, largely, by misinterpreting them.

John's reason, then, for only using the verb and not the noun must be elsewhere. It lies surely in his conviction that true knowledge is not an abstract reality, which could be detached from its object and, as it were, capitalized on. It can only exist in act, in the most personal act we are capable of positing: accepting, through a living faith radiating love, to be carried away with Christ, by the power of the Spirit, i.e., that eucharistic oblation to the Father which can alone coincide with his own eternal self-giving in the Trinity, shown and shared with us by his grace. This is why the book of Revelation gives us the vision of the Lamb slain before the foundation of the world[26] and now become the center of the universal worship of saved, redeemed and consummated creatures.

---

[26]Rev. 5. Cf. 1 Peter 1:19-20.

Part Four

Understanding the Faith

XIII

From Myth to the Gospel and the Converse

From pagan preparation to Gnostic recovery:
The emergence of Neo-platonism
and the prelude to Arianism

Hellenistic Religion and Religious Philosophy

It is a difficult thing, in any age, to appreciate lived religion. Professional sociologists know how hard it is to organize inquiries which do not *a priori* falsify the final results. And even if that hurdle is overcome, there remains the equally problematic question of interpretation. We should not, therefore, be surprised at being so inadequately informed on the real value of Greco-Latin paganism for those whose religion it theoretically was when first challenged by the missionary expansion of Christianity.

It is remarkable how little even convert Christian authors tell us. An apologetic treatise, such as Clement of Alexandria's *Protrepticos*, expatiates at length on the Homeric myths, which we have every reason to believe had little or nothing to do with the actual religion of his age. At the same time, he gives us virtually no information on religious practice in the temples of Alexandria which Clement himself had frequented. This is just one instance of how much easier it is, at any period, to describe and discuss what one might call literary religion—that readily available in the texts at hand—rather than actual religious practice. It is even more difficult to ascertain the meaning that people gave to their practice.

What one can say with a certain amount of assurance, at least as regards the more cultured of the period's most religious spirits, is that they no longer found any real satisfaction for their spiritual needs, at least relatively speaking, in their actual religion. Instead they turned to philosophies. These had been more or less religious from the start and became more so the more the traditional religions dried up. We are not entirely ignorant of how the simple sought God, as we shall see, but such testimonies as have survived reveal, more than anything perhaps, their disarray and inarticulate discontent.

Cicero provides a good example of the religion of the intellectuals. It was he who recorded the witticism, attributed—which is significant—to a professional pontiff, Cotta: "How can two augurs meet without a laugh?" Yet, for all his preoccupation with a host of other things, Cicero was also obviously preoccupied with religion. But this preoccupation ran almost entirely along philosophical lines.

In a certain sense, one can say that philosophy began from religion. The first Greek thinkers, like those of other nations, began from the data furnished by myth, and while attempting to construct a rational vision of the universe, always remained within a mythical framework. Their "physics," that is, their attempts to understand the "natural" development of reality, always presupposed the whole cosmos as one single living thing, while the different "elements" from which in turn they sought to reconstruct it mentally always retained, to their minds, their original character as divine powers. The proof of this was their constant hope of pin-pointing the one element which would explain the whole of reality.[1]

With the Sophists, this wisdom became at once decidedly humanist and irreligious, in the sense that it was reduced to the art of getting on in life at any price. But even this irreligion was practical rather than theoretical. In any case, Socrates was to restore to wisdom a genuinely religious meaning and purpose, while at the same time injecting it with an ethical rigor similar to that which the Jewish prophets gave to Israelite religion.

From Socrates to Plato

Though his cast of mind was rational rather than traditional, Socrates shared with Confucius the express intention of doing no more than recovering the true meaning of words, especially the word Good. But Socrates was as little a rationalist pedant as Confucius was an antiquarian one. Both were concerned, by means of a strict and proper use of language, to regain direct contact with reality. For Confucius, this meant the true relations between men set up by "heaven." For Socrates, it meant a Good which could not be reduced to immediate utility and, least of all, to the egoistic utility of the person speaking about it. It meant a Good connected to that supreme reality which gave meaning to human life and towards which the inspiration of what he called his *daimon* forced him to tend without allowing him to turn aside or come to a halt.

Out of this came Plato's three themes, each of them unquestionably religious. The Good is sovereign; the world of Ideas is superior to the mixed realities which echo them, more or less effectively, in our sublunary world; the world is the work of a "demiurge," a craftsman whose

---

[1] Werner Jaeger, *The Theology of the Early Greek Philosophers*, Oxford, 1947.

specific intention it is to project upon formless matter some image of that superior world which he continues to contemplate while he works.[2]

A question naturally springs to our minds, just as it did to the contemporaries of the apostles. Where exactly, for Plato, does God fit into all this? Is he to be found in the idea of the Good or the ideas in general or the demiurge? We are, of course, being naïve in thinking like this. For Plato, all these things and the whole of reality, in varying proportion, were divine so far as they were real.

From Aristotle to Stoicism

The moderns tend to equate Aristotle's realistic, scientific reaction with their own and therefore to attribute to it a fundamentally irreligious or at least non-religious motivation. If we may believe Aristotle's latest biographer and commentator, Chroust,[3] this is a misconception. It is true that Aristotle made a clean sweep of Plato's ideas, including that of the Good, and of the demiurge purportedly busy contemplating them in order to project something of them into the world we know. Aristotle regarded all this as gratuitous fantasy, lacking justification and essentially superfluous. But his own universe exists only in dependence upon the transcendent existence of a "first unmoved mover." Aristotle, it is true, at least from one point of view, did not regard this unmoved mover as fundamentally immaterial. Nor was he altogether clear as to whether or not it was unique. It could only be such if this were the only cosmos, and this was a point that, as a philosopher, Aristotle left in doubt. However Aristotle attributed to it a genuine divinity far in excess of that which Plato would have conceded to his more or less ideal realities.[4]

Yet, this "thought thinking itself" was no more than that. It was a God that knew nothing of existents other than itself. They, in turn, certainly owed the movement which was their life to it, but the mover moved them not out of any interest it may have had for them but by means of the love by which it was loved by them: *panta kinei os eromenon.*[5]

The god of the Stoics reproduced the same possible materiality and total indifference. It lacked, however, the absolute transcendence of either Aristotle's or the Platonic God, with the increase of immanence meaning a decrease of divinity. In fact, it became immanence itself. It even became confused with the animation of the universe. It was thought of as "pneuma," a kind of ignited air, the tension of which gave

---

[2]A. Diès, *Autour de Platon*, vol. 2, Paris, 1927, pp. 523ff.
[3]A. Chroust, *Aristotle: New Light on His Life and on Some of His Lost Works*, London, 1973.
[4]Werner Jaeger, *Aristotle*, Oxford, 1960.
[5]*Metaphysics*, 1072,3.

everything its life. At the same time, it was the "logos," immanent reason, harmonizing everything, giving coherence to a whole which was adjudged to be *a priori* perfect.[6]

At the time when Christianity appeared, these different systems were blending one with another and provoking mutual reactions. The upshot was a widespread hesitancy between two tendencies. One of them was monist. It looked upon the universe as a dynamic whole and identified it, without qualification, with God. The other tendency was dualist. It removed God from the sense-perceptible world, indeed from the world in general, and located the divine in what was regarded as its only rightful home: the beyond. The universe merely reflected or, rather, refracted the divine. Its matter was formless, though some saw it as inert or in a state of more or less positive opposition to the reality of God.

The Epicureans, who were always peripheral and continually misunderstood, were unique exceptions to both views. They were certainly dualists. Indeed, they claimed to be absolute dualists. They projected the gods into a higher world and stripped them of all influence, good or bad, over the material world. Here below, on the other hand, chance was in charge: irrational combinations of random atoms colliding meaninglessly one with another. Yet Lucretius' poem shows how this materialistic, avowedly atheistic monism in fact resulted in a kind of materialist pantheism as regards this world of ours. In the end, Epicureanism was, in its way, just as religious as Stoicism, and religious in a fashion that was not really very different.[7]

Philosophical Syncretism

These clear outlines, however, should not mislead us. The dominant reality was syncretism. This was the case in the religious philosophy contemporary with early Christianity. It was even more the case, as we shall see shortly, with practical religion. There was a constant interchange of ideas between the various systems. They became so indistinguishable that it is possible to ask whether what is usually called Neo-platonism could not equally be dubbed Neo-stoicism. The only exceptions were the Epicureans, at least to the extent that they were regarded or regarded themselves as irreligious.

---

[6]G. Verbecke, *L'Evolution de la Doctrine du Pneuma du Stoïcisme à saint Augustin*, Louvain, 1939.

[7]For what follows, see *The Cambridge History of Later Greek and Early Medieval Philosophy*, ed. by A. H. Armstrong, Cambridge, 1970, and also A. H. Armstrong and R. A. Markus, *Christian Faith and Greek Philosophy*, London, 1964.

It is true, too, that this interchange had ancient roots. *Epinomis* which, albeit not one of Plato's dialogues, was close in time to the redaction of his spiritual testament, the *Laws*, provided an early articulation of the Logos concept. The so-called *Second Letter*, which came still later, developed the same ideas. And this means that, not long after Plato, the idea of the logos had already been introduced into the Platonic tradition. *Epinomis*, as the Stoics would later, undoubtedly took the notion from Heraclitus, and for Heraclitus the logos seems to have been the continual flux underlying all the changes of the universe, the one constant reality in it all, simultaneously liquid and fiery, thought and divine animation.

In this Platonic environment, the logos became the thought which embraced in itself all the Ideas and projected them upon the world. What had not yet been said or even clearly intuited was that it, or they, were the thought or thoughts of God.

For the Stoics, the logos was God. It was the only god they knew, and it was diffused throughout the universe. It was *logos* as spreading rationality throughout the universe, *pneuma* as the vital principle of it. The Platonist Antiochus of Ascalon, in the middle of the first century before Christ, seems to have been the first to locate the Ideas in the thought of a god who transcended the universe. The same vision can be found in Seneca. It was the key, or rather the heart of that piety which enabled him to resign himself to fate as to a friendly providence. Only with Philo, however, the Jewish Alexandrine philosopher of the first century A.D., did the logos become the intermediary between a transcendent god and the world it had summoned into existence. Philo was obviously inspired by the biblical notion of the creative Word.

With Plutarch, a near contemporary, Platonic dualism became so extreme that God was no longer simply transcendent but in actual opposition to the world. This had already happened with Xenocrates. Plutarch's logos, like Philo's, was both the model and the instrument by which God gave form to matter, but the latter, with Plutarch, was not so much passive as positively inert and capable of resisting the divine plan with relative success.

According to the Stoics, everything was brought about by a material determinism, *eimarmene*. But this was simply the other side of *pronoia*, the benevolent plan of that divine intelligence which was at once totally and perfectly immanent to the universe. The Neo-platonists, for their part, tended to give first place to *pronoia*, ascribing to it a transcendence akin to that of their god, and to regard *eimarmene*, which held sway at the level of the physical universe, as subordinate to it. In Plutarch, on the other hand, the latter seems to be in opposition to the former: unconquerable matter refusing to be permeated by divine reason.

Here we can see how tension could arise between the two possible perspectives on the relationship of the world to God. With the Stoics, an *a priori* optimism drew strength from identifying divine reason with physical necessity. With the Platonists, a relative pessimism set divine perfection in opposition to the increasingly imperfect image of itself which it projected upon the different levels of the world. This pessimism was to reach its acme with the heretical Gnostics, but we can already see it intensifying in Plutarch. For the early Platonists, matter had been a simple amorphous power, foreign to the divine world but wholly passive in relation to it. For Aristotle, it had been the simple counterpart of potential being in dialectical opposition to being in act. But now it had become positively hostile to a divine influence intent on penetrating the world with beauty and goodness.

Following Jaeger, on the other hand, some have wanted to see the first balanced synthesis between Platonism and Stoicism in Posidonius of Apamea, even in Panetius of Rhodes. This would have been achieved by identifying Plato's demiurge with his sovereign Good, and it would have been a decisive step in preparation for Neo-platonism, not perhaps for that of Plotinus but at least for that of his nearest predecessors such as Albinus and Numenius. Reinhardt, however, has questioned the attribution to Posidonius of a hypothetical commentary on the *Timaeus*, in which these ideas would have been formulated. It therefore does not seem that we can anticipate such a synthesis at this early stage. It only seems to have emerged at the end of the first century A.D. and—what is no coincidence—in areas where minds were not unfamiliar with ideas undeniably Jewish in origin and perhaps even Christian.

Similarly, it was only towards the beginning of the second century that we find a preliminary synthesis of Stoicism and Aristotelianism—in the treatise *De Mundo* which was to be wrongly attributed to Aristotle throughout the Middle Ages. *De Mundo* combined Aristotle's first unmoved mover with the "powers" which made it dynamically (not essentially) present in the world. Thus we have a world to which God remains foreign. He only envelops and rules it from on high, while coming down into it by way of manifold echoes in us of his reality, a reality which can only be found in its full purity and authenticity in him.

The blending of Platonism and Aristotelianism happened later still. It first appeared in the work of Aristocles and above all in that of Alexander of Aphrodisias. We shall return to the latter further on.[8]

---

[8]On Posidonius and *De Mundo*, P. Merlan, "The Stoa," in *Cambridge History of Later Greek...Philosophy*, pp. 126ff.

Popular Religious Syncretism

Ordinary people, of course, knew nothing of these speculations. The cosmopolitanism of the Macedonian empire and then that of its Roman successor inevitably engendered syncretism, with the local and national gods becoming increasingly confused with each other. When Stoicism took to popularizing itself, it too served to justify syncretism, by connecting all the gods to the logos. When fully popularized, it was marked above all by a preferential identification of the logos with Hermes, who had always been the god of the word, the interpreter of the other gods. In Egypt, Hermes was identified with Toth, the messenger of the gods and the divine psychopomp who led men to the gods of the after-life. This no doubt contributed to the strictly neo-platonic interpretation of the logos as an intermediary between the transcendent god and this world.

Everywhere at this time, there was a need felt for a god who would come closer to man, be good to him and even save him. This in fact was the most salient characteristic of the period. There was, of course, much vagueness about how all this would work out. But the need was real. It sprang precisely from the general confusing of the gods. Their contours became more uncertain than ever. There was nothing to lay hold of in them. And meanwhile, from the Near East came the fatalism of the astrologers. This, too, spread far and wide, and Stoicism proved itself unable to convince the average man that destiny was ultimately beneficent.

This new need expressed itself in other ways than speculation. Two kinds of cult, at two very different levels, came to reflect it. They were not new. They did, however, at this time, attempt to renew themselves. Their success was uneven but undeniably real. On the one hand, there was the imperial cult. On the other, there were what are called the mystery religions. These latter at first developed slowly. Then, as the second century became the third, they expanded rapidly.

The Imperial Cult

The cult of emperors represented an unexpected re-emergence, in the framework of the hellenized Roman empire, of the extremely archaic figure of the mythical King who was not just a priest but an epiphany of the divine. This could be seen for the first time in Alexander. He conquered the East, but the East also conquered him. He allowed himself to be divinized, even to the extent of his death becoming an apotheosis.[9]

---

[9]L. Cerfaux and J. Tondriau, *Le Culte des Souverains dans la Civilisation gréco-romaine*, Paris-Tournai, 1957.

Egypt had its ancient traditions regarding the Pharaoh. It proved fertile ground, therefore, for Alexander's Ptolemaic heirs to cultivate his legacy further. The Seleucids however, at Antioch and its environs, were the ones who took the notion with the greatest seriousness and exploited it to the full. This was what aroused the ferocious opposition of Macchabean Judaism. Indeed, it made no small contribution to a stiffening of Jewish monotheism, a preliminary to that which would harden it in its rejection of nascent Christianity.

The Roman Emperors were heirs to this divinizing. One might think that there was little more to it, at first, than oriental flattery, provoking in return Nero's or Caligula's or Domitian's brands of megalomania. But it was the populace who adhered to the practice and they did so sincerely. This explains the ease, even the spontaneity, of the anti-Christian reaction subtending the organized persecutions. It was precisely the Christian refusal to take part in the new cult that aroused the reaction. Conversely, there can be no doubt (as there could be as regards the original Hebraic vision of God as the only king) that the Christian reaction against the imperial cult aided the decisive recognition of Jesus as the only Lord, that is, the only king and the heavenly Savior. St. Paul's words on idol worship are sufficient proof of this: "For although there may be so-called gods in heaven or on earth—as indeed there are many 'gods' and many 'lords'—yet for us there is one God, the Father, from whom are all things and for whom we exist, and one Lord, Jesus Christ, through whom are all things and through whom we exist" (1 Cor. 8:5-6).

The empire, the *pax romana*, had no lack of defects. But for a humanity which was already in crisis, was unsettled and uprooted, its order gave the impression of being something miraculous. It seemed to make it possible, in a way no one had dared hope, to live a relatively harmonious existence in this world. But there were of course those who asked for more. There were those, too, whose personal, painful experience had made them see the inadequacy of this politico-religious "salvation." It was inevitable that such as these should look for initiation into some more consoling kind of salvation, some privileged involvement with a god who would show himself closer to the lot of his worshipers. Hence the increasing vogue for the mystery cults.

The Mystery Religions

What is meant by the mystery religions? They too were not, strictly speaking, new. They were a revival. They now spread unexpectedly beyond their original confines, and their exotic character, with the added allure of antiquity, gave these ancient forms of worship a quite new power of attraction.[10]

Yet they contained nothing, either at the ritual level or at that of their myths, which was in any real way different from the old autochthonous cults. But the initiations they offered took people out of their ordinary environment, and their symbols in consequence took on fresh luster, reviving a sense of communion with the powers presiding over life and death, restoring hope in some kind of union with the mysterious divinities ruling the world, and above all making it possible perhaps to break out of the oppressive circle of human fatality.

It was a case of imprecise aspirations, of hopes which were insuppressible for all their tenuousness. In Apuleia's *Metamorphoses* we can see them driving the most pious, or the most superstitious, from one initiation to the next. Nothing evokes these aspirations better than the melodious, though somewhat ambiguous phrase which the hierophant would murmur to the initiates of Attis:

Tharreité, O mustaï: tou théou gar sésoménou
estai kai humin ek ponon sotèria!…[11]

Take courage, you initiates: the god is saved
so for you too there will be salvation from your trials!

Modern authors have claimed to see in these mystery cults certain precise doctrines regarding the salvation they involved. But this was the result of a confusion. Beginning with the initial discoveries of the nineteenth century and continuing into Reitzenstein's over-ambitious syntheses, there has been much retrojection onto the mystery rites of conceptions which were not their own, but the product of religious philosophies and especially that of Hermetism. It is quite true that these latter were not ashamed to make abundant use of imagery borrowed from the mystery religions. Greek religious philosophy, at least since Plato, had done the same. But this does not mean that these philosophies simply publicized the esoteric teaching known to the initiates of the mystery cults. In fact, there is no trace of this. Rather, we have clear proof that religious philosophers grafted onto the mystery religions an interpretation which had different and external sources. They may well have received a certain inspiration from various symbols, but when they

---

[10]There is still no substitute for F. Cumont's great book, *Les Religions orientales dans l'Empire romain*, Paris, 1929. For the state of research up to 1955 see the article of Bruce Metzger at the beginning of that year's volume of the *Harvard Theological Review*.

[11]Quoted by Firmicus Maternus, *De errore profanarum religionum*, 22 (Turchi, *op. cit.*, p. 239).

developed them, they projected ideas upon them which were not native to them, but which came from them later and blended the developed Platonism and Stoicism of which we have spoken above.

It is in this sense that Hermetism, in particular, cannot simply be dubbed, as so many over-hasty studies have done, as a mystery religion. Rather, as A. J. Festugière said so well, it was no more than a "literary mystery."[12] In other words, Hermetism never belonged as such to any of the mystery cults. *A fortiori* it never set itself up as one with its own rites. It was a religious philosophy, expressing itself unreally in the ritual and mythical imagery of the mystery religions.

Religious Hermetism

Nonetheless, when we come to what is called religious Hermetism,[13] we must recognize that, along with the later philosophical speculations described above, we can detect some more directly religious elements which had no small influence in specifying and heightening its fervor. We should first of all point to the Pythagorean influence, which was at this time back at full power, having been noticeable ever since the period of Platonism. The primary source of the Platonic Ideas had in fact been Pythagoras' experience of how the different sounds corresponded to different lengths of vibrating chords. The first conclusion from this was that numbers lie behind sensible qualities. Then came the inference that every physical reality corresponds to a higher reality. From this sprang the spiritual orientation given to thought which was such a striking feature of Pythagoreanism and which made this school a kind of religious order.

Pythagoreanism seems to have had Orphism as a long-standing ally. This latter does not admit of easy analysis. It was a collection of traditions connected with the semi-mythical person of Orpheus, the most significant of them being the myth of the Titans. There were the earthly giants destroyed by Zeus for having devoured his child Dionysus-Zagreus. Human beings had sprung from their ashes and they carried deep within them, therefore, a divine spark, buried as it were in an envelope of clay from which it strove to disengage itself.[14]

None of the above elements had ever been absent from Greek thought, especially the Platonic tradition. But they seem to have been in the full swing of revival at the period we are considering.

---

[12]A. J. Festugière, *L'Idéal religieux des Grecs et l'Evangile*, Paris, 1932, pp. 116ff.

[13]A. J. Festugière's four volumes, *La Révélation d'Hermès Trimégiste*, Paris, 1949-1954, and his volume of essays: *Hermétisme et Mystique païenne*, Paris, 1967.

[14]Guthrie, *Orpheus and Greek Religion*, London, 1952.

However, there were new factors also, more definitely Eastern. It is hard to assess to what extent Indian influences, since Alexander, had affected Hellenism. But Iranian Mazdeaism, with its emphatic dualism of darkness and light, had had an undeniable influence. So had the astrological superstitions, which certainly came from Babylon. But there was another influence, at the very least on a par with those just mentioned, which played a role in late Hellenism that has yet to be fully appreciated. This was Judaism, felt particularly around Alexandria. The Greek Bible, the Septuagint, was widely read, even beyond the circles of proselytes who were particularly drawn by those synagogues that worshiped in Greek. Its influence, at least that of its highly distinctive religious vocabulary, was felt everywhere at the end of the second century of the Christian era. Dom Jacques Dupont[15] has definitely demonstrated that the vocabulary of *gnosis*—i.e., the designation by the expression *gnosis tou theou* of a "knowledge" which is not just specifically religious but salvific—was owed to it. The Greek philosophical tradition had only given this technical sense to *episteme* for "knowledge," and *epistanai* for "to know," and never to *gnosis* or *gnonai*. This means that the whole of religious Hellenism at this time, beginning with Hermetism, definitely derived what it said about *gnosis*, albeit indirectly, from the Jewish prophets' knowledge of God. The fact that this notion was substantially altered in varying degrees does not detract from this.

The religious treatises, attributed to the inspiration of Hermes-Toth and which appeared in the Greek-speaking milieu of Alexandria at this time, were a blend of all the above, served up with a superficial coating of traditional Egyptian religiousness. *Poimandres* and *Asclepius* are examples.

Philo of Alexandria

Alexandria itself was to be the home, too, of the Jewish religious thinker, Philo—an almost exact contemporary of Christ. It was his role to exercise a decisive, albeit not an all-determining influence both on the greater part of early Christian religious thought and on the last revivals of Greek thought. This influence was to emphasize all the more the already growing religious tendency of the latter.

Nineteenth-century studies of Philo tended to see in him little more than an eclectic disciple of the Greek philosophers, a man whose immoderate use of allegory enabled him to claim a spurious presence in the Bible of the whole complex of Greek thought. Contemporary research

---

[15]Jacques Dupont, *op. cit.*

has led to other conclusions. Philo was a profoundly religious Jew. He was faithful to Israel's faith. The only use to which he wished to put his knowledge of hellenic philosophy was the defense and propagation of this faith. It is true, certainly, that Platonism made a deep impression on him, and Stoicism perhaps even more so. But the basics of his thought were always biblical. As has now become clear, even elements which seemed essentially hellenistic, such as his theory of the "powers" by which God becomes present and active in the world, were merely a transposing of Palestinian angelology.

This was true, in a still wider perspective, of his whole conception of intermediaries, beings whose nature did not admit of comprehension, and by means of whom an utterly transcendent God could become no less immanent to everything and to the mind of man in particular. His Logos, whatever may be the elements in it adopted from Platonism or Stoicism, came straight from the Bible's Word, amalgamated with what the Bible, again, says of the Wisdom and of the Angel of the Lord. Even when he went so far as to present him as the high-priest of creation, the "son of God," even as a *deuteros theos*, Philo no more admitted a real distinction from the one God than Palestinian Judaism did with its manifold intermediaries. God was always jealously preserved as supreme and, what is more, absolutely transcendent.

Yet, thanks to his very effort at this preservation, Philo tended to see matter as a reality foreign and even opposed to God as to the point of confusing the state of the creature and the state of sin. His anthropology, though not that alone, showed this very clearly. Against the primitive, heavenly Adam, who tended to be identified with the Logos itself, was set the physical, fleshly, fallen Adam, his successor and our ancestor.

In this regard, Philo certainly confounded, or tended to confound, our salvation by the illumination brought by the Logos with disengagement from what is bodily. Inversely, the contemplative life—first outlined, in his view, among the Hebrew patriarchs—was for him not a simple intellectual contemplation, like Aristotle's, but a contemplation of God, while remaining, like the vision granted Moses on the mountain, a vision "from behind," i.e., only seeing him as he passes by, always escaping at the very moment we would like to take hold of him. This does not prevent this "royal way" from taking us so near to God that Philo (like Jesus!) had no hesitation in using and emphasizing those biblical expressions that give divine qualifications to man, affirming by their means what he called our vocation "to become God"—not, be it noted, gods: *theon genesthai*.

On the other hand, the almost complete disappearance, in Philo, of eschatology and messianism shows the extent to which he was hellenized. Yet there was less hellenization of what was Jewish than judaizing of what was most Greek. He did not suppress history. It was essential, in fact, to what he called the "royal way"—that exemplary history all are called to follow once they have unearthed its tracks in the Bible. Yet for Philo "eulogies of the fathers," already frequent in the Bible's wisdom writings, were the whole key to sacred history. The prophets had already interiorized this history. Philo did that and more. He seems simply to have seen it as something individualized in purely typical persons.

Finally, there was something of which too little account is still taken. Even when Philo took up so apparently Platonic a theme as that of our assimilation to God by way of contemplation of him (Plato, of course, had only spoken of contemplating and being assimilated to the Good), he stood it on its head. He took the biblical point of view. He did not suggest that we become like God through our efforts at coming to contemplate him, but rather that, thanks to his gratuitous revelation, we are able to contemplate him and so come to be like him. This is why in the last resort, as Jean Laporte has shown so well, Philo's whole piety was always set in the context of the Jewish "eucharist": thanksgiving for all God's gifts going up to God with the free giving back of the gift of ourselves, a gift owed only to his own freedom and love.[16]

Gnosticism

The religious treatises of the *Corpus Hermeticum* reflect this same notion of a contemplation assimilating us to the God who reveals himself in a *hieros logos*. This is true whatever be the influence behind them: Philo, Alexandrine Judaism or simply the Septuagint. But what is most striking about them is the emphatic dualism, more marked even than Philo's, which they set up between the physical world, to which we belong through our body, and the transcendent deity to whom they intend to take us. There is no doubt then that here we are on the threshold of Gnosticism. It was at this period that it made an abrupt and ubiquitous appearance. Its own roots were various. We have already mentioned that its vocabulary—centered on *gnosis theou*—was undoubtedly of biblical origin. Apart from that, it had what seem to have been almost pure "pagan" connections and to have involved an esotericism putting itself out as true Judaism or true Christianity. In

---

[16]H. Chadwick has summarized recent Philonian research in the *Cambridge History, op. cit.*, pp. 137ff.

other words, Gnosticism took on various forms. But the same basic ideas reappeared behind the different garbs.

R. M. Grant[17] seems recently to have provided the best explanation of its sudden rise. Gnosticism was not a last, relatively autonomous but still *sui generis* development of Greek thought. On this point, we can trust Plotinus' passionate reaction against Gnosticism. He may have renewed Greek thought, and done so trenchantly, but fidelity was always his intention. Yet, on the other hand, Gnosticism was not, *pace* the suppositions of Adolf von Harnack or Eugène de Faye, a first, jejune attempt at hellenizing Christianity. Rather, it represented a relapse on the part of Judaism as a whole but more particularly of apocalyptic Judaism. Both nascent Christianity and Hellenism were fast contaminated. The cradle of the former was those very Jewish circles whipped to a fever pitch of eschatological expectation by their apocalypses, while the latter was eagerly prospecting for new "revelations."

What in fact supremely characterized Gnosticism was the collapse of the hope nourished by the apocalypses. There had been too many catastrophes. It was no longer possible to believe in a decisive, divine, historical intervention which would destroy the powers of evil once and for all and usher in God's Kingdom. What happened, apparently, was a reversion from the essentially historical dualism of biblical revelation, with its revolt of created wills against the divine plan, to the old ontological dualism of the ancient myths, with their heavenly, divine and ideal reality standing above the earthly, inferior, alien reality of the here below. The result was an exact inversion, within the framework of those apocalypses which had been the final stage of biblical revelation, of what that revelation had been producing from its very beginnings. We saw how, under the impact of the Word of God, the structure of the myths was exploded and their symbols reformed according to a quite new structure, that of a divine, creative and salvific history. This time the opposite occurred. The imaginative description of this salvation history's hoped-for consummation was now refashioned according to the resurrected pattern of the ancient myths, with their earlier pessimism now emphasized and finally hardened.

This meant, in other words, that for all the use of biblical language and symbolism and of the now most thoroughly characteristic concepts of the Bible, including the New Testament, the three confusions we discerned in all the ancient myths reappeared afresh. In fact they reappeared with a vengeance—not just as threads traceable behind the fables,

---

[17]R. M. Grant, *Gnosticism and Early Christianity*, New York, 1966.

but, in these new forms, absorbing everything into a final, unalterable structure.

According to the Gnostic myths, in fact, for all their apparent variety, God, or to be more precise the so-called divine "pleroma," was in itself absolutely removed from this world of matter, darkness, suffering, death and sin. The only way in which something of the divine had come to lodge in this carnal world was by a fall and dismemberment of the pleroma into matter, into this irreversible darkness. In the case of some men, there was a spark of the "mind" or the "logos" shining in them. There was only one way of salvation, i.e., of saving what was imperishably and unchangeably divine within them, namely that of disentangling this element from its fleshly, permanently alien envelope. "Salvation," then, could only mean a restoration of divine "knowledge" within them, a kind of re-acknowledgment of their real nature, that nature which had gone listless and comatose in the material and corporal and was embedded in a remote and hostile world.

The Savior Redeemer was necessarily heavenly, and could only be and remain Savior by coming to us simply in appearance, clothed in what was only a semblance of flesh. This had to be so however much he might have been dressed in the garb of the apocalyptic "son of man," who was equated to a greater or lesser degree with the Jewish Messiah, or have been purportedly found in Jesus whose true reality was supposed to have been unearthed by some esoteric tradition. The appearance of flesh was a stratagem allowing him by his teaching to re-awaken, reanimate, the "knowledge of God" in those who, at the deepest, hidden level of their being, were still *pneumatokoi*, wholly spiritual beings, fallen into flesh as the result of a disastrous mistake. We must understand this as the knowledge of a god of whom they were simply the scattered particles in a dark place. Then, becoming conscious of themselves, apprehending themselves, they would escape with their gnostic "Savior" to the world above, all reunite and become one with him in the reconstituted pleroma.

Such was the Gnostic religion. In it, as we have said, pre-Christian, pre-Jewish, even pre-hellenistic religiosity made its reappearance, reconstituting itself more emphatically but still in a way that followed the outline of the old myths, such as the Orphic one we have just recalled. This re-making proceeded to take up and twist to its own meaning the apocalyptic formulas not only of late Judaism but also of early Christianity. Hence the Gnostic chains of "eons" merely borrowed the title given by the Septuagint to the biblical "ages," i.e., the successive phases of creation and salvation history. But these "eons" now became permanent strata, extending from the transcendent unity of the divine pleroma down through every conceivable kind of gradation or rather degradation until coming to matter, which was always alien, impenetrable and an enemy of the divine.

Creation, therefore, was simply the product of a divine fall into matter. Salvation was a liberation of the "sparks" of the divine furnace from the matter in which they had been lost. They would of themselves go back to their source, thanks simply to that "knowledge" which restored them to the knowledge of their true and abiding nature, hitherto dormant in ignorance.

All that remained in this of biblical teaching was the sense of divine transcendence and immanence, both of them paradoxically pushed to an extreme. Yet they remained as ineluctably opposed as in Platonic or Aristotelian dualism, the one simply negating or relativizing the other. In Gnosticism—and how Greek this was—the infinite, which was something so essential to the God of the Bible, was regarded as merely negative. God's perfection, on the other hand, lay in his limitation. It was this which made him susceptible to being circumscribed, and therefore known.

Yet, even within the narrow framework of Greek thought, and even though it was never let loose, there was a presentiment of the truly infinite. We can discern it in Plutarch as well as in Philo. It lay in the very tendency to consider matter, the physical, the finite not just as non-divine but as anti-divine. Yet, once this road was taken, any reintegration had to mean destruction and any communication self-deprivation.

The Genesis of Neo-Platonism

What we have in the Neo-platonism[18] of which Plotinus was to be the culminating exponent was an attempt to introduce into hellenistic categories something of the Bible's and the Gospel's novelty. Certainly it was only an attempt. The categories were never fully surpassed. Success was limited. Yet here was something incomparably purer and loftier than Gnosticism. Here was something of what we have called prophetism. The actual modification of the old myths was superficial but the tendency, undoubtedly, was to total transfiguration.

Simultaneously, several of the ante-Nicene Church Fathers were striving to express the genuine Christian message about God in a hellenistic framework. Failing to reshape that framework as thoroughly as was required, they produced ambiguous expressions astonishingly akin to those of the Neo-platonists. We should not wonder that these two sym-

---

[18]On its origins in general, P. Merlan, *op. cit.*, pp. 53ff.

metrical developments influenced one another—to such an extent in fact that often what was owed to each one's innate dynamism and what to contamination from the other are indistinguishable.

It has been said that the Neo-platonists of the second and third centuries A.D. aimed at combining Aristotle's transcendent but practically indifferent God with the Platonic demiurge who, as he fashioned the world, had his eyes fixed on the transcendent model of the pure ideas. But there was more to the synthesis than a meeting of Platonism and Aristotelianism in an environment charged with Stoic immanentism. Of itself, this would only have led to such ingenious combinations as we find in the treatise *De Mundo*, with the first unmoved mover superimposed on the powers representing him in the heart of the cosmos.

We have already said that a first step towards eventual Plotinianism seems to have been taken as early as the first century B.C. when Antiochus of Ascalon apparently equated Plato's ideas with the thoughts of a transcendent God. But Albinus, in the mid-second century after Christ, was the first to develop this insight. He worked a bold combination of Platonic ideas and Aristotelian forms, the first existing above and outside sense-perceptible reality, the latter immersed in it and separable only by the abstractive activity of our own understanding. Albinus then lifted this last operation into God and reversed it. First, God conceived the pure ideas; then he formed matter by applying them to it. The result was a threefold distinction between God, the ideas and the world.

But Albinus also tended to distinguish between God in his transcendence and God as thinking and making the world. He therefore opposed what he called "the first God" to "the heavenly intelligence," and this intelligence in turn to the world-soul, constituted apparently by the intelligible forms immanent to the world. Yet his first distinction seems to have been one of reason only, since he immediately went on to affirm that the supreme God and the heavenly intelligence were one and the same. One step more and we would have had the Plotinian tri-partition between the purely transcendent divinity of the One, the Mind and the World-Soul.

Besides this, there was something of particular interest from the religious point of view. Albinus was explicit that the heavenly intelligence was the "Father" of the cosmic soul, maintaining that it was he who implanted the ideas in it and turned it towards himself so that it might contemplate and be filled with them. Once again, we are very close to Plotinus and his doctrine on the *epistrophe*, the "conversion" by which the soul begins its climb back towards the One by turning itself towards the Mind.[19]

A further, decisive step was taken by Numenius of Apamea, who regarded Plato (and even Socrates) as nothing but Pythagorean. With him we have something more than a mere way of thinking of God, the world and some interconnecting reality. We have three gods, three levels, in fact, of a single, divine existence taking it all the way from pure transcendence to total immanence in the world.

The first god is sheer goodness (*tagathon*), the first intelligence, incorporeality, the one who is (*on*) or being (*ousia*). He is, as it were, the idea of the second god, who in his turn is the second intelligence and participated goodness and, at the same time, the world's artist and administrator, ruling the whole of it while contemplating the first god and yet in danger of becoming immersed in it. Thus the first god presided over being, the second over becoming. Consequently, Numenius disagreed with what he thought was Plato's (and even Socrates') conception of second and third gods (found in a famous passage of the *Second Letter* attributed to Plato), and preferred to regard the second god as two who were in fact one—unless, of course, the world itself was to be taken as the third.[20]

At this point, we are only a step away from Plotinus' triad: the utterly transcendent One, the Mind, who was the intermediary between this indefinable, wholly uncomposite One, and the Soul, this latter reflecting the Mind in the sense-perceptible multiplicity of the beings immersed in matter. It was hardly surprising that the ancients accused Plotinus simply of plagiarizing Numenius.

Plotinus, however, could not have made the transition from Numenius to his own system without the help of the Platonizing interpretation of Peripateticism developed by Alexander of Aphrodisias in the wake of Aristocles. Alexander drew a distinction between the intelligence in act, free of all matter, and the passive intelligence which was essentially material. The first corresponded to the transcendent intelligibles (though, to him, these were not exactly Platonic ideas, being individual and not generic) and the second to the wholly immanent intelligible forms. In this scheme, there was certainly such a thing as providence, though God exercised it obliquely rather than directly. He was not turned toward the universe, but since the latter's concrete existence depended on his, it could be said to be governed by it.[21]

---

[19]P. Merlan, *op. cit.*, pp. 64ff.

[20]*Ibid.*, pp. 96ff. (The text quoted from the *Second Letter* of Plato is on 312c.)

[21]P. Merlan, *op. cit.*, pp. 116ff.

All this represented a progressive rearrangement and refinement of some of the traditional material of hellenist thought. However, one cannot help observing, before proceeding, how we are coming continually closer, albeit asymptotically, to Jewish and Christian perspectives.

Nor must we forget that Philo came between Antiochus and Albinus. Philo was explicit and manifestly biblical. With him, we have God conceiving the world in his Logos, regarded as Wisdom, and, by expressing the Logos as Word, fashioning the world in accordance with his eternal thought.

Again Numenius, while following Plato, Aristotle and Plutarch in quoting the ancient Egyptians and the Persian "Magi" in support of his speculations, and even adding the Brahmins, also mentioned the Jews among his sources and authorities. He even said that Plato was simply a Moses speaking Greek.[22] He made explicit reference to the texts of the Septuagint. Further still, he quoted Jesus with favor.[23]

As regards Plotinus, Porphyry has informed us that, like Origen, his master at Alexandria was Ammonius Saccas. The latter had been a Christian. Even Porphyry admitted this, though maintaining that eventually he had ceased to be one. We will see, however, that there is good reason for doubting this last assertion. Be that as it may, there were certainly contacts, and increasingly close ones, between the two traditions, and we can see the results in an ever more evident rapprochement between neoplatonic and Christian positions. Yet a study of the contemporary Christian thinkers obliges us to realize that influences no less forcibly ran the other way.

Irenaeus

After the New Testament, the first Christian thinker to have left us a genuine theological synthesis was Irenaeus.[24] His theology directly opposed the errors of the Gnostics, and did so simply by recourse to the Bible, the latter being interpreted wholly from a Pauline perspective and, more precisely, along the line of the Letter to the Ephesians, i.e., of what, following that Letter, he called the *anakephalaiosis*. Irenaeus understood by this word the reacquisition of the whole of human history by God, the God who had created everything by his eternal Word in the power of the Holy Spirit. Free wills having fallen away, God went about bringing

---

[22]Fragm. 102.

[23]Fragm. 192.

[24]On what follows, cf. *The Eternal Son*, pp. 306ff. and H. Chadwick, *op. cit.*, pp. 137ff. Our summary of Irenaeus is practically nothing but a cento of quotations: *Adversus Haereses* 2,28,6; 3,6,2; 5,5,1; 4,20,1; 4,20,6-7; 5,1,3.

everything back to himself through Christ, the incarnation in time of the eternal Word. In this way, sin had been overcome and death swallowed up by life but, more than that, we have all become sons in the Son, given life with him and in him by the Spirit.

This meant, as Irenaeus himself said, that of himself the Father cannot be seen. But he has created us, then redeemed, adopted and perfected us by sharing his own eternal life with us, all through what Irenaeus called "his two hands," the Son and the Spirit. The first of these, the Son, came to us as it were from the outside, drawing nearer and nearer ever since the fall until finally making himself one with us by the Incarnation. The Spirit, acting in parallel, has taken progressive possession of our whole being at its roots, gradually penetrating it with divine life and so over-coming in us all the powers of death. Irenaeus expressly affirmed that this saving history revealed God making it his glory to give man life with his own divine life. Conversely, man's life was seen to lie in the "knowledge of God," that knowledge communicated by God as he communicated himself.

But this, on the other hand, in no way meant that the Son or Spirit merely appeared in human history or in function of that cosmic devel-opment of which that history was the heart. On the contrary, the Son was one with the Father. He had been begotten by him in an ineffable way. He had the Father within him, just as he subsisted in the Father, and it was only because of this that he could make us know the Father with so living and intimate a knowledge. Even before creation, in fact, accord-ing to Genesis ("Let us make man in our image..."), the Son, and the Spirit also, existed with the Father. Thus, for Irenaeus, there was only one eternally existing God, the same in both Testaments (against the Gnostics, for whom the creator could be neither the supreme God nor the Savior), the Savior and the Sanctifier being one with him, the Creator, albeit eternally distinct.

Irenaeus himself went no further than this. He did not speculate beyond these simple and coherent assertions. They were enough for him to be able to refute Gnostic dualism. And at the same time they attest how the second-century Church, while taking the New Testament's affir-mations on the distinction of Father, Son and Spirit with the utmost seriousness, always interpreted them in the light of biblical monotheism.

The Apologists

The Apologist Fathers, for their part, tried to make this doctrine accessible to minds formed in the Greek mold. They attempted to explain it to them with the help of concepts which were already familiar to their audience.

This was based on the conviction—as Justin, the first of these fathers and a former philosopher, made quite clear—that, even before the Incarnation, the Word, the Logos was present in the world in a diffuse way. This presence could be verified in any man. It was more evident, however, in philosophers like Socrates and Heraclitus.[25] Yet, Justin also said, it was only by having borrowed from the Old Testament that the philosophers were able to speak of the Logos, and this knowledge remained fragmentary and incomplete until Christ's appearance. In him alone was the Logos fully present, the presence even in those who had spoken best of him being no more than partial.[26] There was here, certainly, an echo of the diffuse and ubiquitous Stoic *logos spermatikos*.

Justin, though, was insistent on the full and entire divinity of Christ.[27] He was, too, the first to draw the consequence from it not just, as Irenaeus had, that we are called to become sons in the Son, but that we are to be deified in him.[28]

On the other hand, for Justin, God only became Father when he created.[29] Until then, his Logos remained within him, indistinguishable from him. He only came forth from him and became Son for the purpose and as a result of creation. Hence, he was the intermediary between the transcendent Father and creation, so much so that in his distinct existence he was inferior to the Father and subordinate to him.[30]

It seems to have been the realization of how incompatible these latter affirmations were with the whole Bible, including the New Testament, that led Tatian, originally Justin's disciple, to reject his teaching and along with it any introduction of philosophical ideas into the exposition of the Christian faith.[31]

Theophilus of Antioch, however, went even further than Justin in assimilating the Word of the Bible and St. John to the logos of the Stoics. He set in opposition the Logos who was not distinct from the Father before creation, the *logos endiathetos*, and the Logos who, at the moment of creation, had come forth from him and become distinct: the *logos prophorikos*. Yet he was the first to speak of a triad apropos the Father,

---

[25] *Apol. I* 46.
[26] *Apol. I* 44 and *Apol. II* 10 and 13.
[27] *Dial. cum Tryphone* 48,108.
[28] *Dial.* 124.
[29] *Dial.* 12.
[30] *Dial.* 61.
[31] J. Quasten, *Patrology*, vol. 1, *The Beginnings of Patristic Literature*, pp. 220-221.

Son and Spirit.[32] He was the first, too, to see the Old Testament theophanies as manifestations of the Logos, beginning with man's interlocutor in paradise.

Yet only one of these Apologists expressly rejected any subordination of the Son to the Father with regard to creation, and that was Athenagoras.[33]

The Alexandrines: Clement and Origen

The first of the Alexandrines for our purposes was Clement. He identified Christ the Word with the Logos and therefore as the creative reason of the universe but above all as teacher and law-giver. For Clement, the whole of Christianity was *gnosis*, or at least led to it, to the knowledge of God. Christ for him therefore was first and foremost author of that faith which must lead us to *gnosis*. This *gnosis* was the opposite of that of the Gnostic heretics. It was not knowledge of a god mixed up with our own true nature, but knowledge of the Creator God who, in his Logos, had revealed and communicated himself to those who welcomed him with faith and sought to let this faith penetrate their whole life and being. He only mentioned the Spirit in passing, calling him the Father's mouth and the Son's strength.[34]

Origen's theology was vastly more elaborate. Knowledge retained its important role but as the knowledge of the Pauline mystery of Christ and his cross given us by a faith that has been meditated upon, and which allows us to enter into it with our whole life as well as our whole understanding.

What is more, for Origen, and this was something specifically biblical and Christian, creation was essentially a creation of free wills. But—and this was the Greek and especially Platonic side of this thought—all multiplicity or at least all diversity could only be an effect of the fall, of sin. At its beginning, the whole universe was simply a cosmos of created spirits, perfectly equal and all reflecting the unique divine thought or rather awareness: the eternal Logos. This Logos, through whom and in whom everything had been produced, had proceeded eternally from the Father as his Son, in the way that our deliberate willing proceeds from reason. He was therefore *homoousios* to the Father, a Son not by adoption but by nature (*ousia*).

---

[32] *Ad Autolycum* 2,10.
[33] *Apol.* 10,2,133.
[34] *Protrepticus* 9,82,1 and *Paedagogus* 2,2,19,4. See our *The Spirituality of the New Testament and the Fathers*, London, 1963, pp. 256ff.

Despite these clear assertions, Origen, like Philo, accorded the Son no more than derivative divinity, entitling him to the name *theos* but not *ho theos*. From this point of view he was merely a *deuteros theos*. Only the Father was God by himself, *autotheos*, and in this sense the only truly Good, *alethos agathos*, as Jesus said in the Gospel. The Son was merely the image of his goodness. The Spirit, *a fortiori*, was only an image of that image.

The Kingdom of this Son—who was eternally united, according to Origen, to a human soul, the only one not to have become detached from him, in contrast to the others who therefore fell into material bodies—must, through the Incarnation, eventually extend to the whole universe and so lead all souls back to God through their reunion with the Logos. Thereby the Kingdom of the Spirit would extend to all men. Then the Son himself would return the Kingdom to the Father, in the sense that all souls would be as perfectly united to the Logos as was the soul of the historical Jesus from all eternity. This was the *apocatastasis*, the final re-establishment.[35]

Origen, who could only conceive of creation as eternal, also admitted that there could be an unlimited succession of falls and restorations on this model.[36] Yet we must not forget that he proposed this extraordinary vision as a largely conjectural and wholly provisional attempt to interpret the Christian faith. But, though avoiding the more jejune infelicities of the Apologists, he was clearly out of harmony with the whole biblical tradition in confusing God's inner life with the making and vicissitudes of the world. Hence the Son, and even more the Spirit, were left in a paradoxical position. Although he explicitly called them, the Son especially, "divine" in the strongest sense of the word, he still reduced them to intermediate positions between God in his transcendence and the world, akin to the successive emanations of Middle and Neo-platonism. As regards the world, it seems that God, if he was to be a living God, had no option but to create it.

This means that even in the greatest of the ante-Nicene Christian thinkers who wanted to explicate and explain the Christian doctrine of God in terms taken from Hellenism, there was a hellenization of Christianity as irreconcilable with the New Testament as with the Old. This was the counterpart of the reverse phenomenon which was so marked in the progressive genesis of Neo-platonism, namely a reinterpretation of elements of Greek thought which, however rooted in its tradition, seemed

---

[35]*De Principiis* 1,2,4; 1,2,8; 1,2,9; 2,6,3; 2,6,5; 2,9,6; *Contra Celsum* 5,29 and 5,39. Cf. *In Joannem* 6,39 and 13,25.

[36]*De Principiis* 13,8. Cf. *In Matthaeum* 13,12.

to betray a growing influence of non-hellenistic factors, especially—as Numenius himself avowed—of biblical, Jewish and perhaps even Christian factors.

Hippolytus and Tertullian

The first tendency was so strong in the Christianity of this period that it can be observed even in those Christians who repulsed hellenist philosophy with horror. Hippolytus, for example, regarded contamination of biblical faith by Greek thought as the source of all heresies. This did not prevent him from regarding the Logos as certainly existing eternally in God but only as his immanent reason. He only became the Son by producing creation and his sonship was only perfected in the redemptive incarnation which, in turn, brought about Irenaeus' recapitulation understood by Hippolytus as an assimilation of everything created to the Logos, in the Son made flesh, that is the return of every existent to God's eternal idea for his creation.[37]

Tertullian who, as he himself said, rejected any compromise between Athens and Jerusalem, saw "the whole substance of divinity" as restricted to the Father, the Son being only a derivation from this, a portion of it as it were, although he was the first to speak of a trinity of persons in the unity of the divine substance.[38]

This shows the extraordinary power of suggestion wielded by hellenist philosophy, even upon those Christian thinkers most on guard against it. And this in its turn throws into greater relief the achievement of Neo-platonism and its climax in the person and work of Plotinus. St. Augustine did not hesitate to acknowledge this achievement. It would not perhaps be correct to regard Neo-platonism as an approach to the Christian God, since it never did and never could have envisaged the Incarnation. But it was not far from the God of the Bible.

Plotinus

Neo-platonists and Neo-pythagoreans, like Numenius, who sought a compromise between, or rather to inter-relate, God's transcendence and cosmic immanence, had come closer and closer to a triad of divine hypostases. Plotinus' *Enneads*, in which his disciple Porphyry collated his teaching, represented the climax of the process. Far above vicissitude and every kind of defined or definable being stood the One, the perfect Good. The *Nous* or Mind proceeded from him, and in it he conceived himself

---

[37] *Contra Noetum* 15 and *In Danielem* 4,11.
[38] *Adv. Prax.* 8 and 27,3.

and also every possible thing, but always within his own inviolable unity. The Soul or cosmic *Psyche* proceeded in its turn from the *Nous*. The *Psyche* continually contemplated the *Nous*, and also the manifold ideas enclosed within it. These latter it projected onto sense-perceptible matter, thereby giving it form and beauty.[39]

But to have said this is, frankly, to have said nothing. The first addition must be what Plotinus called the *epistrophe*. The word referred to the conversion of our souls, those particles of the great cosmic Soul in which, as in everything else, it was thought to project and express itself by its logos, its living word. By means of this conversion, our souls climb away from the reflections of the ideas in the sense-perceptible forms yielded by the cosmos, and back to their source, which is the Soul itself in the *Nous*. The *epistrophe*, therefore, takes our souls back to these pure ideas, these ideas which live forever in the unity of the divine Mind. But then it takes them even further, into the ineffable unity of pure divinity, that unutterable Goodness which drew irresistibly towards itself everything proceeding from it.

But to appreciate this properly we must again realize precisely what Plotinus meant. The totally transcendent One, for him, was no abstraction like Plato's Good. On the contrary, in Plotinus' own words, the One was "boiling with life." Similarly, his divine Mind was no cold contemplation of depersonalized, fleshless generalizations. The ideas were not just concrete individuals, as they were with Alexander of Aphrodisias, but individual consciousnesses, each, as Plotinus said, reflecting the others, communicating and integrating one with another within that transcendent thinking which thinks itself by thinking all of them. So, it was hardly surprising that the Soul, the principle of cosmic life, should have proceeded immediately from the *Nous*, nor that its life should have consisted in giving life even to the pure negativity of matter and in triumphing there, at the very root of evil which was non-being, over the very possibility of evil.

Anything that might, even in the smallest degree, turn away from the pure transcendent; anything that would affirm with *tolma*, stubbornness, its own distinctness, would thereby open itself to the growing possibility of evil, an opening which climaxed beyond the pale of the last divine hypostasis, to whom matter was only the limit. Conversion, on the other hand, took back the Soul itself and, through the Soul, the matter it informed by ideas, to the Mind which conceived these ideas, and, then,

---

[39]A. H. Armstrong, pp. 195ff. of *Cambridge History*, is the immediate source for this whole paragraph. See also Jean Trouillard, *La Procession plotinienne* and *La Purification plotinienne*, Paris, 1953.

in the latter's eternal return to the One, took everything back to its unassailable, plenary perfection.

For Plotinus, the One was the perfect Good, and we must never forget what this meant for conversion. Conversion could not be a simple activity of man's mind. Rather, the intellectual activity had to inspire an extremely rigorous moral purification, which in turn rebounded on the former. But there was more and better even than this in the Plotinian concept of conversion: a point underlined by Hilary Armstrong, the most sympathetic and penetrating analyst in recent times of what may be called "Plotinianism." It is not enough to say that this conversion laid hold of the whole man. Nor even to say that it required him to renounce himself, go beyond himself, and accept a quasi-loss of self in order to attain complete and perfect conformity to the Good and so debouch into the one, true life, an "ecstasy" into God in the most literal sense of the word. Plotinus expressly said more. He insisted that however well-intentioned, however enlightened our efforts might be, they can only serve to prepare us for this experience. We can only wait for the actual experience. It depends on the initiative of God, his free and sovereign goodness. He decides when and how.

All this can give us the impression of being on the brink of Christianity, or even into it. This last point, surely, brings us to what Christians call grace and to grace in its highest form.

We cannot deny that this aspect is really found in Plotinus, or that it was a capital element in his teaching. But we cannot forget other elements either, elements which cannot, it seems, be reconciled with what otherwise came so close to the Bible and even the Gospel. It is true that he defended the physical world against heretical Gnosticism. He proclaimed its essential goodness, a goodness reflecting that of God himself. But his concept of matter was, in fact, highly ambiguous. On the one hand, he seems to have regarded matter as completely subject to God, even non-existent apart from his intervention since it was nothing but the outer limit of his *ad extra* activity. But on the other, Plotinus' matter had an alien independence about it. It was, for him, the sole source of evil, every evil, even moral evil. Similarly, all divine activity which happened to escape from the transcendent unity, however fertile it might be in the fruits of God's goodness, was marked by a dangerous ambivalence. This seemed to suggest something uncertain in God himself, if not an actual flaw, at least an embryonic defect. And what was the ultimate reason for the conversion? Was it to cover over the crack? And did it involve a reabsorption of all distinct existence? Plotinus, it is true, has left us in no doubt that his God, especially the One, was not anything less than a person. Nor did he present this mystical return to God of everything proceeding from him as any kind of dissolution of our own personality into the divinity. Rather, it was a consummation in a full union with *the* person par excellence. And yet, on the other hand, he did end by saying: "Then man becomes God, or rather is God."

In any case, there was plenty in Plotinus moving him away from the orbit of Greek thought and towards that of biblical or Christian revelation. Surely the analogies between his treatment of the neo-platonic triad and the first, hesitant elaborations of Christian Trinitarianism among the ante-Nicene Fathers cannot all have been fortuitous. Why should the influences all have run one way? At the very least, one imagines that there might have been a common source.

Ammonius Saccas

Porphyry, Plotinus' biographer and editor, remarked that Plotinus and Origen, at Alexandria, had been contemporary pupils and remained faithful disciples of the same master, Ammonius Saccas. Porphyry further specified that Ammonius had at one time been a Christian, but did not persevere and reverted to philosophy. Eusebius' account agrees with this in substance, though not in detail.

We cannot possibly discuss here all the theories connected with these testimonies. There have been various attempts to reconcile them: suggestions that Porphyry confused a pagan and a Christian Origen or that there were two Ammoniuses, one Christian, the other not. All this seems rather forced. In our opinion, R. Cadiou in his detailed study, *La Jeunesse d'Origène*,[40] came to the right conclusion. There was only ever one Origen at Alexandria, the Church Father known by this name, and a Christian from birth. Similarly, there was only one Ammonius, the teacher of both Origen and Plotinus, and who was, or at least wished to be, both a Christian and a philosopher. Porphyry, the author of one of the most violent and also most poorly informed anti-Christian treatises, could not have acknowledged that the same man could have been both Christian and philosopher. Since Ammonius remained a philosopher, and was even recognized as such by the great Plotinus, he could not have remained a Christian! Only such a prejudice could have given weight to the hypothesis of Porphyry's apostate Ammonius or to that of another, purely pagan Ammonius, purportedly confused by Porphyry with the Christian one.

If this was the case it is easy to see how Plotinus would have treated his master's themes as purely philosophical and Greek while not realiz-

---

[40]René Cadiou, *La Jeunesse d'Origène*, Paris, 1963, pp. 169ff.

ing the Christian content given them by Ammonius. And even if Porphyry was right about Ammonius finally reneging on his Christianity,
this need not have prevented his retaining many Christian elements in
his philosophy, the imprint of which would have carried over into the
thought of his greatest disciple.

Whatever might be one's final judgment on this delicate problem of
the immediate sources behind Plotinus, there remains a definite fact
which, though thrown into special relief by this problem, goes beyond it.
This is that hellenistic philosophy became increasingly religious. Aside
from possible inspirations from Mazdean Persia or even India, it was
affected more or less consciously by other sources as well: either by the
Bible known, directly or indirectly, through the Septuagint; or by Alexandrine Hermetism which certainly was influenced by the Bible; or by
Jewish thinkers of whom Philo was the most conspicuous but (as he
himself affirmed) not the sole representative; or even from Christian
preaching.

This last, especially in Alexandria but elsewhere too in the third century, was beginning to spread widely. The reason why Neo-platonists
usually had only a second-hand knowledge of Christianity was
Porphyry's complete confounding of orthodox Christians and heretical
Gnostics. Plotinus' own treatise *Against the Gnostics* reveals that he
already shared the confusion.

There are, in the end, at least three points in the evolution of Neo-
platonism at which a Christian influence cannot reasonably be denied.
First of all, there is what we may call an increasingly personalist conception of the one and only God. This was very clear in Plotinus, despite the
remains of a contrary attitude. Then there is, not just the simple triadic
character given to God, but an increasing clarity vis-à-vis the two processions, one issuing finally in a *Nous* which has much in common with the
Bible's Word and Wisdom, the other resulting in a Soul which is
remarkably akin to the Spirit. But there is another point too which, more
than anything, reveals how transparently present the Christian faith was
behind the last developments of that current of thought which aimed at
nothing but total fidelity to religious Hellenism. This was the progressive
and quite novel attribution to the transcendent God of a fatherly quality,
not simply or primarily in the sense of a primogenitor of everything existent but rather as a source of divine life to which human creatures are
called to lift themselves thanks to what must certainly be called a divine
"grace." It seems, in fact, that the best contemporary studies of neo-
platonic origins, such as those of Langerbeck,[41] are now taking this line.

---

[41]H. Langerbeck, *Aufsätze zur Gnosis*, Göttingen, 1967.

St. Augustine might have been over-optimistic in claiming to find the essentials of Christian theology, apart from the Incarnation, in Plotinus. But he did, after all, pass from the one to the other, avidly and intelligently. Was he completely wrong?

XIV

The Theology of the
Fathers of the Church
Two approaches to the Trinity...or three?

At the beginning of the fourth century and coinciding with the pre-cipitant conversion of Constantine and his empire, the hellenizing deformation of the Christian doctrine on God suddenly went a stage further. This was the Arian crisis,[1] the second great crisis for Christian theology, the Gnostic heresy having been the first.

The Arian Crisis

Arias was a priest of Alexandria and, like his protectors, especially Eusebius of Nicomedia, the quintessential imperial bishop, and Eusebius of Caesarea, the most learned Christian of his time, was undoubtedly tributary to the most hellenized side of the theology of Origen and his apologists. But the immediate source of the heresy which he was the first to formulate lay in the teaching of the Antioch school, especially that of the martyr Lucian. It was from there that Arianism took the new habit of applying Aristotelian dialectic to theological distinctions and the use of dossiers of biblical and patristic quotations, both to become constants of the eventual Arian tradition.

The Logos was considered, in the Greek way, as the intermediary between God and the world, and since the Bible taught that the world had a beginning in time, Arius concluded that "there was a time when the Son was not." He was not therefore God in the strict sense.

In the next generation, the dialectician Eunomius of Cyzicus im-proved on this line of reasoning. He insisted on *agennesia* as a concept adequate for defining the Father's essence. Like most of his contempo-raries, he failed to distinguish the derivatives respectively of *gennao* (to beget) and *gignomai* (to become), and he concluded that God, who must exist necessarily and immutably from all eternity, could only be the

---

[1]For more details on this crisis, cf. *The Eternal Son*, pp. 316ff.

Father. The Son, being begotten, had therefore "become," was therefore mutable, and so could not be divine.

The final stage was reached with the *Anomeanism* of Aetius or Acacius. This affirmed that the Son was not even like (*homoios*) the Father at this crucial point.

The faithful had been spontaneously scandalized by all this, ever since Arius had first given vent to his ideas. It was not simply a case of their registering an intolerable diminishment of the role and person of the Son as presented by the New Testament. What they sensed was neo-paganism: a polytheism in which the one divinity was degrading itself by reproduction and, as Athanasius would see and say, a failure to understand that God could have his life in himself, independently of the existence or non-existence of the world.

Whether it was Athanasius or someone else, such as Hosius of Cordova, who first proposed to the Council of Nicea the formula *homoousios*, the means for characterizing the Son as one who shared the essence proper to the Father, is not of moment. In any case, it was Athanasius who perseveringly and eventually victoriously defended the Council of Nicea. In rejecting this diminishment of the Son which Christians found so unacceptable, Athanasius was rejecting the return to paganism implied in a progressively descending theogony, complemented by a cosmogony without which, according to Arius and the Arians, God would not have been the living God.

Athanasius and the Cappadocians

Athanasius opposed Arianism with the most profoundly traditional of Christian themes: that of a God who, by grace, has wished to make us his true sons. This presupposes that he who has communicated to us this literally divinizing filiation is himself the Son of God in the full sense of the phrase: from all eternity and by communication of the very essence of the Father.

Athanasius also stressed the converse implication of this: even if God had never created anything, he would always have had a Son like himself and, as he would later show against the Macedonians, a Spirit of life. Because God possessed life in himself, because this life was sufficient in itself, he has been able to offer us the free and generous participation in it that he has.

In other words, we have now arrived at the first, fully explicit affirmation of a transcendent and eternal Trinity, existing in complete independence of created existences and constituting, in and by itself, the life proper to God. It is this, too, which not only makes him a potential source for other beings, but also constitutes the root, as it were, of their potential elevation (at least in the case of free and intelligent creatures) to a gratuitous participation in the life proper to God. So it is that his grace can truly "divinize" us in the Son and through the Spirit without there ceasing to be only one, unique God.

All this seems to have been immediately evident to Athanasius. Yet no doubt he needed time and mature reflection on the various difficulties raised in order to arrive at certain final capital precisions.

In the field of theology in the strict sense, i.e., the doctrine concerning God himself, Athanasius was led on by the need to distinguish his cause and that of the Nicene faith from that of Marcellus of Ancyra who regarded the Son and Spirit simply as successive, temporary modalities in the existence of the divine essence, appearing or disappearing in function of creation and its salvation. Athanasius, therefore, had to complete the formula "one single essence," common to Father and Son (and therefore Spirit), by another, suggested by the three Cappadocians, Basil of Caesarea, his friend Gregory Nazianzen, and his brother Gregory of Nyssa: "in three really and eternally distinct hypostases."

The explicit consequence of this, both for Athanasius and for the Cappadocians (who also seem not to have drawn it immediately) was that the word *homoousios*, "of the essence," applying to the Son and then to the Spirit in relation to the Father, referred no longer to the common possession of the same essence considered merely abstractly but to their undivided possession of a single, concrete essence. Further consequences followed, quickly seen by the Cappadocians but apparently never gauged by Athanasius.

The first and most important was that all divine actions *ad extra*, to use the later phrase, were necessarily common to the three persons. Otherwise, the diversity of operations would give the appearance of introducing a disastrous division into the divine essence and so make us fall back into a kind of tritheism. But, as we shall see, this principle still admitted of a variety of interpretations when applied to the relationships between God, his divine life, his personal life and creation.

Later still, this necessary undividedness of the divine essence, possessed as it is without partition by the three persons, led with irresistible logic to the axiom that the three persons, who are really distinct from one another, are each only logically so from the divine essence. This was a paradoxical formula and proved extremely difficult to interpret exactly.

The *homoousios*, understood as we have explained, had another final consequence which was equally problematic. The divine persons can only be distinct one from another by virtue of the opposition of their reciprocal relationships. Everything else must be absolutely common to all, but the persons can only be what they are in those relationships which define them, so much so that they could eventually be described paradoxically as "subsistent relations."

But, before tackling the difficulties of interpretation raised by these theological developments started in the fourth century, we must underline one consequence of this embryonic theology which was very different from and even corrective of those we have already mentioned. It appeared in full light in the controversy, most notably that of Basil and Gregory of Nyssa, with the rationalism and especially the conceptualism of Eunomius. But it was already there in Athanasius. It was that our application to the Godhead of concepts drawn from our reflections on the created world necessarily involved a corresponding ignorance. This meant, to use a term which came into play at the time of the Eunomian controversy, that all theology which was not deluded as to its real powers was inevitably "apophatic."

The Kataphatic and Apophatic

All the concepts used by us to speak of God, those concepts which are the spontaneous issue of our minds, only strictly apply to creatures. Our application of them to God, however, is not baseless, because there is a certain analogy between the Creator and his creatures. Yet this analogy, as St. Thomas would later underline in one of the most inspired of his treatises, *De Veritate,* is not direct, as that between a father and son, but indirect: a simple analogy of proportionality which enables us not directly to compare two beings but simply the relationships between them and the activities by which they respectively reveal themselves.

St. Athanasius was the first to move towards this notion. He did so in reaction to Arian rationalism and especially to Eunomius' claim to enclose God in a concept regarded as so adequate that it was possible to deduce all the divine properties from it. Athanasius insisted on the scriptural teaching that such treatment of God is simply not possible. Scripture, in fact, deliberately juxtaposes concepts concerning God or rather images, which cannot in their literal meaning be reconciled.[2] These expressions mutually correct one another according to the analogy of faith. Only this analogy of faith enables us, albeit always hesitantly, to apply this fundamental analogy of being and to do so in the direction indicated by revelation. Without it, the mere analogy of being would never allow us to lift our knowledge of God above his work of creation. We would never have been able to arrive at the inner life of God, even in

---

[2] *I Contra Arianos,* 28.

thought, but for God having opened it to us by his Word so as to introduce us into and associate us with it. Such a perspective has meaning only for the believer and not the proud reasoner living in a world of pure abstraction. It is in this perspective that the same being can be at one and the same time God's Son, and therefore a person distinct from him and subsisting in himself, and yet God's Word, and therefore inseparable from God's nature of which he is simply the expression.

Both Basil and Gregory of Nyssa went further, the latter with the greater precision. They did not hesitate to state that everything affirmed of God by transposing some concept necessarily taken from creatures (*kataphasis*) had to be so transfigured in the process that it had to be denied at the very moment it was affirmed, nothing being able to be taken from this world and simply applied to God (*apophasis*).

This was something needing to be done not just once but over and over again, in accordance with a view of God first sketched by Origen and then developed particularly by Gregory. Every time we have arrived at an affirmation concerning God, we must immediately pass on beyond it. We can only know the infinite God by this continual going-beyond. This was, as it were, the translation into dialectic of Moses' vision, commented on by Gregory in his mystical treatise *The Life of Moses*, apparently in the wake of a famous sermon by Gregory Nazianzen.[3] Following Philo, they borrowed from Exodus the idea of a vision "from behind," a vision of God as he "passes" amid his creation, taking us in his train and snatching us away from everything created.[4] After what we said earlier of the biblical vision of God, there is no need to insist how biblical such an idea was, however much the thought of the Cappadocians might have been impregnated with hellenistic notions.

Pseudo-Denys systematized this conception of the knowledge of God by designating it, at its least unsatisfactory, as what he called a helicoidal movement.[5] Progress could only lie in an unceasing alternation of affirmations and negations, going perpetually beyond and above one another.

The Two Configurations of the Trinity: The "Greek" and the "Latin"

If St. Athanasius' remark on the inevitable duality of any attempt to express God in his interior life is taken seriously, we need not be sur-

---

[3]See the summary given by V. Lossky, *The Mystical Theology of the Eastern Church*, pp. 34ff.

[4]Cf. Gregory of Nyssa, *The Life of Moses*, and *Discourse 22* of Gregory Nazianzen, PG 36, especially col. 29, with our commentary in *The Spirituality of the New Testament and the Fathers*, London, 1982, pp. 362ff.

[5]*De divinis nominibus* 4,9; PG 3, col. 705A.

prised to find not one but two theologies, or two types of theology, of the Trinity slowly taking shape in the patristic period. Neither can be reduced to the other. One started from the distinction of persons, the other from the unity of essence. They should be regarded as complementary rather than contradictory, even though neither of them in the end can avoid running into insuperable intellectual difficulties.

At the end of the last century,[6] Fr. Théodore de Régnon, SJ, distinguished and delineated these two theologies with considerable finesse. He called one the Greek theology, the other the Latin theology. But he was the first to be conscious of how much he was inevitably simplifying, first in the descriptions he gave of each of them and then, even more, in the wholesale attributing of the one to Greek tradition and the other to the Latin.

We shall, nonetheless, begin by reproducing his two outlines. They do shed considerable light, even while leaving some things unexplained.

The so-called Greek theology, which he recognized as belonging also to that of the earliest Latin Fathers, began from the persons, as he correctly observed, and only considered nature in dependence upon them and as that which they have.[7] Conversely, the Latin theology, which would better be called Augustinian-Thomist, was not unechoed in the East, to put it mildly, first and foremost by St. Gregory Nazianzen,[8] and even up to the time of St. Gregory Palamas, even if these authors did not enter into all the details of the Augustinian legacy known to the Latin West. It was essentially marked by the fact of beginning with the one divine nature and, on that basis, seeking to reconnect with the persons.[9]

To have apprehended this original opposition will have sufficed to make us realize why the first theology had a greater facility in preserving the concrete, living character of scriptural teaching. On the other hand, its constant temptation was a more or less thinly-veiled tritheism. The second theology had none of the latter difficulty, but it was forever giving the impression of diluting almost to disappearing point the clear, biblical affirmations on the distinction of Father, Son and Spirit. Further, it would tend even more to evaporate almost completely the New Testament presentation of the specific relations with these persons into which we have been brought by the divine grace of adoption.

---

[6]Théodore de Régnon, *Etudes de Théologie positive sur le Dogme de la Trinité*, 4 vols., Paris, 1892-1898.

[7]*Op. cit.*, vol. 1, Etude VI, pp. 335ff.

[8]*Op. cit.*, vol. 1, p. 401, with the texts he quotes from St. Gregory Nazianzen, especially *Discourse 31*, PG 36, col. 144.

[9]*Op. cit.*, vol. 1, pp. 302ff.

Régnon produced two eloquent images of what he called the Greek and Latin theologies. In Greek theology, he said, the three persons appear to follow a straight line, of which the Father is the beginning, the Son the middle and the Holy Spirit the end.[10] On this view, one can see how easily the terminus of the Trinity could also be its point of contact with creation. From the natural perspective of creation, the divine action at the source of its being would inevitably appear to be one, the straight line looking like a point when viewed from its end. But, from the perspective of God, if one may so speak, this creative activity, while common to the three persons, would be radically diversified, each person being involved in a specific way. The Father is the origin of our creation as of the divine life. But he created us *through* the Son, and *in* the Spirit, following the pattern of his own transcendent existence.

Similarly, our adoption—owed to that communication of God's own life which is grace in the fullest sense of the word—while remaining a work common to the three, introduces us into a consciously differentiated relationship with each of these three. The Spirit comes to us as the perfection of the holiness of that love which is the eternal life of God. We are, as it were, transported with him into the Son and, assimilated to the latter's sonship, are finally referred to the Father, through the Son, in the Spirit, just as the Son himself is eternally.

We may say in parentheses that we should not be surprised at sometimes seeing these prepositions, "through" and "in," used in inverse order from that which we have just used and which has been the more common, at least since St. Paul. Our own explanation has brought out how the very fact that the grace of adoption assimilates us to the Son, makes it possible to speak of living *in* him. And, in the same context, one can then say that the Spirit lives *in* us or again that it is *through* the gift made to us of him that we live *in* Christ. These changes of expression, which result from the different angles of vision adopted, only serve to underline how the necessary complementarity of our expressions about these mysterious realities, pointed out by Athanasius, apply to details as well as to the whole.

To return to Père de Régnon: in what he called the Greek schema, grace was certainly distinguished, as such, from created nature, but it also appeared as a kind of final deployment of that divine action which had brought us to be, and to be as image of God, and which now completed the assimilation of this life "in the image" to its model and source.

In the Latin view, on the other hand, the three persons appeared rather as the three summits of a triangle representing the one divine

[10]*Op. cit.*, vol. 1, p. 539.

nature.[11] There could be no difficulty in envisaging the unity and even the unicity of the divine substance subsisting in the three persons, since these corresponded to complementary aspects, imposed upon the latter, as it were, and embracing one another. On the other hand, it was not so clear how they could be really distinct rather than complementary modalities affecting the single essence.

Similarly, it was the whole divine triangle which, undivided and even indistinguished, came into relation with creation. But the consequence was that, from the point of view of the Creator as well as of the creature, the relationship of the latter to the former was completely undifferentiated as to the persons. Things being so, not even the grace of adoption could alter them. Both supernatural grace and the creation of nature relate us, strictly speaking, not to the divine persons in their specificity but to the divine and indistinguished essence. All that one can say is that since the oppositions of relation which constitute the persons are not really distinct from this essence, our participation by grace in the divine nature enables us to attain to the life of the Trinity as such.

But this does not establish us in any particular relationship with one or other of the persons as distinct from any other. In such a situation, our adoptive sonship, as St. Thomas said replying to an objection,[12] makes us strictly "filii totius Trinitatis" and not sons *of the Father*, something which only the eternal Son is. Some of those who claim today, and have done since the sixteenth century, to be his most logical successors have gone even further and said straight out that our relationship in grace is not properly speaking with the three divine persons as such, but simply with their common divine essence.

This, of course, conflicted so brutally with scripture, the earliest Fathers and the liturgy, that it inevitably provoked objections. One way out was by recourse to the idea of appropriations, already developed by St. Augustine.[13] This rests on the hypothesis that, in creation, there are as it were "vestiges" of the Trinity which can only be recognized as such after its revelation in the Gospel. So it is that the creative power, although common in God to the three persons, is especially evocative of the Father, the intelligible order ruling over creation of the Son, his Word and Image, and similarly the life animating it of the Spirit.

---

[11] *Op. cit.*, vol. 1, p. 311.

[12] *Summa Theologica*, Tertia Pars, q.23, art.3.

[13] This whole question of the images of the Trinity within creation has been brilliantly reviewed by Olivier du Roy in *L'Intelligence de la Foi en la Trinité selon saint Augustin*, Paris, 1966, especially pp. 209ff.

St. Augustine claimed to discover three still closer analogies within the structure of the human soul: either in the memory (i.e., consciousness envisaged in its unity and permanence), the intelligence and the will, or, better still, in what he called *mens, notitia, amor*: the mind conceiving thought, the thought itself which is immanent to the mind, and the pleasure with which the mind rests in it. Thus Augustine and, after him, the Latin Middle Ages, said that the first divine procession, that of the Son, was *per modum intelligentiae*, and the second, that of the Spirit, *per modum amoris.*[14]

In such conditions, the special assimilation to the divine life owed to sanctifying grace could be understood as being, in a certain sense, an assimilation to the divine processions. We are given a certain participation in the knowledge God has of himself, a knowledge wholly imbued with his own love.

It cannot be denied that these speculations have some foundation in the biblical and patristic conception of the Son as Word of Wisdom and of the Holy Spirit, in Paul's phrase, as spreading God's own love in our hearts. But the systematic elaboration seems to go far beyond all this.

What is still more serious is that it is hard to see how for all its daring this extrapolation of our mental operations to God allows for any application of the word "person" either to their term or to their beginning. Rather, in this Latin view of the Trinity, especially when it followed Augustine's favorite image, it was the divine nature or essence which appeared to correspond at the uncreated level to our created persons.

Difficulties in the "Latin" Theory and Possible Ways Out

St. Augustine himself, perhaps not fully consciously, seems to have said the harshest things that could be said about the eventual impasse of this Latin theology. At the end of his attempted explanations he had the honesty to admit that we only talk of three "persons" in God for want of a better term to designate these three "quid" which revelation constrains us to recognize in him despite his unbreakable unity.[15] After that, we cannot be surprised if Cajetan who, after all, was the Renaissance Thomist most faithful to St. Thomas, went so far as to say that there must be a single subsistence as subject of the single essence, which he called absolute with regard to the relative subsistences of the three. But once we have come to that point we have surely implicitly ceased to recognize anything in the divine "persons" actually corresponding to that word.

---

[14]*Ibid.*, pp. 436ff.
[15]See the conclusion of *De Trinitate.*

We are left, in other words, with nothing that could be called a subject, a real suppositum for spiritual activity.

It is even less surprising to find that such systems find it extremely difficult to give any effective meaning to the teaching of Scripture and Tradition on the distinct relationships established by Christian adoption between ourselves and each of the divine persons.

It must be said nonetheless that St. Augustine cannot be held responsible for all these disastrous consequences, which were due to an excessively unilateral systematizing of certain suggestions in *De Trinitate*. Above all, he was very far from proposing the analogy of the Word to the intellect or of the Spirit to the will or love as the key for understanding the Trinitarian distinctions. He only suggested it as a particularly enlightening image. But the fact remains that by their rigorous treatment of these images, which they wanted to change into concepts of almost Eunomian exhaustiveness, the Scholastics did bring the difficulty into the harsh light of day. How can the transition be made from the consideration of an intellect or love, necessarily common to the three persons, to a distinction between them admitting of being called real? It is even possible to ask quite seriously how a simple notional distinction can be deduced!

The Trinitarian theory, generally ascribed to Richard of Saint-Victor but now recognized as due to his master Achard,[16] seems to have been provoked by the desire to surmount this difficulty, while retaining the helpful psychological analogy. According to it, the Father is the Lover, the Son the Beloved and the Spirit the real personification of their Love in its reciprocity. We will return later to this new vision, even though, as we shall see, it is not unproblematic. At this stage, we must simply acknowledge that to begin from the divine essence, to consider it anteriorly to their persons and as in some sense their source, however this may be done, is to make it practically impossible to account for their distinction without a latent modalism and, even more, to give a meaning to any kind of differentiated relationship between them and us which is anything more than an empty formula.

But if, as we saw earlier when discussing the cosmological proofs of God's existence, E. Gilson was certainly right in maintaining how fundamental it is in the Thomist view of God's being, to regard it as that (not simply) of an immutable essence (which was the Platonizing approach of St. Augustine) but of the one pure existent, whose essence it precisely

---

[16]On Richard and Achard, see Jean Ribailler's edition of Richard's *De Trinitate*, Paris, 1958, and Jean Chatillon, *Théologie et Spiritualité dans l'Oeuvre oratoire d'Achard de Saint-Victor*, Paris, 1969.

was to exist in total actuality and unrivaled fullness, then everything must take on a different aspect at least in the Thomist interpretation of the Latin view.

The True Thomist Doctrine of the Trinity

This presentiment is verified on approaching the Thomist theology of the Trinity by way of the *Commentary on the Sentences*. Surprisingly the *Summa Theologiae* did not develop all its apparent possibilities and even gives some evidence of a regression, such as the formula mentioned earlier which refers our sonship not *ad Patrem* but to the whole Trinity in its undivided essence.[17]

But besides this text and others more or less like it, there are in any case three points in the *Summa* itself where the persons are quite definitely given priority.

In the first place, it is quite remarkable that St. Thomas formally rejected the idea that Jesus, in his humanity, could be called an adopted Son, although Son by nature in his divinity.[18] The reason he gives is of the greatest interest, because, if taken seriously, it obviously does not apply simply to Jesus. In fact, he says, sonship, although normally linked to the nature, is not a relation which terminates in the nature as such but in the person and, of course, one cannot allow in Jesus any other person than that of the divine person of the Son incarnate in our humanity.

This first assertion, be it noted, supposes that there are in the Trinity, not personal relations which emerge in some vague way from the common nature, but true relationships between persons who possess in common the same concrete nature.

This assertion is completed by another directly concerned with our own grace of adoption. This latter, according to the formal declarations of St. Thomas, has as its exemplar the proper and eternal divine sonship of Jesus.[19] Need we underline how opposed these two assertions are, even taken separately and *a fortiori* when taken together, to the idea that we are adopted sons, not strictly speaking *of the Father*, but of the whole Trinity, meaning, according to some hardy modern "Thomists," of the single essence common to the three persons?

Thirdly, even if the *Summa* is less rich in doctrinal detail than the *Commentary on the Sentences* on the different missions from the Father of the two other persons and on the consequences of this for us, it clearly

---

[17]On this point, see Dom Lucien Chambat, *Présence et Union*, Paris, 1944.

[18]*Summa Theologica*, Tertia Pars, q.23, art.4.

[19]*Ibid.*, q.3, art.5, ad 2; q.23, art.l, ad 2; q.39, art.8, ad 3; q.45, art.4. See Emile Mersch's commentary on these texts in *The Theology of the Mystical Body*, St. Louis, 1951, pp. 353ff.

maintained the essentials. On the one hand, the Father alone sends the Son into the world; on the other, the Father through the Son sends the Spirit. Besides, for a divine person "proceeding" and "being sent" are necessarily the same thing, according to St. Thomas. Hence the Son's historical incarnation has its principle in his eternal procession; and, likewise, the gift made us of the Spirit not only must be recognized as entirely and exclusively proper to himself, but is rooted, so to speak, in his eternal subsistence, in the bosom of the Father, resting on the Son as the substantial gift which he is in the Trinity.[20]

Fr. Leroy, OP, has recently shown with the utmost clarity that one must even say, if one is going to take the principles of Thomist triadology and Christology with full seriousness, that the eternal Son is not the term of the subsistence of Jesus' humanity because of the grace of union, itself purportedly resulting from the exceptional intensity of sanctifying grace. Quite the contrary. It is because Jesus' humanity belongs properly only to the Son, in the name of that eternal generation from which the predestination of this humanity cannot be separated, that the grace of union is able to adapt the humanity to subsistence in a transcendent subject flooding it with an unequaled fullness of graces.[21]

On the same line, it seems to us out of place to ask how sanctifying grace can raise us to the level of that uncreated grace which is the gift of the Spirit. Posed in such terms, the problem does not admit of any solution. But, following the logic of St. Thomas' thought, it is more appropriate to say that it is because the wholly divine "gift" which is the eternal procession of the Spirit makes him proceed from the Father in the Son while embracing us therein in some manner, according to our eternal predestination in the Son himself, that created grace comes to adapt all our powers to that life in the Son and *ad Patrem* given to us. It is only in this way that one can conceive the Son, and only the Son, as personally incarnate, with no loss to his divinity and no annihilating absorption of his humanity. Similarly, our own humanity can be sanctified and divinized, in God's Holy Spirit, without detriment to the unity and unbreakable community of God's actions *ad extra*, and without our persons being absorbed into the person of the Spirit, just as the Son is not

---

[20]Prima Pars, the whole of q.43. Cf. *Com. in lib. I Sent.*, especially dist. III, XIV, XV, XVI, XVII and XVIII.

[21]M. V. Leroy, "L'union selon l'Hypostase selon saint Thomas d'Aquin," in *Revue Thomiste*, Apr-June, 1974, pp. 205ff.

absorbed by virtue of the recapitulation of the whole Trinity, in the Spirit, towards the Father.[22]

The Problem of Appropriations

Yet this should warn us that the "appropriations" of which St. Thomas speaks concerning the persons of the Trinity (unfortunately without expressly going beyond the distinctions found in St. Augustine) need to be carefully cataloged, according to the different ways he uses the expression. Otherwise, his Trinitarianism, even his Christology, not to speak of his doctrine of grace in its uncreated aspect would be reduced to pure *flatus vocis*.

In the first place, of course, there are certain appropriations which, though not wholly devoid of meaning, must not be taken literally, since they distribute the divine attributes among the three persons: creative power to the Father, as the origin of the Trinity itself and therefore of every existent; the ordering of the world to the Son since he, by virtue of his begetting, is the exemplar of every existent; the perfecting of creation to the Holy Spirit, he being the one in whom the Trinity completes and perfects itself.

At the other extreme lies that appropriation shown by Dom Diepen[23] to be the best term applicable, in strict Thomistic thought, to the humanity of Christ vis-à-vis his divine person. It implies a wholly real, direct and exclusive possession.

Between these two, we must situate everything which, in the traditional language and as required by our supernatural adoption, attempts to express our living relation to the Father, the Son and the Spirit, and we must renounce any hope of providing any satisfying definition of these things in Thomist categories. Modern Thomists have, of course, had a field day here. P. Galtier[24] emphasized with intense passion that we cannot speak of a presence within us exclusively proper to the Spirit. Circumincession, i.e., the mutual presence by which the three persons, following the triangle image, are not simply in one another but inseparable from one another even to thought, very definitely excludes any such notion. On the point, it has proved easy to use impeccable syllogisms to refute Petau, Scheeben, even Théodore de Régnon himself, all of whom

---

[22]On this whole question of the Holy Spirit and sanctifying grace, we are much indebted to Fr. Guy de Broglie, SJ, *De Gratia*, unfortunately only available in the duplicated notes of his course at the Institut Catholique, Paris.

[23]Dom H. Diepen, *La Théologie de l'Emmanuel*, Paris, 1960.

[24]P. Galtier, *L'Habitation en nous des trois Personnes divines*, Paris, 1941.

tried to translate the affirmations of the Greek Fathers on the specific nature of the gift of the Spirit into this idea of a special presence.

A fortiori, there can be no question of attributing different efficient causalities, in our salvation and supernatural life, to different persons of the Trinity. This has been established less ferociously but quite as logically by T. W. Sabrey in a remarkable thesis.[25] He even went on to maintain that one must say the same as regards exemplary causality. On this point, however, there is no doubt that both the *Commentary on the Sentences* and the *Summa* itself take a different line.

But what exactly does all this prove? Simply that the notion of causality, as elucidated by Aristotle, and especially his notion of efficient causality, cannot be strictly applied to the relationship established between us and that supremely personal being God. As will be recalled, examination of the cosmological proofs of God's existence compelled us, at the simple level of creation, to the same conclusion. It is no surprise that the same should happen, and even more notably, when seeking to express our gratuitous connection with the life proper to God.

But this does not allow us to reject as ultimately unserious rhetorical formulae the many biblical expressions describing the divine persons in their various relationships with us, and especially the gift made us of the Spirit, closely linked with our adoption by the Father in the Son. The conclusion one can draw is that recourse must be had to another image of the Trinity, to another perspective on the revelation made us of that intimate divine life with which God has willed to associate us. This is necessary to do full justice to the clearest and most decisive expressions of revelation. To fail to do this, as we have already said elsewhere, is not simply to empty our elevation to the supernatural life of its reality, but given the links between the two in revelation and the whole of the history of dogma, to deprive us of our very reasons for believing in the Trinity. Here what Father de Régnon called "the Greek theory" has something to offer.

Benefits and Drawbacks of the "Greek Theory"

We cannot then begin by first considering God in his undifferentiated essence, within which the persons are (at least logically) secondly to be distinguished. God subsists, exists as the pure existent only in the persons, who are distinguished one from another and from the single

---

[25]T. W. Sabrey, *The Person and Work of the Holy Spirit According to the Theories of Denys Petau, Théodore de Régnon and Matthias J. Scheeben*, (duplicated) thesis of the Catholic University of America, Washington, DC, 1952.

228 / The Invisible Father

essence only by their distinct, mutually related ways of possessing it in common. And if this is so, then everything takes on a different perspective, both in the immanent Trinity, the Trinity as it is in itself, and in the economic Trinity, the Trinity as revealed among us drawing us into the dynamism of its life.

If everything in God, and *a fortiori* everything outside him, proceeds from the Father through the Son in the Spirit and returns to him in the same way, then instead of a simple presence of static coinherence, such as evoked by the "Latin" circumincession we have the eternal pulse-beats of divine life. Such is the precise implication of the Greek *"perichoresis"*: each person existing only in his tendency towards the others according to the mode of existence proper to him (*tropos uparxeos*). This is tantamount to saying that God exists and only exists in the permanent interchange of the Trinitarian relationships. If this be so, God, of course, will not act *ad extra* other than in the way he is eternally. Everything will be created from the Father through the mediation of the Son and, as it were, within the procession of the Spirit who, with the Son, recapitulates the whole Trinity within the Father. Correspondingly, our participation in the divine life will only be conceivable as a consciously received giving of him, the Spirit, who is the mutual, substantial, personal Gift in whom the Son yields himself eternally to the Father as the Father communicates himself to the Son.

This possession of the Spirit—far more his possession of us than ours of him, for in giving himself to us he gives us the gift of giving ourselves—this possession is the first and last word of the divine life, and it assimilates us gratuitously to the Word's eternal sonship. Thus, through, with and in the Son, we are referred to the Father, the Spirit resting on us as he rests on the Son, in the very act by which the Father has freely and eternally willed to engender us as members of the Son's body, animated wholly by this Spirit, as he, the Father, engenders the Son and produces the Spirit.

It is clear that in all of this the inseparable Trinity is at work, and, in one sense, no less as exemplary and final cause than as efficient cause of our salvation and eternal life (so far, once again, as these expressions have any meaning at this level). But it would surely be better to say that this kind of causal relationship, already outstripped by creation, is at this level, wholly transcended and lost to view in the paradoxical combination of a total dependence, of which efficient causality can only give a wholly inadequate idea, and a conjunction which no less outpaces any notion of finality. And this is the whole paradox of grace.

As for the exemplarism involved, this can only be conceived—indeed must be here more than anywhere else—in the sense of an analogy of proportionality between our life thus supernaturalized and the life natural only to God. There can be no question of establishing a static analogy between directly comparable essences, thus making each of us participating images of the whole Trinity—a "development" of Augustinian thought that could have made Augustine more than anyone turn in his grave. Rather, we have here an essentially dynamic, existential analogy between the current of life, communicated in a conscious love uniting us to each other (as so many broken pieces gathered together and conjoined in the one divine image, Christ, the Son of God made man), and the current of divine life, of the knowledge of love which is the *perichoresis* in God himself descending eternally from the Father, through the Son, in the Spirit, and eternally reascending, by the same path in reverse, to its inexhaustible source.

However, having come so far, we have to admit that the principal difficulty remains unresolved. In this view, the three persons are considered anteriorly, with at least a logical anteriority, to their common essence. How, though, can we maintain in an intelligible fashion that God is one before he is three, that he is not three Gods who are one thanks merely to a perfect mutual openness, but one, sole God in the three persons? This is perhaps the only irreducible difficulty about the "Greek theory," but once that theory has been entered into it yields no apparent way out of the problem.

More than that—and St. Gregory Nazianzen is a good example here— once one begins from the vision of three equal, coeternal, inseparable persons, one can only, however much one may do, avoid falling into an inevitable tritheism by having at the back of one's mind a prior vision of a single essence in which the persons are *a priori* encapsulated, as it were. Thus, even those who opt for the so-called "Greek" Trinitarian scheme are bound sooner or later to fall back into the "Latin" one, and so once again run up against its insurmountable difficulties.

As St. Gregory Nazianzen said, Christianity must avoid both the judaizing heresy of the modalists and any kind of pagan tritheism. Yet it seems that to do this either point of view is eventually compelled to invoke the help of the other, otherwise it will end with the very difficulties it began by seeking to avoid. We are faced with an alternative or, rather, with a dilemma. Is there any issue?

In fact, there *is* a *tertium quid*. The sagacious Father de Régnon was not unaware of it, although not knowing how to exploit its possibilities.[26] Not that there is anything surprising in that: this third way, which is neither Greek nor Latin, nor narrowly Jewish, is not, nor can it become, a

---

[26]*Op. cit.*, vol. 1, pp. 444ff. and 493ff.

speculative way. Our logic is necessarily unilinear, and this way escapes it.

A Third View of the Trinity: Biblical and Eucharistic

The very thread of revelation should lead us to this view. Faith praying and faith adoring recall us to it continually, for it is the only one which takes us straight to that contemplation in which, in the end, all our most brilliant theories must lose themselves: when we plunge into what Pseudo-Denys called the "darkness of unknowing," which, as we must make clear, is the same as that "inaccessible light" where, according to scripture, God dwells, but to which he wishes to lead us.

One text in particular of St. Basil can tell us in what this way consists, and shows us its inevitability despite the common resistance to it by both Greek and Latin systematizations.[27] This text is especially revealing, coming as it does from a Greek thinker who combines, in an exceptional fashion, full hellenic subtlety with an acute ecumenical awareness, while knowing, as few other theologians of the Trinity, how to guard against all speculative excess, all "hubris." He had arrived at what we can call the classical Trinity of the theologians: three completely equal, coeternal persons, inseparable from one another and each even inconceivable without the others. And then he found himself up against an insoluble difficulty, the very same one we have met following either of the theories, the strong and weak points of which we have been discussing. If the Trinity is as described, we cannot then conceive any order among the persons: not just temporal order, which we would not expect, but logical order also. There is no one, rather than any other, who would be first, second or third. Yet in fact biblical revelation does emphatically disclose an order: the Father is always first, the Son second, the Spirit third.

Even this is not to say enough. True as it is that the same revelation leads us inevitably to affirm a single divinity, possessed equally by and not distributed among the three persons, it is no less clear that there is not only an order of persons but a real "monarchy": the Father is and remains the sole principle (*arche*) of everything, within God as well as outside him. The Greeks would even go so far as to say that he is the sole first "cause" (*aitios*). Basil admitted that he did not know how to incorporate this into the Greek theory, that he could not even see how to reconcile the two data. The Latin theory, where the persons go back, so to speak, into the single essence, would appear to be even more incompatible with this biblical and traditional datum.

---

[27]*De Spiritu Sancto* 44 and 45.

Throughout the New Testament, God, *ho theos*, does not designate the Trinity, even less one or other of the three persons indifferently, but always and only the Father. Théodore de Régnon had already noticed this. Karl Rahner has had the merit of forcing modern Catholic theologians to become aware of it, after having read and recognized as unanswerable the article *ho theos* of the *Theologisches Wörterbuch*[28] of the New Testament. His own surprise, which he did not conceal, speaks volumes on theology's drift vis-à-vis revelation. But the same usage is to be found in all the traditional liturgies, and above all in the Roman Liturgy, when not obscured by the medievals or moderns, and found especially in what is the heart of every liturgy: the great eucharistic prayer and, here once again, most prominently in the Roman Canon.

We must of course hasten to add that this does not prevent both biblical and liturgical texts being perfectly clear on the equal, undivided possession of divinity by the Son and by the Spirit. But it remains true, that in the perspective proper to these texts, the first subject of this divinity is *the Father*, and the Father only. Byzantine and Latin medievals both came to speak of "God the Son" and of "God the Holy Spirit," just as of God the Father. But only this last expression is biblical, is traditional, in the sense of the "Ur-Tradition," Tradition in the strict sense, apostolic Tradition.

Revelation is quite clear on this point: Christian monotheism is neither solely nor primarily that of a single divine essence. It is that of the divine monarchy, of the Father, the one principle of divinity as of all that has come from it.

But, as Athanasius was perhaps the first to conceive and certainly the first to say with such precision, the very fact that God, the God of the biblical Word spoken fully in the Gospel, is Father, and a Father not accidentally but essentially, has a twofold necessary implication. Firstly, his Son, *the Son*, is essential to his life, his existence, his eternal subsistence as Father. Then, this Son is one with him in his term, in his eternal self-realization, just as he is in his principle or origin.

This "coincidence" of the Son with the Father, this recapitulation of the Son in the Father, as Denys of Rome had already called it writing to Denys of Alexandria,[29] has its expression, as it were, its eternal realization, in that Spirit of life who proceeds from the Father at the same time as the latter begets the Son, and who rests eternally on the Son as the Gift par excellence, the Gift of self-giving, one could say, where utter freedom coincides with absolute fidelity.

---

[28]Essay 4 in vol. 1 of *Schriften zur Theologie*, Einsiedeln-Zurich-Cologne, 1954.
[29]Quoted by St. Athanasius in *De decretis Nicenae Synodi*, 26.

In this profoundly mysterious perspective, any representation of the Trinity as three points on a straight line or as a triangle appears ridiculous. Everything comes eternally, within God as well as outside him, from the Father alone, the one invisible in himself as St. Irenaeus would say. Everything that can possibly be comes from him in the Son, comes as eternally enfolded within the Son albeit infinitely surpassed by him. But—or because—everything the Father has gives itself, realizes itself by giving itself through the Son so completely that everything also returns to him, reascends to him, recapitulates itself in him in the Spirit. The whole divine life is nothing other than Love given eternally, or rather giving itself, but this love lives only in the interchange by which everything flows from the Father through the Son and flows back to him in the Spirit.

If this be so, we do not even have a continuous circle, without beginning or end, constantly coursed by an unceasing *perichoresis* of the divinity, such as St. Basil's reflection would tend to have us admit. Pseudo-Denys' vision is better:[30] the *thearchy*, that is the communication of the life essential to God, in itself, and also the *hierarchy*, its out-flowing (if "out" has any meaning in this context) are nothing other than the pulsation of the Father's life. This life does not have to leave itself, strictly speaking, in order to communicate itself through the Father's own Son or to gather itself up in his own Spirit. But it lives through them and in them, both in itself and in the whole of that projection into nothingness of this unique fatherhood, "from which all fatherhood, in heaven and on earth, takes its name," which we call his creation. And it is in the interior of this eternal self-recapitulation of God the Father—of this other self in whom he realizes and so reveals himself, his Son—a recapitulation which is the procession of the Spirit, that this creation, once fallen, can itself be adopted, recapitulated in Christ, the only Son and the First-born.

This is the vision of God already implied in Jesus' first eucharistic prayer, the prayer of thanksgiving for the mutual "knowledge" of Father and Son, transmitted to us by Matthew and Luke. This is the vision that gradually unfolds in the great "thanksgivings" at the opening of each of the major Pauline letters, and which take over entirely in the Letter to the Ephesians. This is the vision opened by Jesus' priestly prayer in St. John, and which remains that of the Church at every eucharistic celebration of the sacramental sacrifice of the Last Supper. And at that moment we all of us come closer to the eternal eucharist of the Apocalypse: when Christ himself, having subjected everything, even death, will hand over the

---

[30] *De divinis nominibus*, ch.V, 1,4; PG 3, col. 589D.

Kingdom to God, his Father and our Father. It is for this that, in the present era, the Spirit and the Bride yearn unanimously.

The Bridegroom and the Bride:
Word and Wisdom in the Trinitarian Vision

If the foregoing has analyzed correctly the theology in the strict sense, that is, the God-doctrine of the Fathers, we would expect to find in them, and in close connection with their theology, a vision of the relationship between God and his creation, especially creation in his image, which would be a prolongation of the Old Testament doctrine on the relationship of God, of God's own life to his work. The theology had been required so as to take account of the New Testament prolongations, so unexpected but so faithful, of the Old Testament doctrine on God flowing from the fact and reality of his Word. One would thus expect that this appendix would issue from an inclusion of Wisdom in the Word, and from the deployment of Wisdom in Apocalypse: in a revelation of the last things sketched in the Old Covenant but sketched, very definitely, in view of the New.

But since the theology which has been fully revealed in the New Testament has already found it extremely difficult to hold together the two ends of the chain, it should not surprise us to find the same antinomic character, even more in evidence, when we turn to cosmology, ecclesiology and finally what we can call theological sophiology or, if we prefer, the definitive theology of Wisdom, of God's great and now fully revealed plan for his work.

In fact, this duality emerges not only from the relationship, within the creature, between his distinction from and union with God, but still more from the relationship conceivable in God himself between the accomplishment of his whole plan and his own inner divine life. Here we straightaway meet an opposition between the Greek and Latin visions concerning the way in which grace joins us to the divine life without abolishing our creaturely status—something that would be unthinkable given biblical monotheism. Yet, whichever way we follow, we run into the same difficulty about trying to define the relationship between the life of God in itself and its communication to creatures. Yet here, paradoxically, it seems that East and West began on the same path. The close parallel between the suggestions of Sts. Athanasius[31] and Augustine[32] are

---

[31]See especially *II Contra Arianos*. We have commented on this and other similar texts in *L'Incarnation et l'Eglise Corps du Christ dans la théologie de saint Athanase*, Paris, 1943, pp. 132ff.

[32]*Confessions*, bk. 12, ch. 15.

proof of this. But on the other hand—and this perhaps is no less paradoxical—both West and East, medieval and modern, seem to have proved hitherto incapable of taking up and developing these original and highly interesting suggestions without falling either into heresy or quite simply into an irreducible confusion of thought.

As for the first point—and we call this the first stage of the problem— we have the East's dominant tendency to start from the reality of deification, and therefore to insist on the uncreated aspect of the grace of adoption made available to us in Christ. But, in order that this deification should not make us "gods" independent of the one and only God, the distinction had to be made between God's ultimate, incommunicable essence and his "energies," which are not just communicable but have their whole raison d'être in uniting us to, without confusing us with him. The Cappadocians were the first to give an outline of this, more than an outline in fact. For, while for them these energies were above all the principle of the divine attributes manifested by God in creation, they were also, consequently and quite clearly, the root of creation's possible participation in the divine life.

Yet, if this distinction is not to be merely verbal, if it is going to resolve the problem concerned, it has to be reckoned a real and not merely logical distinction. This was clearly stated in the theology of St. Gregory Palamas, that fourteenth-century archbishop of Thessalonica, who sought by this means to justify the mystical experience of the "hesychast" tradition. But then, how avoid ditheism: a radical opposition between God as manifested and communicated and God as totally ineffable, as incapable of issuing from his own transcendence, so that at the end we have two gods remote from one another?[33]

Inversely, the Latin tendency found its perfect formulation, in the thirteenth century, in the scholastic notion of created sanctifying grace. As St. Thomas would say, in opposition to Peter Lombard's identification of the charity "poured into our hearts through the Holy Spirit" with the Holy Spirit himself, the concept of created grace intends in the first place to express the fact that it is indeed we ourselves, in our creaturely beings, who are divinized by the active presence of the Spirit within us without being absorbed and annihilated in God. This is not, he said, like a perfume alien to the vase containing it, but rather like one which steeps the

---

[33]See our study *Byzantine Spirituality* in *The Spirituality of the Middle Ages*, London, 1982, pp. 547ff. We have gone into this whole question in *Le Consolateur*. Cf. E. C. Mascall, *The Openness of Being*, pp. 217ff.

porous vessel with its whole substance, its whole aroma, yet without God or man being confused with or disappearing into each other.[34]

But two things are required for this concept of sanctifying grace to remain fruitful. The first is that this grace remain, as it does in St. Thomas' system, a simple accident inserted into our nature and not an additional nature, neither our own nor God's. The second is that it be conceived as *habitus*, that is, as a disposition enabling us to posit acts, each and every one of which is elicited by an actual grace of God, joining us to him effectively in knowledge and in love.

From this point of view, St. Thomas' grace corresponds exactly with the *exis schetike*, for which St. Maximus the Confessor[35] was the particular spokesman among the Greeks and which he explicitly conceived as an actual connection between our personal existence and that of the Son of God into whom we have been incorporated by baptism.

Nevertheless, even while still faithful to this point of view, the moment one separates, even in thought, created grace and the original Gift of the Spirit, it becomes unclear how, as created, it can associate us with the divine life. And even when the connection is consistently maintained, there seems to remain an unbridgeable gap between the grace which is ours and therefore created, and the active presence in us of the Spirit sent to us by the Father through the Son.

Then, of course, the moment created grace changes its conception from a simple accident to a substance, the moment the "supernatural" is spoken of as a self-subsistent reality (and even called "supernature" as from Suarez onwards), deification becomes an empty word.

Here again, we meet two apparently contradictory approaches, in fact at bottom complementary, but each of them limping and incapable of walking with the other.

But whichever be the point of view adopted or privileged at this first stage, the difficulties will prove still more insurmountable the moment one passes from the relationship, so far as we are concerned, between our life as creatures and the divine life communicated to us by grace, to the relationship in God himself between his life *ad intra* and his work of creation and assimilation.

And yet, at the point of departure, we find a remarkable conjunction between the Eastern and Western views. The sophiology, that is, in the biblical line and furthering it, the doctrine of divine Wisdom which St. Athanasius in the East and St. Augustine in the West developed in apparent independence of one another is essentially the same. Both

---

[34]*Summa Theologica*, Prima Secundae, q.109ff.
[35]*Ambigua*, PG 91, col. 1192B.

strove to assimilate into orthodox thought whatever was legitimate in Arianism and, behind that, in second-century Gnosticism, and so doing admitted that the same divine Wisdom by which God eternally thinks himself includes his thought of everything he will ever create. This Wisdom of creation, in its end and in its origin, must be identified with the uncreated Wisdom. God thinks all things only in his Son. He thinks them as destined to be recapitulated in the Son through the Spirit, in view of man's ultimate deification and, through him, not only of the intelligible, spiritual world to which he belongs by virtue of his soul but also of the physical world from which his body is formed and from which he cannot be wrenched away. The Virgin Mary would appear, in East and West, as the eschatological icon of that perfect identification of created, fallen Wisdom with its eternal model. She prepares and presages the wedding of the Lamb: the final union to and in him of the whole catholic, pan-cosmic Church, of the Wisdom of creation with eternal Wisdom, the union at the end of time of what is already one in him in the bosom of the Father.

Yet, undeniably, once the Fathers of West or East had reached this formulation they could only stammer when it came to defining more precisely how, in what way created and divine Wisdom could be one without confusion—how, in other words, the inner life of God, in the Trinity of its persons, includes human and cosmic life in itself from all eternity and will unite itself to them when history reaches its term, yet without absorbing them back into itself.

As we shall see, the first efforts in this direction—unsatisfactory certainly but significant in their general thrust—were made along the axis of medieval Jewish and Moslem traditions. The best of modern idealism, largely, though not exclusively, under the influence of Jacob Boehme, attempted to do better and to reintegrate these sophiological researches into what was intended as a Christian vision. After Schelling, Soloviev, Florensky and Bulgakov made attempts, not all equally happy, but without any of them getting to a satisfactory conclusion. Nonetheless, they all have the merit of progressively outlining a problematic which modern theology can no longer let itself shirk.[36] But, as we shall see, the theologians of our time cannot possibly face this problem fruitfully without first of all agreeing to submit theology as hitherto developed to vigorous self-criticism, the moral of which will be extreme modesty—not a notable characteristic of that theology either at its most timid or at its boldest.

---

[36]On Wisdom in God and in the history of the created world, according to medieval Judaism, G. Sholem, *Les Origines de la Kabbale*, Paris, 1966, pp. 91ff. We have treated this whole question in another volume: *Cosmos*, Petersham, 1988.

XV

The Prophetic Meaning of the Continuance of Israel and of the Revolt of Islam

Between the Absolute Gospel and the Relativity of Theology

Biblical Old Testament revelation is the final victorious breakthrough of that prophetism, that universal pressure of the Spirit, which we have seen behind every religious form in history. The vision of God at last definitively escaped from those mythical confusions, which were the reflection of the human and cosmic fall. God came down, by way of his Word, in search of alienated humanity and finally formed a people who would witness to himself. In Israel his Spirit succeeded for the first time, not just in temporarily cracking the carapace of a world hardened in its fatal introversion, its magic or its idolatry or its narrow, rationalizing skepticism, but in lifting this people's vision and aspiration, despite many relapses, towards the expected fullness of the divine manifestation, the re-establishment of the Reign of God over everything.

In Christianity, more precisely in Christ, this fullness is attained, although the Kingdom as yet appears only in his divine but definitely incarnate person. Then, taking its origin from him, from the eternal Son now become, at the high-point of history, the Head of regenerated humanity, the Spirit radiates out. He does not just lay hold of a series of witnesses to his continual inroads into the human heart. He begins to gather all men, as it were, into the heart of God by integrating them into the risen body of the Son made flesh. Thus an unveiling takes place. Man—in principle every man, in fact, progressively, all men of good will —comes to know this supreme mystery of God recognized, welcomed, re-established in his mystery at the source of all our thoughts and affections: the mystery of the Father.

As we have seen, this Gospel of the Father—*de Patre*, already present in the teaching of the Sermon on the Mount and expressed fully in the Johannine catechesis—is the Gospel of love: *evangelium amoris*. For it is by learning to love with that unique love which is the revelation of God's own life as communicated that men can discover God's fatherhood, being made sons in the Son, receiving from the Son the Spirit of the Father which rests on the Son.

This is the Gospel properly speaking. The dogma of the Trinity was progressively defined so as to provide the necessary safeguard of eucharistic experience in the face of every threat of deviation or incomprehension. In that experience the mystery of the Father is made known to the Church; we are brought into contact through the Son with the reality of that love "poured into our hearts by the Spirit who has been given us," thanks to the saving cross which has expressed the mystery of the Father by impressing it onto, into sinful flesh itself. But only theological effort could define and then justify the dogma. We have traced the two "ways," calling them for simplicity's sake, but of course simplistically, the "Greek" and the "Latin." They are not logically reconcilable, but both were inevitable and ultimately are inseparable. In them critical reflection on the Word of salvation took its irrevocable course. But neither the one nor the other can encapsulate the vision of eucharistic faith. This, as it proclaims and celebrates the mystery, breaks the bonds of all our logic, and its mystery inevitably comes like darkness on our earth-bound spirit in order to cast us towards that inaccessible light in which God dwells.

The act of faith is, in any case, death for our understanding, even if this death be only a prelude to transfiguration. But even if faith needs theology and its gropings to keep itself pure from error, there will be a fresh difficulty, and an extra trial when theology flies as close as possible to its ultimate object and inevitably yields a defective image of that object.

Certainly, to accept in faith God's fatherhood, with everything that the faith (which reveals it to us by applying it to us) can show us to be required of us, does by itself, in its very integrity, call forth and confront the obstinate pride and the terrified egoism of sinful man. And this suffices to explain many cases of refusal of the Gospel, even by the Jews who seemed all set to welcome the Messiah, and, later, the Islamic rejection, despite Islam's veneration of Jesus and its cult of Mary which at times all but equals that of Christians for her who, more than anyone, "believed." Yet both the Jewish refusal and Islam's rejection, which among the most thoughtful of both Jews and Muslims have focused most explicitly less on the Incarnation than on the Trinity, have been massive in character. And this fact should deter a Christian theologian from such an over-facile explanation. Islam's protest, like that of Israel and perhaps even more so, confronts him with a prophetic element. Doubtless, it will have been mingled many times with a real refusal to believe or at least with a sloth towards and a repugnance for believing. But no less often, perhaps even more often, it will not have been so adulterated, and the Christian theologian must bow before the fact.

The Protest of Israel

In the first place, it is not true, as we are inclined to say too often, that Israel as a whole has rejected the notion of a Messiah suffering for the sins of the people. Even when the scribes did so, they would then usually transfer to the people as a whole the mysterious need for innocent suffering if the world were to be redeemed and the Kingdom come. The faith-perception of God's compassion for the sinner, of God's assuming of sin itself, as St. Paul says, in those he sends and above all in the One sent par excellence, even went so far as the paradoxical perversity of Shabbatai Sevi—no doubt for having failed to acknowledge its legitimate expression in Christ Jesus. Such a pseudo-Messiah is a curious, even scandalous witness to this, but a witness who cannot be set aside. He did not just suffer but sinned deliberately, in order to draw upon himself the full force of God's just condemnation of sin, and so let loose a limitless flood of mercy.[1]

Above all, it is not true that Israel has as a whole rejected the interiorization of the Kingdom, if one understands by that our adoption by God, our entry into, our sharing in, in total reciprocity, that very love, that *hesed* which binds him to his creature, even when fallen, and which finally unveils to us the fathomless depths of his own inner life. Perhaps the clearest proof of this is the way in which Hassidism has centered the whole of Israel's piety on *devekut*,[2] that is, confident abandonment in everything, in an all-embracing, unceasing spirit of thanksgiving, abandonment to that love of God which waits for, calls for, actually arouses our own love.

And this shows how much the prophetic glorification of God as Father, which ran through the whole of synagogue worship even before Jesus appeared, has continued to extend and deepen itself.

In fact, these elements have continued to function as a ferment within Judaism, preparing and frequently producing quite unexpected conversions to Christ and his Gospel. Most of the time, the witness of Christians and even of the Church itself have only played a very secondary role in all this. The example of E. Zolli, the great rabbi of Rome, is symbolic here. His conversion climaxed in an illuminating vision of Christ appearing to

---

[1] G. Sholem, *Major Trends in Jewish Mysticism.* New York, 1946, pp. 287ff., and *Le Messianisme juif*, Paris, 1974, especially pp. 139ff.

[2] G. Sholem, *Le Messianisme juif*, pp. 303ff.

him in front of the ark of the Scriptures at the moment when the attendant was taking the Torah from it so that he could read and interpret it.[3]

Conversely the great hurdle for those who follow this way, and doubtless for many who embark on it naturally but cannot resolve to see it through, is the appearance of relapsing into idolatry and above all into polytheism, thanks to the unsatisfactory expressions that we propose of the Incarnation and especially of the Trinity.

For how many Christians does not a certain "Jesus-ism" tend to replace authentic Christianity by holding up a simple man turned into their god by men instead of the Son of God made man to redeem us? How many forms of piety, such as were already denounced by Origen and which continue all the way down to what is called, with perilous ambiguity, "the cult of the humanity of Christ," do not provide ample justification for the legitimate Jewish suspicion of idolatry?

But once past this stage of an infantile or senile Christianity which is usually regressive to the extent it thinks itself progressive, we encounter what is perhaps the greater hurdle: our habitual presentations of the Trinity. The so-called "Greek" formulas, whatever one makes of them, persistently suggest the image of three associated gods whether we speak, like St. Basil, of the colors of the rainbow blending into white light or, like St. Gregory Nazianzen, of three suns whose threefold brightness is one or even, like St. Gregory of Nyssa, of three torches lit from one another (although this admittedly comes closer to the traditional, properly apostolic proclamation). As for the Latin formulas, they are even worse: as if an abstract Godhead only took on a genuinely personal appearance in God-made-man. And it is best to pass over those deformations so justly stigmatized by Thomas Mozley, and which seem to suggest that the Trinity adored in practice by Western Catholics is not that of the heavenly Father, the Son and the Spirit, but that of the Mother, Child and Foster-father!

Figures such as Martin Buber, André Neher and Robert Aron, to mention only these, are abiding witnesses to what we can call the prophetic and certainly providential role of Israel, even if the quality of their protests is not always sustained. Abraham Heschel, given the extreme discretion of his anti-Christian polemic, is perhaps an even better witness. And they should prevent our reconciling ourselves quite as easily as we do to the degradations in our piety. Above all, they should compel us to admit the inadequacy of our so self-confident theology, even when at its most correct and which in its very orthodoxy remains terribly

---

[3]See his autobiography: E. Zolli, *Before the Dawn*, New York, 1954.

abstract and inassimilable for piety unless converted into images which are almost disastrously deceptive.

Yet it must be said, and we will see the same with Islam, that, as long as Israel refuses the Incarnation and the Trinity, its own sense of the divine vitality, of the fatherly generosity of God's communication to men, seems incapable of expressing itself without falling into a dubious gnosis. It can only avoid careering into a heretical, non-biblical gnosticism by the constant check of that unyielding sense of divine ineffability which is the great legacy to Israel from the ancient prophets. No one, in our own time, has expressed this so vividly as the philosopher and mystic Ludwig Wittgenstein. But as is shown by the continual absurdities of his most vociferous disciples, it is not easy, even for so great a mind, to adhere faithfully to such radical apophaticism without falling into simple aphasia.

Yet that there is, nonetheless, a genuinely prophetic element behind Israel's refusal is attested by the definite persistence in post-Christian Israel of that biblical mysticism, the two poles of which are the Shekinah and the Merkabah, between which one could say that the whole internal development of the Old Testament takes place.

The Meaning of Jewish Mysticism

In this context, it is in fact inadequate to speak of persistence. There has been in the Israel contemporary to the Fathers and in the medieval and modern periods an undoubted doctrinal development, in the sense of an irrefutably genuine unfolding of biblical data. This presupposes genuine mystical experience. We should further specify that this experience—as in Christianity, though less intrepidly, Pentecost being something Jews hope for rather than know—simply repeats the exceptional experience of the prophets in some no less exceptional personalities—from those visionaries of the Merkabah in the first Christian centuries down to the miraculous rabbis of Polish Hassidism. Yet it does increasingly tend to propose itself as the normal term of the piety of each of the faithful. This piety fills his whole life. It shapes it through constant recitation of the *berakoth*, which apply the Word of God—permanently relevant, inexhaustibly effective as it is—to every circumstance of the earthly life of the priestly people. It concentrates on the *kawanah*,[4] that is, on the perfect assimilation of a prayer that simply echoes the Word in faith and

---

[4]G. Sholem, *Major Trends in Jewish Mysticism*, pp. 275ff. Similarly, his *On the Kabbalah and Its Symbolism*, New York, 1964.

love. As Rabbi Simeon bar Jochai is supposed to have said so superbly, everything thus becomes a dwelling-place ready for the Shekinah.[5]

It is this that gives such value to the theosophical speculations nourished by meditation either on the *Bereschit*, the biblical account of creation, or on the prophetic visions of the Merkabah, and where the ultimate meaning of God's plan for his work *ad extra* is unveiled in the dialogue between Lover and Beloved in the Song of Songs.[6] In other words, God's relation with Israel has become the revelation of that communion of mutual love to which God wishes to draw, by means of the chosen people, every soul and the entire cosmos.

Doubtless, taking these speculations literally means registering in them the very same decline from Apocalypse to Gnosticism that Grant observed at the time of Christian beginnings. In the second century we see fantasias built around the letters making up the creative Word, in the *Sefer Yezirah*. Later, in the twelfth century, first in Provence and then in Spain, we find developments to the doctrine of the *sephiroth*, i.e., those elements of the Torah and of creation considered as divine thoughts generative of all else. First the *Bahir*, then the *Zohar* are representative here. Finally, the Renaissance Cabbalists and then those of modern Poland expand all this curious theosophy at will. In other words, once the living stream of a revelation moving towards its eschatological fullness has been arrested, as it were, the themes proper to the Word regress towards myth. The history of creation, its fall and redemption, is replaced by the purely imaginary journey of the soul torn between this world, identified with the corruption of the divine, and the higher world to which the soul thinks that it has always belonged, despite a temporary forgetfulness, and which is no longer distinct from God himself.

But even if those who indulge in such speculations have in fact fallen into the old temptation, a genuine Jewish mysticism remains in the midst of it all despite everything. In other words, we should take it as no more than apocalyptic *haggadah*. It is a simple image, utterly inadequate of course, of the tension between on the one hand that flight of the Merkabah which enables God, even when communicating himself to his closest intimates, to escape all their efforts to grasp him and in fact to ravish them after him towards what is at once an ocean of flames and a depth of darkness, and, on the other hand, the reality of the Shekinah which even now, like the Lover to whom the Beloved opens her door, dwells with them or, better, in them, already united to them in the total

---

[5] Guy Casaril, *Rabbi Siméon bar Yochaï et la Cabbale*, Paris, 1961.
[6] G. Sholem, *On the Kabbalah and Its Symbolism*.

reciprocity of the one perfect love which alone is capable of engendering a love like its own.[7]

Jewish mysticism, we are sure, can reach such a point and in many cases certainly has. And if so, then the refusal of the Christian formulations of the Trinity and Incarnation (formulas which, even if corrected to the nth degree, fall far short of adequate expression of the mystery) has not prevented an initial living of that mystery of eternal love extended to creation, even if it has never been possible for Jewish mysticism to express it fully to itself.

Two elements at least, if only by way of an inventory, should be singled out from the more perilous speculations which, in Cabbalism, Judaism's esoteric tradition, have been able to enclose this experience and have tried to translate it, though at the risk of traducing it. Especially from Renaissance times onwards, they have exercised a continual fascination over certain Christians. The first element is the distinction, which can be found as early as the *Zohar*, even the *Bahir* and can be traced back perhaps to the *Sefer Yezirah*, between the *En-soph*, i.e., God considered in his pure infinity, God always outside our grasp and, on the other hand, that quasi-corporeality in which he makes himself accessible to us either in the *sephiroth* or in the *Adam Qadmon*:[8] that ideal humanity which is the filial reflection of his fatherly countenance. There is no need to stress how close this distinction is to that found among Eastern Christians, between the invisible, incommunicable divine essence and the energies through which it reveals and communicates itself.

The second element, no less influential beyond the confines of Judaism, comes from Isaac Louriah, the founder of the school of Safed. This is the *zimzum*:[9] that sort of contraction or voluntary kenosis by which God is thought of as penning himself in, as it were, in order to leave room for the creature to exist and be free. We shall see how indebted to Louriah are Christian kenotic speculations, especially those of the Germans and Russians.

Of course, one can find neo-platonic antecedents to these intuitions, at least to the first of them. But, as we said before, this intimate alliance, especially in Plotinus' God, between immanence and transcendence, seems to have its source in a biblical, possibly evangelical impregnation of Neo-platonism, even if it took place at a semi-conscious or wholly unconscious level. Be that as it may, it is as true of late Jewish mystics as it

---

[7]On all this, see the beautiful book of L. Gillet, *Communion in the Messiah*, London, 1942.

[8]See G. Sholem, *Major Trends in Jewish Mysticism*, the texts quoted in the index under these two terms.

[9]*Ibid.*, pp. 244ff.

is of St. Augustine, that such patterns of thought, whatever their origin, have been given new interpretation, new value in the perspective of the biblical God "whom the heavens and the heaven of heavens cannot contain," yet who has made it no less his pleasure "to dwell with the children of men."

Islam and Its Rejection of Christianity

If it is true, and what we have been saying suggests that it is, that post-Christian Judaism's refusal of Christianity is a genuinely prophetic protest, then that protest has been aimed at a Christianity which has spent itself in speculations that tend towards either tritheism or a kind of anonymous deism which only becomes personal in Jesus' humanity. But in Islam's rejection of Christianity we find instead a prophetic protest provoked by the degradation of popular Christian piety into polytheism and a real, if not theoretical, idolatry. The episcopal preaching heard by Mohammed must be included in this. There was in fact something astonishingly practical and popular in the person and message of Mohammed, and it is this which has given Islam its strength and which has survived often even among his most speculative disciples.

Going deeper still, in the wake of M. Hayek's perceptiveness,[10] we can see Mohammed's and Islam's prophetic protest as directed at not just Christian aberrations, but the fundamental one of Judaism itself: that fatal tendency, hidden in the simple word "Judaism" and fully revealed at present in atheistic "Zionism," to reduce the worship of the one, transcendent God to the level of a simple tribal, racial, not to say racist religion. We need hardly underline how far the same tendency has unceasingly manifested itself in every Christian offshoot, i.e., in the recurrent relapses of the most diverse kinds of Christianity into mere nationalisms or religious ideologies replacing the Gospel while sheltering under its terminology. Even if, in Mohammed's final phase, that of Medina, the first prophetic intuition has been blunted and been overlaid by at least a latent panarabism, it remains undoubtedly true that in his first preaching at Mecca, there was a reassertion of that pure monotheism which the Word of God addressed to Abraham had begun to bring to life out of myth. From the time of Abraham's own *hegira*, his first departure for the desert, it was this which definitively exploded the structures of the hitherto ubiquitous and obsessive myths. And the undoubted charism of Islam has been that of continuously maintaining and continually renewing, in its full requirements, the lightning-like purity of

---

[10]Michel Hayek, *Le Mystère d'Ismaël*, Paris, 1964.

that first Abrahamic intuition: God, the true God, the one and only God cannot allow any "association," as Islam's most faithful preachers have so justly and unwearyingly proclaimed. God cannot—as in defective Trinitarianism—settle into various sub-gods or, contrariwise, evaporate into concepts. Nor can he—as in an incarnationism which replaces the Gospel Christ with the apotheosis of a purely human Jesus—bifurcate into a transcendent God and a wholly immanent "good God." Even less can he be reduced to the status of supporting or glossing over the tribalism of neo-pagan conservatives or the sectarianism of revolutionary ideologues.

Here too what attests the truth, the original and lasting authenticity of the prophetic element, is the quality of the mysticism Islam has nourished. This prophetism abruptly exploded in what one can only call the sublime candor of Mohammed's first protestation,[11] when he was prepared to acknowledge Jesus as not just the hoped-for Jewish Messiah but the fullness of the Word of the only God who had spoken to them in all the prophets; and prepared to acknowledge the descent of the divine Shekinah on his mother, with the Spirit who had animated all the prophets. But in the practical ditheism or speculative tritheism of a Christianity degenerating into Jesus-ism or getting lost in gimcrack speculation, he could not recognize the great God, the true God, the only God, nor find him—even less so perhaps—in the neo-idolatry of a Judaism as introverted as any exclusively Syrian, Byzantine or Roman Christianity.

Mysticism and Speculation in Islam's Two Traditions

In strictly Sunnite mysticism, i.e., that rigorously faithful to the legal Koranic tradition, we see the vision of faith underlying that tradition pushed to its ultimate consequences. Witness the modest, reserved yet wholly self-detached contemplation of God the Creator in someone like Ghazali. In Sufi mysticism, we see rather a bold even foolhardy drive towards an identification of love with the primordial Lover, even at the cost of death. Witness the writings and above all the sufferings of someone like Hallaj. But in either case, R. Arnaldez[12] has surely been right in maintaining that these mystics did not rise to such heights by leaving the orbit of Islamic piety and succumbing to neo-platonic or Christian influences. Rather, it was by the depth and intensity of their realization of

---

[11]See the chapter on Mohammed by R. C. Zaehner in *At Sundry Times,* and M. Hayek, *Le Christ de l'Islam,* Paris, 1959.

[12]R. Arnaldez, *La Mystique musulmane,* in the collective work ed. A. Ravier, *La Mystique et les Mystiques,* Paris, 1965, pp. 571ff.

everything implied by the prophecy of him who remains for his faithful the "Prophet" par excellence.

And similarly, even if it is true, as H. Corbin has shown especially vis-à-vis Suhrawardi,[13] that the mystics of Shiite Iran link up, by way of Islamic prophetism, with that of Iran's first spiritual master, Zoroaster, the principles of the "gnosis" they have sought and found, just like that of the best Jewish gnosis, undeniably remains that of the prophetic "knowledge of God," that which springs into life at the victorious touch of God seizing the soul and which the Hebrew prophets were the first to define.

However, just as with post-Christian Judaism, so—and even more so, perhaps—with Islam, it is revealing that the moment this prophetic gnosis goes in for speculative formulation, it only gets anywhere, while avoiding Christian Trinitarianism and Incarnationism, by constant flirting with heretical or, rather, neo-pagan Gnosticism, and often in fact falling into its arms. In other words, once again there has been a substitution. An imaginary journey, away from an essentially fallen world consisting of matter and bodies to the original inviolate world for ever identical with God: this journey of the soul rediscovering itself in its original purity and divinity has replaced the quest for God the Father who sends his eternal Son and Spirit to a world and man wholly created and wholly fallen, so as to lift them and divinize them gratuitously out of pure grace.

This misunderstanding—and it first showed its head in the exegesis of Zoroaster by his disciples during the Sassanid period—will only be definitively overcome by Islamic and Judaic mystical thought when they are able to see and accept in the Gospel of Christ Jesus, beyond the caricatures of the Incarnation and the Trinity drawn by Christians themselves, the religion of the Father.

Then the rather moving Moslem legend concerning Christ's return—the expectation of Islam as well as the Church—will come true in a higher sense. The Messiah will then wed his eschatological Spouse, who will bear him a new Moses and a new Mohammed. In other words, what the Apocalypse of John calls the Wedding of the Lamb (the consummated union of the eternal Son with the Church of the last times) will consummate the truth of the prophetic protest of Israel and of Islam,[14] and do this within the pure confession of a Christianity which will have overcome every historical temptation.

---

[13]H. Corbin, *En Islam iranien*, vol. 2, Paris, 1971, and the whole four volumes of this fascinating synthesis.

[14]M. Hayek, *Le Mystère d'Ismaël*, p. 254.

XVI

The High Point and the Decline
of Western Theology

Undoubtedly, Western theological thought reached a peak in its development during the thirteenth century, a peak it has never surpassed since. Eastern Christians who know it well, concede that it has not been equaled by them. This is admitted even by those who reject out of court the general development of Western Christianity such as George Scholarios, alias the Patriarch Gennadius of Constantinople, who made the decision that the Greek East should reject the Union of Florence. The twelfth century had witnessed a recovery of the Greek patristic tradition, and the fruit of this was now combined with the still more recent rediscovery of Aristotelian philosophy. At the same time, no small part of medieval Jewish thought, centered around Maimonides, became part of the Christian inheritance, as did still more perhaps of Arab thought, represented by Averroes and even more by Avicenna.

Yet it has to be noticed that the mystical aspects, both platonic and neo-platonic as channeled by medieval Augustinianism, underwent a marked regression. Similarly, everything or practically everything, in Jewish or Islamic mysticism remained unknown. The prodigious *summae* of the thirteenth century abound as the undoubted fruit of a victorious breakthrough on the part of a deep desire to give a wholly rational account of the Christian faith: a desire which, in St. Anselm's case, intended and indeed believed itself to be wholly interior to the one desire not of "sounding the depths" of God but of "understanding some small part of that truth" of God "believed and loved by the heart." This was desire at its most intrepid. But in the young Abelard, on the other hand, it was completely unbridled, until trials broke his intellectual pride.

Why was it these syntheses proved so fragile, despite being the most imposing of Latin and of all Christian theology? How explain the remarkable fact that none of them could impose themselves for more than a generation, and, even then, on very few? The answer perhaps lies in the unresolved hesitation between the two desires we have mentioned. Certainly, the evanescence cannot be explained sufficiently by the natural instability of the fallen human mind. Such an explanation simply does

not meet the case of such thought as original Thomism which, at its most
mature, in the *Summa Theologica* and the great *Quaestiones* (*De Ente et
Essentia, De Veritate, De Malo*), seemed to have attained an equilibrium
that would guarantee its perdurance. Nor, even more conspicuously, can
such an explanation make sense of the way in which what can be called
the classical revivals of this theology, in the sixteenth century and in our
own day, have proved themselves so unsatisfying so fast and have never
been able to retain the allegiance for any length of time of more than a
handful of docile spirits, despite all intimidating and coercive measures.

Neo-Thomist Equivocations on Thomism

Let us take as an example one of the most venerable productions of
the last Thomist or, rather, Neo-Thomist renaissance: the long and great
book of Fr. Reginald Garrigou-Lagrange, OP, *Dieu, son existence et sa
nature.*[1] In it, the theological teaching of St. Thomas is analyzed, carefully
taken to pieces and put together again, with a clarity and a fidelity most
deserving of praise. Yet few readers, putting down the book, will have
escaped the impression that in it the God of the Bible and the Gospel
has been reduced to a *caput mortuum* of frozen abstractions. And yet its
author undoubtedly exemplified in his time that rare combination of
theologian and eminent man of the spirit, and it was his constant concern
to develop spirituality and theology in tandem. How then, we must ask,
could such a theologian have produced a summa about God frankly so
overwhelmingly boring and, more especially, the speculative ramifications of which (practically) never contribute to a genuine enrichment of
thought?

E. Gilson, with such Thomists in mind, was perfectly right in saying
that one can't see the forest for the trees,[2] and that this is an inevitable
result of their systematic effort to separate what is philosophical from
their master's theology, so as to reorganize and rebuild it, purportedly,
according to its own innate exigencies. It is at the very least surprising
that disciples, beyond the Angelic Doctor, of Aristotle himself should
have forgotten that order is of being. Instead, they imposed an order
on Thomas' thought which was not his own, and thereby turned it
into something quite different from his, even if (which is supposing

---

[1] Paris, 1925. (Eng. trans. *God: His Existence and His Nature*, London & St. Louis, 1949.)

[2] Apart from the two books on realism cited earlier, cf. the beginning of his *Thomisme*
and especially his history of Neo-Thomism in *Recent Philosophy, Hegel to the Present*, ed. E.
Gilson, New York, 1966.

a good deal, given such manipulating) the individual pieces were fully respected.

It was not in fact by chance that St. Thomas never separately systematized his philosophy, that he never detached it from Christian theology but always developed it within the latter. However purely rational philosophical developments should be and remain, for St. Thomas it was quite certain that they did not thereby become independent of the situation of the thinker producing them. If the one philosophizing is a Christian, this will have an effect on his thought, even if, while philosophizing, he uses nothing but rational concepts and procedures accessible, at least in principle, to any and every man even unenlightened by revelation.

The result is that when John of St. Thomas, the first to do this, transformed Thomism by developing philosophy independently of and prior to the theology dealing with the Christian revelation, he inevitably created a different philosophy and a different theology, however careful he was to use nothing but elements taken straight from his master. Even when he is scrupulously precise in repeating St. Thomas' words and key phrases, they no longer say the same thing.

That this is true of "John of St. Thomist" theology, right from its very beginning, is revealed by that theologian's understanding of what, following St. Thomas, he calls a "theological conclusion." According to him it is possible, even while adhering to a strict application of syllogistic reasoning, to have two kinds of theological conclusions—one flowing from two revealed premises, the other from one revealed and one philosophical premise. And this latter kind by its very nature will widen the field, if not precisely of revelation as such, at least of the knowledge we can draw from it. This may appear at first sight to be a quite innocuous and legitimate development of St. Thomas' idea of a theological conclusion. In fact, it transforms it to the point of being unrecognizable. The whole meaning of theological endeavor is at a stroke radically altered, and at the same time even our very conception of revelation.

For St. Thomas there are not and cannot be theological conclusions which are not already comprised within revelation. A theological conclusion is and can only be a revealed doctrinal affirmation of which one has established the logical relationship it has with other doctrinal affirmations of the same species. The whole of theology moves within faith and so within revelation. To suppose that it can evade it in order to increase its scope (!) is no longer to understand anything about revelation itself, as if theology could ever flatter itself of having gone so far beyond revelation as to be able to complete it.

This in fact supposes that, according to John of St. Thomas and those who have followed him,[3] revelation is nothing but an accumulation of externally juxtaposed propositions, to which one can further add philosophical propositions, thus aspiring to enrich revelation by philosophico-theological hybrids. It is of course this which purportedly justifies the separation of philosophy and of the theology concerned with the revealed datum, and the reconstruction of the first prior to the second, with, consequently, the naive expectation of "developing" the objects of revelation by artificially inseminating them with external philosophical propositions. But at this point one is miles away from genuinely Thomist views of theology as the science of God, having its whole basis on his Word. One has in the first place lost sight of St. Thomas' strong sense of revelation as the communication of a single mystery, that of God himself, an organically coherent mystery, which speculation can attempt to inventory, to analyze and synthesize but never exhaust, and even less indulge in the grotesque pretension of adding something to it to complete and develop it.

Traveling on such a road—and this has been the mentality, more or less of Baroque Thomism, not to mention modern Neo-Thomism—one inevitably comes to prolong this now bloodless religious philosophy into a correspondingly depreciative theology of revelation. Such a theology ceases to be able to vivify by the vision of faith, and at the same time refine and reform our merely human concepts, and it increasingly tends to yield to the disastrous policy of clearing out the Word of God of everything that cannot be circumscribed by or reduced to pre-formed concepts constructed without reference to the Word.

It is therefore not surprising if such so-called Thomism gives the impression that the philosophico-theological thought of St. Thomas is nothing but a gigantic and futile exercise in tautology which, while claiming to explain and develop the statements of the faith, in fact eviscerates and disjoints them. And it is worth emphasizing that if this can happen in the case of so distinguished a mind and so worthy a man of the spirit as Fr. Garrigou-Lagrange, then how much worse it will be when this kind of philosophy and theology is taken up by some college rector whose chief concern is to bring out the "errors" of his colleagues, and either has no interior life or never dreams (quite rightly!) of nourishing it on his theology!

---

[3]The ultimate issue of this approach is found in the purely syllogistic view of doctrinal development proposed by F. Marin-Sola and criticized to effect by J. H. Walgrave in *Unfolding Revelation*, New York, 1972.

It is thus possible at least to understand, even if we cannot altogether excuse the unjustified reproaches and inappropriate denunciations hurled at St. Thomas by someone like Laberthonnière,[4] particularly the accusation that the living God of the divine Word has been replaced by an intellectual idol, more precisely the God of love by the Moloch of a self-sufficient deity. It is quite true that Laberthonnière's debunking of Thomism was, in fact, aimed at a caricature. Unfortunately however it was not he who had produced the caricature. It had been provided for him by the contemporary disciples of the greatest Scholastic, and by no means by the least among them.

It is highly revealing that the answer to such an attack was all kinds of "theses of Thomist philosophy," meant to lay the necessary foundations for purportedly orthodox theology. The most surprising of this kind of document ever produced by an intending autocratic authority which is nonetheless made a fool of by its would-be servants went so far as to find room for the Leibnizian principle of "sufficient reason." One could imagine nothing further from St. Thomas, nothing more destructive of his idea of God as the pure existent, and of God's work as something wholly gratuitous.

Fr. Sertillanges is another of these undoubtedly estimable modern Thomists and one whose thought is full of instruction (though it would be best not to have too much recourse to him if one wants really to understand St. Thomas or even simply to know about him). He in his turn, wrote an elegant little book on *Les grandes thèses de la philosophie thomiste*, and this was certainly more faithful both to the letter and to the spirit of St. Thomas than the productions mentioned above. But how significant it is that neither he nor any other member of this school for the whole of theology and for the whole of philosophy—a school aiming at the resurrection of *the* "School" *tout court*—apparently never dreamed of first listing "the major theses of Thomist theology"—perhaps because they would only have been simple logical appendices to the theses of pure philosophy. Yet it is quite clear from any unblinkered reading simply of St. Thomas' commentaries on Aristotle's *Metaphysics* that he does not even reduce the philosophical propositions that he finds to simple deductions from the principles received from revelation but undoubtedly consciously reinterprets, even refashions them in its light.

---

[4]On Laberthonnière, cf. Paul Beillevert's volume, *Laberthonnière l'Homme et l'Oeuvre*, Paris, 1973.

The Existential Character of Authentic Thomism

Once we have become aware of all this, and drawn the moral, we are in a position to rediscover St. Thomas' God. He is not simply that first unmoved mover of the universe, blithely indifferent to it, even disdainfully ignorant of its existence, and who in any case is only capable of referring everything outside and within himself to a hideous egoism or egotism expanded to infinite dimensions. Such was Laberthonnière's accusation. The first thing we must realize is what E. Gilson exposed in a history of the Neo-Thomists,[5] far more devastating than anything Laberthonnière ever wrote, and without making the latter's mistake of believing the Neo-Thomists when they claimed to be unfolding their master. This is the fundamental misunderstanding which travesties the whole of Thomism from top to bottom and in particular St. Thomas' theology: that of transposing his thought from the most radical existentialism there has ever been to a deadly essentialism. How could the God whose essence it is to be precisely "Pure Act," the very act of existing without any limitation, possibly be summed up by concepts?

But to realize, in the deepest sense, the significance of this starting-point, one must see St. Thomas' Metaphysics, not as a simple, superficially modified Aristotelianism but as what E. Gilson, fifty years ago, was so bold as to call "the metaphysics of Exodus," without himself immediately grasping every consequence of that insight.[6]

In other words, the point of anchorage and the spring-board for this whole metaphysic is the mysterious saying of the burning bush: "I am who am." This must not be hastily translated in the way that St. Augustine did in his *Soliloquies*, still wrapped up as he was in the cocoon of his Neo-platonism: "I am the being who is always and forever." This is to stay with a platonizing essentialism, even though its contours have been practically pushed out of sight. The phrase must be taken as St. Thomas took it with a rigor no previous Christian thinker had approached: "I am what I am; I am the only one who can define the infinite, ever actual fullness of his existence." This is what St. Thomas meant practically every time he spoke of *Ipsum Esse*.

Yet at the same time one must emphasize the point so few recognize, namely, how laughably illusory are all those well-intentioned attempts to introduce more logic into St. Thomas. We see Sertillanges, for instance, disarmingly doing his open best to expunge from St. Thomas' system any platonic left-overs, especially the theory of ideas, which had now been

---

[5] Cf. his own contribution on this subject in *Recent Philosophy*.

[6] E. Gilson, *The Spirit of Medieval Philosophy*, vol. 1, London, 1950, p. 51.

transported into God and identified with his eternal thought. In such a case, one can see how two things go together: on the one hand, the impossibility some have in accepting the biblical God in his full transcendence, the God who laughs at the concepts in which we try to swaddle him, and on the other hand the inability of the same people to conceive how God can be interested in the world and his creatures for their own sakes, without the fear of his becoming passible like us and in relation to us and so collapsing down to our level and becoming confused with us.

Theology and Grace in Authentic Thomism

But there is worse still than the simple tailoring of Thomist theology to the measurements of an isolated philosophy, such as we find even in a Garrigou-Lagrange. The full consequences of that misleading twist in the whole interpretation of St. Thomas are revealed in those spiritual theologies which combine a masked Nestorianism as regards the Incarnation with a scarcely camouflaged modalism for what remains of the Trinity. Given such foundations, our association with the divine life naturally resolves itself into a simple, special "presence" (but if we ask: special in what way? we are told this question is unanswerable), a presence of the three persons or rather of the single essence which they have in common, and which no more makes us know or love any one of them, properly speaking, than any one of them knows or loves us. In fact, we are told, the one and only uncreated substance must be in the last resort recognized as capable of entering into contact with us, just as only it loves and, of course, strictly speaking only loves itself both within God and *ad extra*.

At this point, of course, one has arrived at something which, though using indisputably Thomist elements, has in fact rebuilt and then attributed to St. Thomas a system justifying all poor Laberthonnière's invectives and which would have made our saint, more than anyone, recoil in horror.

But St. Thomas' work does not have to be treated as a quarry, from which various random elements can be hacked out and then put back together again according to some supposed inner logic of which St. Thomas was manifestly ignorant. If one approaches his doctrine of God, *in se et in nobis*, in function of its historical development, it then takes on a quite different meaning.

First of all, St. Thomas' theology never sought, in an *a priori* way deliberately ignoring Christian revelation, to provide us with a certain number of supposedly purely philosophical rational concepts which could then be imposed like a grid on the theology of the revealed datum, enabling us to file away, even dissolve everything that did not contribute to an essentially abstract idea of God. St. Thomas, rather, as early as the most philosophical parts of *De Ente et Essentia* and even more so in the great synthesis of his maturity, *De Veritate*, established as perlucidly as possible why such a way of proceeding is quite impossible.

Any application whatever of our concepts to God so far as he is known by simple reason applying itself to his creative work can only avoid getting into an impasse, according to St. Thomas, by even at this stage recognizing in him the fundamental mystery of *ipsum esse*. This means that we can only speak of him with an especially cautious and discreet kind of analogy. *A fortiori* is this the case when he reveals the inexhaustible mystery of his own interior life and of the share in it offered us. We must speak because we must confess our faith, and what we say of the mystery is effectively directed at the presence and communication of he who is par excellence because guided by him and his inspiration. But the mystery always obliges us to recognize that whatever we say about it can never purport to contain this presence and communication, nor coincide even imperfectly with what they are in themselves.

The True Meaning of Thomist Theology

Once one has taken one's bearings from these fixed points, the constants and orientation of genuinely Thomist thought become clear, and one can make the transition from the *Commentary on the Sentences* to the two *Summae* without risking losing sight in the latter of the precise and explicit themes of the former. In fact, it cannot be doubted that these dominants persist through all further developments, while not always being reaffirmed in a formal way, sometimes being corrected, sometimes meeting a difficulty not admitting of easy solution and so at least apparently being obscured. But, in any case, the key principle always remains inviolate, thus preventing us from giving undue importance to those occasional non-sequiturs which no great mind, especially one as prolific as St. Thomas, can ever avoid. And the key principle is that no Christian theology worthy of the name can emancipate itself from revelation, from its primary expression in Scripture as understood by the whole of tradition. And this holds no less for conclusions than for the first beginnings.

For St. Thomas, in the first place, wrote a certain number of scriptural commentaries, too often and wrongly considered as secondary not to say negligible by the moderns. But more than that, as we could gather by caring to re-read and take seriously the opening pages of the *Summa Theologica*, St. Thomas conceived his whole theology as an elaborated commentary on Scripture. This commentary never claimed any dispensation from the duty of coming back, again and again to the text being commented. It was not a commentary that had its starting-point elsewhere. St. Thomas would never have held himself authorized to do that, and this holds, and we say this deliberately for the *whole* of his thought, for the philosophical part, in one sense, no less than for that directly concerned with revealed truths.

To put this better: according to St. Thomas, theology should not for a moment be considered as a study of God at a second stage, coming in the wake of a "purely" philosophical study involving simply the application of the latter to the revealed datum. Theology, as St. Thomas quite expressly understood it, is an organic whole, not artificially and as it were externally unified by an independent philosophy, but proceeding from the inner unity of God's revelation and his whole saving design, a unity which is in any case essentially mysterious. And it has the (unending) task of incorporating, correcting, developing and finally surpassing any worthy philosophy through the contemplation of the mystery of God as it lays hold not just of the whole of man's intelligence but of his whole being.

Approached in this way, the real meaning of the words "Thomist" and "theology" become clear. St. Thomas' theology elucidates our vision of man's destiny within the mystery of our adoption. It does so in a way as critically rational as possible, while not afraid to criticize reason as handled by fallen man, by reason salvaged by man as he has been saved and enlightened by revelation. It shows us the photographic negative, so to speak, of the life interior to God, the presupposition of our adoption and something revealed only by being opened to us.

At the same time Thomist theology, like any theology, but with a special blend of reverence and boldness, of humility and intellectual courage, does its best to connect the mystery of our destiny with the essential, all-embracing mystery of God, understanding the latter so far as it can in the chiaroscuro of faith.

This kind of retroverting mutual interaction is what makes the plan of the *Summa Theologica* comprehensible. Above all, it explains the dynamics behind its unfolding. Approached and interpreted in the way we have sketched, Thomist theology emerges as one of the noblest and most successful efforts at making us understand how God in creating and saving us has revealed himself as the Living One who gives life—so far as we can understand in this life and without any claim to dissolve a mystery which will remain for all eternity. That is, he is the living God in a sense far exceeding anything we can conceive, with a fecundity which is that of the infinite itself. But he has only revealed himself by as it were flowing out from himself—and how supremely incomprehensible this is—and becoming the finite being we are, uniting it, associating, identifying it with his infinity yet without absorbing it.

Any and every interpretation or re-exposition of St. Thomas' theology which begins by strangling this inner movement will inevitably be a falsification.

The Historical Weaknesses of the Thomist Synthesis

But if all this is true, it only enhances the difficulty we mentioned at the beginning: why did the theology of St. Thomas initially rally so few to its standard and for so short a time, and why, whenever it has been resurrected as in the sixteenth century or more recently, has it fallen victim to distortion and misunderstanding?

There is, in our opinion, a twofold answer to this question. We have spoken of humility and boldness as the joint characteristics of authentic Thomism. But humility can always degenerate into mere modesty and, curiously enough, when it does, boldness always becomes temerity.

It is, certainly, all the more remarkable that St. Thomas should have developed his philosophy within theology at a time when the practice of teaching philosophy before theology, and without connection to it, was acknowledged and in force in all the universities.[7] But Thomas' temperament was emphatically not that of a revolutionary and despite his vigorous independence of mind, he does not seem ever to have thought himself called to be a reformer and do away with either the strictly syllogistic method of exposition or the typically medieval literary form of the *Quaestio*: statement of the thesis-objections-argument from authority (*sed contra*)—rational justification in the body of the article and reply point by point to the objections. His modesty, therefore, made him accept two or even three aberrant factors from the whole theological development consequent upon Abelard and his *Sic et Non*, despite their being opposed to the spirit and even the explicit principles of his theological thought. In the first place, there is the development of thought by a single-track cascade of syllogisms. *Pace* Spinoza, even though this method has considerable pedagogical advantages when used in the abstract sciences, such as the mathematical, it misleads even there. It conceals the true paths of discovery and merely justifies what has been discovered *a posteriori*. But the moment one is involved with living realities, especially personal realities, and *a fortiori* with the things of God, to be so mesmerized by the power of simple deduction is to

---

[7]On this question of the cultural context to St. Thomas, cf. M. D. Chenu, *Toward Understanding Saint Thomas*, Chicago, 1964.

condemn oneself to working on terms borrowed from our sense-experience as if they could be univocally applied to God. The result will be a perpetual flirting with non-comprehension, if not surrender to non-sense. One will no longer know how to seize the truth. One will pursue it like a man half-blind. St. Thomas, if anyone, should have been conscious of this. It was he who began by establishing so well the wholly analogical character (and analogical at a second level) of the formulas we apply to God. He, further, who showed so clearly that faith enables us to seize divine truth not in the formula itself, as if it could label it, but beyond it: in that inaccessible light where God dwells and which for us, in this life, remains enshrouded by darkness, the best of formulas doing no more than orientating us towards a truth which they themselves can neither embrace nor even touch.

The facile acceptance, then, of the commonly-used method of exposition introduced a discordance into Thomist theology. To this we must add the congenital weakness of any theology which allows itself to turn, at least apparently, into a collection of questions, however ingeniously arranged. It will inevitably come to treat the Word of God or revelation, as it will be called, as a stack of juxtaposed propositions which it will be the whole task of theology to put in logical order. Experience has shown ad nauseam the effect of such an arrangement on pupils, if not on the master himself. Docility to it has the disastrous result of dissipating the mystery of God and our freely-given association with his life, or at least of concealing it under a spider's web of abstractions. First, these last are superimposed upon the harmonious play of imaged expressions found in the Word of God. Then, and soon, they replace them in fact, if not in principle.

It is easy to see that it is only when St. Thomas comes to treat separately a "question" of wide import, as in *De Ente et Essentia* or *De Veritate*, that his thought unfolds with ease, following its own organic demands, and that he gives us a sense of the unity and all-embracing totality of the revealed mystery, the necessary environment of all theological thought whether it makes use of simple philosophical reasoning or fastens itself directly on the revealed datum in its pure supernaturality.

But it is at this point that humility turned modesty turns boldness into temerity. This passive acceptance of questions so alien to the spirit and direction of the Word of God—a fatal legacy of Abelard and his heirs—runs the risk of putting the entire system out of orbit. Not that the theologian ever should or could refuse to answer questions put to him or that put themselves to him. But he must keep in mind the principle, found loud and clear in St. Thomas himself, that revelation has not been made to satisfy our idle curiosity but to lead us to salvation. Thus the answer to be made to many of the questions taken neat by St. Thomas should have been that they were badly put, and that revelation obliges us to modify them before we can think of answering them.

It is astonishing, in fact, that we have had to wait for Karl Barth before arriving at a frank recognition that the Word of God does not restrict itself to answering our questions, whatever they may be, in the way we put them prior to hearing God's Word. Rather, the Word begins by putting them in quite a different way, and by putting different ones, questions we had scarcely or never thought of. It begins by putting us, first of all, in question, especially us who claim to speak of God authoritatively.

Truth to tell, it is hard to imagine an idea more consonant with authentic Thomism. And in fact, one notices that many of the questions St. Thomas takes up he finally quietly modifies in their structure and import. It is all the more surprising and regrettable that he was never so audacious or so simple as to say it out loud and to draw all the consequences of his timidity or his temerity (in fact, simply his fearfulness in face of the absurd pretensions of a quarrelsome theology like Abelard's) that his heirs have developed so disastrously, even while proclaiming themselves his exclusive and integral disciples.

St. Bonaventure's Venture

Given this, a certain nostalgia for an alternative philosophy and theology contemporary with St. Thomas, i.e., that of St. Bonaventure, is only natural. Gilson seems to have felt this at the very start of his career.[8] At first sight, Bonaventure's thought seems, not perhaps more strongly orientated than Thomas', but at least better equipped to withstand the external pressures, the constraints and ultimately the distortions which, once the master had accepted them so easily, the disciples could hardly be expected to avoid.

Gilson reversed the assessment of Bonaventure's modern Franciscan commentators and established beyond cavil that he was not an embryonic St. Thomas, with his development arrested in mid-course, but that he intended to do something quite different from St. Thomas and was fully aware of what he was doing and why.

To begin with, St. Bonaventure was not content to follow St. Thomas in developing a philosophy that would be autonomous in its principles and method of development within a theological, that is, Christian vision of the whole. Rather, he worked for the conjunction and harmonious

---

[8]E. Gilson, *The Philosophy of St. Bonaventure*, London, 1938.

synthesis of philosophy and theology by conceiving philosophy as the path of human understanding, taking it to a knowledge of God inseparable from adoration.

From this issued an interpretation of the whole of cosmic reality as a simple language by which God makes himself known to us and which prepares us for his direct Word in the Jewish and Christian Scriptures. Similarly, the natural enlightening of the human understanding, as Bonaventure conceived it, takes place under an influx of the divine intelligence and directs us immediately towards accepting the grace of a higher illumination, lifting our intellect to contemplate God even as he is himself.

All this is certainly very beautiful, and very Franciscan in the best sense. It was Alexander of Hales who said that, in Bonaventure, Adam seems never to have sinned. He meant this as praise, but it can easily be taken in an opposite sense. Such a philosophy may be fine for contemplatives at leisure to contemplate undisturbed, though even there it might merely encourage perpetual day-dreaming. But it does not meet the need behind speculative theology, the need driving it, willy-nilly, to make use not of some seraphic philosophy but of one capable of being that of every man: of helping the encounter between the Word of God and fallen man's reflection on his experience to produce a real assimilation to revelation of everything we think. A paradisiac philosophy and theology suffer from a double handicap. They have an air of unreality for those still on earth, and in heaven they will not be needed. In other words, they run the danger of shutting us up in what the English delightfully call a fool's paradise. Later developments of Franciscan thought, from Duns Scotus to William of Occam seem to verify this.

The mystical idealism of St. Bonaventure is, after all, only acceptable for those who attribute, both in us and in God, a primacy to the will over the understanding, doing this so that love can have the last word not only within contemplation but over and above it. The conflict with the Thomist thesis, holding beatitude as the business, in the first instance, of the intellect, whereas the Bonaventuran made it primarily a matter of the will, was the sign of a disastrous cleavage. In fact, here we touch the basic flaw in all these theologies: it is not that they are too sublime (what true theology could not but be?), but that they want to be sublime too cheaply. Given the aberrations we see at work in a theology such as Abelard's, with the intellect applying itself to theology while sundered from living faith, the tendency to fall back on a theology that turns everything to loving, as Bossuet would say, was perfectly understandable. But the mistake was to think that this could be achieved by giving the will primacy over the intellect. What this does is oppose the good to the real, of which the intellect is the meaning, in other words, turn reality into a dream while reducing all theological speculation to a wishful thinking which takes the dream for reality.

On this point, the Thomist analysis of truth remains indefeasible. If the Christian God is not primarily truth itself, he will never, whatever we do, be anything more than an idol, and the idol of our capricious fantasies. To oppose "God is love" to the God of truth is to open the way to the inevitable reversal of taking for God any kind of "love" whatever on the grounds that love cannot be submitted to any criterion.

Duns Scotus

In fact, with Duns Scotus,[9] we see the will, in God, becoming perilously autonomous vis-à-vis the intellect. It is true that his undoubtedly winsome philosophy and theology of freedom are held in check by the instinctive prudence of a deeply Christian outlook, and that he does not concede that God's will could ever be anything but in harmony with truth. But he is far too sure about the possibility of such a disjunction in us, while at the same time no longer seeing any meaning in St. Thomas' necessary distinction between essence and existence in everything other than God. And while he admits God's infinity in principle and even underscores it as a result of his voluntarism, the thrust of his thought inevitably makes this infinity nothing but an infinite magnification of what we are.

It would then be all too easy for William of Occam to reproach him for being illogical and to turn the Thomist view on its head. Thomas saw God's act of understanding as the conscious coinciding of the *Ipsum Esse* with himself, the divine will being unable not to delight in this. Occam, for his part, made the divine will, conceived as *potentia absoluta*, the one rule of a being now nothing but total indeterminateness.

William of Occam

By identifying the freedom of God's will with such a total power of doing and deciding, Occam seems at first sight to have exalted God into the most absolute sovereignty conceivable. In fact, he did nothing of the sort. Rather, he reduced God's omnipotence to absurdity and substituted a monstrous tyrant, in whom no one could possibly believe, for the Father from whom proceeds all fatherhood in heaven and on earth.

It must be stressed that we have here an about-turn of the greatest significance. It is hard to believe that someone so clear-headed as Wil-

---

[9] E. Gilson, *Jean Duns Scot*, Paris, 1952.

liam of Occam[10] did not know exactly what he was doing. At first sight, we seem to have reached the ultimate in intrepid logical deduction from the biblical premise of a sovereign and infinite God. In fact, we have come to an explicit break with the tradition of the living biblical God whose holiness, as in Isaiah's vision, is identical with a completely indefeasible moral exigency. Far from contradicting this, Hosea's vision of the God of mercy which, by reason of its very infinity, accomplishes justice in a way beyond our wildest thoughts and dreams. Occam's God, the God of *potentia absoluta*, on the other hand, could quite easily declare the good evil and the evil good. He could, if the fancy took him, do anything whatever, such as incarnating himself in a stone, an ass, even in one of the damned.

At this stage, it is all too clear that the biblical and Christian concept of God has entirely evaporated. Or, to be perhaps more precise, and more discouraging, this concept seems to have been absorbed and then completely emptied of its content by Occam's intemperate dialectic. At the root of everything, this dialectic has set a radical indetermination and perversely confused it with the regal freedom of the God of Jesus and the prophets. Indeed, Occam's work continually conveys an impression of diabolical perversity. There is something monstrous about it. It is the product of a sarcastic, even cynical mind. It is rather like a wonderfully supple, unstoppable, elastic watch-spring which has slipped its escapement and run wild.

How revealing it is that Occam should have defended the tendencies of Franciscan evangelism at their most radical, even anarchic, while at the same time exploiting them for the benefit of imperial absolutism. As such he is the first to spawn one of those modern theologies, where evangelism does away with rationality, does away with the historical inheritance of the society concerned, and all so as to dignify and favor "the poor." But since these "poor" are simply regarded as a mass of unorganized individuals, what happens next is a brazen, theoretical justification of absolute authority. Only this authority is now reckoned capable of representing the oppressed. It abolishes all hierarchy. It levels everything under the crushing weight of its utter irresponsibility, maximalized on behalf of some abstract freedom and an equality which can only annihilate. Such negative eschatologism claims initiation of a "kingdom of this world" freed from any and every restraint and acknowledging nothing beyond itself. And all this can be legitimately

---

[10]E. Guelluy, *Philosophie et Théologie chez Guillaume d'Ockham*, Louvain-Paris, 1947, and L. Baudry, *Guillaume d'Occam*, Paris, 1950.

traced back to the collapse of spirituality climaxing in Occam's conclusion to the theology of the Latin Middle Ages.

The Legacy of Nominalism

So it was that those who continued Occam's work[11] reduced theology, thanks to their theory of a double truth, to logical organizing of an unreal system of revealed truths, truths which their philosophy compelled them to regard as meaningless. As a result of this, Christian spirituality was faced with a disastrous dilemma. It had either to acknowledge itself unreal and merely verbal or to give itself up to moralizing affectivity. And any attempt to make sense of the latter was formally adjudged hopeless.

In Gerson[12] (at the turn of the fourteenth century) and especially Gabriel Biel[13] (in its latter half), we find a definite effort towards exorcizing and ultimately reversing this dialectic. The idea was to restore a higher quality evangelism. But Gerson could only achieve his purpose by striving to justify and by encouraging a wholly affective piety, marginal to and compensation for a theology which was now irredeemably surrendered to gladiatorial combats about self-multiplying abstractions which had less and less to do with the life of the soul—and a soul, incidentally, further and further removed from its own body and *a fortiori* from the physical universe as a whole. Biel, on his part, tried in vain to do a tightrope walk holding together, all too artificially, a dialectic which reduced mystery to incomprehensibility and a legalistic and affective Augustinianism. And as the last word in paradox, this latter sat undecided between a Pelagian moralism and faith in a grace which was merely divine favor, God's view of us changing but we ourselves remaining untouched in our concrete reality.

Here we have Nominalist theology turned pious at its height (and how costly that piety proved!). On the one hand, reaction was inevitable. On the other, the system bore the seeds of a dialectic which laid itself open to the most unpredictable of about-turns. On both counts, it was a simple step to the paradoxes of Lutheranism and Calvinism: a justification justifying us without any need to sanctify us, and a sanctification showing men that we are the predestined just (a privilege of which we are quite certain!) while leaving us sinners in the eyes of God.

---

[11] Jacques Chevalier, *Histoire de la Pensée*, vol. 2: *La Pensée Chrétienne*, Paris, 1956, pp. 501ff.

[12] André Combes, *Jean de Montreuil et le Chancelier Gerson*, Paris, 1942.

[13] Heiko Oberman, *The Harvest of Medieval Theology: Gabriel Biel and Late Medieval Nominalism*, Cambridge, MA: Harvard University Press, 1963.

It goes without saying that in the midst of all these late developments of medieval theology, the Trinity was now no more than an object for dialectical exercises. And the concepts involved were now not even given as much as Duns Scotus' *fundamentum in re. A fortiori*, of course, they lost all bearing on the life of grace within us. One might even wonder whether anyone was still capable of recognizing the reality of grace, such was the atmosphere of the time. On the one hand, monasticism continued but was increasingly Pelagian in spirit. On the other hand, there was an aggressively independent humanism, not yet quite sure of how to justify itself but palpably present in the whole view of man's individual and collective life as found in the work of Occam.

Augustinianism and Neo-Dionysianism

Thomism, then, practically disappeared overnight. The structures it failed to reject gave far more encouragement to the viruses inherited from the university system of philosophy and theology than support, or victory, to the anti-bodies introduced so valiantly by St. Thomas. The Franciscan school, for its part, seemed to uphold the traditional faith against Thomism's apparent secularizing. But given the fallacious character of its dream-theology, no amount of unanswerable logic could do away with the fact that the victory was a purely Pyrrhic one. But it would be unfair to equate the whole history of medieval theology with this. Other currents were present. Augustinianism was an ambiguous factor, and so platonizing was its Christianity that its piety was inevitably misleading, but it did persist. Then again, despite their apparent eventual failure, there were the repeated inroads of another theology, probably best called Dionysian or Neo-Dionysian or even possibly Gregorian. It takes its origin from Gregory of Nyssa and Denys. It was revised by Maximus the Confessor. And in the course of the Middle Ages, it underwent a series of successive revisions at the hands of Scotus Erigena in the ninth century, William of St. Thierry in the twelfth, Master Eckhart in the fourteenth and Nicholas of Cusa in the fifteenth.

The textbooks, however, over-simplify matters by reducing the survival of Augustinianism merely to those theologians who would have nothing to do with post-Abelardian Scholasticism, such as, with their differing emphases, St. Bernard and the great Victorines.

In these two cases Augustinianism did not merely survive, it was renewed. But it is essential to add that it was thanks to the great Scholastic *Summae* of Saints Thomas and Bonaventure that the best of the Augustinian legacy was kept alive throughout the Middle Ages, and that it was in them that that legacy was put to the best use.

Yet St. Bernard on his part showed himself capable of writing *De Gratia et libero arbitrio*, a book in which Augustine's principles are deepened by being developed and even corrected with unusual felicity. St. Bernard showed how Augustine's concept of the Creator God desirous of having his creatures share his own life did not require, as its necessary complement, any suppression of created freedom. Rather it enhanced the vision of that freedom, and showed divine grace simply as the force bringing it to full flower.

St. Bernard, apparently unconsciously, was exceedingly close to Maximus the Confessor at this point. He was also, presumably, the most immediate source of the best of the Franciscan outlook: that awareness of uncreated Love summoning created love, and doing so, not to satisfy some subtle transcendent egoism, but for the latter's own good.

Nonetheless, the most outstanding and potentially most promising development of Augustinian theology (in the strict sense) must definitely be attributed to the Victorines. This is not found so much in their liking for exemplarism (a second source of the Franciscan tradition, but lacking the purity and vigor of the other), which was too much out to edify not to let facile sentimentality impair its vigor. It lies rather in the Trinitarian doctrine still attributed to Richard. Richard, certainly, illustrated it with success but, as we know now, merely popularized ideas received from his master, Achard, eventually bishop of Avvanches.[14] By a stroke of genius, this theology retained the primitive elements in Augustine's psychological analogy—*mens, notitia, amor*—but avoided the high price that had to be paid in insoluble problems. It described the Father as the original Lover, the Son as the Beloved who answers perfectly to his love, and the Holy Spirit as their common Love projected in a person who proceeds from one and rests in the other.[15]

Yet we have to admit that none of the Victorines, not even Richard himself, proved capable of fleshing out this intuition with a total, systematic theology of the divine life in itself and in us. Nor did they ever set out clearly the meaning of that personal love into which their pneumatology flowered. In other words, off the strictly Scholastic axis, the medieval Latin theology's most useful contributions to the doctrine on God owed more to the rediscoveries of the Greek Fathers, however partial they may have been, than to the exploitation of St. Augustine.

---

[14]Cf. the *op. cit.* of Ribailler and Chatillon.

[15]Cf. above pp. 224ff.

Dom Déchanet demonstrated this most impressively as regards William of St. Thierry.[16] But it is already markedly true of Scotus Erigena, three centuries earlier.

Yet there is something that applies to Scotus Erigena, as well as to Master Eckhart and Nicholas of Cusa, namely that the first and most weighty Greek patristic influence on these Latins was Ps-Denys, as translated and popularized by Erigena himself. One should add, too, that the influence of Denys on St. Thomas was hardly less than on the theologians we are about to speak of. This holds particularly for his doctrine on God and on our participation in his life. Many modern Thomists, predictably, find this rather embarrassing.

There is of course a reason for this embarrassment and for the usually marginal place allotted to the authors we are at present concerned with, namely what could be called the discomfiture about Dionysianism in the modern era. After all, the person once enthusiastically regarded as an immediate disciple of the apostles has been revealed by modern criticism to be not merely pseudonymous but an expert forger. Then, worse still, he has become suspect of Monophysitism and generally been categorized as a Neo-platonist in Christian disguise or at least as a Christian soaked in Neo-platonism.

Vladimir Lossky, however, was perspicacious enough to suspect otherwise and some very fine recent works, such as those of Walther Völker[17] (as yet unechoed in France), have given substance to another view. For one, Denys' Christianity is essentially orthodox, and the Monophysitism of certain occasional expressions, such as "theandric activities," is purely verbal, as it was with so many others. But the more important point to acknowledge is that Denys certainly did not passively surrender to Plotinus' or even Proclus' prestigious cosmology and theology. Rather, he recast them and arguably did so with more skill and effectiveness than St. Augustine.

In fact, what applies to Gregory of Nyssa, one of his principal sources, applies also to Denys. Both were in perfect possession of Greek religious philosophy and, more especially, of their contemporary Neo-platonism, and as such, far from being its slaves, were able to use it for their own purposes and do so remarkably freely. As Vladimir Lossky showed, the proof of this lies in Denys' use of Plotinian dialectic. He applied it at the

---

[16]J. M. Déchanet, *Aux Sources de la Spiritualité de Guillaume de Saint-Thierry*, Bruges, 1940, and *Guillaume de Saint-Thierry, l'Homme et son Oeuvre*, Bruges-Paris, 1942. (Eng. trans. *William of St. Thierry, the Man and his Work*, Spencer, MA, 1972.)

[17]Walther Völker, *Kontemplation und Ekstase bei Pseudo-Dionysius Areopagita*, Wiesbaden, 1958.

very point where it had run into the ground: the One. According to Denys, if God is above every concept, he must be no less above the One than above the Good and Being.

This was a very Plotinian way of correcting Plotinus. But it is essential to assess its significance properly. It did more than more or less adapt the Plotinian Triad to the Christian Trinity, more than lift the latter into a rigorous transcendence which would have left even Plotinus gasping. It took away everything that smacked of degrading divinity to the level of cosmic reality and any possibility of identifying the cosmos with a God who could be immanentized into multiplicity.

But this does not mean that Denys had any intention of severing the creature's participation in the divine life. Rather, his conception of the "heavenly" and "ecclesiastical" "hierarchy" gave the created a hope of entrance into the life of God even in its super-transcendence, and at the same time did not compel creation to cancel out its own specific existence. To regard the Dionysian hierarchy as merely transposing neo-platonic *taxis* to the cosmos and the Church is an incredible mis-understanding. The neo-platonic scheme confused the existence specific to every kind of being with their rigorous confinement to the sphere allotted them in a wholly graded universe. Denys' view of the hierarchy, however, was quite different and he could hardly have explained it more clearly or at greater length. According to him, hierarchy means that every gift God gives us, everything which establishes us in being and in the being specific to ourselves, can only be kept, possessed, and exercised by sharing itself with those not as yet raised so high.

He goes on to say that in doing this the created hierarchy imitates the uncreated "thearchy" of the life of the Trinity. And it does more still; it participates in the divine love characteristic of the Trinitarian life, love that does nothing but give, giving not just what one has but what one is. In other words, Denys did away with the compartmentalized, stratified universe of the Neo-platonists, a universe so partitioned that to leave one's proper level was to lose one's specific existence and be reintegrated with the One only at the price of a conversion which was equivalent to annihilation. What Denys set in place of this was an essentially dynamic universe, where life of any kind lives only by generous communication, only as an image intimately associated with its model: the Trinity, that communion of transcendent life.

Finally, it must be stressed—and the very words *thearchy* and *hierarchy* do this—that Denys is not speaking of some kind of simple process of reciprocal interchange, like a series of mirrors reflecting one another into infinity. Rather, communication is what he has in mind, a communica-tion of the greatest liberality springing from the primary source of the invisible Father and imitating and reproducing his generosity in a single movement which ultimately returns to him. It may be that every element in what Denys would have called this cosmic and supercosmic vision comes from Plotinus or Proclus. But every element, no less, has been decisively and Christianly corrected and, for all its Greek clothing, his final picture of the universe, with its likeness to its divine source and its return to that source, is wholly biblical.

Scotus Erigena

Scotus Erigena was not the first Westerner to know of Denys (Gregory the Great, for instance, shows signs of having been influenced by him) but he was the first, after Hilduin's poor-quality translation, to acclimatize him. In this, he was assisted by the commentaries of Maximus the Confessor. These were not just strongly Christian in tone but markedly "Christic." They were a re-reading of Denys in which the keynote of Christ, the Logos made flesh for our salvation, passed from being the ubiquitous presupposition it must have been in Denys to being something continually formal and explicit. Erigena had a fascinating mind, and much could be said of his originality, not to say curiosity. But it is strange that, for once, Gilson lost his usual penetration and let himself be taken in by appearances. The point is that Erigena instinctively sensed the deficiencies in the West's over-narrow Augustinianism (his controversy with Gottschalk on predestination would have brought these home to him) and strove to exploit anything among the Greeks capable of over-ruling such constriction. This is why Gilson could say that he succeeded in collating and synthesizing every isolated formula of the most orthodox Greeks capable of being given a heretical twist. There is a truth in such a witty observation, certainly, but nothing like the deepest truth.[18]

Dom Maïeul Cappuyns' splendid work on Erigena[19] proposed, to our view, a much better assessment. Scotus' manner of presentation is undoubtedly disconcerting, particularly, perhaps, his terminology, while the most deceptive feature of all is his own private way of using the traditional language. But the theology of God and the universe underlying his *De Divisione Naturae* is essentially orthodox. Its great merit lies in its being a first sketch, tributary to Denys, of an original yet synthetic vision of the divine life, both in the economic and the immanent Trinity.

---

[18] E. Gilson, *La Philosophy*, Paris, 1944, p. 222. (Eng. trans. *History of Christian Philosophy in the Middle Ages*, London, 1955).

[19] Dom Maïeul Cappuyns, *Jean Scot Erigene*, Louvain-Paris, 1933.

This is something that the Latin Middle Ages was to find extremely difficult.

As is known, *De Divisione Naturae* distinguishes within "nature" in general four "natures," i.e., four fundamental modes of existence within being, created and uncreated. The first is *natura non creata et creans*, i.e., the divine being, considered primarily in the Father, the creator par excellence, the initial "producer" of every other existent both within the Trinity and outside it. Then there comes *natura creata et creans*, the existence proper to the Son who is eternally produced by the Father and is predestined to be both the model of every creature and to be identified with them through the incarnation. Whence flows *natura creata et non creans*: the existence of the cosmos and especially of man, its summary. And finally everything is recapitulated in *natura non creata et non creans*, the divine being considered as the term of every kind of procession both *ad extra* and *ad intra*: a recapitulation brought about by the procession of the Spirit and the gathering of everything into him.

The all too noisome originality of such a statement can, of course, raise barriers and gives an incongruous sound to many of its expressions. But Erigena's theological vision can be accounted, not just orthodox, but one of the most harmonious produced by the medieval West.

Master Eckhart

At the other end of the Latin Middle Ages we find another, similar synthesis, one on the whole stronger and riper, though weaker on the point of layout. This was the work of Master Eckhart, a man gifted on the one hand with undoubtedly exceptional mystical experience and on the other with an astonishing capacity for expressing it in a popular way. He worked under influences analogous to those of Scotus Erigena, but enjoying the benefits of the Thomist synthesis—something he intended not to replace but to interpret thanks to a full-scale reactivation of the Dionysian inheritance.[20]

At first sight, Eckhart has every appearance of being more neo-platonic or, more specifically, Plotinian, than Denys. Unlike the latter, he seems not to want to go beyond the One in God, but to situate what is most divine in God in a *deitas* that transcends the persons. But, as a counterweight to this, he does something extremely surprising: turning

---

[20]The critical edition of Eckhart's German and Latin works stimulated some excellent reassessments of his mysticism. These have been summarized by L. Cognet, *La Mystique rhénoflamande*, Paris, 1960. But his theology has still hardly been studied. Cf. the chapter of E. Gilson in his *Philosophie du Moyen-Age*, and V.I. Lossky, *Théologie négative et connaissance de Dieu chez Maître Eckhart*, Paris, 1960.

the Augustinian triad: *esse, vivere, intelligere,* on its head and putting *intelligere* at the source of everything in God.

This is the first paradox, the first apparent contradiction. A second one goes with it, namely the marked opposition between his earliest writings and those from the end of his life. In the former, such as the *Questions on Being,* he places God, precisely as *intelligere,* beyond or, rather, on the near side of being, even going so far as to say: *Unde statim cum venimus ad esse venimus ad creaturam...,* "the moment we come to being, therefore, we come to the creature." In his later writings, on the other hand, he asserts that God is not just being but the only being, creatures in themselves being pure nothingness.

These oppositions look like contradictions. But they are easy enough to reconcile when attention is given to the starting-point and thrust of Eckhart's conception of God and existence in general. To begin with, he follows both St. Augustine and St. Thomas, though if anything with more vigor and depth, in equating being in the full sense with conscious, thinking being. But he goes further, taking his cue from the real meaning of St. Thomas' *De Veritate* while not balking at contradicting it verbally. He takes as far as it can go the thoroughly Thomist notion that thought in act, consciousness, in the fullness in which it is found in God alone, is the source of everything, both within the divinity and in every possible existent.

Hence the Father, for Eckhart, is defined by *intelligere.* The Son is the content or, better, the eternal product of this absolute knowledge which is simultaneously absolute self-consciousness, and so is *vivere,* as the principle of every distinct being. God is seen to be *esse,* though, only in the procession of the Spirit, the unity manifest at the very beginning of the processions now reappearing at their term. E. Gilson inclined to the view that Eckhart, in saying this, was doing little more than keeping himself on the right side of Christian tradition while, on the one hand, getting ready to say, in line with that tradition, that being is in God and God is being and, on the other, taking being back only to the term of the divine processions. But this interpretation does not seem to do justice to the coherence of Eckhart's thought.

It would only be valid, in fact, if Eckhart had not affirmed that *esse purum et plenum* is to be found only in God, after maintaining in the most extreme possible form the formula of the treatise *De Causis:* "being is the first of created things," thus taking the opposite line to St. Thomas' more emollient one and even going so far as to say, as quoted above: "the moment we come to being, therefore, we come to the creature." Gilson himself would surely not have admitted that Eckhart had made a radical about-face in the meantime. No, rather, it seems that Eckhart is here connecting up with the common Greek patristic idea that it is in the procession of the Spirit that the inner divine life achieves its unalterable, unsurpassable perfection, and that it is because this is so that God's life can in some sense burst out of itself and be imparted even to creatures which of and in themselves are nothing. But if they alone have mere being—i.e., neither *intelligere* nor even simply *vivere*—then being in its "purity," a word which for Eckhart suggests not just integrity but unlimited fullness, is only to be found in God. But then in God, too, contrary to the development found in creatures, being comes at the term whereas with them it comes at the beginning. God, as it were, completes himself in being and then projects himself, so to speak, beyond himself into the being of creatures. The task of the latter is to ascend from the being simply gifted them by God to life and finally to intelligence or understanding.

But—and here we come to the very springs of Eckhart's mysticism —there is only one way for this last to flower into total, unified consciousness, i.e., one which identifies itself with the one divine consciousness of the Father, and that is by the passing-over of being and then of the living soul into that divine spark, the soul's quasi-entelechy and the force drawing it out of nothingness, in the wake of created being, only by drawing it to God and in God. Such a perspective enables Eckhart to say something incredibly bold: that the Spirit resting on us leads to such an identification of ourselves with the Son that the Father would cease to be Father if he not only ceased to beget the Son but even ceased to beget him *in us*.

But our vocation to involvement with the life of the Trinity reaches its climax in an absorption into the *deitas*, the divine unity which even transcends the distinction of persons. What does Eckhart mean by this? We might think that he has fallen, here, into the standing temptation of Latin Trinitarianism: putting prior to the persons, or over and above them, an essence from which they in turn proceed and which, as is clear from Cajetan, is the equivalent of what we mean by person—a being subsisting in and by itself. But he did not do this. What he did do, in our view, is something quite different. His deity, with its sublime unity, consists in the dynamism, communication, communion which is simply identical with that "pure being," which is the one being of God. Indeed, following the formula which was perhaps Eckhart's greatest stroke of genius, God is being at its poorest, i.e., he who only possesses himself by giving himself. The Father is conscious only of the Son. The Son lives only *ad Patrem* in the procession of the Spirit. The Spirit rests on the Son and recapitulates in the Father the whole Trinity and, beyond that, everything real or conceivable outside the Trinity. And the Father, finally, is thought of as springing forth from or, rather, as the springing forth of the One Who lies beyond all multiplicity while at the same time enhancing it.

Such a view of Eckhart's thought is, in our opinion, the only one which shows its unity and shows that unity as a living and progressing one. It enables us to see how profoundly coherent his thought was: subtle, certainly, but with an integrity to its development and aimed at capturing an exceptional experience. If our assessment is right, Eckhart's thought was quite as orthodox as that of Scotus Erigena, though, if anything, even more unusual. But one can also see how, in a climate of Hegelian or post-Hegelian idealism, it could easily sponsor an irreversible debasement of the Christian God. A misunderstanding of the opposition between the unity of the *deitas* and the irreducible multiplicity of the Trinity could engender any of the modern species of unitarianism, with their claim of transcending traditional dogma by an ecumenism which is in fact nothing more than another version of syncretism. The primacy accorded thought and, specifically, consciousness, plus a parallel isolation of divine self-consciousness could quite as easily produce Fichte's idealism as Hegel's. Finally, there is Eckhart's affirmation of a participation in the generation proper to the Son on the part of the adopted creature, a participation so real that it becomes inseparable from that generation. In the eighteenth century, we have the poet and mystic Angelus Silesius taking up this affirmation and orchestrating it to effect. But when we come to Hegelian idealism, it degenerates into a full-scale immanentizing of the Trinity into the general process of the world's and more particularly human consciousness' unfolding.

It remains true, nonetheless, that these distortions of Eckhart's thought make nonsense of it. Certainly, it was essentially dialectic, but in a way much subtler than that espoused by modern idealists or materialists. Eckhart was at once one of perhaps the most paradoxical and the most coherent Christian theologians, and to quote him in isolation or to base one's interpretations on a few propositions abstracted from the full cycle of his thought is inevitably to travesty him. Indeed, it can be said more truly of him than of almost anyone else that any literal exegesis which refuses to go beyond the letter is bound to misunderstand.

William of St. Thierry

In Erigena and Eckhart, then, we have two disciples of Denys who, though following separate paths, were both outstanding in their originality. Between them, however, there falls another medieval theological opus different by reason of its discretion, a discretion, in fact, that has for long prevented its receiving the attention it deserves. Its importance nonetheless is unavoidable and it is high time it be acknowledged. Much of it was long taken to be the work of St. Bernard, but though its author was friend and admirer of the saint, neither his friendship nor his admiration ever prevented his taking different positions. We are referring to William of St. Thierry, a man whose place in the history of spirituality has been increasingly realized. What still needs to be appreciated is that he is hardly less important a figure in the field of theology properly so called.[21]

William had sat with Abelard at the feet of Anselm of Laon, and one cannot help but wonder whether Abelard conceived the idea of his famous *Sic et Non* after hearing the critical questions which were habitual with William from the very beginning. He read the Fathers extensively, and the Greeks no less than the Latins. This made it possible for him, later, to correct and complete his original Augustinianism through an in-depth knowledge of Origen, Gregory of Nyssa and even Evagrius of Pontus, which was unequaled in the medieval West. One may wonder, too, whether perhaps his monastic conversion was an early reaction to the start of Abelard's clash with their common teacher, a clash that would lead Abelard to replace what was an essentially traditional and meditative theology with one essentially dialectic in character, demolishing the *auctoritates* by opposing them one to another and so leaving the ground free for the construction of a personal theological edifice.

In any case, there is no doubt that William was at one with the greatest Greek Fathers from Athanasius to Maximus in associating true theology with authentic monasticism. William always took *scientia* in the sense in which the Greek Fathers took *gnosis*, and knew full well that the dogmas of faith can only be "known" by being assimilated, that is by becoming the very stuff of a way of life which has been wholly handed over to the rule of a lived faith by way of Christian asceticism. We find this approach systematized in his *Mirror of Faith*. Theological knowledge can only be one thing: a journey towards contemplation of the objects of faith or, better, the one object of faith; a journey accomplished in perfect "unity of Spirit" with the Spirit himself.

As Dom Déchanet rightly showed against E. Gilson, this is the meaning we should give William's favorite formulas: *Amor ipse notitia est, amor ipse intellectus est*: "It is love that is knowledge, love that is understanding." This has nothing to do with the familiar idea of the Franciscan tradition, namely that in this life, where we live by the obscurity of faith, love must replace understanding if we are to come to the knowledge

---

[21]Cf. our *Spiritualité de Cîteaux*, Paris, 1955, pp. 89ff.

of God, knowledge that will only satisfy our intellect in the future life. William of St. Thierry's view is the complete opposite. Only in eternity will love give a perfect consummation to our knowledge. But, in the present world, the necessary condition for an authentic and growing knowledge of God is the progress of our love.

Such is William's view of the relationship between theology and spirituality, the latter being simply the life of faith within us. And this opens our way into his theology of the Trinity, which he outlines modestly but firmly in his *Enigma of Faith*.

William was a spiritual writer whose formation had been thoroughly Augustinian and who had assimilated Augustinianism in depth. This makes it fascinating to meet in him the one Latin theology which completely abandoned Augustine's psychological explanation, while carefully retaining what was so wholly traditional in it and had been so vigorously renewed by it, namely the underlying recognition of the Son as the thought of the Father, and of the Spirit as the gift of love. What William, now mature in thought and experience, offers us is a synthesis but one which, for all his affection for the great Greek thinkers, does more than just reintroduce into the West what de Régnon called the Greek schema and which is only, as he himself recognized, the most ancient pattern of Trinitarian theology, both Latin and Greek. William transcends this opposition. He comes back to what we have described as the eucharistic vision of biblical and gospel revelation, that vision expressed so clearly in the ancient liturgies, beginning with the Roman liturgy.

William begins with the Father, the origin of the Godhead and therefore of every existent thing. But he shows us, too, how an eternal Son can be the thought (*logos*) by which the Father eternally expresses himself to himself while at the same time becoming an externalized word in the Incarnation, the Word made flesh, in whom the Father reveals his fatherhood to us by adopting us in this Son. The Spirit then, proceeding from the Father and resting on the Son, is revealed as substantial, personal love, a love in whom Father and Son, at the term of the processions, rediscover themselves, as it were, as one, just as they are one already by virtue of the eternal origin of the Son.

But we ourselves can only come to a real knowledge of that life which makes for the unity of the Trinity by being introduced into that love, poured into our hearts by the Holy Spirit, assimilating us to the Son therefore and so leading us back with him to the Father in an eternal eucharist.

As we said before, there could be nothing more restrained and yet nothing more deeply traditional than such a theological vision, with its situating of theology within spirituality and so as inseparable from it. But to have recovered such a vision with such integrity and to have conveyed it in such purity required much. It required sensitive perception of and a living sympathy with every current of tradition, as well as a singular capacity for intuitive synthesis. And it seems that the Latin Ages produced no one else with such a combination of qualities, either before William or after him.

Nicholas of Cusa

Turning to Nicholas of Cusa,[22] the last representative of the successive medieval renaissances of Christian hellenism, we leave behind William's discretion (with all its underlying powers, nonetheless, of discernment and free choice). What is striking about Nicholas is his originality. It was such that arguably he even outdid Scotus Erigena in this respect; such, that he could, in every sense, run through the whole of tradition extracting fistfulls of material as he went and then giving what he laid hold of, be it ancient or modern, such a vigorous shine that he seemed to be inventing truths rather than discovering them.

There was, certainly, something very modern, in the sense of journalistic, about him. He flashes through everything, never stopping and never taking the time either to deepen anything or even to develop it. But his genius, albeit somewhat intermittent, was so outstanding that everything he touched he turned to gold, even when it was a matter simply of bringing out a gold already there. Despite his dilettante streak, then, Nicholas was a deep thinker and one possessed of great balance coupled with an extraordinary unconventionality. We can trace these qualities back, presumably, to the fact that he was, by nature, a man of action and, as a result of his first choice, a jurist, and yet at the same time driven by a desire for total truth and insight, a desire that could only be slaked by strictly mystical contemplation.

Hence this man of the Church who championed papal authority so stoutly could be passionately interested in the theology and mysticism of the suspect Eckhart and, though an incorrigible gyrovague, could lavish nostalgia and friendship on his beloved Carthusians at Tegernsee.

He is remembered, in the first place, for his formula: *coincidentia oppositorum*, according to which everything mutually opposed, as contradictory, in the creature is reconciled, as complementary, in God. Were such a formula isolated from the deep experience of contrast that lay

---

[22]E. Vansteenberghe, *Nicolas de Cues*, Paris, 1920 and M. de Gandillac, *La Philosophie de Nicolas de Cues*, Paris, 1941.

behind it or from Nicholas' over-ruling awareness of reality's oneness, an awareness he never lost and which sharpened with time, then, indeed, it could seem to voice the blandest and abruptest kind of pantheism, translatable into the farcical formula: "Everything is in everything...and conversely." But such an assessment would be grossly unjust—a total misunderstanding and a false reading of Nicholas' mind. As precursor of the integral calculus, he enjoyed developing mathematical images such as that of asymptotic curves tending to a straight line. This suffices to show that his meaning lay elsewhere.

What gives cohesion to the thought of this great realist, who was so in love with concrete reality, was, as Jacques Chevalier saw, a quasi-mystical intuition of how, within negative theology, there lies a hyper-positiveness but one which never can be contained by any of our formulations of reality since the reality these express is essentially limited.

Thus, for Nicholas, God is in no way confused with the world or with the human spirit. Rather, he is the "Absolute at its maximum," yet coincident with "Contraction at its maximum," meaning that infinite being is at once so simple and so vast that it cannot be enclosed by the finite. On the human side, the soul is a true microcosm, containing in its original unity everything God contains but in a state of *implicatio* distinct from God's *complicatio*. Then human knowledge, which develops by entering the multiplicity of sense-perceptible reality, proceeds to "explicate" its own unity by way of the universe. But in man, the two activities of *complicatio* and *explicatio* alternate and oppose one another, whereas God, so far as *complicatio*, makes everything be in him by simply being himself and, at the same time, under the aspect of *explicatio*, is personally present in everything there is. Hence, whatever is exists in God's mind as a model, whereas it exists in us simply as an image.

Yet, in us, the world—provided we let ourselves be possessed by Christ who is the coincidence of God with ourselves—will in its turn coincide with God in the Spirit. This is the true *docta ignorantia*, and it opens the way to ultimate knowledge, the knowledge proper to the unitive *intellectus* which does not contradict discursive *ratio* but rather perfects it by going beyond it. Apparently irrational; in fact, supra-rational.

The timing of all this is extraordinary. It was on the very eve of the apparently irredeemable break-up of the Latin Middle Ages that there appeared, in Nicholas, the first and greatest ecumenist of all time, one who was able to foresee an ultimate reconciliation without mitigating in the least the unavoidable demands it would impose nor turning a blind eye to the insurmountable difficulties standing in its way. Yet the prophetic, if somewhat sibylline, expression he gave to his vision was too much at odds with the growing provincialism of his contemporaries for it even to hold their attention, while those who came after, and in turn were at variance with those who had gone before, only patronized it in support of their pseudo-universalism and therefore thoroughly misunderstood it.

Nicholas of Cusa had had hopes for a reconciliation of Eastern and Western Christendom, and even for a resolution of the conflict between Islam and Christianity, and he had progressively turned all his thinking and all his ecclesiastical activity in this direction. But the generations that followed him were to see the very opposite, the break-up of Western Christendom in the Protestant Reformation. And at the same time, there was to take place the so-called "retreat from Christianity," the ebbing of Christianity or rather the ebbing of humanity from it, with unity no longer conceivable except as a cosmopolitanism more and more drained of its spiritual substance.

XVII

From Theology Degenerated into Religious Anthropology to Idealist Philosophy

The Theology of the Reformers

There can be no question about the prophetic element at the root of Luther's protest; it came even more to the fore, perhaps, on many points with Calvin. The whole of culture had been secularized, but its sacredness was patently sham and, in their reaction against this, the Reformers unquestionably restored the true meaning of Christian salvation as a sovereign work of God within us through the grace given in Jesus Christ. Such was Luther's insight, and Calvin, who in turn took it up and systematized it with the greater vigor, was able to draw the consequence: man, once genuinely saved, can henceforth have no other end in life than the glory of God.

Behind all this, surrounding it and sustaining it, there lay, of course, a rediscovery of the Word of God, of its constant, overarching relevance, of its irresistible presence in our thinking and living.

Given such presuppositions, one might have hoped for the resurrection of a theology such as William of St. Thierry had championed with such clarity over against Abelard, i.e., a theology which would not claim to submit and subject God's word to fallen human reason, but which would strive to fulfill St. Anselm's program (a program that he, unfortunately, was on occasion one of the first to transgress) "not of penetrating the depths of God but of understanding, so far as possible, that truth from God which our hearts believe and love."[1]

Yet, surprisingly, if we try to look for the Reformers' doctrine of God, we are forced to admit that they did not have one. Or, to be more precise, they showed a disconcertingly passive docility in repeating that doctrine of the decadent medieval theologians who had been the prime agents of

---

[1]The beginning of the *Proslogion*.

that very distortion of Christianity which the Reformation was intended to reform.[2]

It is this lack which explains the progressively heretical and schismatical bent of the Reformation and its final submersion in a kind of Christianity which even outdid in decadence that which it had begun by counter-acting. And there are two factors, in turn, which explain this strange lacuna. The first was the growing individualism of the late Middle Ages. The Reformers were themselves its unconscious victims. And then, even more in evidence, there was the excessive reflexiveness of the mind, in short, the subjectivism, which had already run riot in the best piety of the period. It speaks volumes that Luther should have reduced Christianity to human salvation or, worse still, to "my" individual "salvation." He did more than make religion merely a private affair; he reduced our interest in Christ and in God simply to what they are "for me." When Kirk analyzed Heiler's fine passages on Luther's prayer, he was able to show with ease how it issued in an egocentricity which was not even remotely Christian or biblical, and often relapsed into a species of magic prayer in which the worshiper praises and cajoles his god simply to get whatever he wants by hook or by crook.

Calvin, while keeping inviolate the primary insight into the sheer divine gratuity of our salvation, realized that this salvation would be totally meaningless unless it became for us, individually and collectively, the principle of a new way of life wholly dedicated to the glory of God alone. And this, surely, was his great merit. On this basis, he was able to make the clear and wholly healthy affirmation that sinful man can only hate been genuinely justified when we see him, in St. Paul's phrase, working out his own salvation with "fear and trembling," while never forgetting that "it is God who is at work in us, both to will and to work."

But this makes it all the more surprising to see Calvin quite as incapable as Luther of freeing himself from the framework of post-Occamist theology. He continued to confuse God's sovereignty with its parody, the *potentia absoluta*. At the same time, he proved himself equally incapable of distinguishing the analogy of being from the merely univocal, and this had the same fatal consequence for him as for Luther, making all intrinsic goodness imparted to the creature by the Creator appear as an unacceptable diminishment of his exclusive greatness.

Here we touch on the permanence of the second factor which was to prove fatal for the Reformation: the separation between theology and spirituality, a separation complete since Gerson and praised so wonder-

---

[2]Cf. our *The Spirit and Forms of Protestantism*, London, 1956; the chapters on Luther and Calvin.

fully but so dangerously by the *Imitation*. A spirituality which holds theology in contempt and, in a flush of false humility, thinks itself able to exist without it *ipso facto* gives a blessing to a theology the principles of which will now be confined to narrow rationalism and which will show itself incapable of expressing the mystery while being all too adroit at travestying and emptying it.

From this comes that kind of theology of which Calvin is the source: with his predestinationism on the one hand and his Nestorianism on the other (so ineradicable that the repeated efforts of piety to go beyond it invariably fail), he separated the human and the divine in Christ, *a fortiori* in the Church, in the sacrament, in the whole experience of the Christian. Barthian theology represents the ultimate in this line: an unconscious theological Tower of Babel set up to justify at any cost a glorification of God that systematically empties his creative and redemptive work of all real content and so, by way of its own catastrophic collapse, opens the door to theories of secularization and of the death of a god congenitally hostile to man.

At such a point, it is extremely interesting to embark on a parallel study of two equally lucid and highly ingenious theological undertakings, one by a Counter-Reformation Catholic, the other by a second generation Protestant. Both were alarmed at the rise of atheistic humanism. Both saw it as already submerging their respective movements of reform and were too aware of its strength to oppose it without taking account of its authentic insight. Both, too, appeared to provide theologians, Catholic or Protestant, with the means of defending themselves against the oncoming flood. In fact, however, they merely provided precarious shelter, an illusion of safety which lulled minds to sleep, and the tidal wave that came swept away the dikes they had built, exposing them as fatally flawed for all their brilliance. We refer to Francisco Suarez and Pierre Ramus. Even though the first sought to buttress the Counter-Reformation and the latter the Reformation, the philosophies they produced are surprisingly alike on many points.

Francisco Suarez

The more one studies Suarez,[3] the less inclined one is to denounce him as the father of every modern heresy. This, though, is what the Jansenists did, what his Thomist Dominican contemporaries had already done and, of course, all those Augustinians who had reformed their

---

[3] J. Chevalier, *op. cit.*, pp. 665ff. has given one of the most positive recent interpretations of Suarez.

ranks after the debacle of the Reformation, those, that is, who had not been carried off by Luther or drowned in the reaction he provoked.

Suarez, in fact, is profoundly worthy of respect, if for no other reason than his philosophy of law. St. Thomas was his starting point, and what Suarez produced remains the most reliable resource available to the modern world whenever it is engaged on a realistic effort towards social and political justice, either in the international or in the national sphere. Behind such an achievement there must have lain a realism of the healthiest sort, matched by an exceptional capacity for analysis and no mean power of synthesis.

Given that, it is no surprise to find that Suarez's philosophy rests on a well-nigh exhaustive analysis of all accessible previous thought in this domain. As has often been said, if one wanted to draw up an inventory of medieval philosophy, it would be best to begin by reading Suarez. One can only admire the incredible ingenuity and infinite patience with which he strove to knit together every thread, even the most divergent, in order to weave his synthesis. Here, if anywhere, we should be on the brink of a reconciliation between tradition and modernity. Yet the results of all this good will and intelligent industry in the last resort have to be acknowledged as unsatisfying. And if one passes from this certainly very honest and astonishingly dexterous philosophy to the theology which it rendered possible, one is a great deal more than merely unsatisfied. One has to master the anger that can take possession at this point and lead one to accuse the Suarezian synthesis of purely verbal concordism. But one cannot suppress one's disappointment. In fact, as regards the focal point of the doctrine of God and of our association with the divine life, the disappointment is so acute that one feels like repeating the words of Mary Magdalene: "They have taken away my Lord and I do not know where they have put him."

If we wanted to summarize everything in a word, that word would be ecumenism. It is this that lies at the basis of Suarez's thought. Its sincerity can hardly be impugned, nor the labor and skill that went into its construction, but it lies at the other extreme, both in its weak and its strong points, from that kind of ecumenism so worthy of note in Nicholas of Cusa. The latter would take any problem and pitch it at such a height or depth as to take one's breath away and leave one puzzled as to how to follow. Suarez, on the other hand, explains everything and resolves everything with such poise and calm that it all becomes instantly and effortlessly understandable. One is even left marveling at how, before one met Suarez, one could have been so intelligent and never noticed it, so adept at understanding everything with such ease and solving any kind of problem so deftly. But then come second thoughts: perhaps one has not solved any issues but merely side-stepped them. They had seemed to have vanished with a wave of the wand, but in fact it soon dawns on one that they have not gone away at all. They are still there and they have not changed. Nicholas of Cusa's ecumenism was so highly metaphysical that one was taken out of one's depth. Suarez's ecumenism is all diplomacy. The only wisdom, in this field, is the wisdom of his political philosophy: not to put the absolute where it is not, not to deprive oneself of any opportunity to do a limited but genuinely possible good thing. But whereas such an attitude could be highly successful in the political realm, it was disastrously unsuccessful in a realm in which the absolute is precisely what is at issue. Suarez's method was a superb tool for avoiding the danger inherent in every ideology, that of substituting a verbal idol for reality. But when applied to theological controversies, it could only resolve them by a discreet abolition of the reality at stake.

Suarez intended to be a Thomist, and it would be as wrong to question his sincerity in this, as that of so many others who have had the same determination. But he was equally clear that the Thomism he espoused was to be of the intelligent kind, not one which confused fidelity to the master with a deliberate incapacity for facing any problem not already diagnosed and resolved by St. Thomas himself. He was determined to save Thomist ontology at any price. But, so conscious was he of the almost diabolical power of Occamist criticism that he believed the only way of safeguarding the essential was by yielding, so far as could be done, to Occam's relentless nominalist logic. It is strange that a mind of Suarez's insight should not have realized how impossible in practice it is to keep ontology and logic in separate compartments. He seems to have thought that he could hold his ground by dint of certain rearrangements on the frontier and thus leave the heart of the country practically or even wholly untouched. It remains surprising that he should have apparently failed to realize the extent of the ensuing and inevitable readjustments.

Once the real distinction in creatures between essence and existence had been abandoned, it was inevitable that the analogy of being between them and God would be reduced to mere univocity, the inadequacy of which could not be palliated by talk of different levels of application. But, having got to that point, the effective dependence of creatures upon their Creator, and even their distinction from him, can only be maintained by undermining the subsistence proper to what has been created. Conversely, every attempt to reinforce the matter will turn creatures, willy-nilly, into little gods all too liable to aggrandize themselves.

Whence the inevitable consequence that there can be no possible action of such a God on such a creation which does not involve its converse: i.e., a possible determination of God by man or the world and one which, if not actually equal to God's action, is at least homologous to it. Hence it proved all too easy to justify Molina's *scientia media*. This latter purportedly reconciles divine grace and human freedom. In fact, it reconciles nothing. It makes grace depend upon our freedom and at the same time fails to show how freedom can be genuinely free as long as it remains created. At this point, Descartes is at the door. This is the very God whom he will lay hold of, mentioning him merely to reduce his creative activity to the initial flick of a switch.

But even before being compromised by his disciples, Suarez himself, with the best will in the world, had perpetrated something far worse. The adverse consequences of damaging divine transcendence were now to be revealed in the theology of the Trinity and grace. If one refuses to regard God and his creature as communicating vessels, it becomes impossible for us not only to be associated in any way with the inter-relations of the divine persons, but even to be made in any real sense *consortes divinae naturae*, "partakers of the divine nature," to use the phrase of Second Peter. Sanctifying grace is no longer a mysterious adaptation of our nature to a real relationship with God as he is in himself. It is merely a super-nature, bringing us one notch closer to God. Our intrinsic capacity for natural love is simply endowed with a higher metaphysical modality, making it a brighter reflection of God's love. Nor is there even any need for us to be aware of this. Nor is there any real communication of God's love because if there were, given the demands of the system, this would inevitably make us little autonomous deities.

But such, in fact, are the perspectives of Suarezian theology, that it would be misguided for the man adopted by God to be overly disappointed by the merely modal and non-substantial supernatural of which he is the beneficiary. Any more direct association with God and especially with the life of the divine persons would simply have no meaning. In the first place, God has ceased to be the Wholly-Other. He has become merely an enlarged and perfect image of what the human mind itself may already be. He has ceased, therefore, to be the Father in any true sense, either within the Trinity or in relation to us. Indeed, the Trinity has now become what there was always the danger of it becoming once the Augustinian imagery was interpreted too literally, i.e., merely a large-scale projection of our own mental operations. In Suarez's view, in fact— and this holds both for God and for us—personal subsistence does not precede nature either logically or ontologically. It cannot be said to possess it. It cannot be said to add anything to it; it merely completes it. Or, to be more precise, it is in fact the nature which, by completing itself, thereby constitutes personhood. Hence not only is there only one true

God, which is unexceptionable, but, if one were to be logical, one would have to say that there is strictly speaking only one divine person who, after all, is not particularly personal! The only objection to this is the established usage of the Church.

So we have no real grounds for complaint on being told that we are not in any sense called to be sons of the Father but simply of the Trinity or, to be precise, of the single divine essence. And, of course, our sonship is not just adoptive, it is in some sense putative and honorific. Not that even that need be of any great consequence, God's fatherhood, even in God, being now no more than a *figmen mentis*, although it would as yet be thought rather unseemly to say so. And, in any case, to want to apply this eviscerated relationship to us, even with the safeguard of every conceivable and possible distinction, would compel the system to collapse into the very emanationism which it strove so laboriously to avoid and avoided, in the end, only to give us precious little instead.

Pierre Ramus

At first sight, Ramus set out to do something completely different. Suarez began from a moderate realism in the hope of persuading the Nominalists to swallow a good chunk of ontology, liberally buttered with their kind of logic. Ramus, on the other hand, began with language, and alternately connected logic and ontology with it. Thus to enter in depth into the processes and erudition of language was to uncover a necessary shape within thought, a shape that must correspond to the structure of reality itself since, though God is free, in his *potentia absoluta*, either to withhold or to give this structure, he has in fact given it and done so, apparently, irrevocably.

Calvinist Protestant theologians, in particular, and more especially the English Puritans of the seventeenth century who took refuge in Holland en route to found New England, grasped at the possibilities offered by this new philosophy.[4] In fact, they exploited them to the maximum, and thus followed Calvin's own line of development and that of what might be called his Neo-Catholicism. They felt encouraged to develop the theology of man's sanctification by grace in the direction of a real association with the life proper to God himself, and so were enabled to justify the revival, among the most ferociously anti-Catholic Puritans, of a genuinely Christocentric and Trinitarian mysticism. Hence those theologies of the covenant, first initiated by Perkins. They sprang, cer-

---

[4]On Ramus and his influence on reformed theology, see Perry Miller, *The New England Mind, The XVIIth Century*, New York, 1961, pp. 335ff.

tainly, from profound meditation on the Bible but they were articulated thanks to the possibilities opened by Ramus' philosophy.

Lost Opportunities

Whether we turn to the Catholics, especially those of Spain and France, or to the Protestants of Germany and Great Britain, it is quite clear that we are apparently on the brink of a reform of the Reformation or of the moment when a Catholic Reformation is about to supersede the Counter-Reformation. There was a general renewal of biblical and patristic studies and, connected with this, an astonishing rediscovery of mysticism at its most traditional, at the practical as well as theoretical level. One thinks of the catechesis of the great Spanish Erasmians like Caranza; of the positive theology of Petau and Thomassin which distilled the best of what has been called, en bloc, the French School; of the great figures of that School. Francis de Sales, the first Port-Royal, Bérulle and Mme. Acarie, all far closer to each other than their quarrels might lead us to think; of the Jesuits of the lineage of Lallemant and Surin; of the Anglican theology of Hooker and the Caroline Divines, even more perhaps of the Neo-Lutheranism of Johann Gerhard and, as already mentioned, of the inner evolution underway in Puritanism. All this seemed to augur a reconciliation on the theological heights, and a common rediscovery of true theology, a theology which would never sever its links with spirituality nor allow spirituality to cut adrift from it. But why were all these hopes dashed and dashed so soon?

One answer is, of course, the political conflicts which exploited and embittered religious enmities, and which resulted in spiritual and moral collapse. One need only think of the ghastly Thirty Years' War for instance. On top of this came the struggles between religious orders or, more widely, spiritual families (often immersed quite as much in the temporal as in the spiritual!), as between Jansenists and Jesuits, Calvinists and Lutherans, Anglicans and Nonconformists, etc. But behind all this lie the inconsistencies of contemporary religious philosophy. In some cases, there had been unthinking regurgitations of earlier philosophies; in others, artificial but inaccurate exhumations; in others again, brilliant improvisations. But in every case, the foundations proved wobbly and fragile and so vitiated the best-intentioned attempts at reconstruction.

How revealing it is, in any case, that, at the beginning of the seventeenth century, use was being made on both sides of the confessional and political divides, of the materials of a return to the biblical patristic resources, and yet that by the eighteenth century, after half-hearted and fruitless attempts at diplomatic rapprochement, everything should have degenerated into a kind of trench warfare. There was a constant cross-fire sustained by the same make-do philosophies. Each side could use them against the other, but what was not realized was that, thanks to them, another enemy was now on the field: relativism and, in its train, agnosticism.

A characteristic case, here, was the use to which Lutheran Scholasticism put Suarez. This led, through Leibniz (though not through what was genuinely new and profound in Leibniz) to the ultimate in systematization, and lifeless formation: Wolff. But in the case of both Wolff in Germany and of the evolving New England Calvinist theology based on Ramus (well described by Perry Miller) what took the wheel were the unexpurgated elements of rationalism in the underlying systems. This eventually led to such unreality that, once sensualism had broken in, radical skepticism was bound to take over. This had been presaged by Bayle and, with Hume, became a reality. Thus it was that Protestant Scholastics, themselves, slid progressively into agnosticism or left their disappointed disciples at the mercy of plain pantheism. The same fatal finality seems to have governed Suarez's direct posterity, beginning with Descartes.

The Debacle of Theology

Our analysis could, in fact, end here. Christian theology seemed to have triumphed in the great thirteenth-century *summae*. But it proved a Pyrrhic victory, and the rout began. It is this we have just been describing. Suarez, in fact, on the one hand, and the Protestant theologians of *Federaltheologie*, who were so like him, on the other, were the last Christian theologians in the full sense of those words. They were the last at least to attempt seriously to produce a doctrine of God that sought clarity and system through use of the resources of contemporary culture and did its best to answer that culture's inevitable questions. Not that theologians as such, either Catholic or Protestant, became extinct. But, leaving aside the manualists who were duty-bound to touch on everything, it is noticeable how modern theologians have shown themselves willing to discourse on practically anything rather than God. It is as if they have sensed that the concepts they have for such a task simply will not work, and that they do not know where to turn to find more adequate ones.

So, they are forever running round the fringes of what, whether they like it or not, is or should be their central problem. Their chosen subjects, these days, are Christologies which, with increasing explicitness, bracket off God and then lead naturally to soteriologies mainly concerned with telling the Word of salvation that it is dispensable. Or, just to make sure they are really safe, they disclaim any attempt even at such low-level flying and confine themselves, at ground level, to a closed circuit ecclesiology before openly transferring to what they call "the theology of earthly realities." They then finally solemnly dig their own graves and, before stepping in, produce "theologies of secularization" and—as a necessary climax—"a theology of the death of God."

What has really died, of course, is a particular type of theology: a theology that had already collapsed in the second half of the Middle Ages before anyone had become aware of the fact, and collapsed simply because it played the frog who wanted to be bigger than the ox: insisting on submitting the Word of God to naively rationalistic "questions" so as to be able to hold forth *de omni re scibili...et quam multis aliis*!

But the curious thing is that modern philosophers have never stopped gathering around the corpse of this theology, and this despite their apparent initial anxiety to exploit to the full the liberation of philosophy from Christian theology—a liberation which the double-truth Nominalists and, no less, the "Thomists" *ad mentem Joannis de sancto Thoma* congratulated themselves as having accomplished while remaining blissfully unaware of what their success would mean for their successors. These liberated philosophers, however, from Descartes all the way to Husserl and Heidegger (and leaving aside their particular contributions), have never been able to liberate themselves from the corpse which has now been poisoning the air for at least three centuries. In fact close examination of even the most professedly independent philosophies reveals that they are each and all composed of organs deriving from this very corpse which no one has, as yet, decided to inter. It is hardly surprising then if these Frankensteins have so far only managed to fabricate monsters that fall to bits the moment they are set in motion.

Any present-day Christian theologian or, more precisely, anyone who rather rashly, maybe, volunteers to help set modern theology on its feet and on its way, cannot dispense himself from at least cursory examination of these disconcerting experiments. There is room, no doubt, for justifiable criticism of the authors of these attempts but at least they had the merit of undertaking a task which even their failure shows to be necessary and which the professionals appear to be, at present, incapable of acquitting. More importantly, still, they show that mankind cannot seriously undertake this task by first making a *tabula rasa* of biblical and Christian revelation.

Descartes, Kant, Hegel and then those two faces of the existentialist Janus, Kierkegaard and Nietzsche, surely represent the principal moments in this strange spectral survival of Christian theology in a philosophical form—a form which, paradoxically, has substituted itself for it while, in fact, merely reworking it in a more or less ingenuous way. When we come to Husserl and his phenomenology, and to Wittgenstein, with what is perhaps the most thorough-going criticism of modern scientific thought, we hardly find any less dependence on the Judaeo-Christian inheritance but we also meet the first precursors, perhaps even the first actual proclamation, of what philosophy could be once it stopped vainly trying to take over from decadent theology and instead prepared the way for a theology that would at last be regenerate.

But, first, let us look at theology's last incarnations in philosophical disguise. For theology, by now, even if not acknowledging the fact, had been exposed as finished once what is called "the modern world" had got underway.

Descartes

Everyone more or less agrees that Descartes,[5] like Francis Bacon though to greater effect, was not just the first to draw up the plans, as it were, of the modern world but the first actually to begin building. His protestations of orthodoxy were certainly sincerer than Bacon's but, however one assess them, there is no doubt that he did not think of himself as destroying so much as reconstructing, His *tabula rasa* was only aimed at obvious encumberments and, in connection with theology, one's reproach would be, as with the Reformers of the previous century, not that he played the aggressive innovator but rather retained far more than he realized of decadent scholasticism.

It is all too obvious that his God is simply Suarez's God, received by way of his teachers at La Flèche. The only reprehensible element here is that he treated him with a fierce logical exactitude which would have horrified the prudent Suarez who was far too intelligent not to be immediately aware of the frailty attaching to his delicate theological constructions.

Descartes had not the least desire of falling out with such a God. He merely wished to carry on his own business without any danger of divine interference while feeling free to have recourse to him when there was no other option. One can hardly pick a quarrel with Descartes for having such a plan. Suarez's God may not have been conceived for such purposes but he all too obviously meets them.

---

[5]The chapter on "Descartes et Pascal" in J. Chevalier, *Histoire de la Pensée*, vol. 3: *La Pensée moderne de Descartes à Kant*, Paris, 1961, pp. 107ff. gives a far more balanced judgment than Christians usually manage in this sphere.

What Descartes wanted, on one side, was an enclosed area where human ingenuity could have full rein and establish its mastery. This is what he called extension, within which the observation of exact measurement was sufficient to explain everything and thus control everything. Hence man must be autonomous within his own field of operation, just as every kind of substantial nature needed to be, and it was precisely such an autonomy that Suarezian ontology had done its best to shore up and protect against any Occamist logic threatening to bury it in God or God in it.

Besides, Descartes' methodical skepticism would have rebounded against his own project without some firm guarantee of the existence of the external world which was to be the scene of his great adventure. The *Cogito* and its logic proved incapable of furnishing such a guarantee. Once again, Suarez's God stood ready to hand, easily invoked by recourse to that Anselmian ontologism Suarez had just resurrected and triumphantly vindicated. In fact, this God could have nothing better to do than to set in motion this great world machine which Cartesian man was intent on turning to his own advantage. But then he would eventually reappear to stop the gaps which, after all, can occur in the best-regulated determinist systems. This is precisely what Newton feared.

It was not Descartes' fault if thereby he exposed to the cruel light of day (without in the least intending to insult his teachers) that Suarez's God was simply a divine plumber: not just that, admittedly, but certainly nothing greater than that, necessary for installing the system and getting it going and even repairing it when it gets stuck, but with nothing to do in the interval.

Descartes' Posterity: Malebranche and Spinoza

The devout Malebranche,[6] by dint of five minutes casual reading in a book shop, lost his soul to the simplicity, economy and flawless logic of the Cartesian system. But he was also acutely aware of the weakness in it that we have mentioned. The remedy he proposed was to bring extension back into thought, and in order to do that he had to bring the world, including ourselves, back into God. This made it possible for us to know the world and besport ourselves in it without ever leaving God.

But Malebranche's *Traité de la nature et de la grace* was aimed at showing to what extent his simplified Cartesianism had the power to simplify theology. But while it purported to bring about the absorption

---

[6]J. Chevalier, *ibid.*, pp. 270ff.

of nature into grace, it in fact gave most people the feeling of having very successfully confused the two.

Such a system inevitably turned into that of Spinoza. The transition was effortless. It was enough to draw a consequence which Malebranche had failed to see, despite "seeing everything in God" as that scoundrel, Voltaire, said. Once one is in Malebranche's position, in fact, it makes no difference whether one says that the whole of nature is in God or that God is simply nature looked at from the other side (the side from which it happens we cannot see it). Thus God is *natura naturans*, which our intellect sets over against *natura naturata*, whereas in fact it is simply the same thing in reverse.

Berkeley, whose thinking owed much to the stimulus of reading Malebranche, and Leibniz, had a very high opinion of Suarez. Both, however, managed at least to point a way beyond the disastrous alternative bequeathed them by their immediate predecessor. Both, in their different ways, revived Bonaventure's concept of the world as the basic language by which God communicates to his thinking creatures. But since their interests lay in cosmology, they themselves did not draw all the latent theological consequences of such a notion. Nor did any of their successors. Hume only approved of the critical side in Berkeley. For the rest, it was easy enough for his own agnosticism to demolish what Berkeley had built, especially after discrediting it by means of a gauche misinterpretation, the speciousness of which has only recently been fully exposed. Worse still, the only thing Wolff preserved from Leibniz was what Leibniz had taken from Suarez, i.e., his tendency to give a facile explanation of anything and everything by saying "everything is in everything …and conversely," meanwhile putting up a subtle smoke-screen of persuasive syllogisms.

At this point, the field was free for Kant.

Kant

Kant[7] definitely had not the least intention of shelving Christianity. In fact, in the sincerest way possible he wanted to save as much of it as he could from the now painfully obvious shipwreck of a theology which had purported to be both traditional and appropriately modernized. His goal was not atheism. It was, quite definitely, Christian theism. It was to find the path to victory for such theism out of an intellectual world which appeared to have thrown road-blocks across every conceivable exit.

---

[7]On Kant, a Catholic exposition of an unusual serenity can be found in F. Copleston, *History of Philosophy*, vol. 17, New York, 1960.

In the first place, while it is no doubt perfectly true that Kant gave away far too much to the opposition and that his "religion within the limits of reason" was in fact religion reduced to subsistence level by reason at its most voracious, one can retort that he was far from being the first to make such a mistake and that, from at least the thirteenth century, the most creditable theologians had continually been doing the same as he and often worse.

Secondly, given the very positive side (ultimately re-expressive of many Augustinian elements) to the *Critique of Practical Reason* and its follow-up, *Metaphysics of Ethics*, the way modern theologians, especially Catholics—though not only Catholics and not the school of Joseph Maréchal—have obstinately misinterpreted it causes one to suspect that they are if anything more narrowly rationalistic, and certainly less profoundly so, than their *bête noire*.

Manual theology, in its holy simplicity, thought that by having debunked the ultimately jejune and inappropriate attempts of Froshammer and especially of Hermes to turn Kant to apologetic uses, it had done for him once and for all. But it has to be acknowledged that Kant in fact reopened ways through to God, ways that have never been entirely blocked even by any of the philosophical developments following those paths to reality privileged by modern, post-Cartesian physics. Above all, however, as we have said earlier, Kant's analysis of conscience, despite being encased in formalism, does include a real awareness of the inescapably religious element within it, and comes very close to the Thomist analysis of "synderesis."

On the other hand, certainly, the Kantian dissociation of the phenomenal and the noumenal—completing something implicit in Descartes' *Cogito*—must be regarded as untenable.

Hence Fichte's immediate reaction: simple abolition of the noumenal. By this, he guaranteed the wholesale imperialism of the subjectivist transcendental *ego*, but only by installing it in perfect solitude, the price of its perfect freedom. This was a "logicization" on the basis of a single, initial principle which for sheer inexorability has never been equaled. But it could only avoid straight solipsism by a last-minute illogicality.

Schelling[8] reacted by restoring the "absolute" to a position over against the ego, not restricting it merely to one at its base. This was a healthy beginning. But ultimate failure was inevitable—as Hegel saw and said so clearly—because, having defined the absolute by its relationship of opposition to the ego, Schelling could not prevent it remaining something purely negative. His second philosophy was a courageous

[8]See Claude Bruaire's good introduction in *Schelling*, Paris, 1970.

attempt to start again from a broader base. Unfortunately it fell between the two stools of Boehmian occultism and a philosophy of nature which proved itself equally incapable of freeing itself from modern science and of gaining the upper hand over it.

Schelling's system, in other words, was more of a project than an achievement (like that of his admiring emulator, Coleridge), but even in its failure it has a splendor, and Soloviev, at the dawn of the twentieth century, was able to salvage from its wreck no small support for his own thought—one which, despite many imperfections or incongruities, has perhaps been the only one hitherto to move at least a little on the way towards that theological reconstruction which has become such a crying necessity.

Hegel

It is a curious fact that the most ambitious attempt ever made to produce a logical explanation of reality, that of Hegel,[9] should have been no less indebted and arguably more so than Schelling's to one who, despite some astonishing and on occasion unforgettable intuitions, was a genius of mental confusion, namely Boehme.

We will come back to this point at the end. But it is a fact that Schelling's first abortive effort and the pathetic (and inevitable) incompleteness of his retractations left a field free for what can well be called the most colossal philosophico-theological enterprise of the Christian era. Alas, this colossus has proved not so much to have feet of clay as to be based upon ineradicable equivocations. We might call it the sphinx of our era. Whether it stand upright or be stood on its head by Marxists claiming to put it the right way up, it has continued, and no doubt will, to exercise a mysterious power of enthrallment over the modern mind, probably thanks to an inexhaustible capacity of taking on any meaning one cares to give it, none of them being completely reliable.

Here, contrary to what has happened concerning Kant, whereas the Catholics, nowadays, are continually swinging from side to side among Hegel's various heirs, it is the Protestants who, insisting on reading him via Kierkegaard, have made a bugbear of him. According to the Danish Pascal, Hegel was the father of all modern unbelief, while the unfortunate bishop Martensen, who was guilty of attempting a Hegelian Chris-

---

[9]See the two diametrically opposed interpretations of Jean Hyppolite, *Genèse et Structure de la Phénoménologie de l'Esprit*, Paris, 1946, and A. Kojeve, *Introduction à la lecture de Hegel*, Paris, 1947. Similarly, P. Asveld, *Hegel Reformateur religieux*, 1793-1796, Louvain, 1952, and *La Pensée religieuse du jeune Hegel*, Louvain, 1953.

tian Dogmatic,[10] simply personified a Christianity duped by the Anti-Christ in person. As a result, who, since Kierkegaard, has taken the trouble to read Martensen? But if anyone were to, he would realize that the bishop's work is one of the very few of its kind and its period which are still readable. Nor is it at all clear that it amounts to a little summa of concealed infidelity. And if not, then perhaps it might be allowed, at least until proof to the contrary is forthcoming, that Hegel, no less than Kant, never deliberately intended to do Christianity down.

And indeed there is no real reason to suspect the good faith of his repeated protestations to the effect that God does not just exist but is the supreme existent and, what is more, personal being at its perfection, we being able to approach him only because we too are persons and, as such, cannot be destroyed and cannot be confused with anything else. The whole early unfolding of his thought, and then its consequent progress, are not just extremely hard to fault; they are incontestably religious and, with equal seriousness, are intended to be Christian.

But it cannot be denied that Hegel interiorized Christianity radically. He formally identified the rational and the real and, conversely, had being resolving itself into thought. But further still, he became incapable of conceiving of any thought that was not homogeneous to, or even immanent with, human thought—albeit transcending any particular, individual thought or thought arrested short of its full development.

Hence when he said that the Trinity (and he meant, quite clearly, simply the Christian Trinity of Father, Son and Spirit) explains everything, he meant that the whole of reality is nothing but the unfolding of a thought which has to objectify, project, situate itself outside itself, and hence alienate itself in order to find itself once again in the human mind. This development is accomplished by the mind entering into full self-knowledge as it progressively assimilates intellectually first, the nature in which it is born and out of which it is born by a process of opposition, and, then, eventually, human society in which it perfects itself by taking it to its true, freely realized perfection, thereby realizing its own freedom. This became objectively visible in the Christ-event (the summit of human and cosmic history) when Christ consummated his self-projection in his death to rise so far as the Spirit draws out the full effect of that death in us. By understanding the ultimate meaning of this event, our mind will manifest the synthesis, the supreme *Aufhebung* (a provisional denial which safeguards the original datum by ultimately going beyond it) in which the one Idea from which everything has come is finally reconciled with itself.

---

[10]H. L. Martensen, *Christian Dogmatics*, Edinburgh, 1898.

This, of course, supposes that the Son's historical incarnation is nothing but a harbinger at the individual level and in the midst of time of a universal reconciliation accomplished as time issues into eternity. *A fortiori* the Church, which conveys the news and knowledge of Christ to men, is destined to disappear into the one definitive human society, of which the Church is merely an initiator, viz. the perfected State.

Thus Hegel was able to congratulate himself on having finally brought the kingdom of God down on to the earth instead of leaving it inaccessible "in heaven" like the historical Church. But it is clear that he interiorizes Christianity so radically that it achieves incarnation only by deifying man. It is not just that the Spirit of God functions only in what he makes of the human Spirit, but that he only becomes himself when our spirit reaches its full development, God appearing to be simply what man—once the cosmos and society have been wholly humanized—is destined to become.

It is all too clear that this is nothing but Swabian pietism taken to its ultimate logical development. Hegel, after all, had been brought up on this pietism. In the Tübingen *Stift* he had shared rooms with Schelling and Hölderlin, and together they had conceived a grand plan of religious and cultural renewal. It was the pietism of Halle, on the other hand, inherited from Francke, which had exerted a decisive influence on Kant. It had convinced him that the key element of Christianity was not objective revealed truth, such as human speculation and dogma vainly try to capture it, but the blind confidence of "regenerated" man in a God only attainable by loving obedience. Hence the trust accorded only to practical reason. Hence the exaltation of the categorical imperative. But Swabian pietism was very different. It remained essentially speculative. But it held that the Christian dogmas—the redemptive Incarnation, the Trinity—were of value, even of reality, only so far as they could be assimilated and lived as a genuine experience.

"Phenomenology" was a word coined by Oetinger, the greatest figure in Swabian pietism—a word Hegel took over and made famous—and its original reference was precisely to the soul's assimilation of these "truths" which, as far as we are concerned, only become such by being assimilated.

What Hegel did, then, was simply to draw out the ultimate consequences of such "phenomenology." It is true that, for all his intransigent immanentism, he did give it back a certain transcendence. But it was only of a relative kind. He merely meant that the individual who engaged on this process of assimilation simply made conscious—by himself becoming conscious of it—the ultimate reality underlying cosmos and society, a reality that only surfaces, that only becomes fully itself, when the human being achieves a final consciousness of it. The unfortunate aspect, of course, to this Hegelian vision of Being realizing itself in Becoming is that, whether he liked it or not, the triune, incarnate Christian God has become no more than a world-soul, and one realizing itself by revealing itself to, or rather within, the human soul, once that soul has reached the term of its evolution, an evolution that takes place wholly within and on the basis of this world. Hegel's philosophy is infinitely more subtle than that of Spinoza; it did its best to absorb the full richness and complexity of human experience as a whole. But in the last resort it comes back to the same thing: God and the cosmos constitute one single reality, whether we consider that reality at its source or at its term. Hegel merely specifies that God and the cosmos only attain consciousness, only realize themselves, in man.

Hegel's mammoth effort, therefore, to assimilate the Christian God to the cosmic life which comes to its climax in and through man, was ultimately a catastrophe. And one can see in this catastrophe the final, most revealing, fruit of the tendency running through the whole of Christian theology since Abelard (not to speak of the earlier Gnostics and Arians), the tendency totally to submerge God's Word in human reason, while pretending to be allowing the latter to assimilate it.

Anton Günther and His Attempt

Christianity could not allow itself to be taken in by the basic equivocation which makes Hegel's system the perfect Gnosticism. On the other hand, it needed to show itself capable of integrating the truth within it: its sense of the essential kinship between the divine and the human, as well as the need of lifting everything human, and even everything cosmic, into the divinizing work of grace. The only clear move in this direction was made by Anton Günther, acting under the immediate inspiration of one of the greatest nineteenth-century saints, St. Clement-Mary Hofbauer.

Günther remains the most tragically misunderstood of nineteenth-century Christian and Catholic thinkers.[11] Yet it was he alone who, in the face of the Hegelian threefold dialectic of thesis, antithesis and synthesis, knew how to express the truth perceived by Nicholas of Cusa at the very moment modern thought was being born, namely, that contraries cannot be reconciled, the *coincidentia oppositorum* realized, not by a purely immanent process but only by a leap from the immanent to the transcen-

---

[11]There is a very superficial introduction by E. Hocedez, *Histoire de la Théologie au XIXe siècle*, vol. 2, Brussels-Paris, 1953, pp. 39ff.

dent, from the finite to the positively infinite. In other words, reasoning on the basis of experience can only resolve or rather get beyond its antinomies by recourse to faith, faith in the Word of God, faith which lets us be taken and taken away up into that Word.

Unfortunately, Günther expressed himself somewhat paradoxically. His thought was at once overly simple and too enigmatic. Hence, almost immediately he was either misunderstood or not understood at all, particularly by freshly resurrected Neo-Thomism, though also, it must be said, by many simplistic and compromising disciples of his own. Hence he was promptly condemned and condemned, most ironically, for a semi-rationalism purportedly akin to that of Hermes, while in fact he was no more or no less rationalist than St. Anselm in his *Proslogion*.

Günther accepted the sentence humbly, but he did not have the heart to attempt any new expression of his genuine thought. For a short while, he aroused an enthusiasm we would nowadays find it hard to imagine, but then he seemed suddenly to disappear leaving no apparent traces in theological history.

Instead it fell to two very different thinkers, far more gripping than Günther but with far less certainty as to what they were doing, to express the inevitable Christian—and human—reaction to the Christianity of Hegel and his meekest disciples. One was Kierkegaard, the other Nietzsche. At first sight, it would be difficult to connect two more alien minds. But in fact, for better or worse, they have so much in common that their separate influences blended into yesterday's existentialism, allowing this to assume two diametrically opposed forms represented in France by Gabriel Marcel and Jean-Paul Sartre.

Kierkegaard

There have been many attempts to brush aside Kierkegaard's[12] objections to Hegel as those of a sick man to a person in undisturbed health; likewise, for all the more reason, Nietzsche's cavalier treatment of him as non-existent while being so closely dependent upon him. But this is too simple a line to take. There is no doubt as to the pathological element present in each, and ultimately vitiating both their endeavors (and Nietzsche's in an especially pitiable way), but it may well have functioned as a violent reaction exposing the unreality of Hegelian idealism which, like all its kind, never really confronts evil.

What Kierkegaard, especially in his *Post Scriptum* which completed his *Philosophical Fragments*, latched on to and denounced, quite rightly,

---

[12]The best biography remains that of T. Bohlin.

was the way in which Hegel for all his good intentions (and there is no reason to denounce his repeated protestations) never managed to guarantee freedom, and hence personality, either in man or in God. He wanted his philosophy to be attentive to history, to be essentially historical, but in fact his uncontrolled and all-absorbing rationalism fossilized the history. Hegel only ever perceived and conceived it as a finished process. Worse still, he made it something artificial from the start by treating it simply as the unfolding of the Idea. And thus the apparently titanic conflict, in which he saw it taking possession of itself by fighting itself to the death, was in the last resort a shadow-battle, lacking substance.

In face of this Kierkegaard made a vigorous and refreshing reaffirmation of the creative gratuitousness of every moment, with the created person being called to realize or lose himself in an encounter with a God who has nothing abstract about him but, on the contrary, is perfectly free and therefore the person who is not just an archetype but source and end of every other person. Nor did he mean that persons can only fulfill themselves by blending themselves with God's personality, as if they were merely emanations from him. On the contrary, he meant that God's own inexhaustible newness continually provokes a completely original "becoming" in those he created.

Unfortunately, Kierkegaard's passionate reaction against Hegel's rationalism and monist totalitarianism made him incapable of distinguishing precisely, or even of discerning the difference between the supra-rational and the merely irrational, and, similarly, between the communion which is necessary for the human person if he is to flower and the simple confusion in which he will inevitably disappear.

Nietzsche

Nietzsche's uncertainty was even more dangerous.[13] Kierkegaard's almost frantic exaltation of individuality left him unclear as to how to reconnect with either the Creator or other creatures. But the Nietzschean individual can only affirm himself by going against the latter, while thinking that he has left God well behind him, like a corpse to be abandoned to those other dead (human) beings. But as Lou Andrea Salome saw so early—and she was the one woman he really wanted to love, without ever quite making up his mind to do so or doing so effectively!— Nietzsche was continually in the grip of a nostalgia for God, the God of

---

[13]Charles Andler's colossal synthesis, *Nietzsche, sa Vie et sa Pensée*, 3 vols., Paris, 1958, has lost much of its value since Mrs. Forster-Nietzsche's distortions have been exposed by recent critical study.

Jesus Christ, and the superman who thought that he had trodden all other men underfoot and moved far beyond them, literally died of a desperate but impotent craving for sympathy.

What Nietzsche, while never freeing himself from Christ's fascination, condemned and rejected in Christianity with its God of love, mercy and pity was in many aspects Christianity such as it had become in the liberal post-Hegelian Protestantism that followed on pietism, i.e., a Christianity totally reduced to the human level, justifying man as he is; no longer opening a road to genuine transcendence, but allowing us to settle down in a self-contentment disguised as divinization. And conversely, there was an unquestionably positive element in his image of the Superman who rises above merely legalistic morality. The image was idealized, but the idealism meant to be effective, and effective in recovering that authentic divinization which only Christianity can offer—a Christianity, that is, where God is really God and, as Schelling saw at the end of his life, only capable of creating and creating in view of such adoption because he is absolute freedom.

This Promethean atheism of Nietzsche, however—even though he only acknowledged the fact, most reluctantly, because his acute critical mind would not permit self-deception—sprang from Feuerbach, the most brilliant yet superficial of those so-called left-wing Hegelians who, prior to Marx and to his advantage, defended their master's dialectic to the hilt while claiming to stand it the right way up, i.e., recognize for what it was that disintegration of the divine which is the shadow, as it were, of the Hegelian apotheosis of the cosmic and the human. For Feuerbach, in fact, a transcendent God had never been anything but an imaginary projection, a sort of prospective, sent in front of itself by humanity, something in opposition to its present condition but which it must ultimately dominate and reabsorb, as it were, in order to reach fulfillment. As in Hegel's famous image, one gives oneself a master and makes him one's slave in order to be his master and the master of everything else as well.

Contemporary Atheism

Marxist atheism is a combination of that of Feuerbach and that of Engels, the latter being an unconscious divinization of matter giving it, in accordance with nineteenth-century scientism, all the attributes of the traditional God and especially those of the biblical God-Creator.

Hence contemporary atheism, be it Marxist or Existentialist in a superindividualistic sense, as in Sartre, retains a revealing nostalgia for the social, for communion, for the absolutizing into transcendence of a truth to which man can consecrate himself. It is this urge that made Sartre ogle at Marxism while never being able to make up his mind to go the whole way with it. And this is the price he paid to be able to say that he is not anti-theist but very precisely a-theist, the God-problem now being a problem only belonging to the past, a problem passed beyond, left far behind.[14]

The Structuralists would have great fun showing the enormous illusion in these claims. This post-Nietzschean man, pretending his existence is his only essence and that he can form himself in perfect freedom, is in fact nothing but an image of the Christian God, an image naively convinced of its capacity to outlive its model. The eloquent honesty of Sartre's confession of final failure in Les Mots[15] needs no commentary. Clarity of mind, and basic uprightness of heart (in Pascal's sense) shine out so brightly in this book that it only makes it more surprising that its author failed to see how the compensating nostalgia pushing him towards Marxism was directed in fact to the latter's transposed biblical Messianism, without which it would amount to nothing but what Stalin exposed without initiating: a hideous compound of pseudo-science and vicious resentment.

Thus, all these post-Christians, atheist or otherwise, are clearly the heirs of a disintegrated theism, fruitlessly disputing over its last relics as they turn to powder in their hands—that theism which Christian theology since Occam (be it Catholic, or purportedly Catholic or Protestant) has been forever rearranging in the hope of producing out of it a man-God rather than a God made man. It was predictable that such a theology would eventually proclaim God dead, and thereby bring man finally to the grave.

The post-Christian philosophies aimed at a far more radical break with Christian theology than did the pasteurized "Thomism" of John of St.-Thomas and his epigons, not to speak of the nominalist philosophers of the double truth. But in fact they merely amount to Christian theologies in a laicized form. In the Thomism of St. Thomas, as in all the Fathers of which he was heir, ancient philosophy—on the brink of a final bang or whimper—came out rejuvenated after a supernatural bath, as it were, in the waters of true theology. But, in their senile impotence, those theologies which have unconsciously relapsed into heretical gnosticism have conclusively proved their congenital sterility, while a seemingly endless succession of barren philosophies continues to burgeon around their corpse.

---

[14] See some good analyses in Paul Toinet, Existence chrétienne et Philosophie, Paris, 1965.

[15] J. P. Sartre, Les Mots, Paris, 1964.

XVIII

Prospects

Pannenberg insists much on what at first sight seems a strange idea, namely that we can only really hope to know God in the eschatological future. This, of course, must not be understood in the sense of S. Alexander's bizarre theology, according to which God will only exist at the and of time. Nor would it be right to take it, as so many of our contemporaries are tempted to, in the sense that God is so much a part of the process of becoming that he can only be known when it is complete. But, in perfectly orthodox fashion, we must realize that the only encounter with God in which—in that Pauline phrase which must be a constant point of reference—we can know him as from all eternity we have been known, will in fact be that eschatological encounter when, his kingdom having come, God will be everything in everyone.

Then, of course, there will be no more need for theologians and their speculative theologies. But, conversely, theologians must in the meantime remind themselves that, if their theologies are not going to be invalidated by their very intention, then they can only be the fruit of faith tending towards vision, faith looking forward, as it were, while fully aware that at present it can only ready itself for vision, not attain it.

Hence every closed theological system purporting to be self-sufficient will fall under the stricture quite rightly passed on Hegel's philosophy, namely that it would only be patient of meaning had history decided to stop when it appeared. Alas, history has not shown the slightest sign of doing so, despite Hegel's aim of bringing the Kingdom of God down onto the earth and his conviction that this was what his work was going to accomplish.

The Son of Man will come like a thief in the night, and God's kingdom when no one is giving it a thought. This is true, and it would be no bad thing if theology could make us live in permanent expectation of this or, at least, point us in that direction. But this does not appear to be the most conspicuous or widespread preoccupation of professional theologians. The resultant need for theology, or at least for what goes under that name, is in our opinion that it should, on the one hand, take up dieting and, on the other, get more exercise, not in replacing mysticism which is capable of anticipating eschatology in a way theology simply is not, but in opening up a path for it.

Many theologians appear, on the contrary, to be preoccupied in closing any such paths as hermetically as possible. This is generally true of Protestant theologians since Ritschl, and it has to be admitted that, on this point at least, the great majority of Protestant theologians, with very few exceptions, are at present in agreement, right across the board from extreme liberalism to the most rigid neo-orthodoxy.

In the face of this, contemporary Catholic theology appears hesitant, divided, and uncertain as to the path it should take. Even when it does still tend towards the vision of God, it does so without much conviction and not in a convincingly efficacious way.

We have already revealed our mind on modern theology's passion for dissertating about and settling everything, especially in areas where it is not possible for theology to have any particular competence. We have even seen one Catholic author unhesitatingly deciding that the inhabitants of other planets are saved, even when no one is in a position to say whether such beings exist or, if they do, that they are. On the other hand, the annual number of books published about God could be counted on one's fingers. What this new theology is admitting in all this is that it is simply the decomposition of the old which, since the Middle Ages, has yielded again and again to the claim to know everything about everything, never failing to give even the most foolish or ridiculous question a suitably apodictic answer.

What still remains of this so-called pre-conciliar theology, or remained until recently, was—at least in part and in its best representatives—preoccupied with telling us how to move, or how we should move from baptism to the vision of God. We have been merciless in our criticism of Fr. Garrigou-Lagrange, so it is only just to recall his *Perfection Chrétienne et Contemplation*, a very worthy book and one of great intellectual and spiritual sanity.

Despite this, it is striking that the very school to which this eminent Dominican belonged, for all its utter self-assurance as to the exclusive value of its own kind of thinking, should as a whole hardly ever have believed that its theology had a close connection with that face-to-face knowledge of God to which we are all called. Worse still, it hardly seems to have realized the necessary relationship between that vision and Christian dogma itself, despite its claim to be all of a piece with this dogma. Take the curious, posthumous work of Jacques Maritain. It amounts to the good old syncretism sailing under the flag of ecumenism. Despite maintaining that the only correct theology, in fact the only theology worthy of the name, is that of him and his friends, he here teaches that neither this theology nor even the Gospel, of which it claims to be the only patented interpretation, is necessary or even of particular use in leading mankind to the beatific vision, to eternal salvation And even now, apparently, the capacity to attain the highest mystical experience is as much and as easily available to a Buddhist by way of his Buddhism, to a Hindu by way of his Hinduism, as to a Christian by way of his Christianity.

At this point, one may be pardoned for finding it hard to see what, from a spiritual point of view, distinguishes Catholic theology as these gentlemen understand it from any religious philosophy or even from some purely arbitrary mental game like charades or a crossword puzzle.

Such theology, nowadays, seems to be condemned and, one might say, it serves it right. It is of little import that its representatives still claim to be called Thomists. In the view of the Fathers of the Church and of St. Thomas himself, the faith has been given us to lead us to salvation and can only be validly interpreted from such a perspective. It is they, then, who would have been severer than anyone on such works.

There is a second characteristic, too, requisite for any Catholic or even merely Christian theology which is genuinely such. It must lead towards encounter with God not the men of some justifiably or unduly idealized past epoch, but those of its own time. If St. Thomas concentrated so much on cosmological arguments, it was not because they seemed to him the only valid ones and the others, such as Augustine's, only doubtfully orthodox or flatly heretical. It was simply because he knew that the great mass of his intellectual contemporaries, and especially there in the universities, to whom he was speaking, regarded Aristotelianism and its methods of approach as the only viable ones. So true is this that, in support of the fourth way, he quotes a text of Aristotle of only doubtful relevance, whereas any historian can tell us that he has drawn this argument straight from a famous page of *The City of God*.

By this we do not maintain, like some, that one can take any philosophy in vogue (Hegelian, Marxist, Freudian, Nietzschean, etc.) and then dress it up, at no great expense, in Christian theology. But there are certain positive data within modern thought that cannot be bypassed whatever the precise character of one's theological endeavor. It is not merely their contemporaneousness which makes them important. Rather, the point is that among the common presuppositions of the best modern thinkers, or at least some of them, there are undoubted and solid values to be found. This, after all, goes for every age, even for those least privileged intellectually. One would be culpable if one failed to take these as a foundation. After all, it is one's aim to gain some hearing from those to whom one is speaking and to lead them by the shortest, surest route to what seems to be essential.

There are three contemporary philosophical acquisitions which a theologian would appear to be particularly bound to take stock of. Once mentioned, it will be clear to our readers just how much they have shaped our own inquiry.

The first is one of which Hegel grasped the full import and to which, first among modern thinkers, he wished to give its full due. Unfortunately, he refused to pay the small price demanded of him We refer to the great importance for modern minds of a historical outlook. This is surely of capital importance. It must embrace human life, in the first place, but also human thought. And not least Christianity itself, for if there is one great source for this universal outlook of ours, it is Christianity itself or, more widely, biblical religion as a whole.

But the prime error of Hegel's whole philosophy, and of all subsequent branches of Hegelianism, including Marxism, has been to continue believing what medieval theologians were all far too convinced of, namely that one can only know the historical, and only know it in depth, by bringing it back, willy-nilly, into some sequence of *a priori* reasoning.

This had been the great weakness of Scholasticism as a whole. But the moment one thinks one can replace history or produce the only scientific view of history by elaborating some wonderful "philosophy of history," then, not merely has one failed to move a single step in the right direction, but one has unconsciously erected a barrier which makes any such movement impossible. And, we must hasten to add, one will go even further astray by replacing this philosophy of history by some equally *a priori* theology of history or other.

The only way to achieve anything of value would be to elicit, *a posteriori* from human history as a whole viewed in the light of faith, some essentially historical theology in the truest sense of the word. In other words, we need that respect for the creative event so well expressed by Kierkegaard, as long as one avoids his mistake of restricting it simply to each individual history but rather finds it in that human history, the inseparable warp and woof of which consist of what, on the one hand, is essentially personal and, on the other, essentially collective, in a cloth which is wholly inter-personal.

The second element in the contemporary intellectual situation of which we think any theologian must take the greatest account is what we might call the phenomenological revolution. Husserl set off a chain-reaction and, for all his subtlety, never quite foresaw all its consequences. He had after all been seduced by the only thing Brentano had taken from Aristotelianism, namely that all intellectual activity is not only inexplicable but incomprehensible and even irremediably impaired if one abstracts from the intentionality behind the mind's every act, the intentionality of an object which the mind regards as transcendent and towards which it directs itself. By moving from a neo-objectivism to a super-subjectivism which did its best to absorb the object back into the subject, Husserl inevitably fell under the ax of Heidegger's criticism: that it is as meaningless to tack an object onto the subject as to make a choice either for the one or for the other. Rather, we need to regain possession of the mind in that existential relationship in which it realizes itself simply as a relation to something else, either a presence or an absence.

Without himself either intending as much or foreseeing it, Husserl did in fact lead his disciples in the direction of that Christianity which he himself spent his life approaching, albeit tangentially, and it was they who grasped the full implications of his reworking of the Cartesian *Cogito*. Reinach, however, died prematurely, before being able to produce a rational justification of something of which deeply personal experience had convinced him. Scheler was, as it were, struck down halfway. He had realized that his thought could not be disjoined from actual living, but he lacked the capacity to live it through to its logical end. It fell, instead, to a woman to draw out the full meaning, with great clarity of vision, of Husserl's inheritance. Edith Stein was undoubtedly a genius at the intellectual level. Above all, she was, if not a saint, at least certainly on the way towards sanctity, with martyrdom calling her to it. It is true, of course, that as a result of circumstances her work was unfinished, promising much but not yet fully matured. Her work of reconstruction was impeded by her isolation. The Christian tradition was something entirely new to her; she had come upon it suddenly, and she lacked trustworthy guides to take her through it. Hence, when she came to interpret St. John of the Cross and St. Thomas and the whole cloud of witnesses they presuppose, she often missed her mark, even seriously, and her work is uneven, unfinished, in some places over-extended and, in others, over-charged. But despite all this, it remains one of the most enlightening as to the path that a genuinely theological and genuinely relevant theology must take.

There is a third element in the contemporary intellectual environment which seems to us as unavoidable as it is enriching. This is the critical analysis of modern scientific thought and its location within the wider problem of language that is owed to Ludwig Wittgenstein. Neither logical positivism, which was somewhat premature in claiming him as its patron, nor the different forms of contemporary linguistic analysis have as yet come anywhere near exhausting the seminal possibilities of this philosopher, comparable to no one so much as to Socrates. It was Wittgenstein's achievement, first of all, to reveal the precise demands and implications and, no less, the necessary limitations of every scientific kind of thought, i.e., of any thinking founded on rational analysis of exclusively sensory experience. But this did not lead him to imprison us in some suffocating species of positivism. Rather, he prepared the only exit which does not issue into simple irrationality. And this was by showing that all our thought systems are merely language games, all of which and each of which have a meaning provided one recognizes it and respects its distinctive logic.

This, of course, does away for good with any chance of constructing a "scientific theology," meaning by that a theology in continuity with modern physical science. On the other hand, neither can theology claim to be *scientia* in William of St. Thierry's sense, i.e., as we have said already, the gnosis of the Greek Fathers which was itself simply the Christian development of the prophetic knowledge of God, and which consists in acknowledging God in the darkness or, better, chiaroscuro of faith while it takes possession of human existence as a whole and directs it towards an encounter with that God who is always ahead of us in revealing his love. But theology could reestablish a solid status for itself, if it limited itself to proposing a phenomenology of faith and thus disposing us for the true *scientia*. Then, while avoiding any kind of neo-concordism with modern science, theology could in fact harmonize quite naturally with the unexpected perspectives opened by in-depth exploration of the epistemological problems which have emerged as an inevitable consequence of science's quite autonomous development. Ian Ramsey realized all this. How sad that such a remarkable mind was taken from us so early.

But at this point we come to what is perhaps the greatest modern temptation for theology: not just an immersion in history (as opposed to disengaging itself from it) but such a highly narrow application of itself to a historical and specifically evolutionary vision of the whole of reality, that finally it wants to make God relapse into the process of becoming. We see this in fictional theology à la Teilhard, but not only there. There seems to be a kind of vertigo which, at least on occasion, has taken possession of even the most powerful and most religious philosophers of our time, Bergson, for example, and even Whitehead.

But a God who becomes will inevitably be a suffering God, and a suffering God will no longer be an Almighty God—in other words (if we are going to take the Bible and especially the Gospel seriously) will no longer be God. Such a God would no longer be the Creator, and would be incapable of being the Savior. How then could he adopt us and lead us to that life beyond a very possible vicissitude?

It is strange that so many gifted modern minds seem to be incapable of realizing what should be as plain as daylight to them. After all, Whitehead himself—the philosopher of becoming and change if ever there was one—said that there could be no "change," let alone "progress," if it were merely meaningless chaos and not founded on something permanent.

Yet this reaction is not those of people who are simply uncritical followers of contemporary currents of thought. The truth is that, behind such a position, there lies a right and healthy reaction to a certain static immobilism, which was precisely what brought the old theology to its death. For the latter, which was trying to be modern for its time, proved incapable of realizing that the divine being cannot be reduced, by abstraction, to a fixed, immutable essence but must always be "actual." And, therefore, he has no need of change since he always has been and always will be actuality in the fullest sense.

Hence the basic importance of the personalism of God. Without it, he ceases to be the God of the Bible and of Christianity. Once this personalism is lost sight of, everything goes. And yet it, also, will not be preserved by being congealed in abstraction. The personality of God, we must say, is the personality of *the Father*, a personality that always and only consists in giving, in that giving objectified in the Son, but not objectified in another, dead way, because the objectivity in this giving simply elicits another subject. Or rather, and here we have the whole mystery of the Trinity, this new subject for the Father while being the Other in person is at the same time nothing but another Himself. How else could he be *the Son*, just as He is *the* Father?

But the full meaning of this only emerges when we see that the procession of the Spirit is inseparably linked with the generation of the Son. For in this procession the very gift that the Father gives to the Son, the gift which rests on the Son and constitutes him as such in his own abiding actuality, becomes the gift of the Son's own self-giving to him who has given him everything and never ceases doing so. Hence the divine life reascends to the Father for the very reason that it flows from him. It is recapitulated in the Father by the Spirit precisely because it proceeds from him in the way that it does. And this does not mean that the divine life comes to a halt or stabilizes.

It is as true to say that in God there is only one fundamental or fontal personality, the Father's, as that God nonetheless exists in three persons. The Father is only Father by reason of begetting the Son. The Son is only Son by acknowledging the Father's gift of the Father's Spirit, given to him by the Father to be his own just as the Father gives him his being Son, and ceaselessly returned by the Son to the Father just as he is ceaselessly received. Hence the unity of God should not emerge as the dead unity of a simple and unchangeable essence, but rather as a personal unity involving, embracing and surpassing multiplicity by gathering it up into the only One who can be both the Good and the True at once and, thus, eternally, the All in the One.

To want to make such a God "come alive" by finding a space in him for becoming or passivity is to fail to see that everything of infinity which our limited, unfinished life seeks to reach by way of becoming or everything complementary that it seeks through passivity is to be found in the Infinite God, found in him from the very beginning, and in a superabundant, wholly transcendent, all-excelling way.

However, in Denys' language, we then have to see how the thearchy of the divine monarchy, the Father's, has only been revealed to us by its ineffable self-communication in the hierarchy of cosmic creation and the eschatological Church, in which all creatures must be re-gathered into their divine exemplar so that God may at last be all in all.

And here we would turn to Eckhart's Trinitarian scheme. God, the Father, is supreme and original consciousness. He is self-consciousness, with the Father's self only realizing itself by giving itself, by losing itself in such a way that it only, unimaginably, finds itself again in the double producing of the Son and the Spirit, a producing which remains within its own infinity. Here we have the original and eternal realization of what Louriah looked for in creation and called Withdrawal: God limiting himself, God never revealing himself as God so much as when he makes room for the Other. This is what Boehme, with greater depth, understood as a contraction which is simultaneously intra-Trinitarian and creative, in the production of the Wisdom of creation. But he never came to see that the first can occur without the second.

This is what, going deeper still, Bulgakov, following Tareiv and Bukharev, thought of as a hidden, intimate "devastation," an eternal kenosis thanks to which the Father only is by communicating himself in the Son, just as the Son only is by restoring himself to the Father in the love of the Spirit, a love which is inter-personal as well as supremely personal. But he too could not conceive of this as separable or ever really distinct from the kenosis of creation, nor even from that kenosis as regards creation in its concrete condition of fall and separation which we call the incarnation. And this latter, too, Bulgakov thought of as no less necessary than creation and, indeed, as a result of the fall, hyper-necessary.

But the Bible, and the Gospel above all, affirm the gratuitousness of creation and salvation, and this obliges us to look for another view, one far more unified but first requiring the acceptance of a far greater diversity.

Thus we come back to Eckhart's scheme. The Father is fundamental intelligence in act. He is all-embracing consciousness. The Son is the content of this consciousness. The Son is his Word and Wisdom in which he expresses himself at once necessarily and yet with supreme freedom; he expresses himself wholly and in one, and thus the Son is his very Name. This is the first aspect. But, under a second aspect, the Father expresses in his Word his free plan to create and for creation. He expresses this in the bridal image of Wisdom, which is at once distinct and inseparable from it. At the same time, the Spirit, who is the divine liberty personified in love and who rests on the Wisdom of creation just as he rests on the Son, gives this Wisdom freedom, a freedom which includes the possibility of sin, this possibility being actually accepted by the whole Trinity. Yet, at the same time, and in the same Spirit, the Son himself wills himself to be what the Father has eternally conceived him to be, namely incarnate in a fallen world. Thus, the Spirit of freedom, pouring himself out over the latter just as he does over the Son, will turn the world back to him by way of his own identification with fallen Wisdom in its very fallenness. Thanks to the eschatological Wedding of their mutual love, fallen Wisdom, creation lost and regained, the Church of the new creation will at last be led back to God, not to be dissolved but fulfilled in him, and led back as the eternal Bride of the Son, his mystical Body for all eternity.

In this view, divine freedom is revealed at its maximum in the creation of free beings, and a creation which accepts their fall, and in the descent of the Son and Spirit who are sent by the Father to the defaced image of eternal Wisdom in order to bring it back to its divine exemplar.

God, from all eternity and in himself, in his living unity, infinitely surpasses all mutability and passivity, and similarly—through time and the history of creation—he at once arouses, encompasses and accomplishes the full, actual realization of our mutability and passivity.

A final word, here, on the person as subsistent relation. There can be no doubt that the formula encapsulates an intuition of lasting value. But there can be scarcely any less doubt about it being, as such, profoundly ambiguous. On the one hand, the revelation of the person of the Father as primordial and supreme makes it clear that personality, just like love, cannot be conceived as self-enclosed. What St. Gregory the Great said of charity can be said of the person, of which charity is the revelation: *non potest esse minus quam inter duos.*

Yet at the divine level, which is not simply the support but in a sense the whole of all existent reality, the Trinity of persons—there everything is finally recapitulated in the Father by the Spirit—suppose that this relativity of the person is only ultimately substantial because the relation returns to its principle (doing so with a simultaneously total necessity and freedom). Otherwise, a substantial relation would be like the smile of the Cheshire cat in Lewis Carroll's story, "subsisting" even when the cat was no longer there, which would of course be perfect "nonsense."

So, we have to say that all existence, created as well as uncreated, only has meaning in the measure that it approaches personal, i.e., relational, being. But all these relations only hate a substantiality of their own because they have come from and must all return, to "the Father, from whom all fatherhood, in heaven and on earth, takes its name," the only one who has known us from all eternity, as he knows the Son, in the Spirit, and as, finally, we shall know him: with a knowledge which is one with that Love which is the definitive meaning of everything there is.

This enables us to understand—not statically, but dynamically, in line with Nicholas of Cusa's *coincidentia oppositorum*—how the distinction between the divine persons is real and even, in a sense, reality itself, whereas they are only notionally distinguished from the divine essence. And, since the created adds nothing to the uncreated, but only participates in the latter's infinity with a finiteness surrounded by the same infinity, we must say of ourselves that, in the perspectives of eternal Wisdom and to the eschatological Espousals to which it is destined with the divine Logos, that, however eternally distinct we may be one from another and in relation to the divine persons, especially that of the Father, we are in a real way intentionally one with them and with him in the one and only *deitas*.

This, of course, does not mean pantheism. We are nothing and have been raised up by God in order to be divinized in him. Thus, there is no symmetry, and he is and is everything without any need of us.

Ultimately, indeed, although God must be all in all, everything is not God for the reason that everything exists only in the mind of the Father which of itself necessarily evokes the two other persons (though with a necessity in which freedom finds its fulfillment by transcending itself), while it is in complete freedom (though a freedom consummated in the Love manifested in that irresistible self-diffusion which is the Good) that the Three call, conform and unite us to their reciprocal knowledge and love, there everything constantly returns to the Father from whom it has always come, and always will.

*   *   *

The most intelligent and sympathetic critic of our previous volume, *The Eternal Son*, was not able to conceal his disappointment at the *Reflections* which concluded it. He had wanted to take a highly appreciative attitude towards them, but, for all that, felt that they did not quite answer the readers' expectations. There had been a historical exposition of the development of revelation and theology. After this, surely, some kind of systematic synthesis would have been in order, rather than what was a very inconclusive conclusion which hardly provided any fundamental principles for such a synthesis. We appreciate such feelings of disappointment, and these present *Prospects* of ours will, we anticipate, renew them, and even increase them.

We must frankly admit that, when we began our series of doctrinal works, we did intend to produce precisely what our critic was hoping for. But, en route, we have come to realize two things, or even three, as the author of Proverbs would say.

The first is that the more we approach the divine at its source, which is the Father, the more we see how laughable must be any attempt at a system of theology. Or, if people prefer, after a genetic exposition of revelation, the only system that is not a snare and a delusion is that of a progressive clarification of the successive, self-generating questions which the divine Word has raised for the Church to the extent that she builds herself up by evangelizing humanity as a whole. To do that as completely as possible is to do a great deal more than simply tell the history of theology. It is to elicit from history what only history can produce: the building-up of what is called positive theology, i.e., the only systematic theology corresponding to the Church's actual assimilation of revealed truth, and thus the only one which would not fall victim to an artificial system or degenerate into a mere mental game.

This does not mean that, at any given stage of the Church's history, one cannot, from that particular vantage point, try to summarize what has been learned in a synthetic way, though such an attempt must necessarily remain provisional.

In other words, it is both possible and desirable for every generation to re-do a phenomenology of the Spirit, but this cannot claim, as Hegel's did, to precipitate (in every sense of the word) the process of mankind's spiritual becoming as if it precontained a summa of absolute knowledge which, as time passed, would only need to be methodically inserted in its appropriate prefabricated pigeon-holes. All that such a phenomenology should do—and to do more would be to surrender to an illusion which would prove disastrously idolatrous—is to draw a dynamic synthesis, and not a static system, from meditation on the experience of the Catholic faith, an experience which cannot be other than incomplete. We mean a synthesis which will direct us from where we have actually arrived towards the place of eschatological encounter and consummation.

But, however much we hope to help towards an eventual union of the human and the divine at the as yet unattainable end of history, such a phenomenology of the Spirit can only be written if we distinguish the human spirit from the transcendent Spirit proper to God and see behind the former that cosmic entelechy which must be its guide and which is the architectonic Wisdom governing the universe.

This is why, in the first place, even to sketch such a synthesis only becomes possible at the close, or rather the double close, of our endeavor, whereas the key of the whole Hegelian synthesis was to be found in the *Phenomenology of the Spirit* such as Hegel understood it, the reason being that the "spirit" concerned was simply the *Weltgeist*, the spirit of a world of which man and human reason were not just the microcosm but the very essence: *Deus sive natura*.

There is only one way of avoiding the idealist vertigo that, in our view, ultimately reduces the *Phaenomenologie des Geistes* to a superbly orchestrated tautology and, worse still, to an unending discourse in the void on the part of the human spirit and that is to tear such a phenomenology in two. We must not reduce the object to the subject and thereby drown the subject's becoming in an exhausting vicious circle. Therefore we must make a bifurcation between what could be called a phenomenology of the Holy Spirit, the Spirit of God in his communication to man individually and in community and to the Church as an interpersonal society, and a phenomenology of that divine Wisdom which is the spirit of the redeemed world: God's plan for the whole cosmos as cosmos, i.e., as that whole in which the invisible Father must eventually be all in all through the incarnation of the eternal Son and his consummated union with the whole Church of the first-born whose names are written in heaven.

Hence our last two volumes, *Le Consolateur*[1] on the Spirit-Paraclete and the grace he gives us, and *Cosmos*,[2] on the universe and the divine glory which is its destiny. Each of these hopes to offer a kind of sketch of each of these phenomenologies, one by considering what anticipates the Kingdom of God, the other by recapitulating that history of salvation which takes us towards it.

Only with these works and, as it were, at their point of intersection, can full sense be made of the *Reflections* which concluded our study of the Word of God and its attempted Christological culmination. With them, too, the common perspective of the two phenomenologies we have

---

[1] English translation to be published by St. Bede's Publications.
[2] St. Bede's Publications, 1988.

outlined in these *Prospects* will, we hope, become a good deal more evident.

But neither path can issue in a system that would allow a theological candidate to pass judgment, in some sense, on the Word of God, as if he could have God's viewpoint upon it.

Nor can we, either at the end or only half-way through our enterprise, have any other ambition than that of merely marking out the necessarily double tracks on which the Spirit of God and the spirit of his creation meet.

And what of this encounter itself? Short of its consummation in the beatific vision of eternity, it cannot be the object of any theology except that mystical theology which is not a theology we can produce on paper but the only theology that constitutes authentic Christian mysticism,[3] the life of grace within us.

---

[3] We hope to be able to offer, not another phenomenology of this, even in outline, but a semantic, as we did for its source, the Eucharist. *Et hoc erat in votis!*...

Biblical Index

Old Testament

New Testament

Index of Authors Cited